THE CONSPIRACY READER

THE CONSPIRACY READER

From the Deaths of JFK and John Lennon
to Government-Sponsored Alien Cover-Ups

Compiled by Al Hidell and Joan d'Arc
Editors of *Paranoia* Magazine

A Citadel Press Book
Published by Carol Publishing Group

A Citadel Press Book
Published by Carol Publishing Group
Citadel Press is a registered trademark of Carol Communications, Inc.

Editorial, sales and distribution, rights and permissions inquiries should be
addressed to Carol Publishing Group, 120 Enterprise Avenue, Secaucus,
N.J. 07094.

In Canada: Canadian Manda Group, One Atlantic Avenue, Suite 105, Toronto,
Ontario M6K 3E7.

Carol Publishing Group books may be purchased in bulk at special discounts for
sales promotion, fund-raising, or educational purposes. Special editions can be
created to specifications. For details, contact Special Sales Department, Carol
Publishing Group, 120 Enterprise Avenue, Secaucus, N.J. 07094.

Manufactured in the United States of America
10 9 8 7 6 5 4 3 2 1

Library of Congress Cataloging-in-Publication Data
Hidell, Al.
    The conspiracy reader : from the deaths of JFK and John Lennon to
government-sponsored alien coverups / compiled by Al Hidell and Joan d'Arc.
        p.   cm.
    "A Citadel Press book."
    ISBN 0-8065-2041-8 (pbk.)
    1. Conspiracies United States. I. D'Arc, Joan. II. Title.
HV6275.H46   1999
364.1—dc21
                                                            98-28228
                                                                CIP

Contents

GOVERNMENT CRIMES AND COVER-UPS

MEDIA MIND CONTROL

CIA MIND CONTROL AND PSYCHOLOGICAL WARFARE

CULTS AND SECRET SOCIETIES

SUPPRESSED RESEARCH AND SECRET SCIENCE

Acknowledgments

THANKS TO EVERYONE who has helped and supported *Paranoia* magazine since its inception, as well as everyone who has written articles for us. We particularly thank the authors whose work appears in this anthology: George Andrews, Anonymous, Dr. Alan R. Cantwell Jr., Barry Chamish, Scott Corrales, R. B. Cutler, Adam Gorightly, D. Guide, Robert Guffey, Allen Hougland, Jorge Martín, Eric Odinson, Ron Patton, Seeker 1, Jerry E. Smith, Wendy Wallace, Mark Westion, and John White.

Introduction

IN THE SUMMER OF 1992, flyers posted in and around the city of Providence, Rhode Island, called to order the first meeting of the Providence Conspiracy League. The loose-knit group which began to meet at Newspeak Book Store on Richmond Street barely knew each other's names or knew if the names they used were real or fictitious. Out of those early meetings came a collection of diverse opinions, theories, information, and backup materials which were collected in several binders. As the binders began to overflow it became evident that the information needed wider exposure.

One night, Conspiracy League member Al Hidell outlined his exciting brainstorm to join the tide of independent magazine ('zine) publishers just beginning to rise on the scene. The new 'zine that would hit the streets of Providence, he proposed, was to be called *Paranoia: The Conspiracy Reader*. Providence Conspiracy League founder Joan d'Arc began working with Al on choosing the thematic content of the first issue of *Paranoia*. With a lot of help from their new friends, the first run of two hundred copies of *Paranoia*'s premiere issue, which focused on the assassination of Malcolm X, was photocopied and sold locally with a cover price of $2.50. When copies were sent to magazine distributors for consideration, the response took the group by surprise. *Paranoia* had to reprint in order to accommodate the orders coming in from the distributors. *Paranoia* was in business.

While it wasn't the first small-press conspiracy magazine on the market, *Paranoia* quickly took its place among the top few 'zines which were opposed to the mainstream "accidental theory" of history. Within this small group of independent publishers, historical events were viewed in the context of alliances between little-known power groups, or thug elements within groups, which exert covert control behind a façade of open democratic information flow. Thanks in part to desktop publishing, similar material began to be published by more and more grass-roots groups, reflecting a growing paranoia which erupted in full force with the massacre of the Branch Davidians at Waco, Texas, in 1993.

Conspiracy Web sites also began to emerge, including *Paranoia*'s stint with Konspiracy Korner on AOL in 1995. The mainstream media decried the commandeering of this new medium to spread distorted "right wing" conspiracy theories and warned people to beware information which They had not branded safe for consumers. At the height of American paranoia in early 1997, Hillary Clinton announced that a "right-wing conspiracy" was out to get the first couple, aided by the mainstream press. The *New York Times* reported in April 1997 that Mrs. Clinton described the Whitewater investigation as a "never ending fictional conspiracy" which reminded her of "some people's obsession with UFOs and the Hale-Bopp comet."

Since it takes the knowledge of only two people to have a conspiracy on your hands, it would follow that a lie written on a page constituting a cover-up can pass as one of those people. In their attempts to brand conspiracy theory theory as trash, the media shot itself in the foot. Conspiracy theories began to tug uncomfortably at America's assumptions of democracy, justice, and the accountability of government alphabet agencies for wrongdoings on American soil and around the world. Waco was the straw that broke the camel's back. People could no longer scoff at the idea of men meeting behind closed doors to concoct elaborate schemes; the conspiracy no longer required meetings now that it had acronyms and national security status.

As the spectacular events of the nineties unfolded, *Paranoia* and other small-press pioneers began to publish alternative views to those proposed by corporate media giants, as well as historical exposés which the mainstream opted to marginalize. Was AIDS a man-made disease? Did Lee Harvey Oswald have a Russian agent body double? Was TWA #800 shot down by friendly fire? Was the assassination of Yitzhak Rabin an open-and-shut case? How are Virgin Mary sightings and UFOs connected? Why was American Indian leader Leonard Peltier framed for murder? Was Gulf War Syndrome caused by forced injection of military personnel? Are Satanic cults for real? How does mind control really work?

With the help of a small army of freelance writers from several continents dedicated to the cause of "correcting the textbooks," *Paranoia* came to be a people's think tank of sorts: a grass-roots response to the official recorders of information and history, a counterattack aimed at the owners of earth's information flow. Thanks to the rare, open editorial policies of *Paranoia,* conspiracy-minded researchers found a venue to freely publish their findings, corroborate their leads, and network with others of like mind.

Today *Paranoia* is the most popular conspiracy 'zine and has newsstand distribution and subscribers in several countries. *Paranoia*'s success has caused some skeptics to question the existence of any conspiracy. "If there's a conspiracy," people scoff, "why are you still publishing?" "Why hasn't someone rubbed you out yet?" Perhaps it is because Americans love their conspiracy theories as much as they love their soap operas. Like soaps, conspiracy theories are often (but not always) elaborate stories with spectacular twists and turns. The players play dirty and sleep around. They're sleazy characters who lie and cheat with a deadpan gaze and go to their graves with their secrets. Conspiracy theories make great screenplays and TV shows, as Hollywood has discovered. As conspiracy theories become more mainstream, the content of *Paranoia* becomes at least slightly more credible and acceptable to the general public, who in turn become better informed. Perhaps therein lies our safety factor.

But the often fantastic nature of conspiracy theories does not necessarily make the scenarios any less plausible. After all, soaps are only a minor exaggeration of real life, a kind of superconcentrated pastiche of the violence, secrecy, and betrayal that exist in the real world. To deny that the absolute lowest in human potential could exist in at least a small coterie of planetary citizens, and then to doubt their ability to gravitate toward each other and to plan, is to be unrealistically naive. Like the rest of us, powerful people have specific goals and desires that they want to keep secret. Is it too much to suggest that these goals do not always coincide with the public welfare, democracy, and justice? These are the core assumptions of just about every conspiracy theory. To us, they seem quite rational. However, some people still have their heads in the sand.

Paranoia has a sense of humor. It doesn't take itself seriously all of the time. Its entertaining blend of the fantastic with the plausible has confused and distanced readers on occasion. They have judged this mind-boggling mixture to be deliberate when it is, in fact, merely a result of an open editorial policy. As editors of *Paranoia,* we are not

there to censor any theory that is internally consistent, logically presented, and well written. For, in the cheesiest of worlds, everything is
possible, even if only some things are probable. *The Conspiracy Reader*
is a chronicle of some of the diverse ideas "Out There" in what has
turned out to be a decade full of unbelievable events. Fortunately, aided
by its readers' forum format, *Paranoia* was writing it all down.

Spanning an awesome premillennial decade full of spectacular current events and historical disclosures just begging for conspiratorial
analysis, *Paranoia*—with its blend of original writings, interviews, and
reprints from various alternative media sources—may come to represent a time capsule of the Clinton era, an era when even the president
invoked "conspiracy" as the cause of his growing legal problems, a time
which might come to be characterized as "the Era of Paranoia."

Welcome to Paranoia.

Al Hidell
Joan d'Arc

A FRESH LOOK AT JFK

Double-Crossed: Who Is Alek J. Hidell?

Joan d'Arc

Two distinctly different ID cards were carried by "Lee Harvey Oswald" upon his arrest by the Dallas police on the day of JFK's assassination. The bogus ID cards are discussed in detail in this article, including proposal of the theory that the Russian-born Alek J. Hidell became a CIA recruit and defected to the USSR as Lee Oswald. Upon his return from the Soviet Union, Oswald's family noted to others that his appearance had changed drastically, including a receding hairline and a two-inch difference in height. They never had time to confront him about it, for he had received a new "assignment" as patsy for the JFK assassination.

"ALL RIGHT. WHAT'S YOUR NAME?" No answer. Bentley reached over and pulled a billfold from the prisoner's left rear pocket. He opened it, took out some cards, and studied them for a moment. "Are you Lee Harvey Oswald? That's what this card says." Still no answer. Bentley pulled out another ID card from the billfold and said, "Hey, this one's got a different name. Alek J. Hidell, H-I-D-E-L-L. Same picture, though." He gestured toward "Oswald."

"Both of the pictures are him."

The preceding questioning of "Lee Harvey Oswald" took place in the backseat of the unmarked police car of Officer Bob Carroll, as reported in a 1969 book written by Judy Bonner entitled *Investigation of a Homicide*. Bonner's book, now out of print, details information obtained from her friend Sgt. Gerald Hill. Sergeant Hill was present at the initial discovery by a Dallas police detective, Paul Bentley, of the two distinctly different ID cards carried by "Oswald-Hidell," as reported by Jack White in the January 1993 issue of the journal *The Third Decade*. The Oswald-Hidell ID cards could have provided a major clue to the identity of the conspirators in the JFK assassination had they been seriously considered by the Warren Commission.

But then again, who on the Warren Commission was looking for a conspiracy? The Warren Commission already had their man and sought only to bolster the theory set in place by the Powers-That-Be. The lone psychopath model was to be the only cloth held up to the sniffing bloodhounds that were the anointed members of Earl Warren's hand-picked commission. This Inquisition already had its cake, and they were eating it, too: a solitary scapegoat and a guilty verdict without a trial. The Hidell-Oswald espionage story would have been the can of worms just busting to crawl on the American psyche.

The Minsk Photo

The Hidell card is a bogus Selective Service card bearing the "Minsk photo" with the Hidell signature appearing at left. Genuine Selective Service cards, claims Jack White, did not have a photo on them. While the ID card found by Detectives Bentley and Hill is not reproduced in the Warren Commission volumes, the photograph does appear, identified as "a photo of Oswald taken in Minsk (Russia)." The commission does not identify the source of the photo or explain how this illustrious body knew where the photo was taken. Jack White surmises that the commission picked up this photo from another source, since they do not connect it with the ID card. He notes that "had they connected the photo and the card, it would have been immediately apparent that the Minsk photo should not be on a U.S. Department of Defense card!"

The Minsk photo, according to Jack White, is a composite of the faces of two different individuals, the real Oswald and the impostor "Hidell," so that the photo used as an ID card looks like both of them. He believes that "the real Lee Harvey Oswald lent his identity (legend) to a trained Russian-speaking intelligence agent who was sent to the USSR as a defector." Mr. White claims that he presented this information to the House Assassinations Committee, but his testimony was ignored.

The Selective Service card was dealt with by the Warren Commission, but only on the grounds that Oswald ostensibly forged the card himself for the purpose of ordering a rifle by mail order under the name Hidell. This is ludicrous on at least two counts: (1) rifles can be easily purchased in Texas; and (2) no postal record was ever produced which proved that a gun was picked up by Oswald or Hidell. Dallas researchers Ray and Mary LaFontaine published an article on November 22, 1992, in the *Houston Post* which stated that "in December 1966, when the FBI finally released Oswald's Defense Department ID card to the National Archives, it arrived nearly obliterated by FBI testing." Apparently there are no pictures of the curious DD1173 card in its pristine condition as published in Judy Bonner's 1969 book.

Alias Oswald

The theory that there were actually two "Oswalds" is taken quite seriously by another assassinologist, R. B. Cutler, in his book *Alias Oswald*, which is dedicated to Alek James Hidell, "who died in an heroic attempt to save his President's life." Cutler proposes that Alek J. Hidell was born in a Baltic country, probably Riga, Latvia, in about 1938. He suggests that the Russian-born Hidell later became an American, served in the Marine Corps, and became a CIA recruit in 1957. This is the Hidell (as Oswald) who defected to the USSR, married Marina Prusakova, returned to the United States, was under orders to infiltrate an existing conspiracy to assassinate President Kennedy, was framed as the assassin, and was murdered by mobster Jack Ruby. What happened to the real Oswald according to this theory?

Lee Harvey Oswald, born on October 18, 1939, in New Orleans, had wanted to be a spy ever since he was a little boy. His father had died two months before he was born. The high school dropout enlisted in the marines in October of 1956, at seventeen, and was assigned as a radar operator in Atsugi, Japan, in September 1957. Cutler states: "Serving with his radar unit overseas in Japan, he turns out to be the look-alike of a CIA recruit training for a spy mission to Moscow. The Oswald name, ID, [and] civilian and military background are transferred to the spy who then lives forty-nine months as Lee Harvey Oswald." Cutler notes that "proficiency in the difficult Russian language appears to have been the primary reason for the imposture." The whereabouts of the real Oswald after both he and Hidell were discharged from the marines in September 1959 remains unknown. Harry Dean, a CIA operative who knew Oswald-Hidell well, states, "He had two outstanding qualities which made him a number one agent. He was intelligent and he knew how to keep his mouth shut."

Alek James Hidell

Next to nothing is known about the Russian-born Hidell before an apparent dental exam in El Toro on March 27, 1958. He spoke Russian with a Baltic accent. Upon his return from the Soviet Union, Oswald's family noted to others that his appearance had changed. His hair had thinned drastically and his hairline had receded. This Lee was much thinner, and there was apparently a two-inch difference in height. During his two years and eight months behind the Iron Curtain as a cold war espionage agent, Oswald's American family was conditioned to accept the double's appearance by photographs of him with Marina and baby June sent from Russia. His mother, Marguerite, told a friend, "Lee's not the same person. He even looks different." The family, however, never had a chance to confront the impostor. He took it upon himself to create a distance with his espionage work. He had received a new assignment.

In March 1963 the CIA heard a rumor of a Communist, Castro-backed conspiracy to kill JFK. The agent Hidell was sent to downtown Dallas to infiltrate the plot. According to Cutler, he "was assigned to monitor the movements of Castro supporters." The CIA-FBI needed information on the backgrounds of these "death squad members." Cutler surmises, "If they were only anti-Kennedy, it was possible that they had been recruited by Castro. If they were both anti-Kennedy and anti-Castro, the conspiracy was undoubtedly a domestic plot." Carrying out his assignment, Hidell launched a campaign in New Orleans for the Fair Play for Cuba Committee. He ordered application forms and membership cards, which he signed as A. J. Hidell, mailing the card back to national FPCC headquarters. Hidell continued to project his Communist image by passing out "Hands Off Cuba" leaflets on the Dumaine Street Wharf in New Orleans. He was later jailed for disturbing the peace in a curious about-face (as agent provocateur?) which entailed passing out pro-Castro leaflets on the same street.

The morning after his arrest, Hidell asked to see an FBI agent. Bail was paid and he was released, to appear in court the next day. Apparently the agent-provocateur had made enough of a spectacle of himself to warrant TV news coverage as he left the courtroom, after paying a $10 fine for disturbing the peace. During the next ten days Hidell was again filmed distributing pro-Castro material in front of the International Trade Mart. Cutler believes that the conspirators' plan was to give Oswald a high profile in the Dallas area. In a televised debate set up with the local delegate of the Cuban Student Directorate, Hidell proved himself very knowledgeable in Marxist theory. Cutler believes that this performance "placed Hidell head and shoulders above any other nominee for the Conspiracy's patsy." He posits that Hidell walked into the trap set up by the CIA-FBI, was branded a Red, and the cogs in the conspiracy to assassinate JFK were set in motion. The Communist "legend" was the setup that would make their story stick, especially if the patsy didn't live long enough to talk. While being led to believe that he was gathering information concerning a foreign or domestic plot to kill the nation's first and only Catholic president, Oswald-Hidell was actually being double-crossed by the Agency. The spy, as Communist defector and lone gun nut, was set up to hold the bag for the murder of the president. As Cutler surmises, "Hidell's successful infiltration was the result of his CIA assignment after his return from the Soviet Union. Apparently he never even smelled the cheese in the trap."

R. B. Cutler's book, *Alias Oswald,* presents a theory that is compatible with known facts and is within limits of reason given the blatant omission of certain other facts by those in charge of the most insidious conspiracy cover-up campaign in America's history. In the world of covert intelligence operations, it is not too farfetched to believe that the "Oswald-Hidell" switcheroo occurred and that the double agent lived in a dangerous world, where he was an "actor" infiltrating a "violently pro-Castro cabal dominated by autonomous intelligence operatives and Mob elements."

Alek James Hidell, alias Lee Harvey Oswald, died at Parkland Hospital at 1:07 P.M. on November 24, 1963, without ever regaining consciousness from the impact of Jack Ruby's bullet. He was buried on November 25 at Rose Hill Cemetery in Fort Worth, Texas, initially under the name "William Bobo." Before her death on January 17, 1981, Marguerite Oswald, Lee's mother, told a Dallas newspaper she had "serious doubts that the man buried in the Rose Hill grave was her son."

Issue 6, Fall 1994

The Center of the Labyrinth

Al Hidell

The labyrinth is thoroughly known. We have only to follow the thread of the hero's path, and where we had thought to find an abomination, we shall find a god. . . .

—Joseph Campbell

The shootings in Dallas were an ancient play, following a script etched long ago into our collective unconscious. Looking beyond specific evidence and theories, Al Hidell finds that the life and death of Lee Harvey Oswald contains intriguing parallels to the lives and deaths of several mythological figures. He asks: Was Oswald a sacred executioner or a mythic hero?

THE KENNEDY ASSASSINATION was a myth. I'm not saying that the events in Dallas did not happen. Just that they happened before. Indeed, the life and death of the alleged assassin, Lee Harvey Oswald, contain several intriguing parallels to the lives and deaths of several mythic heroes. Viewed in this way, the shootings in Dallas become an ancient play, following a script etched long ago into our collective unconscious.

The Warren Commission concluded that the actions of John Kennedy's assassin could not be judged by "the standards of reasonable men." Lee Oswald's life, they declared, had been one of "isolation, frustration, and failure." It was also a life of contradictions:

[Oswald] was never satisfied with anything. When he was in the U.S. he resented the capitalist system. . . . [After his defection to] the Soviet Union, he apparently resented . . . Party members who he

8

thought were betraying communism [and] spoke well of the United States.

Oswald's shifting opinions of the two superpowers were echoed by his shifting political associations. His life, marked overall by left-wing, pro-Castro sentiments, also included contacts with right-wing, anti-Castro individuals. These contacts may have been part of an effort to infiltrate the anti-Castro movement. Or perhaps it was his left-wing persona that was "manufactured," a ruse intended to mask his function as a "false" defector planted by U.S. Intelligence. As Harrison E. Salisbury remarked in his introduction to the Warren Report, "Both right- and left-wing [conspiracy] theorists are apt to cite many of the same pieces of evidence."

Contradictions

The puzzling contradictions of Oswald's life are reflected in this assessment of the life of another historical figure, the Greek hero Heracles:

> We shall not find in the actions of Heracles any consistent development of character or moral attitude. He is a mixture of paradoxical qualities, and these are the main reasons for the random arrangement of his life.

There are other similarities between Oswald and the heroes of what G. S. Kirk calls the "traditional tales" of our past. These similarities suggest that, like the soldiers of the Trojan War, Lee Oswald and Jack Ruby were unknowingly acting out the stuff of myth.

This article will look at Oswald's life in the context of three mythic frameworks: (1) Hyam Macoby's concept of the sacred executioner; (2) G. S. Kirk's suggested folktale motifs; and (3) Joseph Campbell's description of the hero's adventure.

Sacred Executioners

Mythologist Hyam Macoby has described an Athenian ritual that demonstrates society's "desire to shift the blame . . . to find some person or even object that can be . . . punished for an act which, nevertheless, was regarded as an essential observance." The ritual took place at the yearly Bouphonia (Bull Slaying Feast). As related by Macoby:

A bull representing Zeus was sacrificed on the altar of the temple. The priests [then] fled in mock panic, crying out a formula absolving them from the guilt of having slain the god. Afterward, a trial was held in which the blame was attributed to the knife that slit the bull's neck. That knife, having been found guilty, was punished by being destroyed.

A sacred executioner, like the "guilty" knife, absolves society from responsibility. (In Harrison Salisbury's contemporary observation, "There is in each of our hearts some feeling, however small, of responsibility: some feeling that each of us had some share in the crime because we had a role in a society which made it possible.") The sacred executioner is a scapegoat (pharmacost). Or perhaps a patsy.

Of significance (to conspiracy theorists, at least) is Macoby's statement that "the [sacred executioner] may himself be a victim, either of accident or of malicious plotting by which he is tricked into performing the execution." Macoby provides the Norse myth of the death of Balder as an example:

> It is Hother, the blind marksman, who performs the slaying; but the person really responsible for Balder's death is the evil plotter Loki, who performs no deed of violence himself but arranges that it should occur. Yet Loki and Hother cannot be quite separated. . . . They represent two aspects of a single entity: the misfortune by which the victim fell.

For Macoby, such misfortune can be interpreted in two ways: as sheer bad luck or as the result of evil plotting. Often, in the sacred executioner myths, one person stands for bad luck, another for malicious plotting. Applying Macoby's sacred executioner model, strip club operator Jack Ruby could represent the "plotting" component. It was, after all, mobster Ruby's public murder of Oswald that first aroused the suspicions of many conspiracy theorists.

Oswald's role as the assassination's "bad luck" component, and the idea that chance played a role in the assassination, is suggested by the following:

- Oswald gained employment at the Book Depository more than two months before Kennedy's route was selected.
- Oswald was allegedly using an unreliable Italian army surplus rifle manufactured in 1940.

- Many of the crates that shielded Oswald from the potential view of other Book Depository employees had been moved close to the window because work was being done on part of the warehouse floor.

Conversely, Ruby's representation of the "malicious plot" component is suggested by his documented connections to both the Dallas and Cuban underworlds. And, of course, the very fact that Ruby killed Oswald, perhaps to silence him, itself encourages the suspicion that both men were involved in an assassination conspiracy.

Like the scapegoat Oswald, Jack Ruby is also a kind of sacred executioner. As Macoby notes, "The essence of the Sacred Executioner is that he dares to take responsibility for the sacrifice." Oswald never admitted to killing the president, while Ruby proudly took credit for killing Oswald. In addition, the sacred executioner is said to kill "through malice, and yet in fulfillment of a beneficent will." Finally, the sacred executioner is described as being "an outcast from the community, yet representing it." The "lowlife" Ruby, as Oswald's sacred executioner, was clearly doing something that many angry but "respectable" citizens wanted to see done.

Oswald as Folk Hero

Oswald fits at least one of Professor G. S. Kirk's heroic criteria: "Most [mythic] heroes," he notes, "rather expectedly die remarkable deaths, usually violent ones." Citing the adventures of Perseus, Kirk remarks that heroic myths often contain "folktale-type motifs," which include

- defending one's mother from a seducer.
- the meant-to-be-fatal quest.
- rescuing the princess.
- an interest in exotic lands.

Each of these motifs describes an aspect of Lee Harvey Oswald's life:

Defending one's mother from a seducer: Lee's father died two months before Lee was born. Lee grew up living with his mother and slept in her bed until he was ten years old.

The meant-to-be-fatal quest: The events of November 1963 were fatal for both JFK and Oswald.

Rescuing the princess: Oswald made an adventurous defection to the Soviet Union, where he met and married his beautiful wife, Marina. He then took her with him back to America, in a sense "rescuing" her from a drab Soviet existence.

An interest in exotic lands: By November 1963 Oswald had lived in New York City, New Orleans, Fort Worth, Louisiana, and Dallas. In addition, he had served in the marines at Japan's Atsugi air base, origination point of the classified flights of the U2 spy planes. Oswald had also, as stated previously, lived in the Soviet Union. And in the early fall of 1963 Oswald is alleged to have traveled to Mexico City, where he applied for a Cuban visa.

Oswald as Mythic Hero

Kirk might view the assassination as a hybrid, or even clash, of folktale and myth: For him, folktales are concerned with "ordinary people" (such as Oswald), while myths are about "heroes . . . aristocratic figures far removed by birth and context from ordinary people" (such as Kennedy).

So, the life of Oswald-as-patsy does match part of Macoby's definition of a sacred executioner, as does the life of Oswald's murderer, Jack Ruby. Oswald's life also fits at least some of the motifs that Kirk describes as being part of many heroic folktales. But can we really call Lee Harvey Oswald a hero? We can if, like Joseph Campbell, we acknowledge the essential relativity of the term "hero":

> Whether you call someone a hero or a monster is all relative to where the focus of your consciousness may be. The moral objective [of heroism] is that of saving people . . . or supporting an idea. The hero sacrifices himself for something. . . . Now, you might say that the idea for which he sacrificed himself was something that should not have been respected . . . but [that] doesn't destroy the intrinsic heroism of the deed.

Indeed, for many right-wingers and bitter Bay of Pigs veterans, Oswald was in fact a hero. Conversely, the Greek "heroes" of the Trojan War were in no way heroes to the people they killed and enslaved.

Campbell elaborates on his definition of a hero: "[A] hero is someone who has given his or her life to something bigger than oneself." Then, Campbell notes that "when we quit thinking primarily about ourselves and our own self-preservation, we undergo a truly heroic transformation of the consciousness." Oswald, interestingly, expressed just these heroic attitudes in a letter written from the Soviet Union to his brother Robert:

> Happiness is not based on oneself, it does not consist of a small home, of taking and getting. Happiness is taking part in the struggle, where there is no borderline between one's own personal world and the world in general.

In addition, Oswald meets another of Campbell's heroic characteristics: "A hero is usually the founder of something, [for example] the founder of a new age." The Kennedy assassination is often said to mark the true beginning of the 1960s, the end of America's innocence, and the end of our political and moral idealism. When we look back, the assassination seems somehow to have paved the way for the violence yet to come.

Likewise, Oswald's chronic "dissatisfaction" and pattern of defection-return matches Campbell's outline of the typical heroic adventure:

> [It] begins with someone . . . who feels there's something lacking in the normal experiences available or permitted to the members of his society. . . . [His adventure] is usually a cycle, a going and a returning.

Echoing Sophocles

In Sophocles' *Antigone,* Antigone is a hero because she sacrifices her life in order to follow her conception of divine law. The king of Thebes has decreed that her brother Polynices, who died while trying to overthrow the existing Theban rulers, be denied a proper burial because he is a traitor. Meanwhile, Polynices' brother Eteocles, who died defending the city, is given a full state burial. But Antigone defies the decree, mourning her brother and placing upon him a covering of road dust.

In his novel *Libra,* one of the first efforts to mythologize Lee Oswald, Don DeLillo describes his burial and recalls Antigone's heroic action. Oswald was, in this context, a modern Polynices; Kennedy, Eteocles; and Marina, Antigone:

> . . . somebody ordered the body removed from the chapel . . . they called many ministers, Lutheran men of god, but none wanted to pray over Lee Harvey Oswald. . . . They were in such a hurry to bury [him] they forgot to notify the men who carry the coffin to the grave-

side, so news reporters teamed up to move the body. . . . They lowered [him] to the red clay of Texas, burying him for security reasons under another name. . . . Now Marina came forward and picked up a handful of dirt. She made the sign of the cross, then extended her arm over the grave, letting the dirt fall. . . .

Issue 4, Spring 1994

Gem Warfare

INTERVIEW WITH GERALD CARROLL

Joan d'Arc

Is there a connection among Aristotle Onassis, Howard Hughes, Jackie Kennedy, and the assassination of JFK? The Gemstone File, a document privately circulated in the 1970s, claimed to reveal the identity of the JFK assassination conspirators and placed Onassis and Hughes fully in the mix. In 1994 the bizarre claims made in The Gemstone File *and a subsequent book,* The Skeleton Key to the Gemstone File, *were cross-referenced by Gerald Carroll in his book* Project Seek. *This interview was conducted after the publication of his book.*

You state that you can corroborate that billionaire Howard Hughes was kidnapped in 1957, as the Gemstone thesis asserts. How sure are you about this?

It is clear that the real Howard Hughes dropped out of sight during the spring and summer of 1957, never to be heard from again. That much is evident. Proof is abundant. Hughes never appeared again in public after his trip to Nassau, the Bahamas, that spring and summer. Even close aides like Robert Maheu never saw him. Maheu claims that he once "saw" Hughes, but it was dark and Hughes was dressed to conceal his appearance. *Project Seek* deals with this sequence of the Gemstone thesis in great detail and outlines the many pieces of information that point to the Hughes kidnap and switch. Late in 1993, when I was finalizing much of *Project Seek,* I was contacted by Donald Neuhaus, one of Howard Hughes's personal aides. Neuhaus is now a reputable financier, and I have cross-checked his information. It is not only correct, in my view, it is extraordinarily accurate. The reason he waited so long to come forward was to ensure his personal safety and the safety of his family.

Neuhaus confirms much of what the Gemstone thesis says about Hughes. He worked for Hughes during that stormy year of 1957 when the entire Hughes Corporation underwent thunderous upheavals. He relates that during the summer of 1957 he was summoned to an emergency meeting at Hughes Corporation headquarters on Romaine Street, Beverly Hills. It was two A.M. when Neuhaus and other close aides to Hughes were informed that Noah Dietrich had resigned from the company. However, Neuhaus had always suspected there was more to it.

Upon reflection, Neuhaus now feels that Hughes was no longer in the picture at the time of that meeting. Afterward, "Hughes" changed dramatically. Neuhaus never saw him after that meeting. He did talk to him on the phone a few times. Neuhaus also was responsible for keeping tabs on actress Jean Peters at the Beverly Hills Hotel and confirms that the Hughes-Peters marriage never took place. The detail Neuhaus presents is indisputable and cannot be completely related here because of space limitations. It is all included in *Project Seek*, however.

Neuhaus also knew the Hughes doubles and confirms that L. Wayne Rector—mentioned prominently in the Gemstone thesis—was one of them. Neuhaus confirmed that many Hughes employees crossed over to Aristotle Onassis's organization right at that point in 1957 and thereafter, just as Gemstone asserts. One key member of that team was John Meyer, a Hughes attorney and public relations expert who—among other things—helped defend Elliott Roosevelt (son of President Franklin D. Roosevelt) in congressional hearings when Elliott was accused of a variety of improprieties, also mentioned in the Gemstone thesis. Meyer switched allegiances and became Onassis's press aide. One of Meyer's primary duties was to watch over Jacqueline Kennedy Onassis in the 1960s and 1970s. Meyer's career with Hughes started when he was a driver, and Neuhaus worked right alongside him for years.

Hughes's mysterious trip to the Bahamas involved a strange switching of pilots between stops in Montreal and Nassau. This is related by author Robert Serling in 1983 in his book on TWA. The new pilot, Greg Bushey, was called upon in Nassau every time Hughes wanted to fly. The reason? The real "Hughes" was gone, already kidnapped and switched, and the double could not fly a plane. Hughes was an expert aviator, but none of his doubles could even pretend to be pilots. Consequently Bushey had to fly the airplane to keep up the illusion that the real Hughes (who practically lived inside airplanes) was still around and still enthusiastic about flying.

The crude, unforgivable censorship and suppression of Clifford Irving's biography of Hughes by McGraw-Hill in 1972 also covered up much of this conjecture about a possible Hughes kidnapping. My fresh *Project Seek* contacts in that area include Frank McCulloch, an esteemed journalist with whom I worked for many years at the *San Francisco Examiner*. I was a staff editor and reporter, and McCulloch was managing editor. McCulloch was the last known reporter to have talked with Hughes over the phone. That conversation took place with other reporters present in 1972 and was designed to discredit Irving. It worked.

But McCulloch has admitted to me and other writers that he was convinced of the authenticity of Irving's biography because he read the text himself before McGraw-Hill decided to run with it. Keep in mind that advance sales of that book totaled four hundred thousand and that it was practically to the bindery before "Hughes," by phone to McCulloch, torpedoed the whole project. McGraw-Hill lost millions. I am convinced Irving's book was correct, and it was drawn from the computer printout of Hughes's life story that is discussed in the Gemstone thesis. There are many, many more examples of proof of Hughes's disappearance, published in *Project Seek* and other reputable sources.

You state in a letter to me that you are less sure about whether Aristotle Onassis was behind the kidnapping. What are the facts indicating that he may have been behind this? What would his motive have been?

For years Onassis had been hounded by the United States government and military-industrial complex. He made brutal enemies of the U.S. military by aiding and abetting American enemies during World War II. He made enemies of the petroleum establishment in this country by seeking to monopolize all oil shipments from Saudi Arabia. He purchased surplus U.S. ships illegally through fake American shell companies that he controlled. His alliance with the Kennedy family was profitable but controversial. He built huge oil tankers at U.S. taxpayer expense because he controlled the U.S. Maritime Commission with the help of Joseph Kennedy in 1937. He built these tankers mostly through arrangements with Bethlehem Steel, where Gemstone author Bruce Roberts's father worked. But he was hauled before Congress to defend his illegal ship purchases. Among those badgering Onassis was a hawk-ish young attorney named Robert Kennedy, maverick son of Joseph and a man hated by not only Onassis, but the entire Greek shipping indus-try. Cornered over and over again by government and industrial leaders in the United States, Onassis sought a way around these complications. Clearly, if he could exert some covert control of U.S. industry, he could circumvent the U.S. government—an end run if there ever was one. A good way to begin would be to gain control of the Hughes empire.

However, that is the point where much speculation and little proof exists. The one person with that connective information was probably Hank Greenspun, the Las Vegas newspaper publisher mentioned in Gemstone. Greenspun had connections with the shipping industry and had purchased a factory in Erie, Pennsylvania, in the late 1930s with a loan from—you guessed it—the Maritime Commission! This is a critical and little-known fact. That factory rebuilt engines for so-called liberty ships—the very ones Onassis purchased illegally from the United States. Greenspun, of course, was famous for having sensitive documents in his office safe (the Gemstone thesis says that said documents were related to the Hughes kidnap switch and that the Watergate plumbers at one point wanted to break into that safe and find out what was in there). Greenspun died in 1989 at the age of seventy-nine. With him died any firm answers to the Hughes mystery.

One vital point is provided by Donald Neuhaus: Jack Egger, who used to be director of security for Warner Brothers Studio, was Beverly Hills police chief in 1957 when the Hughes kidnapping allegedly took place. Neuhaus said that Frank Egger was under orders by the CIA to keep "Hughes" bottled up in Beverly Hills after "Hughes" returned from the Bahamas trip in 1957. Jack Egger is son of Frank Egger, who in the 1950s was a key executive with the insurance firm of Bailey, Martin and Faye. BM&F was one of the largest insurers of oil tanker hulls in the world. A key client was a Greek gentleman named Aristotle Onassis. None of these connections really proves anything, but if Onas-sis wanted to make a move toward seizing the Hughes empire, he had all the tools necessary to accomplish the task in just the way the Gem-stone thesis implies.

Do you have any information on the strange deaths of Onassis's son, Alexander, who died in a plane crash, and his daughter, Christina, who had a heart attack at a fairly young age? Do you smell any foul play here?

Yes, on both counts, and the facts that follow are derived from a number of reliable, published sources. Alexander Onassis died on January 22, 1973, when his Piaggio seaplane crashed on takeoff. Alexander, a passenger, died, while the pilot, Donald McCusker, survived with injuries. Aristotle Onassis hired a private investigator, Alan Hunter, to pinpoint the cause of the crash. Hunter discovered evidence of sabotage: the aileron controls of the Piaggio had been reversed. McCusker had been instructed to bank left when airborne in order to avoid the wake of a French Boeing 727 that had taken off moments earlier. When the Piaggio drifted right instead, McCusker applied more left wheel and flew the Piaggio into the ground. The Gemstone thesis erroneously blames the crash on a "fixed altimeter." Bruce Roberts stands corrected on this one. Onassis suspected, among other people, the CIA, his shipping rival Stavros Niarchos, and even his wife, Jacqueline Kennedy Onassis. However, he died never knowing who sabotaged his son's seaplane.

Christina died of a sudden, mysterious ailment at the age of thirty-seven in Buenos Aires on November 20, 1989. She had just overcome a multitude of personal problems and had turned her life around. She was a competent executive running her late father's shipping company (Aristotle Onassis died in 1975). She collapsed at poolside and died of what was reported as a "lung disorder, a pulmonary edema caused by an accumulation of blood in the lung." At the time of death she had no health problems. Results of an autopsy and blood analysis were never released, so it is not known if she had been poisoned. A few days after her death, the body being whisked off for burial on the island of Skorpios, a conflicting report was issued that Christina Onassis had died of a "heart attack."

You indicate that Ted Kennedy and Jackie were always running to Aristotle for protection. What was the tie-in with the Kennedys and Onassis? How did he hold the reins of power over them?

The connection began in 1917 when Joseph Kennedy was an executive with the old Bethlehem Steel shipyard in Quincy, Massachusetts. It was evident at the tail end of World War I that whoever owned the shipping lanes would be among the world's most wealthy. Then, as now, three major commodities dominated shipping: oil, drugs, and arms. World War I made many people wealthy, and other conflicts promised to do the same. John D. Rockefeller had monopolized the oil business until the government broke up Standard Oil in 1911. This precipitated a furious battle for control of the world's oil transport. Enter Mr. Onassis.

The next titanic struggle involved control of the world's sales of illegal alcoholic beverages to Prohibition-bound Americans. Alcohol remained legal in many freewheeling nations during Prohibition. The trick was transporting it into the United States. Enter Mr. Kennedy. Joseph, whose father, Patrick, had been a saloon operator and had enriched himself through liquor sales, had no plans to stop that business during Prohibition. But he needed an established transportation network, and Onassis was certainly beginning to see the profit potential from his perch in Buenos Aires and, later, Europe. An alliance was struck, just as the Gemstone thesis describes.

The opium trade routes had been established for centuries, and trade in opium was essentially legal in most of the world at the turn of the century. It was only after passage of antiopium laws in the United States that the opium trade became explosively profitable. Because opiates became illegal in the United States, the price jumped ten times or more compared with what the world market was supporting. It has never been proven that Onassis was a "drug pusher," as the Gemstone thesis bluntly states. However, that is not to say that his shipping business did not carry its share of that contraband—with or without his direct knowledge or approval. Onassis dealt through various levels of government bureaucracies and a web of business associates, so hiding the movement of illegal substances—whether they be Prohibition booze or heroin—would not be difficult.

The Onassis-Kennedy link would strengthen dramatically in the late 1930s as it became increasingly evident that Nazi Germany and the rest of the Western world were on an unalterable collision course. In *Project Seek* we document a connection between Onassis and the U.S. Maritime Commission in 1937, when Joseph Kennedy was named chairman of the commission. He was in that position only briefly—but long enough to approve the sale of surplus U.S. ships to Onassis and other Greek shippers. There was furious debate over this sale, since there was no way to assure that those ships would not be used against the United States in the event of a major European war.

So the connection between Onassis and the Kennedy family has a lengthy history. It was only when John and Robert grew up, entered politics, and tried to establish a Camelot-style empire in the United States that conflict between the Kennedys and Onassis erupted. The Gemstone thesis states that these conflicts led to the violent deaths of the Kennedy brothers and the political assassination of a third. Whether Onassis was directly involved is not as important as remembering that the violence against the Kennedys greatly strengthened Onassis's position as a world economic emperor.

In Project Seek *you discuss the bizarre reports of sightseers boating past a Greek island and seeing a man in a wheelchair with a woman who looked like Jackie O. These sightings may have instigated the tabloid reports that JFK is still alive.*

In my view, the sightings of an old man on two of the Greek islands—Tenos and Skorpios—were legitimate. Indications are the old man was the real Howard Hughes. However, when Canadian journalists leaked that story, some kind of cover was needed to make sure people would not think of the Hughes angle. So it would be easy to leak a version of that story to the American tabloid press saying that JFK had survived and was living on a Greek island. That way, readers in this country could have a few laughs and that would be the end of it.

A similar situation exists now with the "Elvis is alive" scenarios that are resurrected whenever tabloid press sales levels drop below a certain point. What remains intriguing, though, is why the U.S. tabloid press has never parroted the Gemstone thesis, despite its obvious appeal to readers of such material. The reason: The tabloids never wanted to cross Jacqueline Kennedy Onassis. Personally, I believe that Aristotle Onassis exerted certain controls over the U.S. alternative press and was able to plant—through his highly paid media agents—the stories he wanted to see in print. Money was a key factor. Reporters could be paid substantial sums to write stories that skipped quietly around any Onassis-Kennedy connections (historical or otherwise).

Plus, remember John Meyer, mentioned earlier. He was Howard Hughes's crack media contact, and he did the same for Onassis in later years with regard to information concerning Jackie. In short, the story that JFK was alive and living on a Greek island was bogus. However, it could well have been that the real Howard Hughes was the "old man."

Can you comment on the power which Jackie Onassis held with her ties to Random House and how this power may have blocked publication of certain Gemstone-related manuscripts? You mention that Gerald Posner's book Case Closed *was published by the book firm that employed Mrs. Onassis. Why did she want this particular "case" closed?*

Jackie Onassis, while alive, had extraordinary influence on the American book business. Her influence was felt in all literary circles. She was called a book "editor" at Random House, but in my view she was a censor. That is why a full accounting of the Gemstone thesis, until *Project Seek,* was never published by any major house. They did not want to cross Jackie. Now, intriguingly, the thirtieth anniversary of the JFK assassination was "celebrated" in November 1993. Note that Posner's heavily financed and promoted book was released at that time. That book is full of useless information and frivolous attempts to discredit the few remaining eyewitnesses to the JFK assassination. Then, Dan Rather and CBS News came out with a major JFK assassination "historical overview" special, and the highly respected PBS documentary magazine *Frontline* presented an exhaustive life history of accused JFK assassin Lee Harvey Oswald.

The common thread in all three of those major presentations? They all, incredulously, support the Warren Commission Report. Anyone with any common sense and decency realizes the Warren Report is a monstrous falsehood. To again propagandize the American public with that mountain of trash on the thirtieth anniversary of JFK's death is unforgivable. But they all had the blessing of Jacqueline Kennedy Onassis. In the spring of 1990, when I was working on preliminary drafts of *Project Seek,* a friend of Jacqueline Onassis's, a gentleman from New York named Robert Tompkins, visited me at my home, which was then in rural Kentucky. Mr. Tompkins was interested in my Gemstone research. Upon seeing what I had uncovered, he told me I would never get my work published by any publisher in New York because of Mrs. Onassis's position at Random House.

However, he was sympathetic to my situation and added that he believed Jackie had made the decision to suppress any material related to her late second husband, Aristotle Onassis, mainly to protect her children and extended family. That was the major reason, he said, she married Onassis in the first place. If there was one individual powerful enough to offer Jackie the protection she needed, it was Onassis, he reasoned. Further, Tompkins had been a close associate of Dorothy Kilgallen's, the famed journalist and longtime member of the TV game show *What's My Line?* Ms. Kilgallen was found dead soon after she uncovered explosive information about the JFK assassination as a reporter in Dallas. Tompkins was very concerned that the world would never know the real reason behind Kilgallen's death.

In the end Tompkins cautioned me not to pursue *Project Seek* any further, and since he sounded very convincing, I backed off the project for two years. That was how much I respected Jackie Onassis's position in the literary world. I find it interesting that as soon as *Project Seek* was released in the spring of 1994, three major Gemstone-related personalities had recently passed away or were about to: Watergate conspirator and Bay of Pigs operative Frank Sturgis, former president Richard Nixon, and Jacqueline Kennedy Onassis.

So Jackie may not be as innocent as we all want to believe?

Jacqueline Kennedy Onassis is a monumental historical figure. She has had more impact on the history of this country than any other woman. I would compare her with the likes of Catherine the Great, Queen Elizabeth, or Joan of Arc as far as historical importance in relation to the United States of America. But much of that was behind the scenes. She was swept up into history and dealt with it as well as anybody in her position. Personally, she dealt with a very brutal mother-in-law, Rose Kennedy, and an equally demanding father-in-law, Joseph Kennedy. Her husband, John Kennedy, was unfaithful on many occasions, and this led to extraordinary personal suffering. JFK's overall health was always a problem. The whole picture was one of a disjointed, largely political union between two quite awesome and charismatic personalities. This joint charisma carried the JFK presidency. The aura of Camelot was hypnotic, and it did not truly reflect the personal desperation these people had right until the time of the assassination.

Then a person comes along, Aristotle Onassis, who sees all this going on and wants to do something about it. Jackie's well-being became an obsession with Onassis—an obsession that started when Jackie's young son Patrick died. Onassis invited the First Lady on his yacht, the *Christina,* and according to sources in *Project Seek* and elsewhere, these two people started to have feelings for one another. The need was there on both sides. Onassis saw something in Jackie he had never seen in other women, and he was helplessly caught up in it. All things considered, the early relationship between Onassis and Jackie was nothing less than the purest form of raw love and attraction. Passion knows no boundaries and does not recognize individual feelings. In that sense, Onassis and Jackie were destined to have some type of relationship together. Conversely, Jackie saw in Onassis's isolation a kind of eerie security; the voices of history would no longer plague her life and the lives of her children if she were to spend more time on Skorpios than in New York.

As Bruce Roberts asserts, was the Jackie-K to Jackie-O metamorphosis in a perverse way Onassis's "prize" in the Mafia hit on JFK?

The assassination presented an opportunity. Whether intentional or not, the dominant fallout of JFK's death was the inevitable marriage between Jackie and Onassis. In that sense, the assassination was a release point and marked the dawn of a new era in history.

Some evidence points to Jackie having advance knowledge that her husband's life was in mortal danger. After all—as described in *Project Seek* but ignored by mainstream media—there were at least three documented attempts on JFK's life before the actual assassination. In all three instances, Secret Service protection broke down. One of those attempts took place when Kennedy was running for president in 1960; the other two took place while he was in office. They were covered by the media in brief, laundered form and quickly dropped from public view. It's all in *Project Seek,* but few researchers place any emphasis on it. I find that absolutely astonishing.

It is also clear that Jackie received very strong hints that JFK was going to be eliminated when she went on that cruise on the *Christina* in the fall of 1963. Keep in mind, she was with Onassis for about two weeks or thereabouts, and the Secret Service panicked when the yacht disappeared for a few days in the Mediterranean. The government went as far as to suspend payments due Onassis's shipping operation until it was evident that the safety of the First Lady was assured. This is where I think that Onassis was more of a beneficiary of the JFK hit than the person actually behind it. He was aware through his vast international network that JFK stood in the way of economic considerations embraced not only by the Mafia, but by our own government as well. He had advance knowledge of it, I'm sure of that.

The actions of Jackie in the hours right after the assassination were also amazing. She has been described as being "strong" and "noble" through that horrible experience, but I am convinced she knew it was coming and was able to get through it because she had prepared for it. She was always calm and collected—not hysterical and out of control. Which is not what I would expect of any woman who had just seen her husband's head being blown off by an assassin's bullet. Armed with the knowledge that JFK's death was a certainty (although she would not know of the precise day, hour, or method), she was even further motivated to get out of the picture for a while, and Onassis provided an opening with the yacht cruise in October–November 1963.

Gemstone states that the assassination team was poised and ready to knock off JFK in Chicago in early November 1963 but that JFK caught wind of that and canceled the trip. That has been confirmed by researcher Sherman Skolnick of Chicago. All this was happening when Jackie was still on her cruise and just returning from it. Realizing all these circumstances, Jackie used Onassis as security and as a fallback position in case JFK was killed. Onassis, knowing the hit was taking place, probably through his connections, guessed it would be sometime in the fall and most likely thought that whisking Jackie away would keep her safe until JFK had been eliminated.

Personally, I think Onassis felt Jackie herself would be killed in the assassination attempt and tried to protect her from that for as long as he could, keeping her out of the picture and on the *Christina*. When danger passed in Chicago, both he and Jackie might have felt it safe enough for her to return. As it was, Jackie miraculously escaped being killed in the fusillade of bullets that rained upon the presidential motorcade on November 22, 1963. As for Jackie being the "prize" for Onassis after JFK's death, I think that is reaching and a point where Gemstone source Bruce Roberts got caught up with his own passions.

The Gemstone thesis and the JFK assassination are tied into many bizarre and sudden deaths. What possessed you to devote so much time to such a controversial topic?

Anyone who has even been exposed to the Gemstone file—especially when it was first being passed around in the mid-1970s—will tell you there is an indisputable magnetism to the statements. They ring as facts, not fiction, and the writer cares little for his (or her) personal safety in openly describing this alternate view of twentieth-century history. *The Skeleton Key to the Gemstone File* (written by Stephanie Caruano), in its introduction, requests help from other researchers in verifying statements made in the document. However, at that time, in 1975 or 1976, this information was still a little too hot for most people to investigate for fear of losing life or limb. That's what happened to Larry Flynt and *Hustler* magazine, which had gained possession of this material in 1975.

I was told in 1975 that *Hustler* would run the *Skeleton Key* in its entirety. I kept looking for it, and it never appeared. Then, in January 1978, Flynt suddenly announced he would offer $1 million for information leading to proof of a conspiracy to assassinate JFK. He must have had the Gemstone material already and was seeking confirmation of the statements pertaining to Onassis's possible connection to JFK.

Then, shockingly, Flynt was shot and paralyzed from the waist down in March 1978, only two months after his announcing the $1 million reward. That cast a great chill over any Gemstone research. I knew that *Hustler* had the Gemstone writings, that Flynt had been shot probably because he was about to publish them, and it was lights out for any Gemstone research until the situation stabilized. However, *Hustler* eventually did run a version of the *Skeleton Key* in February 1979, almost four years after they'd first obtained that material and nearly a year after Flynt was shot. Flynt announced he had obtained the material from a source who stated: "Everyone who has seen this is now dead." It would appear that Flynt took great further risks to actually publish the Gemstone material, but his version was so drastically trimmed down that many potentially damaging passages were removed. That probably took the heat off enough to go ahead and publish.

However, most versions of the *Skeleton Key* have all the material, including that which was edited out of *Hustler*'s version. A comparison of these versions makes up a large part of *Project Seek*'s initial analysis. My own research accelerated rapidly upon learning how and why *Hustler* published its version. I was very anxious to learn why the magazine left out huge pieces of the Gemstone thesis, and I wanted the general public to know about the entire *Key* so they could determine for themselves whether the statements were correct. Further, I wanted to open the door for more researchers to enter this area, researchers with more data and background than I possess. I encourage a more open debate about Gemstone instead of the current scene of arm's-length, misinformed debunking of it among conspiracy researchers.

What kind of trouble did you encounter while writing Project Seek, *and how are you faring now in the aftermath of its publication? Is the heat off the Gemstone thesis?*

I did encounter many hurdles in producing *Project Seek,* not least of which was finding a publisher. Nobody really seems interested in bringing up this topic, despite the evidence that it is more than simply a distorted rant fabricated by a disturbed mind. Although that could indeed be true, it does not settle the question of the validity of some of the statements it contains. The next problem was staying in the realm of mainstream media. I was a newspaper professional when my *Project Seek* research was hitting its peak: the harbinger of many lies we are bombarded with day in and day out. Morally I could not live with myself being in the news business, knowing that the media establishment purposely distorts the truth on many key issues we deal with today, especially in the area of twentieth-century history.

There is never a day when the information contained within the Gemstone thesis is not hazardous to its researchers. However, with many of the primary characters deceased (Nixon and Jackie passed away soon after *Project Seek* was released), it is certainly less of a danger than in the 1970s when *Hustler* took on this material. There is considerable margin for error in the statements made in the Gemstone thesis, and for the most part I point them out in *Project Seek.* The major difficulty is the simple omission of facts by the mainstream press during this period. The incidents were reported but never included in any historical reviews, especially of twentieth-century maritime history, where the Gemstone file was spawned.

Do you think there's a margin of safety provided by some of the bizarre attributes of the Gemstone thesis? That it's just too "kooky" for some people to accept at face value?

The Gemstone material has earned a "kooky" reputation over the years, but that has to do with people's attitudes more than anything else. There is a hesitancy to discuss ideas and different interpretations of historical events. Most mainstream historical accounts conveniently leave out facts that are vital to the understanding of a particular culture's history. That is exactly the case with the Gemstone thesis. Granted, the wording is blunt and without accompanying support. It's not that such support for the statements does not exist—we certainly uncovered plenty in the process of researching *Project Seek*—it's just that it has been covered up or suppressed in some fashion over the years.

This subtle kind of censorship—that is, omission of facts—is only going to get worse in the coming years with the Internet and World Wide Web. For example, many copies of the old *Skeleton Key to the Gemstone File* are available on the Internet. However, none to my knowledge has the kind of appropriate supporting documentation we have tried to provide in *Project Seek*. In short, the more facts people have in their possession, the more informed they are, the better position they will be in to determine exactly what the history of our culture is and how to improve it.

Do you see any hope of this information making a difference, or do you think it will all get swept under the rug?

Any time you're dealing with information that embarrasses the ruling elites of our nation and world at large, it will get swept under the rug. But that information never goes away. It is always there in some form, and it will always resurface and become an even more powerful force. In the case of the Gemstone thesis, this information has seen the light of day, and when the mainstream press catches up with it, there will be hell to pay as far as the ruling classes are concerned. Look what is happening to the Clinton administration, and look what happened to the Bush administration before that. Criminal activity abounds within our own government, and only through the efforts of a small group of dedicated researchers will the truth ever come out.

Had the old Gemstone theories about Aristotle Onassis, for example, been researched by the mainstream press as soon as they became known, it would have painted a much different picture of maritime history in the early twentieth century and cast the assassinations of JFK, RFK, Martin Luther King Jr., and Malcolm X in a different light. The entire stretch of history between the disappearance of Howard Hughes in 1957 and the Watergate scandal in 1972 would have made more sense. Bruce Roberts attempted to connect these events and make a comprehensible whole out of it. It's too bad much of his work has disappeared. It would be nice for more of his original writings to come to the fore in order to better understand the entire Gemstone story. The Roberts writings are to conspiracy research what the Dead Sea scrolls are to biblical research—a vital documentation of one person's worldview. They deserve a fair hearing and analysis. In that sense, *Project Seek* is only a beginning.

You indicate your book is very popular in Europe. Do Europeans see this huge conspiracy as "rogue Americana," like a cowboy movie, or do they take it seriously?

Europeans have known about this material for decades. Great Britain is where Onassis first cranked up his merchant fleet into high gear following his start in Argentina in the 1920s. The stories about drug trafficking are old hat; it has long been rumored (and documented in some cases) that England's royal family accumulated much of its vast fortune through the opium trade with China, and that trade continues through today, albeit in different forms (heroin, cocaine) and different markets, the United States being the largest.

Australians have been very receptive, mainly because the history of Onassis's involvement in Western Pacific banking circles has been legendary over the years. As the Gemstone thesis declares, Onassis's "involvement in the Golden Triangle drug trade was no secret." Indeed, the biggest problem was finding a safe haven for all the money generated from contraband shipments. Keep in mind that much of this drug commerce remained legal in many parts of the world throughout most of the century until 1963, when opium-poppy growing restrictions were adopted on a worldwide basis. Those restrictions, however, are largely unenforced outside the United States, and the trade flourishes.

The precepts in *Project Seek* have a special meaning to the Islamic world, which has long known of America's drug history and has been hostile toward Americans mainly because of that legacy. Many Islamic nations, such as the lawless government of Afghanistan, now grow opium poppies in large numbers, openly and commercially, and manufacture hard drugs for export into the United States. They justify this practice as a way to fight America from within and destroy U.S. morale without having to challenge the Americans militarily.

Our war with Iraq was no accident, and the roots of that can be found within the Gemstone thesis. Our upcoming war with Iran will also be no accident, but with Iranian access to nuclear weaponry, that war will have far more devastating consequences.

It is no surprise that the United States is hated by many nations on earth. We have attracted this hatred as a people by ignoring such matters as the Gemstone thesis outlines. We don't even know our own history and therefore cannot relate to why most of the rest of the world has a virulent hatred toward everything the United States stands for. That is why *Project Seek* and all related research is so critical. Eventually, when enough mainstream research is directed toward exposing our own hidden history, a reawakening of world consciousness will be inevitable.

Issue 10, Fall 1995

SUSPICIOUS DEATHS

Who Killed John Lennon?

Al Hidell

Mark David Chapman appeared to be a classic "lone nut" assassin. But what led him to shoot ex-Beatle John Lennon in 1980, and did he have help? Al Hidell looks at the evidence for a conspiracy and explores the role the novel The Catcher in the Rye *(written by reclusive former intelligence officer J. D. Salinger) may have had in the assassination.*

MARK DAVID CHAPMAN was the classic "lone nut" assassin. After shooting John Lennon with four devastating hollow-point bullets, he did not make what would have been an easy nighttime escape. Instead he waited patiently for the New York City police to arrive, calmly reading *The Catcher in the Rye.*

The novel's reclusive author, J. D. Salinger, served with Henry Kissinger in the army's Counter Intelligence Corps (CIC) during World War II. The CIC often worked with its civilian counterpart, the Office of Strategic Services (OSS), forerunner of the CIA. Salinger's novel was also owned by Ronald Reagan's attempted assassin, John Hinckley Jr.

When he died on December 8, 1980, John Lennon, the most politically active rock star of his generation, had been due to fly to San Francisco to march in support of striking Japanese American workers. The radical ex-Beatle was "returning to the streets," and as suggested by London lawyer Fenton Bresler in his book *Who Killed John Lennon?,* he "was likely to prove a rallying point for mass opposition to the policies . . . of the new U.S. government headed by Ronald Reagan."

However, the murder of John Lennon was never investigated by a commission. It was not filmed or photographed. And the alleged assassin avoided a trial by pleading guilty. Consequently there is little available evidence, and Bresler can present only a largely circumstantial case for conspiracy.

33

Not Insane

First, he demolishes the popular conception of the "lone nut" assassin, noting that Mark David Chapman was not ruled insane. In fact, between 1835 and 1981, fifteen men and two women have attacked nationally prominent political leaders. Only three have been ruled insane by law. (Three were killed before they could stand trial: Huey Long's assassin, Carl Weiss; Lincoln's assassin, John Wilkes Booth; and Lee Harvey Oswald.)

Bresler then argues against three major theories of Chapman's motivation:

He killed Lennon to become famous and gain attention. If this were the case, why does Chapman continue to turn away "thirty or forty" media requests for interviews every year? And why did he plead guilty, losing the spotlight and attention of a trial?

He believed that he was himself John Lennon, and the act was a twisted kind of suicide.

He was a devout fan who now hated John Lennon because he'd become a "phony," just another rich capitalist rock star.

In rejecting the last two theories, Bresler offers a weak argument: He dismisses them because "both cannot possibly be right." This is like saying, "The sky cannot be both blue and purple, so the sky is not blue." Nevertheless, the "thought he was Lennon" theory does not fit a person who acted "coolly and rationally" and was ruled legally sane. The "Lennon was a phony" theory is plausible, given the odd increase in media coverage of Ono-Lennon's wealth and business dealings in the months before his death. (They owned the entire seventh floor of the Dakota, their New York apartment building. The couple also owned a weekend home on Long Island, a Florida mansion, a 63-foot yacht, and 250 prize Holstein cattle.)

"He Could Have Been Programmed"

Whatever his motive, eyewitnesses saw Chapman pull the trigger, and he freely admitted his guilt. Police officials considered it an open-and-shut case. Yet at least one of them now has nagging doubts. As Arthur O'Connor, NYPD lieutenant of detectives, admitted to Fenton Bresler in 1988, "It's possible Mark could have been used by somebody. I saw him the night of the murder. I studied him intensely. He looked as if he could have been programmed."

YMCIA?

If Chapman was programmed to kill John Lennon, who did the programming? An ex-CIA case officer suggested one possibility to Bresler. He told the writer that the YMCA was possibly one of many CIA-infiltrated front organizations. With offices in nearly ninety countries, it was certainly possible that the CIA may have used the YMCA in its intelligence operations. This also makes sense given the CIA's known history of financing and infiltrating such domestic organizations as the National Students Association.

Perhaps it is merely coincidence, but Mark David Chapman had a clear and long-term involvement with the YMCA throughout his life. In 1975 he went to Beirut for them. (Mark, by then a fundamentalist Christian, had asked to be sent to the Soviet Union.) He also worked for the Y at a camp for Vietnamese refugees (also in 1975) and at a YMCA camp in Georgia (1969–1976). In 1978 he toured the world, staying in several YMCA youth hostels. Despite these connections, Chapman's name does not appear in the YMCA's central archives. The Chapman file, if it ever existed, is missing.

Assassin Training

Bresler cites research conducted by the Christic Institute, which claims the CIA has trained assassins at a location in Hawaii. Hawaii has also been named as a CIA training site by conspiracy researcher Mae Brussell. These islands, with their strong U.S. Naval presence, were also the home of Mark David Chapman in the three years before he killed John Lennon. It is known that Mark was trained as a "security guard" while in Beirut, but could the CIA have programmed this previously antigun Christian to kill? Bresler says yes and cites evidence of CIA mind control experiments begun in the early 1950s.

"It Wasn't an Accident"

After recounting Lennon's increasing involvement in left-wing politics, Bresler reports that the FBI had a file on Lennon of over two hundred pages, some marked "Copy to CIA." The files make clear the government's concern about John Ono Lennon. In April 1972 J. Edgar Hoover directed his New York office to "locate subject [Lennon] and remain aware of his activities and movements . . . careful attention should be given reports that subject is heavy narcotics user."

The files make much of Lennon's "revolutionary activities" and consider him a legitimate security threat. (Lennon was indeed a threat: to Richard Nixon's presidency. He was involved in several left-wing causes, including a planned demonstration at the Republican national convention.) Bresler has found a 1973 FBI memo that refers to "the illegal electronic surveillance" of Lennon's phone calls. And at least one FBI memo urges agents to "neutralize" Lennon's "disruptive" activities. Lennon was well aware of the government's concern and of its relentless surveillance. Bresler reports that in 1972 Lennon told publisher Paul Krassner, "Listen, if anything happens to Yoko and me, it wasn't an accident."

Preferred Rundgren

While Lennon fought government harassment and a threatened deportation based on a 1968 marijuana conviction, Chapman was supposedly his "devout fan," right? Like most teenagers, Mark was a Beatles fan. But according to the New York County assistant DA who prosecuted him, Mark "had no particular interest in John Lennon between age fourteen and twenty-four." In fact, part of the prosecution's strategy, had a trial occurred, was that Chapman simply wanted to kill a famous person, any famous person, to become famous himself. In addition, classmate Newton Hendrix has recalled that "[Mark] never expressed strong views on Lennon or the Beatles. He played the guitar and may have written some songs, but it was not 'Beatle-type' music." Honolulu police captain Louis Souza told Bresler that "he was [not] a John Lennon nut. It appeared that he was just the opposite. He . . . was not a particular fan of John Lennon." And Brook Hart, the Honolulu lawyer who represented Chapman's wife, has stated, "I have more Beatle records in my collection than Mark had." Based on his belongings, Bresler reports that Mark was, in fact, a major Todd Rundgren fan. In fact, it was a Rundgren tape, not a Lennon tape, that he left for police to find in his room.

Altered Evidence

An altered airline ticket is one of the few solid pieces of evidence of conspiracy. The airline ticket conveniently left by Chapman on display in his hotel room suggests that Mark flew straight from Hawaii to New York via a Chicago connecting flight. The ticket found in his hotel room had a departure date of December 5, and it is undisputed that Mark landed in New York on Saturday, December 6.

But the ticket purchased by Mark (on November 28) was not, in fact, for a flight leaving Hawaii on December 5. It was for a flight leaving Hawaii on Tuesday, December 2. Bresler reports that United Airlines had confirmed, to Honolulu police captain Souza, that Chapman used the ticket on December 2. On December 9 Chapman's wife, Gloria, seemed to confirm the earlier date when she stated that Mark had left Hawaii "eight or ten days" ago. In other words, we know that Chapman flew from Hawaii to Chicago on December 2 and from Chicago to New York on the night of December 5. Bresler concludes that someone has altered the airline ticket, which originally had the correct departure date of December 2, to cover up the fact that Chapman spent three days in Chicago before he flew to New York.

Even more puzzling is the fact that the airline ticket purchased by Chapman was for a flight from Hawaii to Chicago on December 2 and a return flight from Chicago to Hawaii on December 18. In other words, it was a round-trip ticket to Chicago, with no mention of New York. Even if Mark purchased a round-trip ticket just to save money (round-trip tickets often cost less than a single one-way ticket to the same destination), this does not explain why he did not purchase a Chicago–New York ticket at the same time. To Bresler this suggests that Mark initially intended to go to Chicago and "decided" to fly to New York only during his mysterious three-day stay in Chicago.

But why would Mark have flown to Chicago in the first place, if not with the intent of flying on to New York to kill Lennon? A possible answer was suggested to Bresler during his interview with Gloria Chapman's friend Ruth Brilhante. She stated, "When we heard that Mark had shot Lennon, we couldn't believe it. Not only because we could not believe he could do a thing like that, but because we did not know he was in New York. We all thought he was in Chicago. That is where he had gone to take his grandmother home after she was visiting out here." It is known that Mark had a grandmother in Chicago, but there is some confusion over whether he was taking her back to Chicago or simply visiting her there. (Of course, the story could have simply been a lie on Mark's part.)

Ringo's Cryptic Comment

As the medical examiner was conducting the autopsy, Beatle drummer Ringo Starr arrived at the Dakota with his fiancée, Barbara Bach. He was there to console Yoko and was the only surviving Beatle to make the journey. As Starr later told *People* magazine, Yoko had asked to see Starr only by himself. In response he said, "Look, it was you who started all this. We're both coming in."

Now what could he have meant by this odd statement? Although Bresler makes no such speculation, and there is no hard evidence to prove it, Starr may have been referring to the highly publicized "feud" between Lennon and his former partner, Paul McCartney. Unfairly, perhaps, the feud is thought to have begun when Yoko Ono "broke up" the Beatles.

If this is the case, could Starr have considered the Lennon murder to be some kind of finale to the feud? Keep in mind that, at the time, McCartney had recently been jailed in Japan on a marijuana possession charge. Facing an extremely stiff prison sentence, he had been imprisoned and humiliated. (His Japanese guards had gotten their kicks by forcing their famous prisoner to sing "Yesterday.") Was this the incident behind Ringo's comment? And had McCartney suspected that John or Yoko had been involved and in turn taken his extreme revenge? Although this theory is farfetched, it is clear that Yoko or her banking family had the means to pull strings in Japan. And it might explain McCartney's seemingly sarcastic comment to a network news crew in response to the assassination: "It's a drag," he said disinterestedly.

Justice Denied

Once again, a liberal public voice has been silenced. (Why is it that violent deaths seem to happen only to left-wing entertainers and politicians? Do their more conservative peers lead charmed lives?) John Lennon's death brought about an unprecedented wave of grief and sadness but precious little investigation. It seems we owe it to his memory to at least ask why. After all, we may know who shot John Lennon, but do we really know who killed him?

Issue 3, Winter 1994

Chappaquiddick:
Water Under the Bridge?

R. B. Cutler

This lecture and interview with New England assassinologist R. B. Cutler portrays the Chappaquiddick incident as a CIA ambush rather than an accident, from which Ted Kennedy walked away and his brother Bobby's secretary, Mary Jo Kopechne, lost her life. After twenty-five years of media distortion and Kennedy family cover-up, this bizarre event may be better understood as the political assassination of the third Kennedy brother. Three years after this article appeared in Paranoia, *A&E televised a documentary in 1997 which concluded that Ted Kennedy was not in the car on that fateful night. Will the Cutler ambush hypothesis finally get its day in court?*

Original Introduction

Dean: . . . if they get those bank records between the start of July of 1969 through June of 1971 . . . there comes Chappaquiddick with a vengeance. . . .

Nixon: (unintelligible)

Dean: . . . if they get to it . . . that is going to come out, and this whole thing can turn around on that. If Kennedy knew what a bear trap he was walking into . . .

Watergate tape, 3/13/73

The Chappaquiddick "accident" occurred just thirteen months after the assassination of Robert Kennedy. It was rumored that Teddy had been drinking heavily during those months, traumatized by the assassi-

nations of both his brothers. A perfect hit on the third Kennedy brother's political career, therefore, did not necessitate killing him. In fact, a third shooting would have been poorly advised, as it would have alerted a sleeping citizenry to the "conspiracy" in charge of America's seat of power.

Using Teddy's weakness for alcohol against him was the perfect way to scandalize him out of the presidential race of 1972. No better trap could have been set than an engineered automobile accident after a party which had involved "booze, blondes, and the beach." But the people never had the chance to hear the whole story. Many questions were never properly answered, many contradictions not addressed. Now, after twenty-five years of distortion and cover-up, the Chappaquiddick accident that killed Mary Jo Kopechne, Bobby Kennedy's secretary, is just water under the bridge.

But for the sake of the facts, and the life of an innocent girl, we believe the evidence warrants a serious reappraisal of the most infamous motor vehicle accident in history, for which Ted Kennedy had no choice but to take the blame. Should we just let sleeping corpses lie? Even though Kennedy is still alive, this CIA-orchestrated ambush left him politically dead. Forced to lie about being behind the wheel, Kennedy dropped out of the presidential campaign nine months later. And that walking corpse has been lying for twenty-five years.

Give us a hint, Teddy. A wink and a nod. With CIA guns at your back, how deliberate were your mysterious hints like "when I fully realized what happened" and "whether the girl might still be alive somewhere out of the immediate area"? Do you know who really killed Mary Jo Kopechne?

Joan d'Arc

THE MATTER OF CHAPPAQUIDDICK is very easy to resolve if you first make up your mind that, of course, Teddy was running after the girls, that he left the party to go to the beach for sex, that he was "plastered," and that the party was in effect nothing more than a drunken brawl. This is the story that the media tried so hard to make it out as. It's simple to say what happened, and to believe what Teddy himself said happened, but if you read the transcript of the inquest and go after the *facts* of the case, you've got a different story.

Here's a test: Sitting in your car on dry land, try getting out from under the steering wheel and climbing out your car window. Now flip your car completely upside-down and try to climb out of that window with water rushing in, on a pitch-dark moonless night. Think about that, and you'll see that it really is impossible. We're down to Sherlock Holmes: "When you have eliminated the impossible, whatever remains, no matter how improbable, must be the truth." There is no question in my mind that it was impossible for Ted Kennedy to have climbed out that window. Therefore Teddy was not in the car and it was an engineered accident.

How do you get Teddy out of that car? How do you get him walking over a mile back to the cottage after the accident, walking past two or three lighted houses and a firehouse? It's unimaginable for a sensible human being not to ask for help when help is available. How about the ridiculous swim over to Hellspont after such a traumatic experience? How can you believe him sitting for a half an hour the next morning with friends and not mentioning one word about an accident, the death of a friend, but instead chatting about the weather, about the race, about what a good time they had yesterday? It's completely ridiculous!

If you read the inquest from the point of view not that Teddy was after the girls, but rather that the incident was engineered, as a political assassination to get Kennedy out of the campaign in 1972, then all the facts begin to fall into place.

I've been going after the facts on all these political assassinations. In fact, I spent eleven years alone on the JFK assassination before I could confidently say that I thought I had the firing sequence, the shots, and the wounds all matched up, and even then I had to revise it. So let's go after the facts of the Chappaquiddick accident which prove that it was engineered.

Engineering an Accident

First you've got the "skidmarks" on the bridge, which are not skidmarks at all because they go absolutely straight. Skidmarks would indicate that brakes were used, so there would be a swerve to them. There are two parallel marks on the rubrail going in the same direction, no swerving. Now anyone coming toward that bridge would have turned the wheel at least a little bit. It's not much; about a twenty-three-degree turn is all that's necessary to avoid going off into the drink. But there are no turn marks. The marks are absolutely straight, so you have to wonder how those marks were made, because they were not made by somebody going twenty-two miles per hour, as Ted Kennedy claims.

The registry report shows the measurements of the marks, where the car was from starting point and where it ended up and all that, all done very scientifically, but nobody paid a damn bit of attention to it. The final report of the Registry of Motor Vehicles in Massachusetts says exactly what Teddy says: that he was traveling at twenty-two miles per hour.

The judge at the inquest never paid attention to those things. Remember, there was no trial for the death of Mary Jo Kopechne. It was just a hearing to determine the facts of the case and whether there was negligence, and that's what the judge found, of course: that Ted Kennedy was negligent in leaving the scene and failing to report a motor vehicle accident.

Also curious is the fact that the car literally "flew" thirty-six feet into the air. In other words, when you measure from the point of takeoff to where the engine landed, you've got thirty-six feet. Now an engine of that weight (Oldsmobile) does not travel thirty-six feet at twenty-two MPH. John Farrar, a fireman and scuba diver, the one who dove down and found Mary Jo, had an engineer friend estimate how fast the car had to be going for the weight of the car to go that thirty-six feet, and it comes out to forty miles per hour. If you think in terms of forty miles per hour, that's not Teddy driving, that's something else. So right away you begin to think of an engineered accident. And when you begin to think about this in those terms, you've got an entirely different frame of reference.

Political Assassination

Now, why would anybody want to engineer an accident involving Teddy Kennedy, and why would Teddy say that he drove off the bridge himself? These aren't easy questions to answer. But nine months after the Chappaquiddick "accident" Ted Kennedy announced, "I am not a candidate for the Democratic nomination in the presidential race for campaign '72." If you begin to understand that this is a political assassination in order to get rid of the front-running Democrat, then you have the answer. If you can assume that answer for a while, you can go back and prove it to yourself, because there is no other answer as far as I am concerned, after looking at all the facts up close.

It took me a long time to take all the facts of the Chappaquiddick case—the damage to the car, the damage to Ted Kennedy, hit on the head and possibly kicked in the back, as the doctor's report suggests. If you take the fact that the car windshield is smashed, the roof is damaged, and every panel on the right side of the car is completely smashed, with all the glass on the inside of the car, the driver-side mirror post hanging by one bolt—if you take all these facts, then you have to ask, how could you have all of that with a car that could only have limped off the edge of a bridge at twenty-two miles per hour? The answer, of course, is you can't.

Ass Over Teakettles

It is physically impossible for a car to do a flip of that sort and wind up with damage to front, roof, and sides all at once. You can, by going ass over teakettles, shatter the windshield and damage the roof, but you can't get the right side. If you fall off the edge, maybe you could get the right side damaged, but those panels are really beat in, and the windows are completely shattered, with the glass on the inside. That doesn't happen at twenty-two miles per hour. Therefore it seems safe to say that Ted Kennedy's Chappaquiddick accident was engineered.

Let's figure out what happened to the front mirror post. If you take a line, secure it to the wheel, pass it out through the vent, and secure it to the mirror post so that the front wheels stay straight, what's going to happen when the front wheel hits the rubrail on the edge of the bridge? Something has to give. So with the car moving at about forty miles per hour by the time it hit the rubrail, going at a slight angle so that the right front wheel hit slightly before the left, there was a shimmy there, a pull. The front wheel wants to turn, but the line securing the steering wheel pulls straight, so the weakest point—that's the bolt holding the mirror post—lets go. I think that if the front wheels hadn't been tied somehow to the steering wheel, the wheels would have turned and the car would have rolled over sideways off the bridge. The car didn't roll; it flipped back end over front. There was, of course, no mention of anyone finding any rope.

One question might be how to get the car going that fast. There are some very smart people who could figure that one out. It could have been a wedge holding down the gas pedal, or maybe they just boosted up the carburetor or got into the linkage somehow. There's plenty of ways to engineer an accident. But in this case, I'm thinking once the friction is gone from the rear wheels and the engine goes from, let's say, two thousand to five thousand revs, you've got a tremendous force. It must have been fairly loud. With the front end heavier than the rear end, the weight of the engine weighing the front down, the rear end flies up and over.

Mary Jo's Blouse

The facts of the victim, Mary Jo Kopechne, are also important: The victim had, I believe, a .10 blood alcohol level. That is not consistent with Mary Jo's behavior. All of her friends, the so-called boiler room girls, stated emphatically that she was a nondrinker. Therefore, when you've got .10 alcohol, which was practically legally drunk in the state of Massachusetts at the time, something doesn't jibe. Put that with another fact, that on the blouse, around the collar, almost all the way down the back, and on both sleeves, a very large area, residual traces of blood were found in testing about three weeks after the accident.

I found out about it at the time, and I called the coroner's office at the Public Works Department on Commonwealth Avenue in Boston. I spoke to the coroner on the telephone. I explained that I was writing a book on Chappaquiddick and would like to make a drawing of the blouse and the areas where the residual blood traces were found. He initially agreed to provide the information and wanted me to call him back the next week. When I called back for verification a week later, he was very upset and stated in no uncertain terms that he could not speak about the Kennedy case. He wanted nothing to do with me. The fact that I had even gotten through to him was bad news, apparently. So in my book, *You the Jury In Re: Chappaquiddick,* I have a sketch which approximates where the residual blood traces were found according to the available published reports.

Where do you suppose all that blood came from? John Farrar is the diver who pulled Mary Jo out of the car, and she came up and he held her and passed her up to Jim Arena, the chief, who was sitting on the upturned car near the gas tank. Jim Arena held her and then put her in the boat and took her over and laid her on a white stretcher, and the doctor had a look at her. Not one of those people said anything about blood. I even established from the hospital people at the time that no blood was seen on the white stretcher where she had lain on her back.

Not a trace. So what happened, I propose, is that the bloodstains had been there when she went into the water (I'll jump ahead a little bit) at about one A.M., and John Farrar didn't get her out until five minutes to nine, so she'd been there about eight hours. In the interim, the saltwater tides coming in and out washed all the bloodstains out of the blouse. It's very simple: You're in a big Laundromat; salt water is excellent for that kind of thing.

As soon as District Attorney Dinis found out about the residual bloodstains, he knew there was foul play, and that prompted him to request an exhumation. He went to her family and said he wanted to exhume the body to see if they could find anything. Well, if you consider the the level of alcohol in the blood and the fact that the girl was not a drinker, it's obvious that you've got to get alcohol into her somehow. How was that done? The only way I can think of is some type of needle and syringe. And I'm thinking that perhaps they hit a blood vessel when they punctured the neck. They got the alcohol in but punctured something, and the blood ended up all over the back of the blouse when she was lying in the backseat.

The Ambush: A Scenario

The mortician, Walter Frye, went over the body very, very carefully and found no bumps, no scratches, no nothing. Just a little something under the fingernails where she had been clawing in the footwell of the upturned car. Quite peculiar. What happened? You also have to try to figure out how Teddy got his wounds. He was hit on the head and on the back and was in a neck brace for a time. His medical exam indicated that he was more damaged than Mary Jo, except, of course, that Mary Jo lost her life. So if you put all these facts together, a possible scenario emerges:

Teddy and Mary Jo left the party at the same time—most in attendance at the party say it was eleven-fifteen. Mary Jo was tired and Teddy was tired—he had raced that day—so he offered her a ride back to the hotel, which meant they had to make the last ferry before midnight. Somewhere between the cottage and the ferry, somebody intervened. I call it an ambush (although it depends on what you mean by ambush). It could have been a roadblock, they could have taken Teddy out forcibly or pretended to be Secret Service. Curiously, Teddy said in a magazine article a few years later, "I always thought Mary Jo got away." So somehow they were separated, and he didn't know where she was. They took Ted out from behind the wheel, and they took Mary Jo in the Oldsmobile.

I say "they" because this scenario needs a team of maybe five people: two people to take care of Mary Jo, two people to take care of Teddy, and one other person. There is no way that this could have been pulled off without this person: the one who impersonated Ted Kennedy. So the ambush occurs, two people take the Olds with Mary Jo in it, and the other two take the car they've got and go right across on the ferry. I have no problem with that way of getting Teddy across to his room at the Shiretown Inn, as opposed to his ridiculous claim that he swam across. Just knock him out, a blow to the head and a kick in the back and whatever else it takes, and hide him in the backseat. He was drugged the whole night, and the way I see it, he was just another passenger that night on the ferry. There was no moon, it was very dark.

One of the facts not very well known is that Teddy's wallet was in fact missing after the accident. He did not have his wallet when he got to the station. Go back and ask, Why? Because they'd gotten his wallet to prove to Kennedy associates Gargan and Markham that they had him in hand. They may have even forced Gargan and Markham to write Kennedy a note telling him not to do one damn thing until they got over to him on the first ferry in the morning. That explains Ted's inactivity until morning. The operatives may have engineered a spoof kidnapping of Mary Jo. In other words, "We've got Mary Jo; wait by the pay phone at Chappaquiddick for ransom instructions." When they got there, the body had been found in the car, and there went the ransom story. It was all over. They had been had.

What Did Look See?

Of course, the ambush team had radios and communicated to each other all night. The other two meanwhile plied Mary Jo with alcohol and had her slumped in the backseat. At about twelve-thirty the Olds drove right past the cottage, and when it got to the corner, they did the wrong thing. They drove straight ahead down Cemetery Road. At that particular moment, as fate would have it, Huck Look, the deputy sheriff and a bouncer at the Yacht Club, sees the Olds driving onto Cemetery Road, which everyone knows is a dead end. The Olds stops and backs up, appearing to be lost. Huck Look stopped his car and got out to give directions to the driver, but the driver apparently did not want directions, seeing that Look was a cop or some kind of official, and he sped away down Dike Road toward the bridge. The time according to the testimony of Huck Look was twelve forty-five. The car had a Massachusetts license plate beginning with the letter L, and the number contained two 7's, one at the beginning and one at the end.

When Huck Look heard about the accident in the morning and drove down to the bridge, he found the dark Oldsmobile sedan he had seen the night before, with the license plate L78-207. He was the one who put his finger right on it. With his testimony, you've got the car on dry land at a quarter to one. Teddy says he drove straight down toward the ferry, took a wrong turn onto Dike Road, and drove off the bridge at eleven-thirty, at most fifteen minutes after the leaving the party. You've got those two conflicting statements made at the inquest, and nobody ever looks at them and says, "Wait a minute!"

The Cover-Up

Huck Look has never changed his testimony, and Ted Kennedy has never changed his testimony. He's a politician and he wants those people off his back, and that is what he is going to continue to say. That is always going to be his position, but his position is incorrect. It's correct for him only because he was told that he damn well better say he was driving or someone else will lose their life. I'm sure that the word he received, through Gargan and Markham via (Ted) K-2 the impersonator, was that if Ted Kennedy goes to the White House, it's not going to be very healthy for him.

Ted surely must have realized it was curtains for his political career. He's got a great big family, from Rose all the way down to the youngest grandchild, to worry about. They could take any one of them or even Ted. It was the perfect political assassination, where the victim is politically dead, but he's alive and breathing and walking around, and he's having a hard time mentally. If you put yourself in Ted Kennedy's position, you would realize that he has really had a bad time, because he knows what happened. I don't know if he knows who killed Jack or who killed Bobby, but we know it wasn't Lee Harvey Oswald and it wasn't Sirhan Sirhan. And it sure as hell wasn't Edward Moore Kennedy who killed Mary Jo Kopechne.

I don't know whether Teddy's ever been able to find out who engineered the accident at Chappaquiddick, but we can guess what would happen if his inquiries went anywhere near the FBI or the CIA. You know, Hoover was terribly interested in everything that was happening at that time. He was absolutely certain Ted Kennedy was driving that car before any information had been gathered. Here it is three-thirty on the afternoon of the accident, and Hoover already knew it was Teddy driving, so we know damn well it was Hoover behind the whole thing. Aside from the FBI, where else do you find a bunch of guys who can engineer an accident like that? You look for the CIA.

Kennedy's attorneys, Ropes and Gray of Boston, went to the Supreme Court to keep the inquest secret. They had to do all kinds of things to keep information from the press. There had to be an effective cover-up to make Teddy's story, as stupid as it was, pass as what really happened. In effect, Teddy's story itself operated as the cover-up for the engineered accident. The cover-up story was so effective that the media bought into it and reacted exactly as the people who engineered the accident expected them to: a blonde, booze, and the beach, that's all they needed. You're not able to think about what really happened after you're bombarded with this stuff for three months in the newspapers, radio, television. The Teddy bashing was phenomenal. There's no way anybody can think straight after the media gets through with their character assassination. The media is part of the whole problem!

Issue 7, Winter 1995

Accident or Ambush?

INTERVIEW WITH R. B. CUTLER

Joan d'Arc

There was a lot of talk about how much Ted Kennedy had to drink that night, but has there ever been any proof?

I don't think there was much booze at the party. It was mainly a cookout. I interviewed Ross Richards, who sat with his wife and talked with Teddy at the Shiretown Inn for half an hour the morning after the accident. He said, "Ted didn't have a hangover. I had the hangover. I wish I looked like Teddy!" This was just before [Kennedy associates] Joe Gargan and Paul Markham showed up and dragged Ted off to speak with him in his room.

Did anyone ever see Kennedy's wet clothing?

No, I don't think so. Had he really swum back to the other side of the channel, he would have staggered home all by himself.

Ted would have had a very long walk back to the Inn, if he did swim, according to your analysis of where the current would have carried him.

That's right. Of course, he didn't swim at all. He was taken across either by boat or on the ferry, hidden in the backseat of someone else's car.

So why does Ted lie about it?

He has to. Because they've threatened to kill him or another family member, of course, the same way they killed Bobby only thirteen months before.

And his sidekicks, Gargan and Markham, know the truth as well?

Oh hell, yes. They were told to tell Teddy to keep his mouth shut or we'll get someone else in your family.

So they told Ted to say he swam back to the Inn?
I don't really think so. I think they were basically free to say whatever they wanted as long as Teddy said he was driving. I think Gargan and Markham made that one up, that he swam across.

So let's get back to the morning chat with Mr. and Mrs. Richards. Teddy is talking with them and in walks Gargan and Markham . . .
Yes, soaking wet, and they quickly usher Ted into his room to speak in private.

Is this the first Ted knows about Mary Jo's death?
This is the first possible time. They may not have known for sure yet at that time, but their clothes were soaking wet, indicating that they had been diving around in the water. They may have seen her body in the car in the early morning and got on the first ferry at seven. The first thing the three of them do is zap right back over to Chappaquiddick to wait by the public pay phone. I think they probably were going to get some ransom money for Mary Jo, so they went to the phone to receive a call, not to make a call, as others have assumed. I believe that Gargan and Markham had been instructed to be at the telephone by nine A.M. to make arrangements to get Mary Jo back.

So when Teddy states in his police report that morning, "When I fully realized what happened, I immediately went to the police" . . .
That was the only truthful statement he made the whole day; that's the most important statement.

He didn't know anything about Mary Jo until Gargan and Markham informed him in the morning?
He knew they had been separated, but that's all he knew. As I said, he may have been told she had been kidnapped and was awaiting further instructions on that. I think that those two, Gargan and Markham, were up all night looking for Mary Jo and that sometime after sunrise they finally spotted the car and dove in and may have even seen that she was in there. Because when they showed up at the inn and grabbed Teddy away from his nonchalant conversation, they were soaking wet! And the judge wouldn't allow that, the inquest records state that they were "damp." If they were allowed to be "soaking wet" on the record,

then that would be inconsistent with Ted's story that they had dived in for Mary Jo around midnight. I don't think Ted ever went swimming at all.

Didn't Kennedy make several phone calls during the night?

I really don't think so. I believe he was out cold all night. They certainly had his wallet, so they could have done anything they wanted. K-2, the Kennedy impersonator, could have made phone calls. I believe he had Ted's wallet. Some calls were made by Gargan and Markham from the police station. Teddy didn't even have money for a phone call in the morning from the station. He borrowed a dime. His wallet was definitely missing. I don't believe he personally made any phone calls during the night.

So Chappaquiddick happened thirteen months after Bobby Kennedy's assassination.

Yes. And I might add that a third Kennedy hit would have stretched the lone nut theory to the breaking point. It had to be a scandal, not a straight hit. People would have been convinced of a conspiracy had Ted been assassinated. So what could scandalize him out of the presidential race? On the front of the *Boston Herald,* in early 1969, Ted was talking about getting the hell out of the Vietnam War. In other words, Teddy had picked up the torch and gone right on doing what Bobby and Jack would have done. And by this time they figured out this guy has got to go. Nixon was paranoid about Ted Kennedy, absolutely bananas.

Yes, I notice a quote in your book which comes from the Watergate tapes about Chappaquiddick.

Yes, basically I think Nixon knew that something was going to happen at Chappaquiddick; he didn't know exactly what, but Hoover was planning something. Hoover was behind the whole Chappaquiddick hit. There was a document that clarified that Hoover got the information at three-thirty in the afternoon from somebody who had notified the FBI earlier, and the FBI sent a notice to Hoover to the effect that nobody's saying Ted was driving the car but, rest assured, "he was." And it's blanked out as to who sent it. I tried to find out who informed the FBI, because that had to be around twelve-thirty or so the night of the "accident." Teddy would have just gotten off the island around that time. Somebody made sure the director of the FBI was perfectly content that everything had gone the way he expected it to. That's what I infer.

So you don't believe a renegade faction pulled off the ambush at Chappaquiddick?

Well, however they pulled it off, they've got a bunch of people in the CIA who've been doing this sort of thing all over the world. All they do is sit around and figure out how to pull it off. And they have a wonderful time. I still maintain that they had a boat; a small outboard was seen at about two-thirty by a few witnesses. There are so many details. The information is there. You aren't able to follow every single one, so you make the best scenario possible given the facts. You can't bother with every single little piece of information. Basically, I think my solution is the best one. Some small details need to be worked out; maybe it was done this way, maybe that way. I think there was a Kennedy double I call K-2 who got Gargan and Markham to get in the Valiant with him and took them and gave them the kidnapping story, then got over to Shiretown by a small outboard and talked to "Peachey" at the inn. K-2 would be the guy at the bottom of the stairs who asked Peachey what time it was, and Peachey responded it was two twenty-five A.M., establishing "Kennedy's" whereabouts at that hour. Actually, Kennedy was probably still out cold in his room at that time.

So when "Kennedy" or K-2 walked back to the cottage for help, how did he alert the rest of the party that something had happened? He requested help from a distance in the dark and slipped into the backseat of the Valiant?

Yes! Can you imagine him doing that? He'd never do a thing like that. If he was serious about getting Mary Jo, he'd come up and say, "Hey, gang, I've got a problem, let's go!" It's totally ridiculous to believe he would stand in the dark shadows and request Ray LaRosa to "get me Paul, and get me Joe" and slip into the backseat of the Valiant. He would have walked right up to Ray and requested assistance. Ray is a fireman, a scuba diver, a rescue man just like John Farrar. He would have said, "Ray, we need you!"

Was there ever any question about identification of the voice?

Nobody even brought it up! What happened to me was I suddenly realized that Ray LaRosa did not really see Ted Kennedy as he stood in the dark, he only heard him. The same with Russell Peachey at the Shiretown Inn. And there you solve the problem with K-2, the Kennedy double.

So in the dark, in the shadows, someone the same build, same height as Kennedy . . .

He could even have had a voice box of some sort, for all we know, or a mask, or a tape recording. They have those, you know. E. Howard Hunt had a voice box when he talked to Dietre Beard in the hospital. They have ways of making your voice, when you talk, sound like someone else's. The CIA has some great technology.

Do you think these agents stopped the car shortly after Ted and Mary Jo left the party and said something like "Senator, come with us, we'll take the girl home"?

Well, I think there must have been more to it than that. The car was badly damaged along the right side. Kennedy may have put up a fight, because he was hit on the head. In effect, it was an ambush, but it's hard to say exactly how it was done. A roadblock of some sort, perhaps. They probably did not have guns, because residents would have heard something, and bullets would indicate murder rather than "accident." So they had to do it by force. Maybe Mary Jo even got away, scrambled away for a short time, and was caught up with.

Kennedy's television statement a week later claimed that somewhere in the back of his mind he wanted to think she was somewhere else, not in the car.

Yes, that's why I wonder if she got away. They had definitely been separated, and he wasn't sure where she was until morning. It was very well done.

What good it does knowing this twenty-five years later, I don't know. Do Mary Jo's parents suspect any of this?

If they do, they don't believe it. They have my book, and they won't read it, I don't think. I've tried to get to them, but it doesn't work.

Why did they fight the exhumation and autopsy?

It has a good deal to do with religion, I guess. To leave her in one piece. It's totally emotional. Also, the implications, rumors, what are they going to get out of it? What were they going to prove with an autopsy? There was nothing they could find. As far as the needle mark in the back of the neck, maybe [for intravenous alcohol delivery]. Now that would have been something. But they already knew she had a high level of alcohol. Maybe they wanted to know if she'd been raped; that would be one thing.

So the official cause of death was not drowning?

No. Asphyxiation was the cause of death. That means she used up all the oxygen and couldn't breathe anymore. Drowning is asphyxiation by immersion. There was less than a cupful of water in Mary Jo. The water was secondary to her running out of oxygen in the pocket of air she had been breathing in the footwell. She was alive a couple of hours, at least, at most three. You can pinpoint that by going backward from nine A.M. when she was found underwater in almost complete rigor mortis. Her body floated up with no effort. A drowned body would not float for at least one hundred hours.

So when the car flipped over, it held a pocket of air in the footwell for her to breathe in?

Yes, but the judge at the inquest wouldn't allow any of that. The trunk was completely dry. They couldn't allow people to find out about that, because then you have the girl alive in there all that time. It looks really bad then. It's much easier to say she just went in and Teddy couldn't get to her in time and she drowned. John Alba, the guy with the tow truck, was going to testify about all the bubbles that came up from the trunk and the footwell, but they wouldn't allow any of his testimony. It would have screwed up Ted's story that she drowned and nothing could be done to save her. They didn't want people to know that she had been alive for at least two hours. The story was that she drowned. Who wants to go into the details of how long it took her to drown?

And Teddy claims he can't remember how he got out of the car, he just somehow emerged?

I can't see how he got out of the car! That's why I can't see him in the car at all.

If he was so drunk he can't remember, then why didn't he drown along with Mary Jo?

Absolutely! And if he was that drunk, he couldn't have been driving fast enough for what happened. I think applying the brakes is a natural reaction, even for a drunk. He couldn't have had that much to drink; there wasn't that much booze at the party, unless he was drinking it straight.

Could he have gotten out of the passenger window somehow?

Well, then you'd have Jack Olsen's story *(The Bridge at Chappaquid-*

dick). He's the one that put Mary Jo behind the wheel. He figures they got out, waded in the poison ivy, and then Teddy let her drive. Then he just floats out the passenger window. According to Olsen, she didn't know how to work the car and drove it off the bridge, got into the backseat, and drowned. Now how do you do that?

Typical "dumb broad"?

Oh, yeah. There are a lot of theories out there. And so many facts to keep track of.

So Mary Jo had been Bobby Kennedy's secretary?

Yes, Mary Jo had been very upset about Bobby's assassination. She was a very respected girl, smart, and doing exactly what she wanted to do. Everybody said she was going with some fellow who wanted to marry her, and some tried to say she was pregnant. All kinds of rumors. She lived in Washington and shared a place with one of the other girls. They were Kennedy campaign workers, the so-called Boiler Room Girls. They worked tremendous hours. I have a lot of respect for those people. This was not the first party the Kennedys had thrown for the girls. Teddy couldn't make it to the last one they had held in D.C., so he suggested to his cousin Joe Gargan to fix up a party for them the weekend of the boat races at the Vineyard. So Joe got the cottage. There was nothing hanky-panky about the party at all.

One of the most important witnesses was Huck Look.

Yes, he saw a black sedan, which appeared lost, and as he approached the car to offer directions, the car sped off. He has never changed his story one bit, and nobody has really tried to make him, except the judge at inquest. Here's Look's story with Ted's car and occupants alive and well at one A.M., and here's Teddy's story, off the bridge at eleven-thirty. Totally at odds, and nobody does anything about it.

Ted also claims he took a wrong turn on the way to the ferry and ended up at the bridge. Didn't he know his way around the island?

Certainly he did. They had been around that area since they were kids. He knew the area like the back of his hand.

So how many people did Look claim to see in the car?

He saw two people in the front and "something" or a "shadow" in the backseat, but he wasn't sure what it was.

Maybe a slumped figure?

He didn't guess at what it was. He never said.

And the people in the car appeared lost?

Yes, they were the ones who didn't know their way around, not Teddy Kennedy! I don't believe Ted was driving the car at that point. They attempted to drive straight down Cemetery Road, stopped, backed up and turned down Dyke Road toward the bridge. Teddy would not have done that. He knows the island very well.

So there are no streetlights out there?

No, just poison ivy, six feet high. There were some who asserted that the stains on Mary Jo's blouse were grass stains. Pig's eye! I can't see any hanky-panky going on in the poison ivy. The place is loaded with it.

Have you ever spoken with Huck Look?

No, I almost made it, but not quite. He didn't want to give any interviews. He knew he was in contradiction with Ted's story, and that's not a happy position to be in.

So you believe that Mary Jo could not have been sitting in the front seat and got thrown to the back during the flip?

I don't think it's possible. With the car upside-down, she would have had to dive down deeper to get over the front seat and into the back. It's unnatural to do that. You wouldn't dive down deeper to save yourself. She was already in the backseat and scrambled up to where the air pocket was in the footwell. That's exactly where she was found, in rigor mortis, by John Farrar at about nine A.M. He had someone make a drawing exactly as he had found her. It's a very important document.

Could this hit have been done by the Mob?

The CIA knows better how to engineer an accidental death, I think, than the Mafia. The Mob only knows how to take a nine-millimeter and shoot a guy in the back of the head behind the ear. That's what they are much better at. The CIA has been engineering accidents all over the world. But nobody can believe the CIA operates in Massachusetts. These things don't happen here. Maybe in Vietnam, Africa, Europe, South America (it happens all the time down there), but not in Massachusetts!

The Pope Must Die!

MURDER IN THE VATICAN

Seeker 1

Pope John Paul I, who "died in his sleep" after thirty-three days of papal rule in 1978, was a reformer who had made many enemies. Was the pope murdered, and does his death have any connection to the 1982 attempted assassination of Pope John Paul II? In this article, Seeker 1 looks at the history of Vatican scandals and its links to Nazis, the Mafia, and the Masons.

IN 1982, WHEN THE WORLD found out that an attempt had been made on the life of Pope John Paul II, there were immediate cries of conspiracy. Right-wing observers, noting the new pope's anti-Communist stance and support of Solidarity in Poland, suggested that behind assassin Mehmet Ali Agca there was a "Bulgarian connection." The Bulgarians, who were suddenly thrust into prominence as international traffickers in arms, heroin (despite the fact that even today most of U.S. heroin comes from the Golden Triangle in Southeast Asia), and terrorism, were also supposed to have wanted to kill the pope on behalf of the Soviet Union.

In 1983 three Bulgarian Secret Service operatives—Antonov, Aivazov, and Vassilev—were tried and acquitted on insufficient evidence. Despite concerted propaganda efforts by right-wing Catholics and others in the Reagan administration, the "Bulgarian connection" just wouldn't stick, although they succeeded in convincing many that such a conspiracy existed and that a supersecret group called "Kintex" was behind the whole affair. (Which sounds strangely reminiscent of

"Permindex," the dummy corporation that Jim Garrison tried to show was behind JFK's assassination.)

In fact, if one looks closely at the matter, Agca's background is clearly fascistic. He belonged to the pan-Turkish group Gray Wolves, which has ties to the CIA and many fascist groups in the "Black International." Agca clearly changed his story whenever his whims so moved him; though he claimed Bulgarian backers at one point, he also testified to being Christ at another. So much for his credibility. Nonetheless, Celik, Ozbey, and other members of the Gray Wolves who knew him said he had written a note stating quite clearly that his goal was to kill the pope, whom he saw as "another representative of the anti-Islamic Crusades," in order to create unrest and other conditions for a fascist coup in Turkey.

Many of the supposed points of evidence for Agca's travels in Bulgaria are specious, but it is clear he has been to Italy. Agca and other Gray Wolves also may have met with Cuban exiles in Miami in 1981. If anything, Agca's attempt on John Paul II has striking connections to the death of that pope's immediate predecessor, the first John Paul.

The Poisoned Pope

John Paul I, who "died in his sleep" (very likely he was poisoned) after thirty-three days of papal rule in 1978, was a reformer who made many enemies, even within the walls of the Vatican, because he had started to probe the Vatican Bank scandal. The disappearance of millions of Church dollars into the black hole of Roberto Calvi's Banco Ambrosiano ended up costing Calvi his life (a "suicide" that required a considerable ability in self-hanging, as well as knowledge of Masonic ritual murder) and resulted in a major Italian political scandal when it was found that many magnates of finance, the army, parliament, and industry were members of a supersecret Masonic lodge, Propaganda Due (P2). Also implicated in the affair were Michele "the Shark" Sindona, Licio Gelli (grand master of P2), and even some archbishops, such as Paul "the Gorilla" Marcinkus and Luigi Mennini. The Church stood accused of allowing its money for "charitable works" to disappear into a world of dummy companies, organized crime, and even drug money laundering. It was further discovered that Marcinkus as chairman of the IOR (Institute of Religious Works—the Vatican Bank) had written letters of confidence to enable the insolvent Ambrosiano to stay afloat and that the Vatican had in fact owned eight of the many ghost companies Calvi had created for transferring money covertly.

When the full dimensions of the Banco Ambrosiano scandal become clear—and much of those millions are still unaccounted for—the Church may have much to answer for. The P2 revelation shocked the Church, because an eighteenth-century papal bull said that Catholics who became Freemasons were to be excommunicated, and many of the names on P2's Masonic Lodge roster were bishops and archbishops.

The Vatican and "Il Duce"

How did the Vatican get into this mess? Some people feel that, as with many scandals, it started with a deal with the devil. In 1929 the Vatican and Mussolini signed the Lateran Treaty and Concordat. As a result, Vatican City became a sovereign state within the confines of Rome and independent of the Italian government, and the Church received a windfall of millions of lira from "Il Duce." In return, a certain quietness on Italian political affairs—especially the growth of fascism—was expected from Church leaders. The Church, wanting to invest this money for paying off debts and religious charity, created first the APSA and then the IOR. The IOR became a haven for wealthy Italians wanting to expropriate their money in violation of Italian banking laws and helped many Italians prevent their money from falling into German hands. But the cardinals and bishops were not content with merely working with the country's "Catholic" banks (so-called because they loaned money at low interest rates, claiming this did not violate the Church's rule against usury). They needed lay financiers to find savvy investments for the Church—men such as Michele Sindona and Roberto Calvi.

The Church at first obtained holdings in Italian corporations but was soon embarrassed when it was found that some of their holdings included businesses involved in gun, pornography, and contraceptive manufacturing and that they almost blundered into buying illegal American securities in 1974 from the Mob. Soon the Church found itself in the difficult position of defending its tax exemption, given its many worldly possessions.

Some Italian political analysts believe that P2 and "Ordine Nuova" may have cooperated with the CIA to bomb a train station in Bologna in 1980 and blame it on leftist groups. Many think the CIA has had a history of manipulating "terrorism" in Italy and that it may have even used the ultraterror of the Red Brigades to discredit the Italian Communist Party.

Overlapping Circles

There are clearly overlapping circles of membership among P2, the CIA, and the Knights of Malta, a "sovereign military order descended from the Knights of St. John-Hospitallers," and whose membership in the United States has included Bill Casey, Alexander Haig, and Prescott Bush. The Knights, along with Opus Dei, reactionary Jesuits, and traditionalists (who resisted the Vatican II Council reforms) form the nexus of the Catholic "hard right wing." In the shadowy world of spookdom, there are many links among this faction of the church, organized crime, the Mafia and Camorra (a Neopolitan Mafia), intelligence agencies, arms dealers, and "chivalric" groups working for a united Europe and a monarchic restoration in some Catholic countries.

P2 was also involved with Latin American fascist military coups and the death squads controlled by them; it is even thought that P2 helped transfer Exocet missiles illegally to Argentina during the Falklands War. Klaus Altman, alias Klaus Barbie, was an associate of Gelli and part of the Bolivian military junta. He was one of many Nazi war criminals smuggled into South America (which had a large German and Italian immigrant community before the war) by Vatican elements after World War II.

The Church and the Nazis

Many who have looked into the Kennedy assassination have seen how the CIA and Mafia became associated in the 1960s; they had a mutual interest in eliminating Castro. But what about the CIA and the Vatican? Initial ties already existed during World War II between the Office of Strategic Services (OSS; the CIA's precursor) and the Vatican, partly because OSS founder "Wild Bill" Donovan thought that priests hearing confession were a blessing for the spook trade. (Interestingly, the OSS and the Vatican worked to get Italy to surrender a week before the Axis, perhaps to prevent Communist partisans in the north from taking control.) Even more dark, some "rogue" elements in the Vatican may have worked with the OSS to smuggle former Nazis (such as Nazi spymaster Reinhard Gehlen) into Latin America or into the Eastern-bloc spy network, the Kamaradenwerk. Arch-Catholic traditionalist Marcel Lefebvre has harbored accused Nazi war criminals for some forty years.

The role of the Church during World War II is somewhat suspect. Even though it was forced to compromise with Mussolini's fascism, and it may not have done enough to save European Jews, it cannot be said to have "supported" fascism. Some Catholics, however—notably those in "Catholic Action," the clergy in Croatia, the Knights of Malta, and U.S. radio personality Father Coughlin—were openly fascist.

The Direction of the Church

In the post–Vatican II era, the CIA had become worried about the "direction" of the Church. Liberation theology, promoted by many Catholics in Latin America, contains many "Marxist" elements. Many thought that with *Pacem en Terris,* Pope John XXIII moved the Church more toward sympathy for the Soviet Union and communism. The pastoral letters of the American bishops, which condemned the arms race, capitalism, and nuclear weapons, certainly were a cause for concern.

As Malachi Martin has noted in his book *Keys of This Blood,* the Jesuits, originally created as the shock troops of the Counter-Reformation, were beginning to be a thorn in the side of the Church, as many drifted toward modernist scholarship on biblical questions. Many were afraid that John Paul I would be too liberal on many issues, such as ordination of women, contraception, homosexuality, and perhaps even abortion, and that Catholic support for "pro-family" values might erode. The CIA, then, was interested in working with right-leaning Catholic elements to counterbalance this perceived leftward tilt within the Church. The possibility that John Paul I was murdered—either to prevent the uncovering of the P2-IOR scandal or to retraditionalize the Church—is not so remote.

His successor, the Polish archbishop Karol Wojytla (John Paul II), was thought to be unconcerned with "cleaning house" in the Church and to be very anti-Communist because of his support of Solidarity. Indeed, he turned out to be staunchly anti-Communist but critical of "unreformed" capitalism as well (this is made fairly clear in *Keys of This Blood.*) The John Paul II murder attempt may have been motivated by people who were dissatisfied with his amenability to the capitalist cause. (The fact that he took his immediate predecessor's papal name was probably distressing to those who thought he was going to distance himself from the first John Paul's reformist crusade.)

John Paul II is an enthusiastic promoter of the idea of Catholic unity, but he appears to have disdained both global capitalist and Communist hegemony as ungodly. If we pin his attempted assassination on the Bulgarians, the role of other forces in the matter become obscured. The Bulgarian connection to the drug trade was big news for a while, helping to obscure the more important Colombian and Panamanian connection and the potentially explosive fact that America's freedom-fighting Contras were sending back dope to the United States.

The Propaganda Mill

Certainly the "plot to kill the pope" became big grist for the Reaganite propaganda mill. A book of this time, Claire Sterling's *The Terror Network,* spun a vast web of conspiracy, suggesting the KGB controlled terrorist groups ranging from the IRA in Ireland, to the ETA in Spain, to the PLO in Lebanon, to the FMLN in El Salvador. Why the Communists would support terrorist groups espousing such ideologies as nationalism, ethnic or racial separatism, or Islamic fundamentalism was never made clear. For Sterling it was all simply a matter of their united hatred for the "West" and its foul values of democracy, liberty, and justice.

The papal "plot" was cited as proof of the so-called Soviet web of terrorism and was one of the main justifications for various "antiterrorist" legislation as well as crackdowns on domestic groups. A piece of legislation written in 1984 that would punish domestic groups in support of "terrorist" nations narrowly avoided passage. As anti-Soviet propaganda, the "Bulgarian connection" did more to set back arms control and detente than any "missile gap" or "spending gap."

Leftist groups like the Christic Institute see the "kill the pope" conspiracy stretching the other way, to Oliver North's "enterprise" and a host of plots by the "shadow government," from Cointelpro to the October Surprise to Iran-Contra. Others cite P2's shadowy links to international finance and "cult groups" like Reverend Moon's organization as evidence of a wider conspiracy beyond the Vatican Bank scandal.

Battle in the Church

Today the Catholic Church is torn between two contingents. One wants to return to the Tridentine mass, dogmatic absolutist biblical morality, and feudalism—the time when the Church shared hegemonic power with the State, when the pope was the coequal (especially in wealth) of any king. The other wants to modernize the Church and make it a force for peacemaking, resisting the power of the State and promoting social justice: dignity in work, fair wages, and empowering the poor. A Church controlled by this progressive contingent (exemplified by the Liberation Theology movement previously mentioned) would be a great threat to those in power.

The key players in the struggle for the future of the Church are represented by the Sovereign Military Order of Malta (SMOM) on the Right and the Jesuits on the Left. After the Crusades, the Knights Hospitaller gained possession of much of the Templars' wealth and property when that order was dissolved in 1314. They came to set up their headquarters on the island of Rhodes in 1309. In 1522, retreating from Sultan Suleiman, they came to Malta and defeated several attempts by the Turks to seize it, notably at the Battle of Lepanto in 1571. Having been driven from that island by Napoleon in 1798, the Knights are still recognized as part of a "sovereign nation" on their passports in over forty countries, and currently their official "residency" is within Vatican City itself.

Their progressive opponents appear to be the Jesuits, who, curiously enough, as Loyola's "soldiers of Jesus," were supposed to be the "shock troops" of the Catholic Counter-Reformation. The Jesuits engaged in many anti-Protestant intrigues throughout the seventeenth century in England and elsewhere, for which they came to be seen as conspirators extraordinaire and masters of psychological warfare. Today, as Malachi Martin notes, they seem to be in covert war with the Vatican (or at least its conservative elements). Many Jesuits are involved in the dissemination of liberation theology in Latin America and in effecting the reforms of Vatican II.

The dark history of the SMOM is illuminating. Originally a strictly aristocratic, chivalric, European order, they accepted an American contingent in 1927. Those admitted to the "American National Association" of the SMOM, unlike earlier members, did not have to provide a genealogical pedigree of royal blood. Members of the American contingent included important industrial leaders who formed part of the "Fraternity" in the United States, which, toward the end of World War II, was actually providing the Nazis with strategic and material support, trying to replace Roosevelt by coup with General Smedley D. Butler, and using "Project Paperclip" to bring Nazi scientists and doctors into the United States. The careers of some Knights were less than illustrious.

SMOM Knight Magistral Franz von Papen convinced von Hindenburg to offer Hitler the chancellorship in 1933 and served as Nazi ambassador to Austria and Turkey. SMOM Grand Cross recipient Joseph J. Larkin, vice president of Chase Manhattan Bank, helped finance General Franco's "counterinsurgency campaigns." Also, SMOM members Roger Pearson and James Jesus Angleton have edited the right-wing *Journal of International Relations*. Pearson, former editor of the racist journals *Western Destiny* and *Mankind Quarterly*, currently sits on the board of trustees for the American Foreign Policy Institute. In 1977 he was removed as head of the U.S. branch of the World Anti-Communist League, a Reverend Moon–financed organization, because he was "too extreme." Angleton, meanwhile, had worked with Luigi Gedda of Catholic Action to fight communism through the civic committees and rig the 1948 Italian elections. Interestingly, SMOM Angleton was fired by CIA director and Jesuit-educated William Colby in the mid-1970s.

SMOM baron Luigi Parrilli became the go-between of Allan Dulles, U.S. general Lemnitzer, and S.S. general Karl Wolff in 1945. SMOM members De Lorenzo and Prince Borghese each supported fascist coups in Italy in 1964 (the Solo plan) and 1970. In the 1980s a joint project of the SMOM, Reverend Moon's Nicaraguan Freedom Fund (NFF), and Pat Robertson's Christian Broadcasting Network, called the Americares Project, shipped over $15 million in "humanitarian aid" to Latin America. Some of Americares's "aid" went, via SMOM houses, to Guatemalan peasant "resettlement" programs, Contra-backed Miskito insurgents in Nicaragua, and the Salvadoran air force.

And what about John Paul II? To the pleasure of conservatives, he does not want to yield one inch on morals, dogma, or doctrine in the Church. Unfortunately his geopolitics aren't so good and may have even gotten worse after Agca's failed shot. Unlike some twentieth-century predecessors, he does not condemn communism in favor of capitalism: as he sees it, any state in the future will have to be based on "the laws of Jesus," and if there is to be a unified Europe (a new Holy Roman Empire), it must be under the banner once more of the Church Catholic and Universal. He has spoken out against war, particularly the Gulf War, and poverty, and clearly sees a geopolitical role for the Vatican once more, standing in opposition to both Eastern atheism and Western amorality.

A Church in Crisis

If the Church is in fact tied in with organized crime, the international intelligence community, and shadowy groups with covert goals like P2, then it is hard to see its power and credibility growing. From the Donation of Constantine to their role in the Dead Sea Scrolls investigation, there is much in the Church's history that is suspect and scandalous. There are the prophecies of St. Malachy and Nostradamus which suggest that at the end of this century the papacy may face its crisis moment and possibly its own dissolution.

The rift between American clerics and the Vatican hierarchy, still largely a stomping ground for Italians and a few other Europeans, grows daily. The Vatican's concerted opposition to population control is making it difficult for developing nations to take measures to alter their birth rate and causing some concern among American groups like Catholics for a Free Choice. As to whether the Church will move left, right, or into the ashbin of history, nobody knows for sure, but some momentous changes are clearly in the wings.

Issue 13, Summer 1996

Love and Power

Al Hidell

What if you learned about a seamy drug and prostitution ring, and you believed the ring involved high-level public officials, including a United States senator? Would you talk or keep your mouth shut? Indiana cab-driver Joe Love decided to talk, even after he was harassed by police and imprisoned on bogus charges. For those who suspect that the American "justice" system serves power rather than justice, Love's 1995 beating death inside an Illinois courthouse was sadly predictable.

AMID INCREASING EVIDENCE of official lies and cover-ups, a key question remains unanswered: Why is the national media keeping its mouth shut about the death of Joe Love?

Joe Love was killed on June 14, 1995, by a choke hold administered during a brutal police beating. The beating was his most severe, but by no means his first, lesson in American justice. And the lesson is this: The police, the lawyers, and the judges don't always "protect and serve" you. In fact, if you step on the toes of the powerful, they can become your worst enemy.

His first lesson had been different. He learned it the time he knocked out an armed man during an attempted store robbery. The police came, arrested the bad guy, and Joe Love was a hero. Textbook justice, with the scales in perfect balance.

The scales began to tilt when Joe Love came into conflict with the International Laborers Union and sued one of its union attorneys. While the suit was pending, Love was arrested at the local union hall by the Indianapolis Police Department (IPD). Determining that he was a "nut" in need of immediate detention, the police took him to Indianapolis's Wishard Psychiatric Hospital. Ironically, because he had not been charged with a crime, the normal rules of timely bail release or appearance before a judge didn't apply. He was finally released after his father, Johnie, agreed to place him in outpatient counseling, even though by all reports he was quite calm and rational during his Wishard incarceration.

Later, during his case against the union attorney, Joe began to name names. Conveniently, a psychiatrist was brought in to testify that Joe was "delusional."

Soon after this experience, Joe became a taxi driver. Like most cabbies, he began to learn some things about his city's seamier side. He kept detailed records, including information about a male and female prostitution ring, drug running, and how the profits of this drug and prostitution ring had corrupted politicians, judges, and cops.

One night, when he picked up a man at a local hotel, Joe Love was once again arrested. The arresting officer later claimed that Joe had a marijuana joint and that Joe threw the joint on the ground. The cop then picked up the joint and placed it on the hood of a car. Then, the officer claimed, Joe proceeded to eat the joint. Incredibly, they charged Joe with theft of state property (presumably because the joint had been "seized" by the arresting officer as evidence). This was considered a class "D" felony. He was also charged with obstruction of justice.

Love, who suspected he was being set up, was given a public defender. According to Love's parents, the public defender told them it was a bogus case and the state had no evidence. However, when the case was heard, the public defender pursued a different strategy. He pleaded that Love was "incompetent to stand trial." Of course, this was done without Love's permission.

The plea was inexplicable, as it allowed the state to put Love away indefinitely. Unlike a "normal" criminal, who is at least given a possible release date during sentencing, those deemed mentally incompetent are imprisoned for as long as the state defines them as "unsafe," which could well be forever. And remember, Love's crime was, at most, the possession of a single marijuana cigarette.

That, and the fact that he had told his public defender about the drug and prostitution ring.

The Birdseed Raid

If you still doubt that Joe Love was a target of the authorities, consider his arrest a few years previously—for the possession of birdseed.

It was part of the Illinois State Police's infamous "Hydroponic

Sting," in which they set up a bogus hydroponics store, tracked and spied on 114 customers, and raided their homes. (Hydroponics is a technique for cultivating plants using materials other than soil. It can be used to cultivate marijuana, but it has other uses. Essentially the ISP set up a feed and fertilizer store.)

As reported by the AEN News Service, which is associated with Love family attorney Linda Thompson, "Anyone who came into the hydroponics store was followed home by Indiana State police. Their electric and phone bills were scrutinized, they had their garbage searched, their house filmed with infrared cameras." The paranoid mind-set of the investigators is perhaps best illustrated by court documents which indicate that "the police stated that the paying of cash for a purchase indicated a criminal mind-set and a fear of being tracked." Most of these cases, based on twenty-two warrants—six of which were defective— were ultimately thrown out.

Joe Love had two 50-pound bags of birdseed, as well as all his guns and money, seized by state police. (The seeds were sterilized marijuana seeds—legal birdseed. Yet police claimed they were a "controlled substance.") Love was never convicted of a crime, but his guns and money remain in the hands of the police.

Joe's Last Sentence

On June 14, 1995, Joe Love went to his sixth court appearance, dealing with the issue of his competency to stand trial. Fearing for his safety, he had hidden a book containing the lowdown on corrupt government officials in a place someone knew to look if he was killed. He called his mother and father the night before and told them not to come to court the next day.

Love's judge in this case was Charles A. Wiles. Like all municipal court judges in Marion County, Wiles was a political appointee, answerable to the power brokers rather than the people. On the record, Joe said during the hearing, "If you're going to kill me, just go on and do it now." The judge replied, "All right."

What happened next is in dispute. The police say Judge Wiles ordered Love taken into custody for contempt of court, when Love apparently interrupted the judge and began to speak of the crime ring and the corruption of Mayor Goldsmith, Senator Richard Lugar, and others. According to the police, Love "became agitated" when two deputies approached him. They admit that they then jumped on him, maced him, and put him in handcuffs.

Judge Wiles later told the Love family he had told Joe he was free to go and that Joe Love "suddenly collapsed on the way out of court." This was apparently said to support later official claims that Love had "had a heart attack and died." In another statement, though, the judge admitted that police had "subdued" Love and that he had been "surprised to learn Joe was dead." Clearly a cover-up was in the making.

According to the AEN News Service, courtroom witnesses have said that what actually happened was that from the moment Joe arrived in court, a mace-wielding officer stood behind him. They report that, rather than releasing him, the judge told Love that he was going to put him in jail until they could find room for him in a hospital.

Witnesses in the courtroom have stated that the mace-wielding officer and five others took Love down to the floor, sat on him, kicked him, and maced him, then dragged him out of sight, as at least another dozen officers ran in to "assist."

"In over thirty witnesses interviewed, not one witness who is not one of the police suspects has said Joe was fighting or resisting at all," AEN reports. "Even the sheriff's department investigator, Detective Sergeant Mike Smith, said at an early press conference that Joe didn't hit or fight anyone. However, apparently scrambling to toe the official line, Smith would later state that Love had in fact been "resisting with his weight."

In fact, witnesses in the hallway have said Love was cooperating and asking for water. Another said he complained of being hurt but was not fighting police. Another said the police were elbowing him in the elevator. Another said the police had him "jacked up in the back, pushing him," that he had been "escorted" by the shirt and belt. (His cut belt and bloodied shirt were later given to his family.) Downstairs witnesses have corroborated Love's lack of resistance, saying that the mace-blinded victim was docile.

After being "escorted" from the courtroom, Love was thrown into "the hole," a six-by-five-foot cell with a slimy concrete floor, no lights or windows, and a hole in the floor in one corner for a toilet. (In a bit of Orwellian wordsmithing, officials call it "the quiet room.")

It is not known for sure exactly where Joe Love's death occurred, but there is no doubt that he died while in police custody. The result? In AEN's stark summarization, "He was beaten from head to toe, black and blue, up the backs of his legs, his sides, his back, his armpits, and his groin. The insides of his upper thighs were a solid mass of ugly blue and purple welts, the size of dinner plates. His inner arms were a mass of welts and bruises. His back was a kaleidoscope of huge bruises."

For the record, it must be noted that the official sheriff's department statement states that Love had "no signs of being beaten," that he had "only a small bruise on his forehead," and that he was "never struck by anyone." The Marion County coroner concurred that Love had not been beaten.

The official "investigation" of Love's death lasted all of forty-eight hours and consisted of a single interview with the police officer who had filed the police report on the matter. Meanwhile Love's notebook disappeared, along with his keys. His home, heavily alarmed and protected by a padlocked gate, was entered the next day. Along with the Love family, the police were the only ones with the key. Police had first told the family that they hadn't found Love's keys. However, a few days later the keys were "found" on the shift captain's desk. Despite the fact that Joe Love's name was engraved on the keys, the desk sergeant claimed that he had not known whom the keys belonged to.

Meanwhile, media reports were painting Joe Love as a violent criminal. Reporters falsely claimed that Love had been in court that day for "resisting arrest." Generally, they parroted and even embellished the official story, indicating that Love had "had a heart attack" after "tearing up the courtroom" and "scuffling with police." End of story.

An independent autopsy by the chief medical examiner of Kentucky, performed the day the Marion County coroner released the body, pointed unequivocally to a cover-up. The report, by Dr. George R. Nichols II, states that Joe Love was choked to death by an arm choke hold and was beaten. According to the AEN News Service, the list of welts and bruises goes on for four pages. After Nichols's report was released, the Marion County Coroner's Office modified its tune, in effect saying, "Well, he had some bruises, but they were insignificant."

The office of Marion County coroner Karl Manders then began leaking what can only described as disinformation: Love may have "choked on his own vomit." Love may have been taking some sort of dangerous prescription drug, which could have contributed to his "heart attack." (However, the coroner claimed he "couldn't remember" where he had sent Love's blood for analysis.)

Two days after the independent medical examiner's results were announced, Indianapolis newspapers and television began praising Scott

Newman, the Marion County prosecutor, because he had "acted quickly to investigate" Joe Love's death by "calling for a grand jury investigation." This despite the fact that Newman has never spoken to the family or their attorney and, according to them, refuses to do so. At any rate, he has not filed charges against any of the police involved in the Love case. And as legal observers point out, the true power in most grand jury investigations lies in the hands of the prosecutor, not the jury.

Love's family and attorney are seeking an independent prosecutor, in an independent county, to impanel a special grand jury to investigate Joe Love's murder. They have requested the public's help in bringing this about.

Maybe then the scales will finally come back into balance.

Issue 10, Fall 1995

Who Killed Yitzhak Rabin?

Barry Chamish

The U.S. media has portrayed the assassination of Israeli prime minister Yitzhak Rabin as an open-and-shut case. However, in Israel itself the issue is being debated much like the Kennedy assassination is here. In this article Israeli investigative reporter Barry Chamish names names and exposes the holes and incongruities of the official story.

THE SLOPPY SHABAK (Israel's General Security Services) conspiracy to assassinate Israeli prime minister Yitzhak Rabin is slowly being exposed. The most unlikely Israelis are becoming convinced that Yigal Amir did not murder Rabin. Rather, he was killed in his car after Amir shot two blank bullets. Amir's literary agent, Avi Feinstein, says, "Amir was a government agent, and he will expose the whole conspiracy in his book."

The most convincing evidence that Yigal Amir did not kill Yitzhak Rabin came from police forensics expert Baruch Glatstein, who testified at Amir's trial. After examining Rabin's suit and shirt, he concluded that two shots from point-blank range killed the prime minister. Amir was filmed shooting from at least five feet away. One shot came from a twenty-five-centimeter distance, while the second was a contact shot. Glatstein explained rationally that Rabin's shirt was torn to shreds in a way that could occur only if the gasses from the cartridge exploded on his skin. Further, Glatstein tested the shirt of Yoram Rubin, Rabin's bodyguard who was shot in the forearm. He found traces of copper and lead in the bullet hole, while Amir's bullets were composed entirely of copper. In short, Amir didn't shoot Rubin, either.

Glatstein's testimony agrees with that of Dr. Skolnick, a surgeon who operated on Rabin and said that his injuries were caused by contact shots. In July the Supreme Court heard testimony from a Tel Aviv taxi driver who picked up a passenger on the day Amir was convicted. After hearing a radio report on the conviction, the passenger said he was a pathologist at Ichilov Hospital who examined Rabin. He insisted that Amir could not have shot Rabin because his wounds had been inflicted from point-blank range. He then produced his Ichilov ID card, proving he was, in fact, a pathologist working at the hospital.

Dozens of witnesses heard five shots fired, but their testimony was not welcome at the Shamgar Commission's official cover-up of the event. In July, Yossi Smadja, a police officer assigned to the rally where Rabin died, told the press that he also heard five shots. Amateur film of the Rabin assassination has since been examined by numerous people in frame-by-frame sequence and found to have been sloppily cut and edited. More sinister is Rabin's reaction to being shot. Instead of lurching forward from the bullets, Rabin turns back alertly, seemingly aware of the events taking place. Most sinister of all, during the final seconds of the film while Rabin is supposedly being laid on the backseat of the car, followed by the wounded bodyguard, someone closes the opposite back passenger door of the car from inside. Clearly that someone was awaiting Rabin from inside the car.

Then there is the testimony of Shimon Peres, who saw Rabin's body in the hospital. He claimed in *Yediot Ahronot* that Rabin's forehead was swollen and bruised, he thought from being pushed on the pavement after he was shot. This is in direct contradiction to the eyewitness report of Miriam Oren, who was beside Rabin after Amir pulled the trigger. She told Israel Television news moments after the incident that Rabin walked into the car under his own power. Where and how, then, did the bruises that Peres claims he saw occur?

Finally, there is the indisputable proof offered unintentionally by Rabin's aide Eitan Haber. While Rabin was being operated on at Ichilov Hospital, for reasons still unexplained, Haber rifled through his suit and shirt pockets, looking for something, and pulled out the song sheet Rabin had held at the rally. Haber produced it for the cameras as he announced Rabin's death, and it was deeply bloodstained. Unless Rabin put it in a nonexistent back pocket of his suit, he was likely shot from the front. Backing for the contention came from a most unlikely source. On the night of the murder, a close Rabin compatriot, Member of Knesset Ephraim Gur, left Ichilov Hospital and told a Reuters reporter that he had seen that Rabin was shot through the chest and abdomen.

Reports Ignored

On September 20, 1996, two Israeli newspapers printed interviews with unexpected advocates of the conspiracy thesis. After nine months of silence, Shlomo Levy gave an interview to *Yerushalayim*. Levy, an associate of Amir's at Bar Ilan University, was a soldier in the Intelligence Brigade of the Israeli Defense Forces (IDF). After hearing Amir's threats to kill Rabin, he reported them to his commander, who told him to go to the police. The police took his testimony very seriously on July 6, 1995, and transferred it to the Shabak, where it was ignored until three days after the assassination. The newspaper's report concludes, "Levy's was only one of a number of reports the Shabak ignored about Amir. . . . The fact that the Shabak let the reports gather dust until Rabin was murdered lends credence to numerous conspiracy theories." Levy was asked, "If you did the right thing, why have you been hiding in your home out of fear?" He replied, "The Shabak is big and powerful, and I'm a little guy. The assassination is an open wound with them, and who knows how they'd react if I let myself be interviewed."

Also on September 20, Rabin's son Yuval was interviewed in *Yediot Ahronot*. Asked if he believed his father was killed in a conspiracy, a question that said much about the public's interest, he replied, "I can't say yes or no. It's not hard to accept it. . . ." One thing is certain, no one was punished. The worst that happened to any Shabak agent was dismissal from the service.

How Many Shots?

October 1996 saw the blatant inconsistencies between the official version of events surrounding the Rabin assassination and the truth clash publicly. Early in the month, *Maariv*'s weekend magazine published a remarkable collection of testimony from seven policemen and security agents on duty at the assassination scene that fueled suspicions of a conspiracy. On October 18 the author of this piece was the victim of an eight-minute hatchet job on Israel Channel Two Television's weekend magazine show that was shown again the next night. Despite the blatant attempt at character assassination, as *Yediot Ahronot* reported the Sunday following, I succeeded in igniting renewed national interest in the possibility that Rabin's murder was not as officially reported.

The *Maariv* report began with the issue of whether the alleged assassin's bullets were real or not. It is not denied by the Shamgar Commission that "Blanks, blanks!" was yelled by someone while Amir shot his weapon. The official conclusion is that Amir yelled it to confuse Rabin's bodyguards, a contention he denies.

How many bullets were shot? A.H., an agent assigned to Yoram Rubin's staff, declared, "I heard one shot, followed by another." The *Maariv* correspondent then asked another agent called A.A., "Are you certain you only heard one shot? "A.A.: "Absolutely certain." Avi Yahav: "I heard a number of shots. I'm not sure how many." Agent S.G.: "As I approached the car, I heard three shots." The inability of security and police personnel trained to testify in court to agree on the number of shots is puzzling, but on one issue all agree: None thought Rabin was hurt.

Y.S., Shabak head of security for the Tel Aviv rally, stated, "I heard Rabin was wounded only when I arrived at Ichilov Hospital some minutes later." S.G. says he "didn't hear any cry of pain from the prime minister and didn't see any signs of blood whatsoever. . . . It wasn't until some time after that I was told that Yoram Rubin was hurt." A.A.: "Only after a number of inquiries as to whether Rabin was hurt, did I drive in shock to Ichilov." None of the security or police personnel detected any sign that Rabin was hurt, quite inexplicable when one considers that he was not merely hurt but supposedly shot in the lung and spleen by two hollow-point nine-millimeter bullets. However, the amateur film of the assassination exonerates these witnesses.

Who Was Waiting in the Car?

After we see the blast from Amir's gun, Rabin is not pushed forward by the pressure of the bullet, nor does he evince pain. Rather, he keeps on walking and turns his head quickly to his left. Before examining the next issue of the *Maariv* article, let us skip to the report on my research on Channel Two. Despite the snow job, one of my points came across loud and clear and went a long way to keeping my name from being totally besmirched. I showed the assassination film and pointed out that as Rabin entered his car, the opposite-side passenger door is slammed shut. I said the only way the door could be shut was if someone was inside the car, shutting it. This would be in contradiction of the Shamgar report, which has Rabin and Rubin entering an empty car.

Channel Two explained that the door was shut by the vibrations caused by Rabin's entrance. Throughout the country people opened their back car doors and started shaking their vehicles. Nothing could make their doors shut. Further, Rabin's door was armored and weighed several hundred more pounds than the average car door. Add to these facts that the open front door of Rabin's car did not shut with the back door, nor is any shaking of the vehicle in evidence on the film, and you have someone, perhaps the real murderer, waiting for Rabin inside the car.

Now let's examine the testimony of Yoram Rubin, Rabin's head of personal security. On November 8, 1995, he was quoted in the *New York Times* that Rabin's last words to him in the car were that he was hurt but not seriously. Let's look at what Rubin told the police on the night of the murder and later testified to the Shamgar Commission and at Yigal Amir's trial.

Rubin to the police, 1:07 A.M., November 5, 1995: "I lifted the prime minister and pushed him into the car." To the Shamgar Commission: "He [Rabin] helped me get up. That is to say, we worked together. . . . We jumped, really jumped. I'm surprised, in retrospect, that a man his age could jump like that." At Amir's trial: "I grabbed him by his shoulders and asked him, 'Yitzhak, do you hear me, only me?' " In this version Rabin did not answer at all. In previous versions he said he wasn't hurt badly or actually helped Rubin to his feet.

Perhaps the most confusing piece of testimony concerns the critical moments when Agent Rubin enters the car with Rabin. The assassination film shows the opposite back passenger door being closed from the inside and the other back door being pushed closed from the outside. Yet Rubin testifies, "We fell onto the seat together, and I slipped between the front and back seat. His legs and mine were dangling outside as I yelled to the driver, 'Get out of here!' He started driving, and I lifted his [Rabin's] and my legs inside and closed the door. This all took two to three seconds."

The Long, Strange Trip to the Hospital

A most curious incident occurred on the way to Ichilov Hospital, normally less than a minute's drive from the supposed murder site. The trip took from 9:45 to 9:53. With a minute and a half driving time to go, Rabin's driver, Menachem Damti, picked up a policeman, Pinchas Terem, to help direct him to the hospital. Damti, an experienced driver, needed no help in finding Ichilov, but even that isn't the main point. With the prime minister dying beside him, the altruistic Yoram Rubin reportedly said to the policeman, "I'm wounded. Bandage me." As for Rabin, we can only guess he didn't care that his wounds needed much more urgent attention. Terem completed his bizarre testimony by noting that Damti did not notify Ichilov by radio that he was coming, and thus the hospital staff was totally unprepared for Rabin's arrival.

An Honest Inquiry

One possible conclusion suggested by the testimony of all these witnesses is that Rabin was unhurt by Amir's blank bullets and was shot inside the car. Rubin took a harmless arm wound to cover his role in the event, and Damti picked up a policeman as a witness in case of future disbelief. If this scenario or something more insidious is not to be believed, all the contradictory testimony will have to sorted out properly at an honest commission of inquiry.

Perhaps then we will finally learn how the back passenger door of Rabin's officially empty car closed as he entered the vehicle.

Update

A division of the Israeli General Security Services (Shabak), called the Non-Arab Anti-Subversive Unit, planted agents throughout the territories, supposedly to surveil radical Jews and restrict their activities. The unit was perhaps in the best position to learn of and prevent a Rabin assassination plot. Yet the duty of the unit's most famous agent, Avishai Raviv, appears to have been to provoke rather than prevent the murder of Yitzhak Rabin.

He formed an organization called Eyal, which had no members but himself. He convinced a student on the campus of Bar Ilan University, Rabin's future alleged assassin, Yigal Amir, to help him organize study groups in or near Hebron. Four teenage girls witnessed Raviv prodding Amir to kill Rabin, calling him a coward and a fake hero. This testimony was heard by the Shamgar Commission but was not included in the publicly released conclusions. (Notably, much of the commission's report was withheld from the public.)

Raviv was no minor provocateur. He had posters of Rabin dressed in a Gestapo uniform printed and distributed at a large rally. The so-called

Eyal members vowed to kill anyone who betrayed the land of Israel. Later, participants in an Eyal performance testified that Raviv told them what to say and where to stand and that the whole production was viewed as a put-on. They did not realize they were setting up Amir as a patsy by creating a radical group with which the public could identify him.

In the most obvious cover-up of the Shamgar Commission, seven Shabak agents and officers involved in the "snafu" that led to Rabin's death received notices that they were liable for criminal prosecution. Barak did not. In fact, he was not even called to testify.

A few persistent reporters tried tracking down Barak at his home in Kochav Yair but were turned away by the Shabak officers surrounding his block. The key to uncovering the truth of the Rabin assassination clearly lies with Eli Barak, but he has been protected, overly protected, by the government. And because of this glaring cover-up of his activities, not a few people have speculated that he was the mystery man who closed the back door of Rabin's car from the inside before the "wounded" Rabin entered the backseat.

Issue 16, Spring 1997

THE UFO ENIGMA

Like a Virgin: Virgin Mary Sightings, Prophecy, and UFOs

Joan d'Arc

Descriptions of Virgin Mary sightings reveal a curious connection between religious phenomena and UFO manifestations, including alien abductions. Joan d'Arc compares the various "stages" of alien abductions with those of Marian apparitions, concluding that the motifs contained in both "visitations" are surprisingly similar.

A sudden flash of light and tremor of excitement in the crowd made me turn and look in the direction of the sun. Almost to my horror, I witnessed what so many have called the "dance of the sun"—the sun moving back and forth as though on a yo-yo string, its central incandescent white disk surrounded by spinning circles of yellow, green, and red light, for all the world like a Catherine-wheel firework. All around us, people were on their knees praying. To my regret, I felt no such impulse. I had no sense of the numinous, only of the passing strange. . . . I felt that somewhere there must be a rational explanation.

ALTHOUGH UNRECOGNIZED AS SUCH by its author, the preceding description of the recent apparitions of the Virgin Mary at Medjugorje, Yugoslavia, penned by Mary Craig in her book *Spark From Heaven*, reveals a curious connection between religious phenomena and UFO manifestations, as do the phenomena documented at Fatima, Portugal, in 1917.

For Those Who Believe

Dr. Jean Mundy, studying the apparitions at Fatima and believing since childhood that they were divine revelations, had fully accepted that three children, Lucia, Jacinta, and Francisco, and approximately seventy thousand adults, witnessed the Blessed Mother's apparition. In high school, she states, she "would have felt it impertinent to ask the good Nuns for newspaper reports of those strange events or for interviews with eye witnesses." She believed in the motto "For those who believe, no explanation is necessary. For those who do not believe, no explanation is possible." However, later in life, after receiving a Ph.D. from Catholic University, she viewed the video *The Miracle of Fatima: Documentation,* which interviewed, years after the event, three eyewitnesses to the miraculous appearances at Fatima: Carolina and Maria Dos Santos, sisters of Lucia, and a brother of Jacinta.

Their memories of the event were still fresh. As the translator described the event, Carolina stated: "It seemed the sun was saying goodbye to the sky and coming down like a saucer singing and working, and coming down, and stopped only when it almost reached the ground. . . . We saw a shadow, and it was like lightning." Jacinta's brother stated: "The sun, like a disk in the sky, trembled, and made brusque movements outside of all cosmic law." The local newspaper reported at the time:

> The sun zigzagged for twelve minutes, and then plunged down, almost to the ground, and then it suddenly reversed itself. It was seen by witnesses as far away as 40 kilometers. Certainly beyond all cosmic laws, were the sudden trembling movements of the sun, and dancing as it were, before the astonished multitude who gazed in awe, with spectators crying, "Miracle! Miracle!" Other witnesses saw a second sun spinning and giving off fiery fingers of light extending across the sky.

That's No Lady

Estimates of the crowd watching this spectacle vary in the reports from fifty thousand to seventy thousand, but in all the reports it was only Lucia, now Sister Maria das Dolores, who claims she saw a bright light in the form of a woman in white. The "Lady" urged the children to keep her presence a secret and to continue to meet on the thirteenth of every month until October, when she would reveal her identity. Lucia concluded it was the Blessed Mother.

No one else, including the other two children, saw this apparition. As Lucia herself wrote in her memoirs:

> Opening her hands, she [the Blessed Virgin] made them reflect on the sun, and as she ascended, the reflection of her own light continued to be projected on the sun itself. . . . I wanted to call the attention of the crowd to the sun. I was moved to do so under the guidance of an interior impulse.

The Mother of God, states Dr. Jean Mundy, did not appear to thousands of devout Catholics in 1917 in Portugal. Only little Lucia Dos Santos saw what she claimed was the Blessed Virgin, while thousands of others saw only a fiery disk in the sky moving contrary to all known physical laws.

"Miracle" at Medjugorje

In his book *Extra-terrestrial Friends and Foes* (IllumiNet Press), George Andrews discusses many recent apparitions of the Virgin Mary, like the one in Cameroon, which he claims had numerous indications of UFO involvement. However, he states, the most persistent and well-known of these manifestations have occurred in the little village of Medjugorje in Yugoslavia. There, six youngsters between the ages of ten and seventeen had ongoing contacts with the Virgin since 1981. One of these six now has a cyst on her brain and has refused medical treatment, stating that the Blessed Mother wants her suffering offered to God.

These recent phenomena at Medjugorje resemble the occurrence at Fatima in 1917. One witness describing the miracle of the sun claims: "It came down out of the sky. The center of it was like a white host circled with gold and a path led down to us." Although people stared at the sun for thirty minutes, their eyes were not harmed.

The Australian edition of *People* magazine recently featured an article about a Melbourne millionaire who took his videocamera to Medjugorje and captured on film "an immense green disk obscuring the sun, then pulsing as it floods the sky with bands of colored light." Many of the witnesses at Medjugorje describe the sun "dancing in the sky." Also reportedly seen was a "grayish disk" slightly smaller than the circumference of the sun, which appeared to draw near the earth, pulsate, spin, and change colors. George Andrews has an interesting explanation for this phenomenon:

> It seems to me that the occupants of that grayish disc must have become overconfident of the gullibility of the spectators they were performing for, and neglected to align the disc correctly between the sun and the spectators. A single sloppy maneuver can destroy the effect of a whole series of impeccable performances, in this case allowing a witness to perceive and describe what had been so long and carefully camouflaged.

Zone of Strangeness

Dr. Mundy, now a psychologist, has compared descriptions taken from *Secret Prophecy of Fatima Revealed* with suggested stages of the contemporary alien abduction scenario. Analyzed as such, the phenomena offer some interesting parallels. For instance, in the Captured stage, the children at Fatima were herding the sheep when suddenly there were two flashes of lightning. They looked up and saw a globe of light, and eventually Lucia sighted the figure of a woman. During this psychic intrusion they were "frozen with fright," as is reported in alien abduction cases. In this case, capture can also be termed "rapture."

Similarly, in a stage called Zone of Strangeness, a "twilight zone" of strange events isolates the witness. During this experience, it seems to the witness that natural law has been suspended and reality is dreamlike. The motif of secrecy runs throughout abductions, as though they are admonished not to tell; even couples abducted together do not discuss the event between themselves. As will be discussed later, to this day there is a secret still held by one of the three children at Fatima.

In the stage best understood as Time Lapse, the witness's memory of the abduction blanks out, and he or she suffers paralysis or uncharacteristic behavior following the event. In this respect, the introverted boy, Francisco, became an extrovert after the miracle, Lucia refused to reveal many details of the Lady's requests for ten years, and Jacinta, disobeying her parents, returned quite often to the grotto, neglecting her flock of sheep. This compulsive return to the scene is prevalent in contemporary abduction cases.

In a stage called Procurement, a beam of light strikes the witness, capturing his or her total attention. This drawing force pulls the human into a one-on-one meeting, procuring or grabbing the human in order to instruct, reassure, pacify, and control the abductee. As seen in film footage of the sighting at Fatima, the children were struck so inanimate that onlookers pricked them with pins and otherwise tried to draw them from a strange compelling force without success. They remained looking straight up into the sky, with heads tilted back and necks bent like ostriches, their eyes glazed over with religious "rapture."

While some abductees are subjected to an Examination stage, some are not subjected to a medical exam but instead feel that they have been given a message which they are to reveal to others at a preordained time. The children at Fatima do not report being taken anywhere for an examination but appear to have skipped this stage in the place of becoming Messengers.

The children at Fatima were instructed on many details, among them to say their rosary every day in order to obtain the end of the war. Typical of the Conference stage of abduction, they were told, "In October Our Lord will come, as well as Our Lady of Dolors and Our Lady of Carmel. Saint Joseph will appear with the Child Jesus to bless the world."

Abductions seldom end when the spaceship sails off and may leave the witness "scarred for life." The lives of all who witnessed the sightings of the Blessed Mother at Fatima, as well as at Medjugorje, were permanently altered. Lucia later became Sister Maria das Dolores (Mary of Sorrows) as a direct result of the "visitations." Typical of modern alien contact is the Return stage, the continuing visitor experience. In fact, Sister Maria, now living in the Carmelite convent, has continued to experience precognition of deaths and world events and has had visions of Jesus Christ. Also revealed to her was the secret mystery of the Most Holy Trinity, which she is not allowed to share with others.

The Ultimate Scam: Third Prophecy at Fatima

Of the three prophecies Mary of Sorrows was told to reveal, the first two were a plea for people to turn away from sin and save the world from destruction. She was warned: "Many nations will disappear from the face of the earth." The third prophecy at Fatima was to be opened in 1960 and given by the bishop of Fatima to the reigning pope. This event took place behind closed doors, after which, it is reported, the cardinals filed out of the room with "a look of horror on their faces."

The Catholic Church decided not to reveal the final secret of Fatima. Rumor has it that Pope John Paul I had decided to reveal the final secret of Fatima, but, although in perfect health, he died suddenly the night before he was to reveal it. Requests for an autopsy were denied. What could have caused the look of horror on the faces of the cardinals when they learned the final secret of Fatima? Dr. Jean Mundy believes it was not the threat of war, or even nuclear disaster, stating that humans are "strangely accustomed to large-scale dying." She adds: "Death, collectively, is banal. Besides, the first two prophecies were about war, and no one squelched the message or the messenger." The stark horror, she suggests, is a complete disruption of a belief system. It would conceivably constitute the most sacred betrayal to believe that the Roman Catholic Church was established by Jesus Christ, the Son of God, and to learn after a lifetime of devotion that Jesus was an "alien" being. It is the ultimate scam.

If the logical conclusion is that otherworld beings staged an elaborate demonstration involving a Catholic deity, the next progression is to question why they needed such a complex and time-consuming plan to relay secret messages to the cardinals of the Catholic Church. We must also presume that if the miracle of Fatima in 1917 was staged, then the revelation in 1960 was meant to give credit to the scam operators, presumably a race of alien beings. Another possibility involves the occult aspect of UFO phenomena. Does the "fallen angel" named Satan have license to fly such a mobile? Some believe that the Lord of the Underworld is involved with this scheme, especially since, as follows, there is abundant proof that appearances of the Virgin are associated with war as a sacrificial blood rite.

Sacrificial Lambs

Mary Craig, writing in her book *Spark from Heaven,* brings to light some religious historical facts which contain a significant clue to the Medjugorje "sightings." George Andrews comments:

> Long before Yugoslavia became a nation, a struggle for dominance went on between Croatian Catholics and Orthodox Christian Serbians in the Balkans. During the early part of the Second World War,

the influence of the Catholic Church was aligned with the Fascists. On June 21, 1941, Croatian Fascists took seven monks out of the Orthodox Monastery at Zitomislic along with over seven hundred Orthodox women and children. Forced into a large pit at the nearby town of Surmanci, they were all buried alive. Forty years after this atrocity, on June 21, 1981, a plaque was erected at the Monastery in commemoration of that day. Just three days later, on June 24, 1981, the first apparition of the Virgin Mary occurred at Medjugorje.

In 1992, eleven years after the original apparition of the weeping Virgin at Medjugorje, in a nightmare reversal it was the Serbs who turned Fascist, while the Croats remained Fascist, both sides perpetrating the most abominable atrocities. The sacrificial victims numbered in the hundreds of thousands with no end to the killing in sight. In the midst of this religious holocaust, the apparitions of the Virgin continue to occur.

Not surprisingly, the Madonna's road shows can be easily mapped by instances of human mayhem and are associated more with suffering and mass death than with universal blessings. Apparently the Blessed Mother's tears of sorrow for humankind, shed alongside her threats of war and natural calamity, are nothing but "crocodile tears."

Religious Mayhem

As demonstrated by George Andrews in *Extra-terrestrial Friends and Foes,* apparitions of the Blessed Virgin are closely linked to UFO phenomena as well as to religious mayhem. I asked George for his take on all this, and in a letter to *Paranoia* he responded:

Although genuine miracles of healing have also occurred at some of these sites, there is an obvious correlation between these apparitions and large-scale human death. The first of the apparitions was at Guadalupe, Mexico, in 1531, at a time when about three quarters of the indigenous population had just been slaughtered. The apparition at Fatima in 1917 was near the climax of World War I. The apparition in Cameroon was only a few months before the mass deaths near Lake Nios. And look at what has been going on around Medjugorje, what a horrifying bloodbath that whole region has been drenched in, as well as the curious relationship between the beginning of the apparitions at Medjugorje and the massacre of 700 Serb women and children forty years before.

George Andrews feels that there are abundant indications that alien technology is involved in the Virgin Mary apparitions. In a discussion of the book *Keys of This Blood,* George writes that author Malachi Martin, a Vatican insider, devotes considerable space to the manifestation at Fatima. He notes that

> Martin never once uses the term "UFO," but the way he describes the "miracle" on the final day could easily be interpreted in terms of UFO phenomena, so easily that Martin must have been aware of this. While deliberately refraining from being too specific, he describes a spaceship without calling it a spaceship, however, he does call it a disc! He also points out the extreme importance attributed by the Pope to the apparition at Fatima. Martin says the present Pope is not concerned about the fact that his positions on a number of key issues are unpopular, further weakening the Church at a time when its membership is already shrinking, because he expects an event of a miraculous nature to occur in the near future that will cause the entire world to convert to Catholicism. . . .

Could such a "miraculous" event be merely a convenient method for the Grays (that is, extraterrestrials) to take complete despotic control of the planet by giving absolute power to a single human being: the pope?

Catholic Battle Standard

Guadalupe, Mexico, in 1531 was not the first theater of war over which the Virgin presided. Going back to the ninth century, according to Marina Warner in *Alone of All Her Sex,* the defenders of Chartres against the Norsemen flew "the Virgin's tunic" from the staff, which, legend has it, was the trick that defeated the invaders. In Byzantium at the turn of the seventh century, the "awe-inspiring image of the pure Virgin" flew from the ships of Emperor Heraclius as he sailed into battle. During the siege of Constantinople by the Avars in 626, the patriarch had the Virgin and Child painted on the west gates in order to "commend the city into her hands." In 717, during the Arab attack on Constantinople, a relic of the Virgin and Child with Cross was carried around the city walls as a "charm against the besiegers."

In Byzantium, during the Crusades, Christians were generally fighting heathens, and in medieval Europe the armies who invoked the Virgin's favors were fighting fellow Catholics. In the Counter-

Reformation's holy wars, horrors were perpetrated by Christian upon Christian in the name of the same God. At the battle of White Mountain near Prague on November 8, 1620, the Catholic army of Holy Roman Emperor Ferdinand of Austria advanced crying, "St. Mary!" and defeated the Calvinists, turning the tide of the Protestant Reformation in Europe and recovering Bohemia (now Czechoslovakia) for Rome. In the years following that victory, Ms. Warner writes, "Austrian armies established Catholic authority over the country, Jesuits assumed control of the universities, thousands of Protestants were banished, and those that remained were deprived of their civil rights."

The use of religious ritual as a battle standard was combined in the Church's fostering of devotion to the rosary, a necklace of beads on which the Hail Mary is recited over and over. The exact point of entry of the rosary into Western Christendom is not known but is generally attributed to the Crusaders. By the end of the twelfth century, Marina Warner writes, "the Franciscans and Dominicans had spread the use of the rosary among the laity and encouraged its use among the illiterate to obtain the Virgin's mercy and protection." By the fifteenth century the practice had spread zealously throughout Europe.

The notorious witch-hunter Jacob Sprenger formed the first lay confraternity devoted to the rosary in Germany in 1475. After Pope Alexander VI, the first pope to mention the rosary, gave his official approval in 1495, the practice spread like wildfire. In 1573 Pope Pius V instituted a feast of Our Lady of Victory to commemorate the defeat of the Turks at the battle of Lepanto, a victory that "destroyed the power of the heathen Turks in the Mediterranean." The pope believed that by the rosaries offered by the confraternities of Rome, the Virgin's intercession had given the battle to "God's side."

This proclamation affirmed the sacred power of the rosary for all time. The evidence cited by the pope to authenticate this was a vision of the Madonna to Saint Dominic. According to the story, while conducting the inquisition against Albigensian heretics at the beginning of the thirteenth century, Dominic had been given the rosary by the Virgin herself.

Her claim to the divine through the physical "immaculate conception" of the Son of God gave the Blessed Mother powers of intervention, or the ability to work both sides. The Son could not refuse the Mother's imploring pleas to intervene on behalf of her favorite children, as long as they utilized the power of the magic beads. Thus the direct intervention of the Virgin in human affairs gave the rosary a claim to divine ordinance. Nineteenth- and twentieth-century visions of the Virgin Mary have since confirmed her special love for the rosary. At both the visions in Lourdes and at Fatima, the apparition urged the recitation of the rosary, and pilgrimages are now committed to the recital of the Hail Mary.

Communism and the Antichrist

The Virgin and the rosary have over time become associated with the Catholic struggle against its archenemies. In 1717 the Feast of the Rosary was extended to the entire Church after the defeat of the Turks at Petrovaradin (now in Yugoslavia). Exactly two hundred years later, during the visions at Fatima, Our Lady of the Rosary spoke of an Antichrist. Lucia dos Santos revealed in 1927 that the Virgin had warned:

> I shall come to ask for the consecration of Russia to my Immaculate Heart. . . . If my requests are heard, Russia will be converted and there will be peace. If not, she will spread her terrors throughout the entire world, provoking wars and persecution of the Church. . . . But in the end, my Immaculate Heart will triumph.

In the propaganda that followed the visions, this Antichrist was identified with communism and used to spread fanatical anti-Communist paranoia. Many Catholics believed that the Fatima vision prophesied World War II and, further, that it influenced the pope's attitude toward Russia. In 1942 Pope Pius XII dedicated the world to the Immaculate Heart of Mary and soon afterward instituted a new feast of that name, celebrated on August 22. According to Marina Warner, the horror with which the Vatican viewed Russia contributed to its alignment with Nazi Germany, Russia's enemy. As one Catholic author stated: "Against Satan in his red threats, we have Mary."

When Statues Cry

Now we arrive at the ultimate question: Do the apparitions "cause" war, as George Andrews and others have suggested, or does war "cause" the apparitions? The psychoanalytic aspect of these phenomena is studied by Michael Carroll in *The Cult of the Virgin Mary*. He suggests that when populations are faced with danger and destruction, it is understandable that an attempt to reduce anxiety might occur. Religion is the oldest remedial standby for the lack of control people feel at certain times. For instance, the arrival of French troops into Italy under Napoleon in 1796 instigated a rash of "miraculous events," mostly associated with the Virgin Mary. Statues and images of Mary began to do strange things: she cried, she turned luminescent, her eyes opened and closed, and fiery sparks flew from her eye sockets. The Blessed Virgin "coming to life" would reassure people on the verge of calamity that "the forces of the supernatural world are on their side."

Likewise, an apparition appearing in the sky to several children in Pontmain, France, on January 17, 1871, occurred in the final stages of the Franco-Prussian War, after France had suffered a series of defeats. As Michael Carroll explains, "Paris had been under siege since September and under bombardment since December . . . the city's population was starving and on the verge of surrender. . . ." In addition, thirty-five males from the small town had gone off to fight the Prussians, who were expected to enter Pontmain in a day or two. This anxiety-ridden community would be especially receptive to believing that clouds in the shape of the Virgin Mary, and messages written underneath, meant that their boys would come home safe and all would be well. Also, it is important to note the attention and control that children command from adults in these "can't you see it?" scenarios.

As George Andrews suggests, we should "not refrain from asking any questions that come to mind when presented with paranormal phenomena of a religious nature, nor should we go to the opposite extreme of systematically debunking religious manifestations." We should, then, approach these phenomena with an open mind, rather than through a screen of conventional preconceptions.

Space Oddity: David Bowie, Whitley Strieber, and Aliens

Anonymous

This intriguing article analyzes the themes and lyrics of David Bowie's popular music, concluding that perhaps Bowie has had "visitor" experiences—in other words, has been abducted by aliens.

> I've always felt like a vehicle for something else, but then I've never really sorted out what that was. I think everybody, at one time or another, gets that kind of feeling: that they aren't here just for themselves, and more often than not they turn to . . . religion. There's a feeling that we are here for another purpose, and in me it's very strong.
>
> —David Bowie

IN 1987 A BOOK was published called *Communion*, written by Whitley Strieber, a well-known and very successful author of fiction. He maintained, however, that this book was not fiction. It concerned encounters he had experienced with "non-human beings," creatures he has described as "visitors" and others have called "aliens." *Communion* was a number one bestseller in the United States and stayed in the listings for most of a year.

As many people reading this statement will know, that book and his follow-up book, *Transformation*, generated a great deal of publicity for Strieber and for the questions he was asking regarding the possibility of nonhuman beings interacting with terrestrial humanity.

Among all this publicity and controversy, there is one singular and significant missing aspect of the alien equation as it relates to Strieber and to all of us. That is the life and work of the rock star and actor David

Bowie. It is a simple fact that for many years before Whitley Strieber wrote *Communion,* Bowie had been associated with the idea of extraterrestrial life forms existing and having a relationship with humanity. It is a simple fact that in 1981 David Bowie was one of the stars of a film called *The Hunger,* which was based on the book by Whitley Strieber. Taking these two facts together with a third fact, that Bowie is one of the most well-known and influential entertainers in the world today, we can see why the lack of any mention of David Bowie in connection with Strieber and his experiences might be regarded as a serious omission.

Following is an overview of the more obvious aspects of David Bowie's work over the years (pre-*Communion*) which seems to have been influenced by aliens.

Space Oddity

In November 1969 Bowie's second LP, *Space Oddity,* was released. The gatefold sleeve featured, on the back, a picture by George Underwood which included an alien figure with, on the right, a spacecraft and to the right of that a representation of Bowie himself, resembling a human-type alien. Writing about this record sleeve, Kenneth Pitt, Bowie's manager at the time the LP came out, has said:

> The back cover was a drawing by George Underwood from an idea scribbled on a piece of paper by David; it illustrated aspects of the lyrics and a likeness of Hermione in the left hand corner. It seems that David had a vague notion to recognize people who were working with him, for the original sketch included heads of Calvin and myself, but insufficient space caused us both to be omitted from George's final work.

Given Pitt's account of Bowie's "notion," you may ask whether the inclusion of alien figures and spacecraft on the sleeve were supposed to indicate that aliens were working with Bowie or whether their depiction was less consciously indicative of alien influence.

The Starman

In 1972 the same central alien figure turned up on an advertisement drawing by George Underwood for a Bowie Concert at the Rainbow Theatre, London. In this ad the alien was identified as "starman."

Alien aspects are easy to find in the lyrics of the third and fourth Bowie LPs, *The Man Who Sold the World* and *Hunky Dory*. The fifth LP, called *The Rise and Fall of Ziggy Stardust and the Spiders from Mars*, was his big breakthrough LP in Britain and was in the UK charts for two and a half years.

The first single released from this LP, "Starman," was extraterrestrial in its concerns. Bowie sang that there was "a starman waiting in the sky, who would like to come and meet us, but he thinks he'd blow our minds." In the lyrics "he told me let the children use it, let the children lose it . . ." Bowie intimated, within his Ziggy persona, that some degree of communication had been established between himself and an "alien race." This writer suggests that there is a real and meaningful basis to these lyrics in Bowie's own experience.

The Man Who Fell to Earth

In 1976 a major film release called *The Man Who Fell to Earth*, directed by Nicolas Roeg, starred David Bowie as a visitor from an alien world. The *Daily Express* film critic began his review by saying of Bowie: "When I think of him at all, which isn't very often, I always think of him as an alien being from outer space."

As has already been mentioned, seven years after he played the part of an alien visitor in *The Man Who Fell to Earth*, Bowie starred along with Catherine Deneuve and Susan Sarandon in a film adaptation of Whitley Strieber's book *The Hunger*. In this same year, the *Let's Dance* LP came out, which topped the UK charts and sold one million copies in the United States within three months of release. The Serious Moonlight world tour that followed the LP release was one of the most successful rock music tours of the 1980s.

Loving the Alien

Bowie followed this vast success by recording an LP entitled *Tonight* with a hit single from this in May 1985 called "Loving the Alien." The promotional video for "Loving the Alien" (directed by David Mallett) includes a curious moment in which Bowie is singing to the camera, and for no apparent reason his nose starts bleeding. Two years later we would read in *Communion* of nosebleeds being associated with the effects of a nasal probe by Visitors.

Perhaps Bowie's nosebleed in the video may have significance. (Another scene in the video involving an explosive sound also resonates with Strieber's experiences described in *Communion*). Two months after this apparently alien-influenced video emerged, Bowie starred on the UK side of the Live Aid event in which many music celebrities participated. Live Aid focused on world hunger and purportedly was watched by the majority of the earth's population. Was he influenced in some way to participate in this event?

The information in this statement is just "the tip of the iceberg." A great deal of evidence has been found in David Bowie's work which shows beyond any reasonable doubt that he has been influenced by aliens. This writer suspects that this fact will be made known to the world by David Bowie sometime in the next decade or so.

The Jean Genie

Bowie's hit song "The Jean Genie" was recorded on the road, as Bowie made use of RCA recording facilities in New York, Los Angeles, and Nashville before approving the master for pre-Christmas release. This 1969 LP, *Aladdin Sane,* is a strange and likable amalgam of musical influences ranging from Bo Diddley guitar licks to Lou Reed–style lyrics. Bowie has always laughed at critics' interpretations of this song's meaning, especially those that bring in the name of French writer Jean Genet. "In the past, Bowie has usually been willing to help the press dissect his songs, but now he was enjoying their guessing games," stated Ed Kelleher in his 1977 book *David Bowie: A Biography in Words and Pictures.*

The myth about "Jean Genie" is that it is a song about Jean Genet, or it is a song about Iggy Pop, or partly about Genet and partly about Iggy. The idea that it is about Jean Genet must be due largely to the title. The idea that it is about Iggy Pop may be, in my view, partially correct in that some of the lyrics could be inspired by him. When questioned about this by disc jockey Nicky Campbell on Radio One in 1990, Iggy Pop also stated this was his view on the matter.

After looking carefully through the lyrics and consulting dictionaries, I am convinced that most of the song's lyrics do not relate to Pop or Genet any more than they relate to any other specific individual. What I have found is that the song more than anything else describes an alien being.

According to the *Oxford English Dictionary*, the word "genie" was adopted by French translators of the *Arabian Nights* from the Arab word "jinnee," meaning "one of the sprites or goblins of Arabian demonology," as the rendering which it "resembled in sound and in sense." In English "genie" has been commonly used in the singular and "genii" in the plural.

Among examples quoted by the *Oxford English Dictionary* is this from Tobias Smollett, 1748: "If the plot . . . had been whispered by a genie, communicated by a dream, or revealed by an angel from on high." *Chambers 20th Century Dictionary* gives under "genie" a jinnee (see jinn), which is defined as "a class of spirits in Muslim mythology, formed of fire, living chiefly on the mountain of Kaf which encircles the world, assuming various shapes, sometimes as men of enormous size and portentous hideousness."

Meanwhile, *Collins English Dictionary* gives the following definitions: "1. (in fairy tales and stories) a servant who appears by magic and fulfills a person's wishes; 2. another word for jinni." Under "jinni" it gives alternative words jinnee, djinni, or djinny, defined as "a spirit in Muslim mythology who could assume human or animal form and influence men by supernatural powers."

A longer description of "jinn" is to be found in the *Brewer Book of Phrase and Fable*:

A sort of fairie in Arabian mythology, the offspring of fire. They propagate their species like human beings, and are governed by a race of Kings named Suleyman, one of whom built the pyramids. Their chief abode is the mountain Kaf, and they appear to men under the forms of serpents, dogs, cats, monsters, or even human beings and become invisible at pleasure. The evil jinn are hideously ugly, but the good are exquisitely beautiful. According to fable, they were created from fire two thousand years before Adam was made of Earth. The singular of jinnee. . . .

"The Jean Genie" was one of Bowie's biggest hit singles of the early 1970s, going silver in the United Kingdom. As stated previously, it was taken from the *Aladdin Sane* LP. It is obvious from the lyrics, however, that it is not simply a song inspired by the genie figure in the Aladdin myth (although Bowie had, in fact, attended a pantomime version of *Aladdin* starring Cliff Richard on March 1, 1967).

A curious coincidence worth noting here is that in 1968 and 1969

Bowie would perform a song called "Life Is a Circus," which Kenneth Pitt states in his book "was a song that Tony Visconti had heard performed by an American Group called Djin." The *Oxford Illustrated Dictionary* gives a definition for jinn and djinn (with two *n*'s, unlike the group's name): "Order of spirits lower than angels, with supernatural power over men. . . ."

Once it is understood that the song's title refers to a kind of supernatural or "alien" being (although the "Jean" part cannot be adequately explained as yet), many of the song's lyrics can be understood within this context. All of the verses of the song end with the line "poor little greenie," which seems to have been consciously derived from the well-known alien description "little green men," perhaps combined with the Chuck Berry song "Little Queenie."

The fourth line, "talking 'bout Monroe and walking on Snow White," may point to the fairy tale of the human Snow White and her seven dwarves, beings who are all small in size (as aliens are commonly described). In the chorus "the Jean Genie lives on his back, the Jean Genie loves chimney stacks," there is a link with the Father Christmas legend, in which he is supposed to come down the chimney with his gifts after traveling through the skies.

Aliens have been described as being in some manner reptilian (in alleged autopsy reports and so forth). The first line of the second verse connects with this apparent characteristic: "sits like a man but smiles like a reptile." The fifth line resonates with the experiences of the alien contactee Howard Menger: "He says he's a beautician, sells you nutrition."

The next line is "and keeps all your dead hair for making up underwear." It has been reported by some people who have encountered aliens that a sample of their hair was taken by the beings. It could be that some alien clothing resembles a mesh of human hair, visually and/ or texturally.

The first two lines of the final verse are "so simple minded he can't drive his module. He bites on a neon and sleeps in a capsule." A relevant definition of "module" in *Collins English Dictionary* is "3. Astronautics: any of several self-contained separable units making up a spacecraft or launch vehicle, each of which has one or more specified tasks."

Chambers 20th Century Dictionary has the following definition: "A unit of size, used in standardized planning of buildings and design of components. A self-contained unit forming part of a spacecraft or other structure."

In his famous earlier song "Space Oddity," David Bowie had used the word "capsule" in the line "It's time to leave the capsule if you dare," in connection with Major Tom's flight in a spaceship. For the word "capsule," *Chambers 20th Century Dictionary* offers "A fibrous or membranous covering (Zool) and a metallic or other container and a self-contained spacecraft or part of one, manned or unmanned, recoverable or non-recoverable."

Collins English Dictionary gives as its sixth definition of "capsule" "A vehicle, sometimes carrying men or animals, designed to obtain scientific information from space, planets, etc., and to be recovered on returning to Earth."

In conclusion, it can be said that a significant portion of the lyrics to the song "The Jean Genie" as well as the title itself have an unmistakable alien connotation. It seems to be almost impossible that David Bowie could have written, for example, the line "poor little greenie" without intentionally associating it with the phrase "little green men" rather than with Jean Genet or Iggy Pop or any other human being. The alien aspect of the song, therefore, seems to have been something of which Bowie was conscious when he wrote his lyrics.

Issue 13, Summer 1996

UFOs: Chariots of the Damned?

John White

The religious dimension of UFOs and abductions has long been investigated by researchers as the most perplexing aspect of the phenomenon. The premise of this article by a well-known author and researcher is that the deception practiced by the abductors can be seen in the light of a Satanic plan which has as its ultimate motive the takeover of the world through brainwashing and mind control.

> Flights of angels came and we called them hordes of demons.
>
> Whitley Strieber, *Majestic*

THE REVEREND BARRY DOWNING's 1968 book, *The Bible and Flying Saucers*, is a seminal work in the field of ufology. There he argues that some biblical passages, especially miracles in the Old Testament, are best understood in light of UFO research, including accounts of angels or God's messengers. His later commentary on the UFO experience ("The Rock of Ages Principle," *MUFON UFO Journal*, May 1990) is important because it further directs the attention of the ufological research community to the religious implications of UFOs.

However, while Downing's perspective is a highly plausible explanation for some ancient events, I do not find it acceptable as an explanation of contemporary abductions. I am especially concerned that he tries to convince us that "disguise and deception" should be regarded as benevolent. He says we may have to decide whether UFOs are good or evil, and he opts for the "good" position, arguing that UFO reports, including abductions, are best understood in light of the biblical doctrine of angels.

I find Downing's position flawed because the Bible recognizes "fallen" angels as those who retained their superhuman capacities but

101

turned from their allegiance to God. Since then their paranormal abilities have been used for evil rather than good. Thus the choice Downing would have us make with regard to UFO entities is not a simple either-or. Both good and evil are possibilities, depending on the sorts of angels with which one is dealing.

Downing is well aware of the "fallen angel" perspective on UFOs; his contribution to the 1980 *Encyclopedia of UFOs* entitled "Demonic Theory of UFOs" is an excellent survey of the topic. Despite that, in "The Rock of Ages Principle" he arrives at what I regard as an unsupportable conclusion. My response to it focuses on the phenomenon of alien abductions and examines that in the light of biblical doctrine.

I disagree with Downing's interpretation for several reasons other than the one just given. First, there is nothing in the Bible which indicates that God or God's messengers use deceit as standard operating procedure. Due care for human limitations, yes; deceit, no. Only the primal adversary of God, called Lucifer-Satan, does that and is therefore known as the Great Deceiver. Second, nothing in the Bible indicates that contact with God's messengers results in the wild stories and wounded psyches of contemporary abductees. God's messengers identify themselves as such and state their purpose. They present their credentials without equivocation. Last of all, God's messengers show respect for the sanctity of human life and do not overpower human will. Yes, one can point to the Angel of Death, acting at God's command, as the slayer of the Egyptian firstborn when the Hebrews were in captivity, but that is the exception, not the rule. Any deaths which have occurred in connection with alien abductions—and I'll discuss some later on—simply cannot be compared to that biblical circumstance. Abductees are not contemporary pharaohs, and the God of the Bible is a God of love and life enhancement.

My interpretation contrasts radically with what Downing calls his "God hypothesis," while retaining his framework of religious concerns. And although it may seem that I am merely offering the simplistic Christian fundamentalism which Downing rightly rejects, I maintain there is an enlightened fundamentalism—that is, a grasp of true fundamentals—which is congruent with that position but has greater depth and solidity because it is grounded in ufological data, metaphysical understanding, and spiritual insight. That is what I offer here. It is a "worst-case scenario."

Before proceeding further, however, I want to acknowledge that my interpretation is also similar to some scaremongering science fiction novels and movies. And I acknowledge that it has underpinning assumptions which are open to challenge. (To name just two: Are the alien abductions physically real events or psychological projections from the mythic-imaginal level of the human unconscious? Are the MJ-12 documents authentic?) Moreover, the data on which I build this scenario are few, tenuous, and far from indisputable. The evidence for my position is difficult to describe to an audience which is not psychologically sophisticated and parapsychologically educated. I've circulated a draft of this paper to a handful of UFO investigators and theorists. Some agree with me, in whole or in part; others think that, as one put it, I am "completely off base" and "lapsing into a kind of primitive supernaturalism and an infantile paranoia."

Perhaps so. I acknowledge the possibility, but at this point I'm not convinced to see things differently. Therefore I present this statement as a hypothesis for discussion of what is a perplexing aspect of the UFO experience—and potentially the most important. I welcome critical feedback in the interest of reality testing. I don't claim to have the "final" answer to the UFO question. (I've said before that I think there is no single answer to that question.) And I am not "locked in" to this hypothesis. I claim only that this statement is the result of thoughtful observation and analysis by a seasoned investigator of the paranormal which draws out reasonable implications and leads logically to a plausible conclusion. I recognize, however, that a chain is no stronger than its weakest links and that this chain of logic has various weak links. So I simply offer the following with sincerity, the most rigorous thinking I can bring to it, and a wish to provoke further discussion and investigation along the line I'm developing. Of course, it's possible to be sincere but deluded. I am willing—indeed, eager—to be shown that this is so in this case because if I'm right, even partially, we're all in big trouble.

The thrust of UFO research is into the metaphysical, where things are not always as they seem. Downing sees UFOs—meaning, in these circumstances, the gray abducting aliens—as benevolent, superior who compassionately take into account, through "disguise and deception," our inability to directly perceive their "vastly superior reality." In Downing's interpretation, that reality is traditionally known as the full glory of God. In my judgment, however, the gray abducting aliens are demonic and untrustworthy. "By their fruits ye shall know them," Jesus said about evaluating spiritual credentials. Saint Paul added that the fruits of the spirit are peace, joy, and love. Judging by the fruit of the gray abducting aliens, I see aspects to the UFO abduction experience which indicate there may be profoundly sinister dimensions to it. I get a strong of sense of conspiracy by the abductors—a vast, subversive plot of long duration and careful coordination which aims at nothing less than the complete enslavement of humanity. I see nothing about their words and deeds which indicates anything except lies, evasion, misdirection, manipulation, exploitation, and total disregard for human values, personal property, and our concept of respect for the inviolability of personhood.

We humans consider kidnapping and violation of civil rights to be criminal, rape to be loathsome, brainwashing and mind control to be heinous, lying to be despicable, deliberate infliction of pain to be sadism, unauthorized surgical invasion and unauthorized impregnation of people to be monstrous, mutilation of bodies to be savage, and damage to personal property to be vandalism. The gray abducting aliens exhibit such behavior—and possibly even murder. On the other hand, I know of no behavior by them which is clearly intended to show respect for our physical or psychological personhood, property, civil rights, moral values, and concern for truthful speech; the abducting aliens routinely violate all that. As I view the situation, it's a ghastly picture which emerges. It is not merely alien; it is profoundly evil in precisely the sense given in the Book of Revelation and other sacred scriptures which describe a battle between the forces of light and the forces of darkness for the salvation or damnation of humanity and the planet. So when abducting aliens allegedly say, "We're here to serve you," I take it to mean they have something like cookbook recipes in mind.

I want to make clear that I am limiting this discussion to one class of UFO entities: gray abducting aliens. I am not condemning all gray aliens. I'm willing to believe there may be good ones, just as there are good and bad people. And speaking more generally, my assessment of ufology's data leads me to conclude that earth is probably one of the major crossroads of local space, with many alien life forms visiting us. Some of them may indeed be motivated by vision and values in keeping with our own most transcendent insights and sacred wisdom. Others, however, are not; and that is my point. If alien abductions are the work of angels, let us be clear about who they are: fallen angels, which are demonic entities.

To get specific about what I think may be going on, consider the humans or humanoids who have been reported by abductees to be present on UFOs, apparently working with and for the aliens. There are many such reports, most notably that by Travis Walton. If the grays have been conducting a genetic experiment or an interspecies breeding program for at least several decades—which is what Budd Hopkins's work indicates—then there could be adult humans who have been raised under alien control since infancy and who are thoroughly alien in their loyalties and psychology, although they certainly would be able to pass as "real" people. While seeming to be ordinary citizens, they would nevertheless be at least programmed, if not naturally inclined through psychological bonding, to identify with the alien culture. Such people could have been raised in an off-world site—say, a base on the Moon or Mars or even a gigantic "mother ship"[1]—and then reintroduced to human society, with sufficient training and ongoing support from aliens to make their way into careers in many fields. Depending on the scope of the aliens' work—which I take to be happening on an enormous scale, since abduction reports are worldwide—the abducting aliens could have hundreds or even thousands of their people infiltrated in science, industry, finance, government, education, the military, and so on, with some undoubtedly in positions of great power and influence. These people, in turn, could have recruited others to various degrees, creating in classic fashion the "cells" of a subversion movement preparing to overthrow the establishment. More likely, though, they would have made their true identity known only to other "aliens among us" and committed true-human collaborators who have been working voluntarily with the aliens.

How might the aliens begin to infiltrate and recruit? The MJ-12 group offers a point of entry. A crashed flying saucer would be "bait" to hook the military-government-scientific complex into contact. Of course, this infiltration activity would not be limited to the United States. If the aliens are doing it here, they're probably doing it elsewhere. If they've made contact with MJ-12 or its successors—as the Project Aquarius, Project Snowbird, Project Sigma, and Project Garnet reports indicate[2]—we can be fairly certain they've contacted other major powers. (Timothy Good's *Above Top Secret* demonstrates a worldwide cover-up of the UFO phenomenon, although he doesn't take that to the extreme I do here.) However, being scheming, untrustworthy, and bent on planetary domination, the aliens would not have told MJ-12 anything about their communication with other scientific and governmental-military officials or groups they have contacted over the decades. It wouldn't do to let each know about the others. In terms of the intelligence community's operations, they would keep knowledge compartmentalized and would reveal it only on a "need to know" basis. Infiltration would be the hidden agenda behind their contact with MJ-12 and the governmental-military-scientific elite of the world until the time was right to let all parties know of the others' participation.

In the meantime, since "loose lips sink ships," the military-intelligence community would have undertaken counterintelligence, disinformation, and media influence programs to discredit anyone on the inside who might come forward to tell the truth and anyone on the outside who might surmise the truth. Thus the ridicule and harassment which people who tell stories about ETs or UFOs encounter may have been started or aggravated by MJ-12 or its successors. Once the attitude "caught on" with the public, anyone who broached the subject was considered a lunatic and his or her claims or data disregarded. How could there be a "Hanger 18" at Wright-Patterson Air Force Base or Alternative 3–like colonies on the Moon and Mars when everyone knows that UFOs are sheer fantasy, hallucination, or misperception?

In parallel with the aliens' infiltration movement would be *Manchurian Candidate*–like programming of the true-human abductees and collaborators, as well as alien-human hybrids produced through interspecies breeding. My thinking is this: If the grays' ultimate intention is world control, they have several ways to get there. Their last resort would be violent takeover, using open warfare. That would certainly unite true humans in opposition, and even if the grays conquered humanity, we would continue to resist them by any and all means, even if our condition were reduced to the status of POWs at a Hanoi Hilton. No, the aliens would seek a bloodless takeover by conquering through deception, manipulation, and propaganda. Remember that American POWs in Korea and Vietnam were continually subjected to brainwashing because their bodies were captured but not their minds. The aliens would recognize that and, in order to make their victory complete, try to indoctrinate us, through covert means, to accept them as we walk down a garden path, rather than have to "reeducate" some five billion people in effect held captive as POWs.

So the more intelligent approach to total control would be to coopt the human race—to subvert it through a cultural conditioning control system such as Jacques Vallee suggests in *Messengers of Deception and*

Dimensions. (To be flip about it, we can call it the "crock of ages principle"—meaning a crock of you-know-what.) MJ-12 and its counterparts in other nations would be the starting point.

Here's where the plot thickens. In fact, it ties in with more mundane conspiracy theories in the political sphere which allege that groups such as the Rothschilds, Rockefellers, Trilateralists, Bilderbergers, Council on Foreign Relations, and others are the hidden powers and secret establishments directing world affairs through international banking and control of the media, education, science, and military-political institutions in order to set up a one-world social order with themselves at the seats of power.

There are some plausible arguments for the political conspiracy theory made by responsible, credible thinkers and scholars such as Carroll Quigley, Antony Sutton, and Eustace Mullins; there are also some absolutely bozo claims made by head-for-the-hills redneck survivalists and fringe Christian fundamentalists. I try to assess them all to see what looks viable, weighing them against my standards of reason, logic, and evidence. Now, it's perfectly clear, thanks to the Iran-Contra affair, that international conspiracies can and do happen. The real question is to what degree and how well coordinated and controlled they are by the alleged secret powers.

Until the last decade, I dismissed the notion of a generations-old international conspiracy to set up a one-world society controlled by international banking-financial interests such as the Rockefellers and Rothschilds. I reasoned that if there were one conspiracy, there would be others, and the net result would be to negate or at least neutralize each other. No one would gain total control or unassailable ascendance. The vagaries of world affairs would be too unpredictable; too many things could go wrong; people wouldn't stay loyal to such a cause all their lives; evidence of it simply couldn't be covered up forever.

Then the abducting gray aliens came into view, and the situation took on a wholly different complexion. If the aliens have secretly planted their agents throughout civilization for decades and if they are pursuing contact with the top echelons of power around the world for purposes of infiltration and subversion, then over the years they have been playing out a hand which was strategized nowhere but in hell.

Look at MJ-12's roster. The members and their probable successors lead straight into the heart of the most disturbing "conventional" conspiracy theories about international finance and military-political-scientific intrigue. For example, consider the Skull and Bones Society at Yale University. It is, from the political conspiracy theorists' point of view, the quintessential "evil empire" within the United States. George Bush, McGeorge Bundy, and a large number of the Trilateral Commission members and the Council on Foreign Relations were tapped by this secret society while they were undergraduates at Yale and were bound by an oath of secrecy to be loyal to the "Bones" purpose. That purpose goes far beyond simple collegial fraternity and the typical "good ol' boy" network's interests.

The conspiracy theorists say that the aim of all this is to covertly create a new world order in which the secret establishment becomes the hidden power controlling global affairs—its economy, science, industry, religion, education, technology, and so on, even while maintaining a façade of increasing freedom and prosperity for the world's masses. Nationhood would wither away, but political power would not. It would be consolidated behind a screen through the fraternal bonds of men (Skull and Bones presently excludes women) whose aims and loyalty are not to any country or group, but only to their own supranational cabal. They would be "the power behind the throne."

Imagine that such a conspiracy has been going on for decades. That would explain U.S. State Department approval of high-technology transfer from American industry to the former Soviet Union, even when it ends up being used against America in military situations—as has happened. It would also explain multimillion-dollar bank loans to the Soviet Union with no assurances sought that they wouldn't be used to underwrite anti-American activities—as has happened. Then imagine that the aliens not only know of the conspiracy and understand its operations, but have also cunningly planned to coopt it by pretending to establish friendly relations with it. What would be the nature of the directing intelligence behind the aliens' scheme? It seems to me that the gray aliens alone are not smart enough or powerful enough to pull it off, despite their technological edge. They appear to be rather robotic or hivelike in their capacities. They appear to lack the intellectual creative flair for such scheming. A greater intelligence is required. I see it like this:

The alien abductors are glad to let the secret establishment continue its work aimed at world domination because the humans involved don't realize the danger they've gotten into by making what is in reality a diabolical pact—in the most literal sense. The secret establishment thinks it's simply got an edge by making contact with the aliens because the aliens can provide advanced technology[3] to help the power brokers advance their scheme; all they have to do is let the aliens continue with their "scientific" work of abducting people for "examination." But the aliens' intention is to be the power behind the power behind the throne. And the MJ-12 successors played right into their hands.

UFO conspiracy theorist John Lear says that a team amalgamated from MJ-12 and the CIA have had a longtime joint venture in which hidden underground bases for alien activity play a part. He also says the team is now scared of that alliance because they have begun to realize the magnitude of the deadly game into which they've been suckered. From the perspective of this hypothesis, that makes sense. Just as they and their fellow conspirators see their "final" victory nearing—that is to say, global affairs are tending well for the establishment of a one-world order, exactly as the conspirators have been working for over decades—the aliens trump them, and in effect the secret establishment itself becomes secretly, subtly, but inescapably enslaved, exactly as they sought to do to others. A delicious irony is there, but don't laugh too loud about it, because if this hypothesis is correct, the situation is appalling. It's the Book of Revelation coming true: A titanic war is being waged in "the heavens"—invisibly, metaphysically—between the powers of light and the powers of darkness for the liberation or enslavement of all humanity.

I'll say more about the powers of light in a moment. For now, return to those alien-raised humans and humanoids. If the aliens are as knowledgeable about human psychology, physiology, and anatomy as UFO research indicates, then they are wholly competent to "program" human beings and humanoids to react in certain ways upon signal. Under hypnosis, abductee Betty Andreasson stated repeatedly in *The Andreasson Affair—Phase Two* that she would reveal something in the future when the time is right as determined by the aliens; quite independently, her future husband, Bob Luca, received exactly the same mental programming from abducting grays. All the hypnotist's skill could not retrieve the unrevealed information from Andreasson because there was or is a second, deeper-level block in her mind to prevent people from learning the truth about the aliens' intention, even after the primary block was removed and her abduction revealed. The hypnotist, Fred Max, agrees with me on this point. After speaking with him, I was gratified to see that Raymond Fowler's *The Watchers* confirms and greatly elaborates on this point. Fowler initially titled the book *The Andreasson Affair—Phase Three* because it reveals much more about the Lucas' experience and their precise, profound programming by the aliens ("they have been and are in control of all the information stored within the deep recesses of Betty's mind," p. 128), as well as Fowler's own. On the basis of these further revelations, Fowler states, "They know more about our overall makeup than we do ourselves." (p. 183)

Think about the so-called medical exam given to abductees. Isn't it perfectly obvious now that the "abduction as medical exam" scenario is merely a cover for something else? How many skin samples do alien "scientists" need before they have sufficient data? As David Jacobs, author of *Secret Life*, pointed out in a lecture at the 1988 "UFO Experience" conference in Connecticut, why hasn't their data gathering become more sophisticated over the decades?[4] It hasn't changed since Betty and Barney Hill were abducted in 1961. Why the now stereotyped, unvarying, and well-rehearsed routine for thousands of abductees? While performing—in the sense of theatrical acting—their seemingly elementary examination of abductees, the aliens demonstrate that they actually have a deep and highly detailed knowledge of human psychology, physiology, and anatomy. Abductee reports show that the aliens can completely control the human nervous system. When aliens want to abduct them, abductees are routinely paralyzed instantly and placed in suspended animation. When they are on alien examination tables and report feeling pain from some operation, the mere touch of an alien hand can block the person's perception of pain. Reports also show that aliens can effect instant healings, alter memory, distort a person's sense of time, and perform precise surgical operations on the brain and visceral organs, not to mention the wide range of gynecological procedures they employ. I conclude that the alien "medical exam" is a sham and a cover for something else—namely, brainwashing and mind control.

For what purpose? I suspect this: The alien-humans would undoubtedly be programmed to rise up violently in armed warfare if the aliens felt it necessary to achieve their aims in extremis. Imagine hundreds of thousands of Manchurian candidates, each programmed to assassinate or otherwise eliminate designated leaders and officials so that the aliens' hand-trained agents can come forward. Is that far out? Not in the shadowy—or should I say gray?—world of political intrigue, subversion, and life-or-death struggle for conquest of planet Earth.

Here I must state emphatically that I do not mean to have people regard all abductees with suspicion and fear, which might lead to a modern witch-hunt against them. My sympathy for them is genuine and strong, and I trust that this essay makes that clear. I say so because Betty Andreasson Luca and Bob Luca, who are friends of mine, do not agree with me concerning the possibility of Manchurian candidate programming—of themselves and others. They do not believe the grays are evil, including their abductors, and have asked me to refer people to two quotations from Raymond Fowler's books about them. Betty points to her statement from *The Andreasson Affair* as evidence: "He [Quazgaa, leader of the alien abductors] says my race won't believe me until much time has passed—our time. . . . They love the human race. They have come to help the human race." (pp. 110–111, Bantam ed.) Bob points to his statement in *The Andreasson Affair—Phase Two:* "[Fred Max, hypnotist] Why do they need to meet other people?" [Bob] "Prepare us for something good. Going to be for mankind." (p. 40, Prentice-Hall ed.) Since our conversation, *The Watchers* (Bantam, 1990) has been published, and it amplifies their position greatly.

The Watchers also reveals that the 1977 automobile accident in which Betty Andreasson lost two sons was "foreseen" by the aliens, who told her of it three days before their death. However, they claimed they could not intercede or do anything about it. Moreover, they suppressed Betty's conscious knowledge of it until afterward. I cannot accept that situation as simple precognition by the aliens. Parapsychological studies of precognition indicate that warnings can be given to alert people to impending danger and thereby avert tragedy; that, if anything, is the biological purpose of extrasensory perception: survival. Common sense leads to the same conclusion. So why should the aliens refuse to let Betty recollect their warning before it was too late? Moreover, since the aliens have legendary capability for tracking people and likewise have technology capable of controlling our own, they were not powerless to intercede; ufology abounds with stories of vehicles' electromagnetic systems being overridden. Last of all, since they are masters of mind control, capable even to the point of programming precisely timed and exact behavior in people, I reluctantly conclude that the aliens knew about Betty's sons' death in advance because they deliberately engineered the "accident." That can be described quite simply as murder. The aliens also told Betty that her religious faith would bring her through the tragedy. That proved true, but it was not thanks to the aliens. It seems to me that the situation had the effect of conditioning Betty—and, through her, Fowler and his readers—to the notion that the aliens are allied with her spiritual outlook, thus making even death an acceptable action in support of the aliens' hidden agenda. I therefore regard the situation as profoundly deceitful. It cleverly and completely undermines Betty's spiritual sensibilities.

Where would all the alien-humans come from? Many would have been bred in vitro from sperm and ova or raised from fetuses, as Budd Hopkins's research indicates. But many others could have been obtained the easy way—by kidnapping children. An estimated one million children are missing in the United States each year. Where could they all go? If just 1 percent of them were abducted by aliens, that's a sizable population to work with at off-world bases. If you grant the plausibility of this admittedly fantastic scenario so far, it then makes sense to say that the grays are not the "ultimate" type of beings contacting us in this matter. The grays are alien, and perhaps they're extraterrestrial. (I present the case for grays as extraterrestrials in "ET or MT? A Response to Kenneth Ring," *MUFON UFO Journal,* July 1989. That statement was deliberately devoid of the considerations made here.) They may also be what UFO researcher and author J. Allen Hynek called metaterrestrial. Whatever the case, it appears there is another "race" behind the abducting gray aliens, directing their activities. This "race" is not merely "alien"—it is evil. It is truly sinister, malevolent, and unswervingly committed to the damnation of all humanity—and it is definitely not extraterrestrial. These intelligences have been characterized in ancient scriptures and sacred traditions as native to earth, diabolical, hostile to our very existence as free people, and intent upon dominating us totally—physically, mentally, and spiritually.

St. Paul spoke of humanity contending with "powers and principalities." My reason, research, and personal experience lead me to conclude that such entities are ontologically real, albeit paraphysical. I see the hand of such intelligences behind much of the UFO phenomenon. I will even name the chief entity, using its Judeo-Christian appellation: Lucifer-Satan. To say more than that in a meaningful manner, however, would take far more space than I have here. I am prepared to get into the issue of Lucifer-Satan and its nature, purpose, and role in the UFO experience, but that will depend on my assessment of the response to this article.

Taking the widest possible view of the situation, I will say that in my judgment we humans are not alone against forces of darkness. I see benign and even benevolent "alien intelligences" here as well—forces of light—trying to assist us in this struggle for psychobiological integrity, spiritual advancement, and true planetary unity—not a new world order but a new world community. We are "surrounded by angels, unaware." These agents of godliness seek in gentle, noncoercive ways to guide us, protect us, and enlighten us.

For example, the beings of light whom people meet during a near death experience (NDE) are providing tremendous support for humanity. The light beings' nature is clearly evident by the effect they have upon human lives. Completely unlike the abducting grays, the NDE light beings produce no traumatic or ambiguous consequences on humanity. People who meet them while in the near death state report later that they sensed only unconditional love and forgiveness for their misdeeds radiating wordlessly from these spiritual entities, along with heightened understanding of life. Abducting aliens induce fear and long-lasting anxiety, discomfortable dreams, intellectual confusion, and a disturbed personality in their victims; NDE light beings have an aftereffect which brings people a sense of ultimate peace, cosmic goodness, reverence for life, deepened spirituality, concern for fellow humans and the environment—a general revaluing of a materialistic, egotistic lifestyle in the name of God and love.[5] Here in America alone, according to a Gallup poll, an estimated 14 million people have undergone an NDE. If America is at the leading edge of a millennial demonic invasion directed by the Prince of Darkness, as I'm postulating, it is also the site of an even greater number of transformative, uplifting, inspiring encounters with entities traditionally called angels, saints, and enlightened teachers. And, like UFO abductions, such activity is happening around the globe. Altogether, this indicates a colossal support system of metaphysical forces which intend salvation—spiritual freedom—for humanity, building in opposition to what I have posited is a hellish plot aimed at complete enslavement of humanity and planet Earth. In conclusion, I must acknowledge that some abductees disagree strongly with my hypothesis. They regard their abductors' behavior as benevolent and intended for human betterment. (In *The Watchers*, Fowler explicitly equates the abducting aliens with the NDE light beings.)

I do not deny that abductees, on the far side of their traumatic experience, often demonstrate psychological gains, and occasionally even extraordinary physiological health gains, as in the case of John Salter of

North Dakota. All that does not negate my position. I attribute such
transformation—such real benefits—to the innate human urge to health
and the body-mind's self-reparative capability rather than to the aliens'
noble intentions. Holocaust survivors are stronger for what they've
been through, but they don't thank Hitler for it. Likewise, recovering
alcoholics don't thank the bottle. And while I'm mentioning the Nazis, I
remind readers that the last attempt to "improve" the human race
through a genetic breeding program such as the aliens apparently have
was engineered by Adolf Hitler and the Third Reich.

To put it simply: I am concerned here with spiritual discernment and
denouncement of evil. I am concerned with truth, freedom, and public
safety. Downing's stance—that all ETs are from God—is representative
of a widely held view whose variations range from "ancient astronauts"
through "space brothers" to "saviors from space."[6] I see that as one
which unwittingly "glorifies the devil" by giving legitimacy to alien
abductions. Legitimacy goes beyond merely establishing their reality; it
passes into the moral dimension and makes or implies a public judgment of the aliens' benevolence and trustworthiness. This gives aid and
comfort to "the enemy," who, the Bible tells us, disguises itself as an
"angel of light." Yes, we called those flights of angels "hordes of demons" because they really are that—fallen angels.

Lest I be accused of thinking in simplistic black-and-white, good-or-
evil, us-vs.-them terms of Christian fundamentalism, I hasten to say that
is not so, as readers of my book *The Meeting of Science and Spirit*
(Paragon House, 1990) will see. What is so is this: In keeping with
Jesus' teaching about the proper attitude toward others, I regard the
gray abducting aliens and all other life forms with unconditional love.
However, unconditional love is different from acceptance and respect.
My acceptance and respect is entirely conditional; it must be earned.
Unconditional love is directed at personhood; acceptance and respect is
directed at behavior. The abducting aliens have not earned my acceptance and respect. I judge their behavior, not their personhood, to be
unworthy of it. I am not casting them out of my heart; I am using my
critical faculties to discriminate behavior from beingness and to condemn the sin, not the sinner.

Therefore, if I am anywhere near correct in this analysis, our best
defense is to put on the armor of love and to wield the sword of dis-
crimination, while making full public disclosure of the activities of the
aliens and their human accomplices.

The abducting aliens always come to us under cover of darkness. They never tell us precisely why they abduct us. The whole thing is as suspicious to me as a Trojan horse, so I'm simply voicing my concerns. If the aliens change their ways—if they reveal themselves in the light of day, unequivocally disclose their business, and allow us to convince ourselves of their benevolence—I'll welcome them into human society. But until they present themselves to us in unambiguous circumstances and without veiled intent, until they present themselves as trustworthy visitors to earth who do not violate and harm its human inhabitants, I shall continue to regard them as cunning, predatory creatures from a netherworld bent on evil disguised as good. And whether they ultimately prove to be physical, paraphysical, or metaphysical will have no bearing on that conclusion.

Issue 11, Winter 1996

Alien Corpse in Puerto Rico

Jorge Martín

Just what was the long-dead corpse that investigator Jorge Martín saw in Puerto Rico? Its physical features are reminiscent of the "Grays" of UFO literature: small body, large head, wide and dark slanted eyes, and a lipless mouth. Martín takes us along on his investigation, which featured a mulattolike Man in Black who told an associate, "I've been told you deal with flying objects. Be very careful with that."

A YEAR AND A HALF AGO, in the middle of a presentation I was giving at the Metropolitan University in Cupey, Puerto Rico, a young man showed me four photographs which left me deeply impressed. They depicted the strange corpse, in a variety of poses, of a creature which had obviously been dead for a long time.

Intrigued by the snapshots, I asked the young man about their origin, since the visible details were reminiscent of the alleged extraterrestrial humanoids known as Grays in the world of UFO investigation—small beings with a maximum height of three to four feet, large heads, and wide, dark, slanted eyes. The eye sockets were similar, but this being's eyes were submerged within them. The corpse barely had a nose, only nasal orifices, and it had a lipless mouth with no visible teeth.

Other details in the photos reminded me of other descriptions given of the Grays, such as the extremely slender and long arms. The mysterious corpse's hands had only four fingers with a membrane between them, the digits ending in sharp little nails. The young man pointed out that a person known to me had given him the photos and proceeded to hand me copies of them. Armed with this information, I set out to investigate the matter.

I contacted the person who had supplied the photos, and he told me an incredible story. According to him, the snapshots were of an alleged

116

extraterrestrial slain by a relative of his around 1980–81. This relative was a cattleman in the northern part of the island who had lost a sizable number of heads of cattle in a bizarre manner, mutilated in an indescribable fashion (since 1975 a considerable number of animal mutilations have taken place). He decided to keep a vigil along with two friends, all of them armed with .30-30 rifles, in an effort to discover who or what was responsible.

One night, four small, strange creatures, similar to the one in the photo, appeared out of a mountain stream. The cattleman and his friends saw the creatures enter a stable and remove a small heifer by levitation. The heifer was rigid and floated between and above the four creatures, who moved with a wobbling gait. Still unable to believe what he was seeing, the cattleman fired upon the creatures several times, striking one of them. The creature fell to the ground, emitting weird shrieks. The heifer fell to the ground simultaneously while the beings tried to succor their fallen companion, who was writhing in pain and struggling to get up.

The cattleman and his friends fired again, prompting the creatures to flee and desert their wounded companion. Upon noticing that the wounded being was trying to get up, the cattleman shot it in the neck. The group moved closer to look at the creature, which still writhed on the ground, and one of the cattleman's friends gave it a strong blow on the head with a piece of wood, crushing its skull and finally killing it. One of the friends took off his jacket immediately after and wrapped the creature in it; they took it to the cattleman's residence, where it was stored at first in formaldehyde and later frozen for ten years. It was shown only on certain occasions, as the cattleman was fearful that the U.S. authorities would learn about his concealed item and take action against him to cover up such a piece of evidence.

On one of the few occasions in which his relative thawed out the corpse, he allowed the individual with whom I was speaking to take several color photos of it, which he kept in his possession. The reader must understand that if this story should turn out to be true, it represents a milestone in UFO research not only in Puerto Rico, but around the world. On many occasions I asked him to arrange an interview with the cattleman, but my requests were always met with hesitation on his part, assuring me that his relative "was scared."

I explained to him that I was aware of another story concerning the origin of the corpse, but he insisted that his relative's account was indeed true, and he refused to arrange another interview, making several excuses. Although the body in the photos resembled that of an alleged Gray, I didn't believe him, because of the story that follows.

Previous Contact With the Case

In fact, before speaking with this person, I recalled having been shown a similar photo, but with a different detail: The corpse was contained within an elongated, transparent glass receptacle. This was in the summer of 1980, during a conversation with two friends from Salinas, Puerto Rico, on UFO incidents which had taken place in the region around that time. They showed me an interesting black-and-white photo in which the same corpse could be seen inside the container.

They stated that it was the corpse of an extraterrestrial which had been slain by a youth at a hill behind Camp Santiago, in Salinas, in 1980. According to this version, the youth ran into several little men while taking a walk through the hills. The little men tried to seize him, and in fear he reached for a piece of wood on the ground and clobbered one of them, shattering its skull. Immediately after, while the other little men fled the scene, the youth took the tiny corpse and abandoned the area. Upon reaching his home, he placed it in a container filled with alcohol and later transported it to a friend, who placed it in a container of formaldehyde.

They gave me the photo as a gift, and we later paid a visit to an individual who—they said—had the preserved corpse in his possession. We went to a neighborhood in the "Las 80s" sector of Salinas, and the individual in question, Mr. C——, a professional chemist, substantiated the story but denied having the corpse. My friends assured me that he indeed had it but was fearful of the authorities.

There was no way of seeing the "extraterrestrial" corpse, a fact I found suspicious. It could easily be the corpse of a small Tití monkey, for which reason I put the matter aside until recently, when I saw the new photos, which were in full color. I researched the matter for a year, and recently a merchant from the city of Cayey told me about R—— B——, a friend of his from Salinas who years ago had shown him a series of photographs of the corpse of an alleged alien slain in that town. Surprised, I showed him the photos in my possession, and he said that they were the very same, but that there were many more! Armed with B——'s name and phone number, I contacted him two months later by phone, and he stated that he indeed had twenty-two photographs of Salinas's dead alien! We arranged an interview at his home to discuss the matter and met a few days later.

He disclosed that the incident involving the "little man's" death was true and that he'd learned of the affair in 1981 from a woman, Mrs. A—— Z——, who had discussed the subject at his place of business. She alleged that her husband, a Salinas police officer, had in his possession the body of dead extraterrestrial which he'd confiscated from a local youth.

Intrigued, Baerga asked her if she could bring him the container with the little creature so he could see it, and she obliged. Later on she returned with the container, and to everyone's surprise, it held a strange little creature that could not have measured more than twelve inches in height when alive. It had a very large skull, which had been crushed by a massive blow to the head, and its description was the one mentioned earlier.

He asked Mrs. Z——'s permission to remove the corpse from its container and placed it on a desk, taking over twenty-two color photos from every angle and placing the corpse in a number of postures. Baerga explained that the story he learned both from Mrs. Z—— and from "Chino," the young man who killed the creature, was that while "Chino" was looking for archaeological artifacts in an area of the mountains behind the Santiago Military Camp in Salinas, he suddenly became aware of several tiny creatures, some twelve to fourteen inches tall, who tried to grab him by the legs. Terrified, he picked up a piece of wood from the ground and killed one of them by striking its head. The others fled quickly and vanished. Scared, "Chino" picked up the creature's body and took it home, where he placed it in a jar filled with alcohol and then took the corpse to the aforementioned chemist, who placed it in a container of formaldehyde.

According to B——, both he and the others present agreed that the corpse was neither a human fetus nor an ape. It was something entirely different, with a human shape (having a head, torso, arms, legs, and so forth) but clearly nonhuman. He also pointed out that the creature's skin had a strange color and was extremely resistant. The old Channel Eleven TV station was notified, but before network personnel could arrive to do a report on the discovery, Police Officer O—— S——, Mrs. Z——'s husband, arrived on the scene, demanding the return of the corpse, which was part of an investigation.

Later on, C—— P—— turned up at Mr. Baerga's establishment, angrily demanding that the jar with the being be turned over to him, since he was going to write a book about the discovery. He also demanded that B—— turn over the photos he'd taken of the corpse. After consulting with a judge, B—— gave him a few prints of the photos, although he was under no obligation to do so, while retaining other prints for himself.

B——'s photos, which were in color and clearer, enabled me to see that the corpse in the container was certainly not that of an ordinary fetus, or that of anything known: The head is too large for the being's body, which also had excessively long arms that ended in four-fingered hands joined by a membrane (palmate) and tipped with sharp little fingernails. The eye sockets were very large and almond shaped, and the face's bone structure, while somewhat similar, was unlike a human face. It lacked defined ears, only auditive orifices with a little piece of flesh stuck to the skull behind the hole.

When I interviewed Mrs. A—— Z——, she stated that her then husband, Salinas police officer O—— S——, had died two years after the "little man" incident, attacked by thugs in Salinas. She added:

> . . . he turned up one day with the container that held the creature, and explained that a kid had called him at the station to register a complaint about something he had in his house, in the Las 80s sector. He went to investigate, and the kid told him that he had run into "those things" in the hills behind Camp Santiago, and that he'd killed one of them high in the hills. The fellow also explained that he'd brought "the thing" home, but that at night, both he and his sister heard strange noises outside, as if someone were trying to break into the house, and they were convinced that someone or something had come after the little corpse. They got scared and called the police. That's when my husband went, found the situation curious, confiscated the container from the kid, and took it back to the station to investigate.

Mrs. Z—— stressed that as far as she and her husband (who had experience in dealing with aborted fetus cases) were concerned, the thing was not a human fetus. It gave her the impression of being an adult figure, but only twelve inches tall. Later on, the chemist went to the police station and demanded that Santiago turn over the container with the creature, alleging that it was his property. S—— turned it over.

Days later Officer S—— told Mrs. Z—— not to discuss the matter anymore. Higher-ups in the police force had told him to leave the matter alone, as upper echelons were taking care of the situation, apparently at the military level, "and that they [the military] would deal with the matter from that point onward."

Back Where We Started

Faced with all the aforementioned details, I tried once more to locate C—— P——, whom I'd visited in 1980. Thanks to a confidant in Salinas, I was recently able to contact him, and he confirmed the story of the young man and the beings in the mountains: "That took place in an area known as La Explanada near the 'Tetas de Cayey,' close to some caves that exist up there." And he added something else:

> I had the jar with the little man in my house for a while, and I can tell you it was no fetus. I was fed up with seeing baby fetuses in different stages of development while at the University of Puerto Rico, and that did not resemble a baby in the least. No, sir.
> Its skin was glossy, coarse, and with a tone like our own, but mixed with clear greenish shades, and let me make clear that it wasn't a result of the formaldehyde. Its skin was indeed that shade. It had only four fingers and very long arms. It wasn't human. I think it was something extraterrestrial.
> Its skull, its head, was too big for the body, which was flimsy, and its eyes were too big. It had no nose to speak of, only the two nasal orifices, and I can say that it wasn't because it was decomposing and its nose fell off; it simply had no nose.

C—— had the mysterious corpse in his house for a while, planning to write a book on the discovery and other strange incidents that had taken place in the area, but he was threatened by neighbors when it was learned that he was the one who had the being. In one instance, a black Chevrolet pulled up at his house, driven by a tall, thin, mulattolike individual, who told him: "I've been told that you deal with flying objects. Be very careful with that."

C—— continued:

> The tone in which he said that led me to interpret that my life was in danger. He tried to pursue the conversation, but I remained silent. He got back in his car and left. Sometime later, the photos and the con-

tainer with the creature disappeared from the place in which I'd concealed them. Maybe someone I'd taken into my confidence broke into the house and retrieved the evidence . . . either that, or it was the authorities.

Due to the threats and the twist taken by the entire affair, P——, frightened and concerned with the risk to his safety, opted against writing the book.

Commentary

The witnesses interviewed alleged that the preserved creature vanished mysteriously, something that occurs frequently in these cases, but we have confidential reports of a person in the northern part of the island who has the creature hidden. According to this source, the person is aware of the importance of these remains but is equally fascinated by them and refuses to turn them over for scientific analysis out of fear that they won't be returned or that government agencies that conceal these matters will take action against him. Even so, we are trying to convince him, by means of go-betweens, to allow us to take a skin and bone sample in order to have them analyzed by a professional laboratory to settle once and for all any doubts about the origin of this enigmatic corpse. This author's initial suspicion—that the remains could have been those of a fetus—has been discarded for the following reasons: All the witnesses, for the most part serious persons, are certain, after having seen the figure closely, that it was not the fetus of a developing baby.

Years ago Mr. B—— presented some of his twenty-two photos of the corpse to a renowned veterinarian in the San Juan metropolitan area, who pointed out that it was neither a human nor an animal fetus. He was unable to identify it. Mr. B——'s son, who was a medical student at the time, showed the photos to different teaching doctors at the University of Puerto Rico's Medical School, who were also unable to say what was being shown in the photos.

One thing is certain: Something did transpire in the hills high over Salinas. There are more witnesses in this case who do not wish to be publicly identified, but who attest to the veracity of the creature's discovery. Bear in mind that Police Officer S—— informed his wife that he was ordered not to pursue the matter by higher levels in the police force, since apparently everything was being taken care of by U.S. federal and military personnel, which leads us to other implications in this most significant case.

The Camp Santiago Connection

The area of "Chino's" encounter with the tiny beings is notorious for a high incidence of UFO sightings. This region and that of Camp Santiago, a base belonging to the Puerto Rico National Guard and the U.S. Army Reserve, have been the focus of UFO incidents of all description over the years, ranging from sightings to encounters with strange creatures. Soldiers and officers stationed there permanently or during maneuvers have told us about these incidents. Among them is the case involving a giant boomerang-shaped UFO, which hovered at a low altitude above a tamarind tree located in the base's maneuvers section, to the astonished eyes of a considerable number of GIs, as well as the presence of UFOs on the base's airstrip. On other occasions they have seen the sides of a nearby hill "open up" and disgorge luminous UFOs, which disappear into the heavens.

Personnel of the Albergue Olímpico, located nearby, claim to have seen large "flying saucer"–type UFOs entering the base's perimeter in the early morning. This has been confirmed by policemen, toll booth operators at the Salinas toll barrier, and civilians traveling along the Las Américas Expressway. Many drivers have seen huge triangular objects and saucer-shaped craft over their cars and flying above the mountains containing the rocky promontories known as "Las Tetas de Cayey." There are also stories of encounters between drivers and creatures slightly larger than the one described in this article (some three to four feet). Among these cases is that of salesman E—— A—— G—— in 1977, in which the being—enveloped in a brilliant ball of light—pointed insistently at the nearby mountains and spoke in an unknown language. The mountains indicated were those where young "Chino" slew one of their number.

Mr. J—— G—— of Caguas had another fleeting encounter with a similar being at the same location while at the wheel of his car. It was late at night when he noticed a "Volkswagen" with brilliant lights at the roadside and what seemed to be a child standing beside the vehicle. When he came up to the presumed car, he realized that it was really a small oval object with an open section that emitted a yellowish light.

The "child" was a large-headed little man in a one-piece white outfit. G—— continued to drive without stopping.

For almost two years the mountainous area near the Tetas de Cayey, where the caves are in which the creatures allegedly live, has been controlled by military personnel. The only explanation given was that the area was going to be "used as a practice range." Local residents claimed seeing military personnel entering the caves located at the base of the Tetas de Cayey.

Coincidence? We can only ask ourselves if the authorities are aware of these creatures and have taken action in the matter. This angle is still under investigation.

Issue 9, Summer 1995

GOVERNMENT CRIMES
AND COVER-UPS

Urban Warfare: A Victim Reflects on the 1985 MOVE Bombing

Allen Hougland

Twelve years ago a standoff with a "cult" ended in a deadly inferno. Eleven people, including five children, perished. Sixty-one houses burned to the ground. It was, in short, an urban precursor to Waco. Except in this case, everyone admits that it was the government officials who started the fire. In 1996 Allen Hougland interviewed the only adult survivor of the siege and reviewed the events of May 13, 1995, in light of Ramona Africa's then current court battles.

FOR THE FIRST TIME, the men who ordered a satchel bomb dropped on the home of MOVE members at 6221 Osage Avenue in Philadelphia, and let the resulting fire burn, are answering in court for their actions of May 13, 1985. Ramona Africa, the only adult MOVE survivor of the siege, and relatives of slain MOVE members are now suing the city of Philadelphia for millions in federal court. Wilson B. Goode, mayor at the time of the bombing and the city's only black mayor, has been granted immunity from lawsuits in the case by U.S. district judge Louis Pollack (who claimed the bombing was reasonable under the circumstances). But Goode's police commissioner, Gregore Sambor, and his fire commissioner, William Richmond—who were in charge of operations in the field—have been named as defendants along with the city itself.

Court watchers believe the trial will drag on for months and expect a media circus, especially given MOVE's confrontational style, which Ramona Africa demonstrated when Judge Pollack debated curtailing the amount of time counsel could question potential jurors: "It is an insult to me when you intimate that time is of the essence," the former paralegal admonished the judge. "I spent seven years in prison, and nobody seemed to care about that time."

Ramona, now forty, recently related what happened after she, along with a nine-year-old boy named Birdie Africa, survived the 1985 bombing:

> They put me in jail, charged me with everything that *they* did: possession of explosives, arson, recklessly endangering other persons, risking a catastrophe, aggravated and simple assault. Everything that they did, they charged me with. I ended up doing seven years in jail. I had a sixteen-month to seven-year sentence, and when my minimum sentence was up the parole board interviewed me and told me that they'd be willing to parole me, but only if I agreed to leave MOVE. I had to agree to not have any contact with any MOVE person, and I was not going to do that. None of my sisters and brothers did that; every single MOVE person who became eligible for parole was given that same stipulation, and not one of us would accept it.

"Unrelenting Conflict"

Why did the city of Philadelphia drop a bomb on a rowhouse and let the fire burn for over an hour? What led the city to commit acts of war upon its own citizens? Was the city, or even the federal government, determined to wipe out MOVE? To answer these questions, it is necessary to understand who and what MOVE is.

While not all are black, all members take the surname "Africa." Some call them radicals, lunatics, or terrorists. One award-winning journalist, however, death row prisoner Mumia Abu-Jamal, recently gave me a different description:

> MOVE is a family of revolutionaries, of naturalist revolutionaries, founded in Philadelphia in the late sixties to early seventies, who oppose all that this system represents. For years in Philadelphia, there's been continual and unrelenting conflict between the MOVE organization and the city—that is, the police, the judiciary, and the political arm of the system. They have fought [MOVE] bitterly.
>
>   When I began covering MOVE as part of my work as a reporter for a radio station in the seventies, what I found were idealistic, committed, strong, unshakable men and women who had a deep spirit-level aversion to everything this system represents. To them, this

system was a death system involved in a death style. To them, everything this system radiated was poison, from its technological waste, to its destruction of the earth, to its destruction of the air and water, to its destruction of the very genetic pool of human life and animal life and all life. MOVE opposed all this bitterly and unrelentingly.

The first time I heard about MOVE was a television report about some MOVE people who had gotten busted. And the gist of the television broadcast was, "These nuts, these crazy people, were protesting outside the zoo for no reason." Of course they didn't explain what MOVE's position was. The reality was that according to the teachings of MOVE's founder, John Africa, all life is sacred and has worth, and should not be exploited for money and profit. MOVE people were busted because they were protesting the reality of the zoo, which they called a "prison" for animal life. Today you have groups like Earth First and so forth, across the world, who embrace many of those same positions that were once called bizarre. MOVE did it twenty years ago.

What I found was a remarkable and incredible family that continues to thrive, to grow, to grow stronger, to build, and to touch bases with people. I mean, if someone told me twenty years ago that there would be MOVE support groups in London and Paris, I'd have said, "Get out of here, you're out of you're mind."

While not a MOVE member himself, Jamal "without question" considers MOVE founder John Africa to be his spiritual leader.

I found in the teachings of John Africa a truth that was undeniable, that was powerful, that was naked, that was raw. And it talked about this system in a way that I wish I had the guts to talk about it and I wish I had the clarity to talk about it. MOVE members talked about it uncompromisingly, and not just talked about it, but lived it every day. To MOVE, all days are holy days, because all life is holy. When you're out fighting for your brothers and sisters, you're practicing your religion. If you ask a MOVE person, "What is your religion?" he will say, "Life."

"MOVE 1, Police 0"

The city of Philadelphia's first major confrontation with MOVE came in 1978, when Mayor Frank Rizzo, who liked to brag that his police force could if need be successfully invade Cuba, ordered police to surround MOVE's house in the Powelton Village section of the city. On August 8 gunfire erupted at the barricaded house, killing Police Officer James Ramp with a bullet through his neck. Nine MOVE members were tried and convicted of third-degree murder; all nine were sentenced to thirty to one hundred years. But not only do they deny shooting the officer, saying he was hit by his own colleague's bullet, they also demand to know how nine people could all shoot one man with one bullet.

In the six years after the shoot-out, nevertheless, police seemed to be waiting for the chance to even the score. David Fattah, of the Muslim community center House of Umoja, recalls seeing graffiti inside a Philadelphia police station that read "MOVE 1, Police 0."

Annoying the Neighbors

Fast-forward seven years to 1985. All nine convicted MOVE members were then, as now, still in prison. Other members had moved into the house on Osage Avenue, which they had fortified with planks out of the belief that they needed to protect themselves from further attack by the city. They committed themselves above all to the release of their incarcerated brothers and sisters. To this end they installed a high-powered loudspeaker on the front of their house and used it to broadcast their attacks on the city.

Neighbors grew weary of listening to MOVE's demands hour after hour, day after day, especially considering that MOVE used obscenities as attention-getting devices. Attention they got: Neighbors began petitioning the city to evict the group, claiming they disturbed the peace and created health hazards by keeping so many stray animals in the house.

These neighbors could not have known that the city would respond to these disturbing the peace and sanitary code violations by bombing the house in question and by burning down the entire neighborhood.

According to Ramona Africa, neighbors' complaints only gave the city an excuse to do what they had been itching to do for years. She says:

> The root of the May 13 confrontation had nothing to do with MOVE's lifestyle; it had nothing to do with the fact that we don't comb our hair; . . . it had absolutely nothing to do with complaints

from neighbors. All people have to ask themselves is: Since when does the system care about people complaining about their neighbors, particularly black people complaining about their neighbors?

I mean, black people have been complaining since we've been in this country. Who listens? Who cares? Who takes serious action to do something about our complaints? Nobody. But they want people to believe that what happened on May 13 happened because the neighbors complained.

Mumia Abu-Jamal concurs with Ramona Africa's assessment:

On May 13, 1985, the city of Philadelphia literally shot tens of thousands of rounds into that house on Osage Avenue, and dropped a bomb, and let the fire burn for ten or twelve hours. And it consumed sixty-one houses, at last count. Was that disruptive of neighborhood rights? Was that disruptive of life itself? Was that disturbing? I think that many people found themselves suckered by a political and police system that used neighborhood conflict and intensified it into urban war and almost Armageddon.

Is the neighborhood alarmed when some drug-addicted punk pulls out an Uzi and shoots at a competitor? You got crack dealing, you got prostitution, you have all the ills of society. But you know what you don't have? You don't have the government come down as if in a war as they did on May 13, 1985. You don't have that. Unless you have MOVE rebels and revolutionaries in their homes.

Moving in on MOVE

Then why did the city bomb MOVE? Ramona Africa tells it this way:

What the May 13 bombing and confrontation were about was the fact that MOVE people had nine sisters and brothers who had been in jail since 1978 for a murder they did not commit. Officials like the current mayor of Philadelphia, Ed Rendell [who was district attorney in 1978], and the current district attorney, Lynne Abraham [who was a judge in 1978 and who signed warrants that ultimately led to MOVE's 1978 confrontation with the city], know that MOVE is innocent, that MOVE did not kill a cop. And these same people had the same jobs in 1985, when they were players in the May 13 confrontation.

DA Ed Rendell said the day after the 1985 bombing that he had been advising Mayor Goode for an entire year on the legality of forcefully evicting MOVE. Lynne Abraham approved search and arrest warrants for four MOVE members, including Ramona Africa, on Saturday May 11, 1985, the day before police moved in on MOVE.

Ramona outlines MOVE's tactics during the years between the two showdowns:

> MOVE had been keeping the pressure on these officials about our family. Our family filed all the appeals available to them, not looking for justice in this system, because we know that there is no justice, but certainly to exhaust all the system procedures available to us, to give the system every opportunity possible to do the right thing. And what the system did was prove that it wasn't interested in doing the right thing. At that point, after the appeals had been exhausted, MOVE people stepped up our own campaign for the release of our family. That involved starting our newspaper, called *First Day*. It involved going around talking to people one on one, it involved sending documentation in the form of information packets to media. We did radio programs. We did everything we could to call attention to the situation. And we were doing such a successful job of it, such an expert job of it, that the system was feeling the pressure. People started to question officials instead of questioning MOVE. And because of that the system felt it had to do something to shut us up.
>
> They knew they couldn't bribe us, pay us off. They had tried that before, in the early days, even before we had got any commitment in us. It didn't work then, and it certainly wouldn't work later. So what they did was decide they had to come out there and shut us up any way they could. It didn't matter if it meant killing us, killing our babies. All those who represented the system knew they had to shut us up, they had to stop MOVE. And that's what they came out there to do May 13.

Mother's Day 1985

Ramona Africa's insider account of what happened that day contains few facts the Philadelphia police's report would contradict. The difference lies in her interpretation of the motives behind what the city did:

It started on Mother's Day, Sunday, May 12, 1985. We were listening to the radio, the all-news station, and they started talking about cops gathering at Cobbs Creek Park, basically for a showdown with MOVE. That's when we first heard about it. Slowly but surely the block was being evacuated. People were leaving, cars were being removed from the block.

We were planning to protect ourselves as much as possible, and toward that end, late that night I took all the kids down into the basement, because that was the strategy, that's where we were supposed to go. I remember around eleven or twelve that night, before anything started, various members were talking on the loudspeaker, just making it clear that this government was out there to kill us. We even made it clear that we were willing to negotiate with three certain people as mediators, who were never allowed to mediate.

An anonymous top city official later told the *Philadelphia Inquirer* that three days before the confrontation, MOVE had agreed through a mediator to leave the house peacefully if the city could guarantee they would face no arrests. But Mayor Goode would promise only no immediate arrests, leaving open the possibility of future arrests. Talks with MOVE fell apart. MOVE members reverted to their demands that all nine of their imprisoned brethren be released. While Goode maintained a conciliatory public tone, Judge Lynne Abraham was busy signing MOVE's search and arrest warrants.

Ramona continues her account:

In the wee hours of the morning, while we were down in the basement, the police commissioner, Gregore Sambor, is said to have made an announcement, something like this: "Attention MOVE: This is America. You have to abide by the laws of the United States." He went on to say that he had warrants for the four of us, myself and three of my sisters and brothers. I personally never heard this announcement; I read about it later. Not that I would have come out if I had heard it. We knew that their intent was not to arrest. So from midnight on I was down in the basement with the kids, and other people came down, after everything was locked up as tight as possible.

The first thing that happened was they trained deluge hoses on the house. The water was just pouring down into that basement. It had to be from the roof down. After an hour or two, that stopped. Then, they claim, they tried to insert tear gas, they wanted to breach three-inch holes in the party walls on both sides of our house to insert tear gas. Well, "breach" to them meant to explode, to blow holes in the walls. And by the time they finished their explosions, they had blown the whole front of the house off. Then they did fill as much of the house as possible with tear gas.

When that didn't work, they shot over ten thousand rounds of bullets at us, according to their own estimate. At one point they used up all their ammunition and had to send back to the armory for more.

Who Fired First?

As in the 1978 confrontation with MOVE, the city claimed MOVE members inside the house fired first. However, when city workers combed the debris the next day, they found no trace of the automatic weapons the police had accused MOVE of firing to initiate the battle.

Ramona describes the calm before the firestorm: "After the shooting, it was quiet for a long time. I guess that's when they were preparing [the] bomb. They want to call it an "entry device" or put some name on it that will soften the context, but you can't soften the context of what they did."

At approximately five-thirty on the afternoon of May 13, they dropped that bomb on the roof of the house, and it ignited a fire. Mayor Goode later said it wasn't a bomb; it was a "percussive device." He said he would never have approved dropping a bomb, seeing that police had seen MOVE members placing gasoline on the roof of the house some days before the confrontation. The city's arrest warrants against MOVE had mentioned the danger from gasoline, ammunition, and other inflammable materials believed to be inside the house.

This Means War

The mayor claimed the plan had been to blow open a hole in the fortified roof so that tear gas could be inserted there. But the entire façade of the house had already been blown off, and tear gas had been used unsuccessfully in an attempt to force MOVE out. Whatever the mayor's plan really was, Goode acknowledged that he "knew from the very beginning that once we made that decision to go in there, it would in fact be war."

Ramona recounts the city's reaction, or more precisely the lack of it, to the spreading fire:

> The Fire Department had been out there from the beginning. They're the ones who had trained the deluge hoses on our house. But when that bomb ignited that fire, they made the decision that they weren't going to fight it, they weren't going to extinguish it: they were going to let it burn, knowing that innocent men, women, and babies were in that house. Innocent not just by my standards, but by their standards; we had not been convicted of any wrongdoing. But they decided to let that fire burn innocent people.

The next day Mayor Goode, Police Commissioner Sambor, and Fire Commissioner Richmond conceded that the city did not begin to battle the fire for over an hour, even as it spread to adjoining houses. Goode claimed that firefighters had been prevented from fighting the inferno by armed MOVE members who had escaped from the house into a back alley, from where they shot at firefighters. But the water cannons that had poured 640,000 gallons of water on the house had been unmanned. Even if armed MOVE members had been shooting at firefighters (and this has never been corroborated by any impartial witness), why did the fire department not turn the cannons back on and let them continue to deluge the house as they had done earlier that day?

By Fire or Firing Squad

Ramona Africa's account grows even more disturbing:

> We didn't realize initially that the house was on fire. We were still down in the basement, while the fire burned down from the top. Then it got a little smoky, and I thought it was tear gas. But it became apparent that something else was happening, because the smoke started getting thicker and thicker, and it started getting real hot. And when we realized the house was on fire, what we did, contrary to any intimation that we're suicidal and masochistic, we didn't make some death pact, we opened the back door and immediately tried to get our kids and animals and ourselves out of there.
>
> And our brother who opened the door, at the point he became visible, the police deliberately opened fire on us. I mean, just started shooting. They didn't intend for anybody to get out of there, knowing the whole place was on fire. Our brother tried to get out a couple of

times; I know I tried at least twice, and was shot back inside. Firing was just going on all around, and we had to back up real quick. Finally, about the third time or so I tried, it was getting so bad . . . you either die by fire or firing squad.

At the next day's press conferences, Mayor Goode and Police Commissioner Sambor contradicted each other about whether police had fired on MOVE members coming out of the back of the house. The mayor appeared startled that Sambor was admitting to the firing. At that point an aide stepped in to inform Sambor that the police had not fired any shots at escaping MOVE members after all. As Ramona relates:

We made another attempt to get out, and I was able to get one of the little boys, our brother Birdie, out of there. And really, to this day, neither one of us can explain why any of those bullets did not hit us. I mean, we were burned pretty bad my left arm, my leg, my back, I had to have grafting done. Just a small portion of Birdie's face was burned, plus his arm and leg. We suffered pretty bad burns, third degree burns. I can't explain why we're alive today.

But there's a force greater than any or all of us, that coordinates everything. And it was just meant for us to survive. And had we not, this system could've said anything about what happened, and who would've been there to dispute it? Nobody. So it was necessary for someone to be here to speak to what happened, to remind people.

Ramona Africa then traced the plan to bomb MOVE beyond the Philadelphia police and mayor's office:

They obtained their weaponry of war through the Federal Government Bureau of Alcohol, Tobacco, and Firearms. That bureau waived every requirement they had to dispense this high-powered weaponry to the Philadelphia Police Department. The C-4 [the military explosive used in the bomb] was supplied by the FBI. An FBI agent named Michael Macy finally admitted to providing 37.5 pounds of C-4 to the Philadelphia Police Department. No municipal police department is supposed to have C-4; but he supplied 37.5 pounds of it. So you can see the conspiracy involving not just the local government, but on up to the federal government.

After May 13, when it was known that babies had been burned alive, that innocent people had been killed, then–U.S. attorney general Edwin Meese applauded the Philadelphia Police Department, he commended them for the job they did. So that tells you how far up the conspiracy against MOVE went. Reagan was the president and he never uttered one word about what happened on May 13. Are you telling me the president of a country which has bombed its own citizens doesn't say anything? His silence spoke louder than anything he could have possibly said.

"Perfect . . . Except for the Fire"

Mayor Goode, who after the bombing described the whole operation as "perfect except for the fire," also garnered the praise of Los Angeles police commissioner Daryl Gates, who called Goode "an inspiration to the nation. I hope he runs for national office. He certainly made my heroes list." Frank Selgrath, editor of the police union newspaper *Peace Officer,* made the questionable assertion, "Every action was taken to see that there was no loss of life or property."

Ramona Africa continues:

> They came out there with fifty-caliber machine guns and M-60 automatic rifles and .30-06 sniper rifles with silencers and twenty-millimeter armor-piercing antitank guns to arrest four people! What did they need silencers for? That's the tool of an assassin, a silencer. This was a major confrontation. Why would anyone feel the need to silence a shot? They clearly came out there for war."
>
> This was not about an arrest. They could have arrested us at any time. We weren't hiding. We went food shopping twice a week, every week, same place; we took our kids to the park pretty much every day; we went from MOVE house to MOVE house taking care of whatever activities we needed to take care of. We were accessible. I remember walking or running certain places by myself, and stopping and talking to some of these cops, just giving them information about MOVE's position and how we knew what they were up to. I could have been arrested at any time. Most of us had outstanding bench warrants on us by 1984. They could have arrested us at any time. But they didn't do that. Because their interest was not in arrest.

Money Mad

Mumia Abu-Jamal contrasts the attack on MOVE with a more recent siege:

Interestingly, there's a case that just arose in Philadelphia, Delaware County. I'm talking about the case of the multimillionaire John E. Du Pont, one of the principal heirs to the chemical company fortune, who has been accused of killing Olympic wrestler David Schultz on his estate in January [1996]. It's very interesting to note what was common and what was uncommon between those two experiences, between what happened on May 13, 1985 and what happened on Du Pont's estate.

Here you have a man, according to at least one eyewitness, the wife of the Olympic wrestler, who said she saw him shoot her husband dead, and she left the house and told this to the police. John E. Du Pont went into his home and refused to come out. He had a few telephone negotiations, conversations with high-ranking police officials. It went on a day. It went on for forty-eight hours. And he was finally arrested after he went out to fix his heater, because the police had sabotaged his heating system and he got cold in that big mansion and he went out to check the boiler and they nabbed him. But he wasn't hurt, wasn't beaten up. Here's a man who while it is legally improper to say he was guilty, I don't know. All we know is what we see in the media and who can trust the media? We at least have one eyewitness who said, "I saw him kill my husband." But here's a man who is a suspect in a murder who was allowed forty-eight hours to rest, to wash, to shave, to sleep, to talk on the phone to whomever he wished. And there was not even the suspicion that police would raid the home of this man, who was said to have been heavily armed.

Who did MOVE kill on May 13, 1985? What witness came forth and said, "He killed (or she killed) my husband"? And look at those two responses. And I think that you cannot look at those two realities outside of what race and power mean in this society, of what wealth and influence and poverty and lack of influence mean in this society.

The role of the police, of course, is to protect the interests of the wealthy, not to protect the interests of the poor. I just told you about neighborhoods all across America where people are shooting sub-machine guns and Uzis and M-10 MACs every night—well, that's not a problem. But if someone gets on a bullhorn and talks about the conditions and realities under which people live, the oppressive realities, they become public enemy number one.

Still Alive

Since her release from prison in 1992, Ramona Africa has once again been spearheading MOVE's crusade to free their nine brethren imprisoned for the 1978 shooting of Officer James Ramp. "The issue now, as then, is our family in prison. We are not going to sit back and watch our innocent family members rot in prison for something we know they didn't do and that the government knows they didn't do."

Ramona says her purpose in suing the city of Philadelphia in federal court is to draw attention to the continued oppression of MOVE members by the police and government. She has her own view of Mayor Goode's intentions:

> Wilson Goode said in a radio program on WDAS before the confrontation that he did not want MOVE people arrested on minor charges where we could be back on the street on bail in a couple of months. He wanted a "permanent end to MOVE." That's what he was attempting to do, and it didn't work. MOVE is still here, alive, strong, thriving, more committed than ever, still exposing this system and more determined than ever to bring our family home.

Issue 13, Summer 1996

FEMA: Fascist Entity Manipulating America

Mark Westion

FEMA is much more than the government's "natural disaster response agency." Everything is in place for the crackdown. FEMA computers compile information. Specially equipped "doomsday vehicles" stand on alert. Representatives of the shadow government are poised in top-secret underground bunkers, waiting for the green light. In this article Mark Westion looks at the U.S. government's chilling "contingency plans" for threats both external and internal.

FEW AMERICANS REALIZE that agents of the New World Order have infiltrated a government agency which was originally chartered to protect and serve them. This agency was initially set up to coordinate communication and rescue efforts during times of man-made or natural disasters.

Nixon started the ball rolling by signing Executive Order 11490, which allowed federal departments and agencies to draft plans for emergency preparedness functions. By 1979 the avalanche of paperwork that this executive order created caused the birth of a new government agency known as the Federal Emergency Management Agency (FEMA).

The new agency plodded along in typical bureaucratic fashion until the newly elected president, Ronald Reagan, decided to use it in furtherance of the agenda proposed by such groups as the Trilateral Commission and the Council on Foreign Relations. Thus in 1982 he signed National Security Directive 58. This directive allowed the National Security Council to use FEMA to carry out the objectives of Directive 58.

The Reagan Administration managed to divert massive amounts of taxpayers' money. They did this simply by submitting a yearly budget request to Congress for disaster relief and other items "submitted under a separate package." These separate packages of itemized expenses were never presented to Congress. At any rate, Congress never seemed to notice. Neither did anyone in Congress ever question the fact that these "separate packages" amounted to more than twelve times the legitimate requests.

Where Did the Money Go?

For the ten years between 1982 and 1992, Congress gave FEMA $243 million for disaster relief. During the same period, the Administration's "separate packages" amounted to $2.9 billion.

Much of the secret funding went into a program known as Mobile Emergency Response Support (MERS.) This program supplies three hundred specially equipped and nuclear-hardened vehicles designed to shuffle the president and his cabinet around the country so they can maintain control after a nuclear holocaust. These expensive toys are kept in the states of Texas, Georgia, Colorado, Washington, and Massachusetts. Thus they are within immediate striking distance of anywhere in the continental United States.

Make no mistake. Although ostensibly a disaster relief agency, FEMA is in actuality a highly sophisticated organization which has been set up to take over the government of the United States. Everything is in place for the crackdown. FEMA computers gather information. Specially equipped "doomsday vehicles" are on "alert" status. Representatives of the shadow government are poised in top-secret underground bunkers, waiting for the green light.

Special Facility

Not far from the nation's capital there is a large natural feature known as Mount Weather, located on Highway 601, just outside the bucolic town of Berryville, Virginia. This mountain sits in mute testimony to the human propensity toward the exercise of total control. Deep inside the mountain the shadow government develops its devious plans, collecting information on the citizenry while comfortably ensconced in what FEMA euphemistically calls the "Special Facility." This facility appears to be very special indeed. It comes equipped with all the computer power and satellite uplinks necessary to control all the communications systems in our country and beyond. The security measures are so stringent at Mount Weather that anyone entering is subject to being searched for such proscribed contraband as cameras, sketch pads, or any other item capable of recording the interior layout.

Although only a handful of insiders know exactly how big the facility is, those who have gotten a glimpse inside Mount Weather describe a huge underground city. It is known that contained within the mountain are all the supplies necessary to keep FEMA running for months without contact with the outside world.

Why would our government feel the need to hide in a cave now that the threat of nuclear annihilation no longer hangs over our heads? To answer this question, one need look no further than the agency's own writings, in which FEMA allows itself to bypass our constitutional guarantees during "peacetime or wartime national security emergencies . . . accidental, natural and man-made occurrences." Please take note that FEMA does not need an all-out war as an excuse to trample on the Constitution. Any "peacetime emergency" will do, such as a repeat of the L.A. riots.

President Clinton's Omnibus Crime Bill restricted gun purchases while at the same time putting one hundred thousand new police on the streets. Meanwhile, prisons are the new growth industry of the nineties.

El Generalissimo

To get a grasp on how an aberration such as FEMA could have been spawned, a short history lesson is in order. The agency's policies became official after the appointment of Louis O. Giuffreda as director of FEMA by his old buddy President Ron Reagan. Giuffreda (who prefers the title "General") had the agency's powerful computers across the country tied into a vast network capable of gathering information on dissidents and potential troublemakers via records obtained through local police departments. Therefore the agency is engaged in a constant data-gathering frenzy via the FBI, Department of Energy, National Military Command Center, CIA, National Security Agency, and the Defense Intelligence Agency.

At huge FEMA campuses located in Emmitsburg, Maryland, and Carson City, Nevada, agents attend seminars in "continuity of government" and workshops on "nuclear weapons accidents." These colleges are also used to inculcate officials from towns and cities across America in "counterterrorism tactics." For good measure, foreign police and military officials are trained in FEMA techniques. Thus, in Giuffrida's own words, "we have made joint military-civil planning far more effective both here and overseas."

At this point you might ask yourself just what all this espionage training has to do with disaster relief. The answer is simple. Nothing. In fact, when winds reaching 160 MPH devastated Homestead, Florida, in August 1992, the city manager requested one hundred handheld phones. FEMA responded by sending one of the high-tech, nuclear-hardened MERS vehicles. Although capable of communicating with an aircraft on the other side of the globe, it could not place a simple phone call to Miami. More recently, FEMA failed its relief mission after the earthquake in Los Angeles. The official excuse was, "We didn't expect so many victims." The above incidents are just two examples demonstrative of this evil agency's true agenda. Far from being established as an aid to America's citizenry, FEMA has been created as an agent of repression working solely for the elite hidden government.

Justified by Law

A short listing of some of the policies ready to be implemented by this agency of repression is well worth reading. The following is taken directly from a FEMA document entitled "The Defense Resources Act."

• Section 1001: "Whenever the President shall deem that the public safety demands it, he may cause to be censored under such rules and regulations as he may from time to time establish, communications by mail, cable, radio, television or other means of transmission crossing the borders of the United States."

• Section 903 empowers the president to "limit employment opportunities to activities essential to the national health, safety or interest."

• Sections 201 and 501 give the president authority to requisition, condemn, or seize property for the "national defense." The government is required to compensate property owners, but those "unwilling to accept" the price determined by the president will get "75%" of such amount; they can go to court to recover the rest.

• Section 1213 regulates the personnel practices of government and federal contractors. They are prohibited from employing "any person who engages in a strike against the government of the United States, or who is a member of an organization of government employees that asserts the right to strike against the government of the United States, or who advocates, or who is a member of an organization that advocates the overthrow of the government of the United States by force or violence." Loyalty oaths are authorized; federal workers who have illegal affiliations "shall be fined not more than $1,000 or imprisoned for not more than one year, or both."

The agency also has another trick up its sleeve called "Plan D." This 364-page document refers directly to the takeover of the media by ensuring that "all telecommunications resources of radio and television licensees are available for use and responsive to a war situation." FEMA is also involved in planning exercises with the Pentagon such as "Operation Night Train," which establishes prison camps along the Mexican border to be used in case there is a sudden and unacceptable influx of immigration by our southern neighbors. This is a program close to the agency's black heart. While still an army student in 1970, Giuffreda wrote a paper detailing just how these prison camps could be set up. It should be noted here that Clinton's crime bill called for "boot camps" for youthful offenders.

FEMA also worked closely with the Pentagon in trying to determine ways in which to bypass constitutional rules, such as the Posse Comitatus Act. This is the law stating that no military equipment or personnel may be used against civilians. Anyone who watched army tanks equipped with flamethrowers torching "cultists" in Waco has to figure that their efforts must have borne fruit.

Just what kind of man is General Giuffreda? What kind of person would be so ready to roll a tank over the Constitution? The legacy left by this one man should give pause to all lovers of freedom. Is our democracy headed for history's scrap heap? Will the New World Order determine our future from the bowels of some nuclear-hardened sanctuary reminiscent of the movie *Doctor Strangelove?*

For an indication of what might be if we drop our vigilance, simply let Giuffreda speak in his own words: "Legitimate violence is integral to our form of government, for it is from this source that we can continue to purge our weaknesses."

Issue 3, Winter 1994

Who Framed Leonard Peltier?

Joan d'Arc

How far can you go in opposing the policies of the U.S. government before you have to be "neutralized"? Joan d'Arc examines the case of American Indian Movement (AIM) leader Leonard Peltier, imprisoned for over twenty years for a killing he says he did not commit. Along with reviewing the strong case made by Peltier's many supporters, d'Arc also puts the events of June 26, 1965, in the context of the FBI's larger campaign to "neutralize" the American Indian Movement.

DRESSED CASUALLY IN JEANS and T-shirts, one wearing moccasins, two men clutching AR-15 rifles climbed out of their unmarked vehicles and began shooting. The two FBI agents were chasing a red pickup truck into the extremely tense Pine Ridge Reservation in South Dakota on June 26, 1975, ostensibly to arrest one Jimmy Eagle for the theft of a pair of used cowboy boots. However, the FBI's actual plan was to trap members of the militant American Indian Movement (AIM) who were camping in an area known as Jumping Bull to protect the Oglala-Sioux community during a period of increasing political violence.

With the neutralization of the AIM leadership a prime motive, Special Agents Jack Coler and Ron Williams had been sent to test the situation, and perhaps to provoke a gunfight, but were then "cut off and abandoned by their colleagues." Some 150 heavily armed agents sitting barely 200 yards away on Highway 18 were the "backup" for their fellow agents' suicide mission. Persons in the AIM campsite, thinking they were under attack by the reservation "GOON squad" (Guardians of the Oglala Nation) or by white vigilantes, state emphatically that they returned fire in self-defense while attempting to surround and capture the transgressors. The agents took cover behind their car, expecting to be backed up immediately, but response was slow to the agents' desperate radio calls for help after one of them was hit. It was not until both agents lay dead, and AIM members got close enough to look into the car to read the words "FBI DENVER," that they realized who these two men were.

The shoot-out ended in the deaths of Special Agents Coler and Williams and eighteen-year-old Joe Stuntz Killsright (Lakota tribe). AIM members escaped the FBI-invaded reservation on foot through the woods. Four Native Americans were subsequently charged with the murder of the two agents, yet only one, Leonard Peltier (Chippewa-Lakota), was convicted.

The ensuing trial in Cedar Rapids, Iowa, of two AIM members, Bob Robideau (Chippewa) and Darelle "Dino" Butler (Tuni), resulted in acquittal on grounds of self-defense in the summer of 1976; charges against Jimmy Eagle were dropped in September of the same year. There was no official inquiry into the death of Joe Stuntz, although there is some indication that he may have been wounded initially and later executed by FBI agents.

Leonard Peltier remained in Canada until December 1976, when he was extradited on FBI-fabricated affidavits coerced from his "girlfriend," Myrtle Poor Bear, a woman unknown to Leonard who later recanted all of her testimony. In a separate trial in Fargo, North Dakota, early the following year, with a different judge under a different set of circumstances, Leonard Peltier received two consecutive life sentences.

Anna Mae

The impetus for Myrtle Poor Bear to sign three fraudulent and conflicting affidavits without even reading them, was the way Special Agent David Price kept bringing up the death of AIM member Anna Mae Aquash. Anna Mae had been actively pursued by FBI agents for her involvement in the Pine Ridge shoot-out. On November 24, 1975, she appeared at a hearing on weapons charges and was released on personal recognizance pending her trial the following day. She did not make her trial. She remained missing until February 1976, when she was found dead, her death attributed to exposure by a Bureau of Indian Affairs coroner. In a typical and gruesome display of its attitude toward Native Americans, Anna Mae's hands were cut off and sent to Washington, D.C., for fingerprint identification, even though the FBI knew who she was and her fingerprints could have easily been identified by other means. She was buried in an unmarked grave until her family was notified of her death and demanded another autopsy, which revealed that she had been shot in the head.

Holed up in a hotel room and badgered for over a month, Myrtle Poor Bear claims that agents threatened to do the same thing to her and to her daughter if she did not sign the affidavits. The third affidavit successfully extradited Leonard Peltier from Canada on the false grounds that Poor Bear had witnessed his savage, close-range execution of the two agents, when in fact she was not present in the area at all.

Reign of Terror

The shoot-out at the Jumping Bull community caused a media blitz because of the death of two government agents, but the truth of the matter is that shoot-outs of this sort were going on all the time before and after that day. Since the election of the "nontraditional" Dick Wilson as president of the Pine Ridge Tribal Council in 1972, the Jumping Bull community had the highest murder rate per capita in the United States. The rate of political murders on the reservation for the period 1972–76 was 170 per 100,000 (almost exactly the rate for Chile following the U.S.-supported coup of Pinochet). The FBI's use of private gangs (GOONs), and its secret cooperation with the military in the ongoing persecution on Pine Ridge, was eerily reminiscent of the death squad repression in Latin America. Two hundred murders in three years in this small community went virtually unnoticed, with no official inquiries, investigations, or convictions by any body of the U.S. government.

The Pine Ridge Reservation is the poorest in the United States, with the lowest level of income, high levels of alcoholism, and conflict between a growing spiritual, traditional movement and a government-affiliated faction containing "mixed bloods" (usually half or less Indian ancestry). Dick Wilson controlled scarce jobs and administered government funds on the reservation, using government money to enrich his administration with no intention of meeting the needs of the people. The feds and the Wilson regime worked hand in hand to intimidate and control the men, women, and children on this reservation with violence. In Dick Wilson's own words: "We have our own way of punishing people." Members of the so-called GOON squads were heavily armed with government-issue automatic rifles. Women, children, and elders lived in a constant climate of fear, brutality, and murder. AIM members were asked to set up a spiritual camp on the reservation because, in Leonard Peltier's words, "it was an intolerable situation; the killing had to stop."

FBI Disinformation Campaign

Founded in Minneapolis in 1968, AIM's purpose was and is to protect the lives and treaty rights of all Native American tribes, although propaganda efforts by the FBI, GOONs, and groups like the John Birch Society convinced some people that AIM was just a Communist front. The tactic used to neutralize the American Indian Movement was to take out its leadership, either by killing them or effectively immobilizing them behind bars on a federal rap. Leonard Peltier now sits in Leavenworth prison as the lone scapegoat for the events which occurred at Pine Ridge on June 26, 1975. The FBI's disinformation campaign blamed the ongoing violence at Pine Ridge on AIM members, when in fact the FBI had orchestrated a continuous flow of mayhem with its informers, infiltrators, and agent provocateurs and its camaraderie with Dick Wilson and Company. Even the relative body counts point to this conclusion: hundreds of AIM and Native American casualties compared with none among GOONs, BIA police, and FBI prior to the shoot-out of 1975.

Immediately after the firefight, the FBI issued a series of field reports indicating that the Jumping Bull compound was in fact a sophisticated AIM military fortification featuring "fixed defensive positions" and dispatched a planeload of SWATs, along with its own media specialist, Tom Coll, to Rapid City from Quantico. (Why does this sound familiar?) They needed to explain why the FBI was suddenly conducting Vietnam-style search-and-destroy operations on an obscure South Dakota Indian reservation. The disinformation campaign claimed that the agents had been executed at close range by thirty or more revolutionary "guerrillas" in a "cold-blooded ambush." Coll made statements to the press claiming the agents were dragged from their car, stripped to their waists, and shot fifteen to twenty times each at close range. Early reports even made the fantastic claim that the agents were "scalped." Since the press was banned from Pine Ridge for two days, the public was forced to accept the propaganda it was fed by the FBI.

In reality, as the press found out soon afterward, the "compound" was better described as a broken-down farm community, the "bunkers" were root cellars or cattle shelters common to this rural area, neither agent had been shot more than three times, and Agent Williams had ripped off his own shirt to provide a tourniquet for Coler's arm. Furthermore, at no time did more than ten AIM members participate in the firefight, including two mysterious men in a red pickup truck. One of the men has since gone on film, with a black hood and his voice altered electronically, to admit to firing the two fatal shots.

South Dakota attorney general William Janklow dubbed the killing of the agents as assassinations, although he did not refer to the slaying of Killsright in the same terms. He stated publicly that it was time to stop being "soft on Indians just because they're a minority group." In his 1977 resignation letter, David Holman, commissioner of the South Dakota State Criminal Justice Commission, stated his awareness of the fact that traditional Native Americans who are politically active are singled out for harassment by the South Dakota criminal justice system.

The Cowboy Boot Caper

The events of that week in June make a confusing scenario. What began as a friendly party on June 23 had ended in a wrestling match between four Indian teens and two white teenagers, resulting in the theft of a white youth's cowboy boots. Ordinarily a matter for tribal court, the FBI instead issued a warrant to search the Pine Ridge reserve for nineteen-year-old Jimmy Eagle. Based on the petty theft of the boots, he was being sought for "kidnapping, aggravated assault, and aggravated robbery" when in fact the kidnapping charge (a capital crime) had no substance at all and was soon dropped without explanation. A thorough search for Jimmy Eagle in the residence closest to Highway 18 on the morning of June 26 by Agents Coler and Williams was made without producing any such search warrant. Shortly afterward the same agents picked up three young Navajo AIM members and questioned them. It is widely believed on Pine Ridge that "the cowboy boot caper was contrived by the Bureau as an expedient to gathering tactical intelligence and establishing a prior justification for an already decided upon confrontation."

Remember Wounded Knee II

The occupation of the Bureau of Indian Affairs (BIA) Building by two hundred people in Washington, D.C., on the eve of the 1972 presidential election had begun the wave of anti-AIM propaganda. The occupiers at what came to be known as Wounded Knee II rightfully requested the U.S. government to investigate its treaty violations over the past one hundred years. In keeping with their treaty, Native Americans have served in this country's armed forces in numbers far exceeding their proportion of the population, with ten thousand serving in World War I, more than twenty-five thousand in World War II and Korea, and forty-two thousand during the Vietnam era. The U.S. government can claim no such honor in its agreements with Native Americans.

The following year, as the occupation dragged on, the standoff escalated. Prepared to conduct a press conference to protest treaty violations and expose Dick Wilson's association with federal authorities, the AIM group at Wounded Knee awoke on February 28 to find itself completely surrounded by GOONs and U.S. marshals, reinforced soon afterward by FBI, BIA police, white vigilante groups, and advisers from the army's elite 82nd Airborne Division. Instead of a press conference, AIM members were trapped inside with restricted media access. Reporters from the mainstream press were barred from the scene, and alternative press personnel were threatened with criminal prosecution. In substitution for direct coverage of events, "press briefings" were conducted, which resulted in headlines such as "Armed Indians Seize Wounded Knee, Hold Hostages."

AIM members awoke to an unprecedented show of military force, including over 130 M-16 rifles with 100,000 rounds of ammunition, 75 high-powered sniper rifles, mine detectors, M-79 grenade launchers with 100 rounds of high explosives, 600 rounds of CS gas and 600 rounds of red smoke (to target air strikes), 750 pounds of dry CS and air delivery canisters, and, of course, military helicopters, sending over 500,000 bullets into Wounded Knee in 71 days. The firefight claimed the lives of two Native Americans and wounded many more, while many still remain missing, presumed dead and buried by Dick Wilson's GOONs. Just in case this show of force fell short, the Defense Department issued a memo to Richard Nixon recommending a full-scale invasion with tanks and fifteen thousand troops. (Nixon would later defy a court order and refuse to release tapes of conversations relating to the AIM situation, citing reasons of "national security.")

The importance of the 1973 accumulation of military hardware becomes apparent when we realize that, once in the hands of the FBI, these toys were theirs "for the duration of its exercise on Pine Ridge," evidenced by the APCs and Bell UH-1B "Huey" helicopters used by the FBI in the summer and fall of 1975. It is this largely unaccounted for military weaponry which answers the question How did Dick Wilson's GOONs become so well armed?

GOON Squad

The Wounded Knee trials dragged on through the court system over the next two years, while more than sixty AIM members and supporters were killed by GOONs and hundreds more were assaulted. The Wounded Knee leadership trial of Russell Means and Dennis Banks was "riddled with government misconduct." Charges in this case were dropped by Judge Fred Nichol, who stated that "the waters of justice have been polluted" after he found that the government "knowingly presented false evidence [and] infiltrated the defense team with an FBI informant." Unfortunately, few federal judges with this degree of integrity can be found.

One might ask if there was ever any effort to depose Dick Wilson legally through the election process. The answer is yes. When AIM leader Russell Means ran against Dick Wilson in the 1974 election, the results were rigged to give Dick Wilson the seat by two hundred votes. An investigation by the U.S. Commission on Civil Rights decided the election was "permeated with fraud." Nothing was done about it, however, and Wilson's violent regime continued for a second two-year term with renewed ferocity. Although civil rights complaints were filed with the Justice Department, not one GOON was ever arrested, indicted, or prosecuted. The FBI claimed it was too understaffed to look into the matter, yet in reality its ranks nearly quadrupled in one year. Pine Ridge claimed the "highest ratio of agents to citizens anywhere in the United States" after the FBI's ten-man SWAT team assigned specifically to the small village of Pine Ridge in 1973 was tripled in 1975.

Injun Hating

Racism systematically verifies itself when the "slave" can break free only by imitating the "master" and contradicting his own reality. Peltier and other AIM leaders were "targeted for neutralization" for their refusal to homo-gene-ize with the white man and bow down to imperialist, corporate statism. In typical divide-and-conquer style, Dick Wilson's "colonial regime" appears to have been fostered, if not created, by the United States in order to "administer the reservation for the benefit of non-Indian ranchers and corporations." What does it mean that only six months after the 1975 FBI shoot-out Dick Wilson signed over one-eighth of the Pine Ridge reservation land, rich in uranium, gas, and oil, to the U.S. Department of the Interior?

Is it a conspiracy of silence so evil the white man has no word for it? While the FBI compiled huge files on AIM members and harassed and jailed them for even minor offenses, the GOONs enjoyed year-round open season to assault, rape, and murder their own people on this reservation. Government inaction and FBI collusion, not to mention free military hardware, was responsible for a brutal secret war within our own borders upon America's precious indigenous population.

What happened in June 1975 on the Pine Ridge Reservation is the fault of the U.S. government's racist attitude toward Native Americans, a pervasive ignorance which has not changed in five hundred years. This "One Nation Indi-invisible" has no right to boycott any other nation for inhumane treatment of its minority groups or indigenous populations until it is willing to look at the demographics of its own political prison population "For Which It Stands." The U.S. government's approval of the FBI's secret political war on minority groups, its consistent inaction being proof thereof, should be called exactly what it is: racism.

Caged Warrior

An appeal of Leonard Peltier's conviction, based on documented FBI misconduct, was rejected by the U.S. Eighth Circuit Court of Appeals. The U.S. Supreme Court refused without comment in February 1979 to hear an appeal. As a result of a Freedom of Information Act suit in 1981, twelve thousand pages of FBI documents in the Peltier case were released to his appeal team, several of which seriously contradicted testimony heard at the trial. A motion for a new trial was filed in April 1982 and rejected in December of the same year. An appeal filed again with the U.S. Eighth Circuit resulted in a new hearing which was conducted in North Dakota in October 1984, where FBI agents were questioned on ballistics evidence. It was decided that the new ballistics evidence would not have changed the outcome of the trial. Thus the

Eighth Circuit rejected the motion to rehear the case, and in 1987 the U.S. Supreme Court again refused without comment to hear the case.

Owing to the major appeals efforts that have been made in Peltier's case, it has become of prime concern to the Bureau that documents illegally withheld at his trial remain hidden forever. Although the FBI has been quite lucky that the courts have mainly glossed over their "improprieties," Peltier's death would neatly "close the books" on this case once and for all. Peltier alleges that the FBI has already orchestrated an assassination attempt on him, enlisting fellow inmates at Lompoc prison as undercover assassins. Five days after escaping to save his own life, Leonard gave himself up without a shot from his defensive position in the woods outside Santa Monica. Leonard could tell that the men coming after him were "local cops, not FBI," and he figured he would live through a surrender. He could easily have taken down a few of them, but to his honor he thought, "I never killed nobody . . . I might as well not start."

Senior Judge of the Eighth Circuit Gerald Heaney has stated that the U.S. government overreacted at Wounded Knee II with a military response to a request to hear legitimate grievances of Native Americans, culminating in the firefight of June 1975. He states: "The U.S. government must share in the responsibility because of its role in escalating the conflict." The fact remains, more than one person was involved in shooting the FBI agents. The "proof" that it was Leonard is based on nothing but FBI contrivance, collusion, and the fact that "someone had to pay." With his life in jeopardy behind bars, and after having now served almost fifteen years, Leonard Peltier has become a cause célèbre to literally millions of people worldwide, who are behind a surge of petitions and letters demanding he be granted a new trial. Fifty members of the U.S. House of Representatives and fifty-one members of the Canadian Parliament are among those who believe that Leonard Peltier deserves what all Americans are promised: a fair and impartial trial.

Issue 4, Spring 1994

TWA 800: No Single Missile Theory

Al Hidell

The November 8, 1996, removal of a conspiracy-minded reporter from an FBI press conference was a blunt demonstration of the government's attitude toward TWA 800 conspiracy theories. However, some do indeed have more credibility than we've been led to believe. In this article Al Hidell separates the fact from the fiction in this widely debated contemporary conspiracy.

"WHY IS THE NAVY not a suspect?" the person shouted to FBI assistant director James Kallstrom.

"Remove that man," was the lead TWA Flight 800 investigator's only reply.

Then security guards quickly escorted reporter Hillel Cohen from the room. The November 8, 1996, incident was a blunt demonstration of the government's attitude toward the unpleasant yet plausible theory that the U.S. Navy accidentally shot down the airliner off the coast of Long Island with a surface-to-air missile.

However, the government has also been close-lipped about another theory: that TWA 800 was downed by a terrorist attack. If it was a missile, was it "friendly" or "unfriendly"? And why is the issue still being debated?

Damage Control

The friendly fire missile theory—widely discussed on the Internet almost since the day of the July catastrophe—was pushed into the mainstream by Pierre Salinger, the former ABC News correspondent and press secretary to John Kennedy. The day of the above-mentioned press conference, Salinger made headlines when he cited a "secret document"

154

that he said proved navy culpability. He made his revelation in Cannes, France, while speaking at an aviation conference.

Salinger, however, was soon attacked both in the press and by some cyberspace posters as a pathetic buffoon, the clueless promoter of a half-baked conspiracy theory based on a single public Internet posting. When *Newsweek* dismissed the theory as a "rumor" in a December headline, the possibility of mainstream media debate on the issue was effectively squashed. (The magazine also took the opportunity to discredit the entire concept of conspiracy theory, decrying the "darkly deluded" conspiracy "freaks" who believe in the carefully selected "wacky" conspiracy theories that *Newsweek* chose to highlight.)

Salinger has stressed that his TWA 800 theory was confirmed by interviews with confidential sources within the intelligence community. Likewise the author of the Internet posting that Salinger apparently cited—retired aviation accident investigator Richard Russell—will say only that his information came from a confidential source who attended a "high-level" briefing on the incident.

Russell's message, which he says was sent as a private e-mail and was apparently posted by a recipient, began: "TWA flight 800 was SHOT DOWN by a U.S. NAVY AEGIS MISSILE fired from a guided missile ship which was in area W-105 about thirty miles from where TWA flight 800 exploded." Russell made a minor correction in an interview with reporter Robert Davey, stating that Aegis is the name of the missile's launch and tracking system, not the missile itself. However, he stood by the rest of the post.

Of course, intelligence agency sources are not known for providing 100 percent accurate information to their media contacts. They always have an agenda, which is often to spread "disinformation" (in other words, lies) about an issue. And Russell's refusal to name his source makes it impossible to corroborate his claim. On the surface, then, the mainstream media's skepticism is understandable.

Lost in the Salinger furor, however, was the simple fact that the friendly fire theory is based on much more than a single document or source.

The Friendly Fire Scenario

Ian Goddard has gathered several reports from different sources to back the friendly fire scenario, and he is the researcher most often cited by other proponents of the theory. It should be kept in mind, however, that evidence of a missile hit on TWA 800 could also support the terrorism theory and does not necessarily prove navy culpability.

Goddard's analysis, available at his Web site, begins with the question of whether the navy was active in the area of the TWA 800 disaster. According to Goddard, the flight did in fact explode near the naval warning zone W-105 (also named in the Salinger/Russell document) and the nearby zone W-107. Goddard quotes an August 28, 1996, report in the professional aviation publication *Aerospace Daily:* "FAA sources and the Navy acknowledged yesterday that the area known as Whiskey 105, or W-105, was activated at the time of the TWA accident. . . ." In addition, *The New American,* published by the John Birch Society, reported in its October 14, 1996, issue that the FAA's "Warning and Restricted Areas Information Log" shows that area W-107 was also activated that night. A warning zone, according to the *Airman's Information Manual* (Section 3:43), is an area "of unusual . . . hazards to aircraft, such as artillery firing, aerial gunnery, or guided missiles." Finally, a Discovery Channel report on the investigation (November 17, 1996) stated, "The Navy had a P-3 [antisubmarine plane] and a guided missile carrier in the area on some kind of exercise."

According to the Associated Press (November 8, 1996), navy spokesman Lieutenant Commander Rob Newell acknowledged that an Aegistype missile cruiser (the USS *Normandy*) was 185 miles south of the TWA 800 crash site. It was, according to the Navy, too far away to strike the airliner. However, Goddard reports that a state-of-the-art SAM known as the SM-2(IVA) could have been launched by the cruiser and that it has a vertical range of over 320 miles. The SM-2(IVA) locks on to the center of mass of its target and thus would have likely hit TWA 800's central fuel tank.

A February 1997 CNN report gave indirect support to the friendly fire theory when it described the controversy over planned "antimissile exercises" off the coast of Florida. The exercises described were similar to those suggested by Goddard's general scenario, but no connection was made to the TWA 800 incident.

The "Anomalous" Blip

An early Associated Press report (July 19, 1996) stated that "radar detected a blip merging with the jet shortly before the explosion, something that could indicate a missile hit." The radar image was confirmed by *Newsday* on September 1, which reported that the radar showed "something rising, tracking toward the plane, circling to the front of the plane, and then disappearing in the plane's underbelly." Finally, the *London Times* on July 22 related a *New York Post* report: "An American spy satellite positioned over the Brookhaven National Laboratory on Long Island is said [by a law enforcement official] . . . to have shown an object racing up to the TWA jet, passing it, then changing course and smashing into it." Federal investigators have dismissed the radar blip as "an anomaly." Presumably the satellite data is also "an anomaly."

And what of the over one hundred eyewitnesses—including two National Guard pilots—who, according to several mainstream media reports, saw what was variously described as a "streak of light," a "white trail," "a missile," or "a rocket" shooting up from the ocean and hitting TWA Flight 800? By definition, so many eyewitnesses cannot be dismissed as an "anomaly."

The Krieger and Kabot Photos

The night of the explosion, boater Heidi Krieger photographed a thin "white line" rising upward toward TWA 800. Unfortunately, the FBI took possession of the negatives and has not released them. Noting the stark difference between what she saw and what the mainstream media had been reporting, Krieger told *Newsday* (September 1), "I think it is a missile only because I have this photograph; otherwise, I would believe whatever is on television." Recently, however, Goddard has been able to examine the Krieger photo and now doubts that it shows a missile.

Another photo taken minutes before the crash, though, backs the friendly fire theory. Linda Kabot was attending a Long Island Republican fund-raiser and was facing north when she snapped a picture of what appears to be a long, cylindrical object in the sky, pointing downward and to the left. If it is a missile, it would have been coming from the direction of warning zone W-105.

Because Kabot had her back to the crash site, the missile could not have been the one that took down Flight 800. (Media reports and Internet postings that have stated or implied that the Kabot photo shows the missile that hit the airliner have only added to the confusion.) Incredibly, official investigators have dismissed the photo, as if the sighting of a possible missile—any missile—in the sky minutes before the disaster has no bearing on the investigation. The FBI's official explanation of the photo: "This could have been a cigar thrown away by a guest."

Goddard has a more disturbing explanation for Kabot's missile: "Missile defense against incoming ballistic and cruise missiles is the latest 'arms race.' If there were missile test firings off the N.Y. coast, it would likely [have been] part of anticruise missile-missile tests." If so, says Goddard, the apparent missile photographed by Kabot may have been a "target" drone that went off course and left area W-105. In Goddard's scenario, the navy attempted to intercept the Kabot missile with another cruise missile (which is a standard missile defense procedure), but the second missile missed the wayward drone and hit TWA 800. This would explain both the timing and positioning of the Kabot photo, which Goddard believes shows a Tomahawk missile. This theory would be bolstered if witnesses came forward saying they actually saw the wayward drone missile, and in particular its presumed crash into Long Island Sound.

Yet Goddard's drone missile scenario doesn't fully mesh with his previously stated SM-2(IVA) missile theory. Although it has been test-fired off the coasts of North Carolina and Virginia, it does not seem likely that this state-of-the-art SAM would have been used during relatively routine missile defense testing to intercept a wayward Tomahawk. At this point it is also unknown whether one was even on board and ready to launch from the navy carrier.

The physical evidence cited by Goddard is mixed (though he does not claim that it all supports a particular missile scenario). The Discovery Channel documentary of November 17 reported that investigators had found several "fist-sized" holes above the center fuel tank. The SM-2(IVA) is, according to Goddard, a fragmentation warhead that would have left such holes in its target. However, Goddard also cites an Associated Press report of September 23 which quotes an anonymous source as saying, "There's metal bent in, metal bent out. . . . I see a hole going in and a hole going out" of the central fuel tank. This, Goddard believes, would indicate that a "practice guided missile with no warhead" hit and went through the fuel tank.

Unanswered Questions

The fact that some friendly fire theories conflict with other friendly fire theories doesn't make the whole idea invalid. And it is certainly possible that the navy is simply lying about the 285-mile distance of its cruiser from the TWA 800 crash site. Or there could have been another cruiser in the area closer to the site. Also, the Kabot photo may in fact show something other than a missile. Finally, there may be different yet equally plausible interpretations of the physical damage.

While Ian Goddard's friendly fire analysis has many persuasive elements, too many questions are still unanswered. Some that need to be pursued:

- What is the average distance from shore of the missile launch, according to eyewitness testimony?
- Did any eyewitnesses report a source for the missile launch or see more than one missile that night?
- Exactly why was zone W-105 activated that night, and what kind of testing—if any—was planned?

However, as Goddard would be the first to admit, his is an ongoing investigation, one that will ideally develop into a single detailed scenario.

An Earlier Cover-Up

If TWA 800 was the victim of a navy missile, the motive for a Pentagon cover-up is obvious. However, some might ask how long such a friendly fire cover-up could last. As it turns out, sixteen years is about right.

On June 27, 1980, an Italian DC-9 passenger jet exploded over the Mediterranean, killing all eighty-one people aboard. At the time, the explosion was blamed on a "terrorist bomb," and for sixteen years that was the official explanation. Finally, in early 1996 Italian military officials revealed that the plane had been accidentally shot down by either a U.S. or a French aircraft, both of which were chasing a Libyan jet fighter at the time.

Another Missile Theory

The Internet has hosted some heated debates between friendly fire proponents and those who believe the downing of TWA 800 was an act of international terrorism. One proponent of the terrorism theory has even suggested that some friendly fire theorists are Iranian agents. Ironically, the two camps have much in common, since evidence of a missile launch might support either theory. The real question: Whose missile was it?

Unlike the friendly fire theory, the terrorism theory has not even merited a *Newsweek* hatchet job. Even the Internet-based TWA research community seems to have lost interest in the idea, if the lack of terrorism-oriented TWA Web sites is any indication. This really isn't a fair reflection of the terrorism theory, which deserves to be pursued.

The Unfriendly Fire Scenario

The most likely scenario for a terrorist attack involves a shoulder-launched surface-to-air (SAM) missile fired from a boat, and early reports had the FBI investigating several boat rentals and operators in the area. Also, as Ian Goddard has noted, "Witness accounts indicate that the missile was fired from very close to the Long Island shore." While the term "very close" could mean anything from a few yards to a few miles, it seems to better fit a small boat launch rather than a launch from a navy missile cruiser. More details of the eyewitness reports are clearly needed.

Despite the repeated refrain that the 747 was flying too high (13,000–14,000 feet) to have been struck by a terrorist SAM, several modern SAMs are capable of the task: the British Javelin and Blowpipe; the Russian Strella; the Swedish Bofors RBS-70; the French Simbad; and the U.S. FIM-92 Stinger.

Not Uncle Sam's SAM

Terrorism theorist and former military intelligence analyst Ron Lewis believes that the little-known Bofors RBS-70 (which is not heat seeking and would have struck the main fuselage, which is where the initial explosion is now thought to have occurred) is the most likely weapon. He states that a heat-seeking (infrared-guided) SAM known as the SA-18 Grouse is another possibility, noting that the much discussed Stinger actually has a poor record of downing enemy aircraft. (Indeed, the Stinger has been used as a straw man by some friendly fire proponents, including the *Jerusalem Post*, which declared soon after the disaster that a Stinger could not have caused the Flight 800 damage but that the U.S. Navy had missiles big enough to do the job.)

In addition, wreckage of the tail section shows little burns or soot, suggesting that it separated from the jet early on. Also, the lower section of the vertical stabilizer shows small chips in the paint which appear to have been created by a backward and upward force. According to Lewis, this damage is similar to that seen in photos of aircraft struck by small, shoulder-fired SAMs.

Although it is widely assumed that a heat-seeking SAM would have struck one of the 747's four main engines, Lewis stated in a July 23, 1996, article that the engines' trail of hot exhaust gases could have guided the missile toward the aircraft's center, where the initial explosion most likely occurred.

Also, despite the official denial of significant damage to the engines, which remain a likely target of a heat-seeking SAM, the *New American* (10/4/96) quoted a federal air crash investigator as stating that the fourth engine looked as if it could have been hit by a missile. Another observer was quoted as saying, "I watched the television coverage when they brought up the fourth engine and half the engine was gone, as if it had been hit by a missile, even as they were announcing that it was entirely intact."

So the use of a shoulder-fired SAM, either heat seeking or more likely laser guided, is clearly possible. This scenario in turn casts suspicion not on the U.S. Navy, but abroad.

The Terrorism Conference

International events in the weeks and months before the TWA 800 incident also suggest a terrorist attack. That summer Iran hosted what Ron Lewis calls a "terrorism conference" in Tehran and a second one after the incident. In addition, the United States had recently imposed increased economic sanctions against Iran and Libya. Also, the Iranian-sponsored Hezbollah movement was not pleased with the United States' support of Israel after Israel's 1996 massacre of civilians at the UN compound in Qana, southern Lebanon. Throw in U.S. sponsorship of the revived Israeli peace process and the World Trade Center bombing trial and subsequent convictions, and there certainly seems to have been sufficient motive for a terrorist attack on Flight 800. Indeed, Lewis reports that the day before the downing of the airliner, a group called the "Movement for Islamic Change" distributed a fax warning of an imminent attack. Finally, the terrorist bombing of a U.S. military base in Dhahran, Saudi Arabia, less than a month before suggests that the

230 passengers on TWA 800 could well have been the victims of a wave of anti-American terrorism.

The main problem confronting terrorism theorists like Ron Lewis is that if their theory is true, federal investigators would have a very practical reason for withholding supporting evidence and for avoiding the public naming of suspects. As Lewis says, "Information has been withheld, but I strongly suspect that it is so they don't blow the criminal investigation. They want [the perpetrators] to relax and get sloppy." He notes that when Pan Am 103 bombing investigators named two Libyans as suspects, the two men remained in Libya and avoided extradition. The TWA 800 investigators do not want to repeat this mistake and may simply be waiting until they have evidence strong enough to win a criminal trial. For now, though, the rest of us are limited to largely circumstantial evidence.

Other Theories

There are, of course, other TWA 800 theories. As of this writing, the National Transportation Safety Board (NTSB) has virtually declared the incident a case of catastrophic mechanical failure, which happens to be its area of expertise. Similarly, the FBI says it is still pursuing the possibility of a domestic criminal attack. Moving beyond official government theories, former presidential candidate Lyndon Larouche has pointed a finger at England, declaring that "London is the center of world terrorism today" and that "a number of governments have lodged formal protests with the Major government over British protection of and bankrolling of terrorist groups." Certainly these theories reflect the area of expertise—and perhaps bias—of the theorists. All, however, deserve to be considered and investigated beyond the few sentences provided in this article.

"I Know a Lot More Than I'm Telling"

And what of FBI agent Kallstrom, who had thrown reporter Hillel Cohen out of his November press conference for daring to mention the friendly fire theory? Ironically, he lent his support to all TWA 800 conspiracy theorists, albeit unintentionally, during a recent interview: "It's not that I'm trying to play games with the public," he confessed, "but I know a lot more than I am telling. It serves no value to us to tell potential co-conspirators what we are doing."

Update

On November 5, 1997, the coauthor of a report that claimed the U.S. Navy shot down TWA Flight 800 told CNN the charges were "reckless and a mistake." Ian Goddard, in a written statement to CNN, apologized to "all those in the Navy I have wrongfully accused" and to "those who believed in my efforts and who are now upset with me for my change of mind." In an e-mail to his supporters, Goddard, a Libertarian, stated that he "wanted to give the government a black eye by any means that looked opportune." However, he denied CNN's labeling of his effort a "sham," saying that he has always promoted what he believed and that now he believes that "the evidence is not sufficient to blame the Navy." He also noted that "all claims I've made were meticulously referenced so that readers could check up for themselves." In other words, the navy missile theory, while certainly not conclusive, was hardly a made-up sham. In addition, Goddard's coauthor, Pierre Salinger, has said he still believes in the theory. Unfortunately, the story has seriously damaged the credibility of conspiracy theories, in particular those expressed on the Internet, in the minds of the general public. For his part, Goddard is at this writing continuing to gather evidence to support the navy missile theory.

Issue 16, Spring 1997

Drugs and the CIA:
From Ho to Hasenfus

Eric Odinson

In 1997 the mainstream media finally began discussing the CIA's possible role in the importation of crack cocaine into the nation's urban areas. However, the connection between covert operations and the world of drug trafficking has a much longer history. In this overview article, originally published in 1992, Eric Odinson exposes the CIA's past drug dealings, including the CIA-Contra cocaine connection.

THE INTERSECTION OF "REVOLUTIONARY" GROUPS, bankers, criminals, and U.S. intelligence has a long history. More often than not, the area of activity just happens to be the location of large-scale drug cultivation and processing (such as the Southeast Asian Golden Triangle and Latin America). One example is Vietnam.

In *OSS: The Secret History*, R. Harris Smith states that American-educated Vietnamese revolutionary Ho Chi Minh made contact with OSS colonel Paul Helliwell during World War II and was recruited as a U.S. agent. Ho's reports soon received top priority at the OSS (Office of Strategic Services, forerunner to the CIA) and were placed directly on OSS head General Donovan's desk. In addition, the Thai government-in-exile in Miami, and Major Austin Glass, a Socony Oil official, sent arms to Ho for his revolutionary struggle.

Journalist Robert Shaplen reports that an official of Chase Manhattan Bank once parachuted into Ho's remote headquarters, where he found the guerrilla leader dying of malaria and dysentery. Ho's life was saved by OSS medic Paul Hoagland, who administered the new sulfa drugs and quinine. He later served at CIA headquarters until the 1970s and was known as "the man who saved Ho's life."

A special OSS contingent, the Deer Team, was sent to Ho's head-quarters in November 1945. The team claimed that Ho was a great statesman whose nationalism transcended his communist loyalties. They boasted that it had been decided at the highest levels in Washington that the French had to go.

Ho was informed that OSS director William Donovan represented large economic interests (the World Commerce Corporation) which planned to rebuild Vietnam's railroads and highways in exchange for "economic privileges" in Indochina. Consequently, in October 1945 the OSS sponsored the "Vietnam Friendship Association" headed by OSS lieutenant colonel Carlton H. Swift.

The French were dismayed to learn that their American "allies" were training and arming Ho's Viet Minh forces. The OSS armed them with the latest weapons and gave intensive training in infiltration and demolition to selected men of General Giap's army. It was these men who later led the attacks against American troops in the Vietnam War. They were given training in the most advanced techniques of guerrilla warfare, training which our own troops never received before being sent to Vietnam.

After World War II, the OSS-trained, -financed, -organized forces of Ho Chi Minh kept up a steady onslaught against the French colonial government. John Foster Dulles, playing a double game, met with French minister of foreign affairs Georges Bidault, promising support and urging the French to make a stand. When the French forces were surrounded at Dien Bien Phu, Bidault, to explain his strategy, read Dulles's commitment to the French Parliament. Dien Bien Phu collapsed after a seventy-seven-day siege, and the French colonial government was lost. The French magazine *Le Figaro* claimed that the White House and the Kremlin had made a secret deal to partition French Indochina into U.S. and Soviet zones, as had been done in Korea.

The Real Struggle

In reality, the fall of French Indochina was a behind-the-scenes struggle to control the drug trade in Asia. In *The Politics of Heroin,* Alfred McCoy points out that during World War II, mobsters Charles "Lucky" Luciano and Meyer Lansky secretly worked for the OSS. Through their influence, the OSS became deeply involved in drug running.

So how did Golden Triangle opium and heroin get into the United

States? It didn't until the so-called French Connection was shut down. Before World War II the Lansky-Luciano syndicate had overseen opium cultivation in Turkey, the processing of the crop into heroin in the French Mediterranean port of Marseilles, and its export to New York, Havana, and elsewhere. This opium processing and exportation center in Marseilles was known as "the French Connection" and is known to many Americans from a popular movie of the same name. As war began to heat up in Southeast Asia (where Communist insurgents were struggling to free the region from French colonial rule), the Marseilles crime bosses, in league with corrupt French intelligence officers, began to eye the highlands of Laos as a new source of opium.

French intelligence needed a source of revenue for semiofficial military operations against Communist guerrillas, and the French crime machine wanted a source of opium under their own control, so they cut themselves loose from the rest of the Mafia, who were not pleased. The U.S. takeover of the Indo-China War effort from the French in 1954 led not only to the Vietnam War, but also to the Lansky-Luciano syndicate, in league with the CIA, gaining control of the Indo-Chinese heroin trade and finally breaking the French Connection. Meanwhile, Meyer Lansky moved the processing of Turkish opium into Lebanon, where it remains today. The French tactic of using drug money to finance covert operations was also used by the OSS to fund Chinese Nationalists and was later used by the CIA in Vietnam, Central America, and Afghanistan.

Inside Miami

Miami plays a crucial role in this closing down of the European shipments of heroin and the substitution of the Asian heroin. It is the center of a huge conspiratorial milieu whose personnel wind through the Bay of Pigs, attempts on Castro's life, the JFK murder, and the international drug trade. Miami became the nerve center of an alliance comprising Thai and Chinese Nationals, mafiosi, CIA agents, Cuban exiles, and Mafia money-laundering bankers, whose common interests were Asian opium and a thirst for political might. This last factor led to a common denominator in which the alliance invested heavily: Richard M. Nixon.

After World War II, Meyer Lansky moved the headquarters of the drug trade to Miami, where Paul Helliwell, OSS chief of special operations in Asia and the man who recruited Ho Chi Minh into the OSS, was allegedly his front man. Helliwell also operated a CIA front in Miami called Sea Supply Inc.; one of his agents was Howard Hunt. Helliwell later served as paymaster for CIA sponsorship of the Bay of Pigs operation. Helliwell was also attorney for General Development Corp., Lansky's real estate firm, which was run for him by Louis Chesler. After the war Helliwell also became counsel for the Thai government-in-exile in Miami. In the 1950s and 1960s much Thai and Nationalist Chinese capital was invested in Florida's explosive development, a great deal of it by way of the General Development Corp.

After leaving U.S. intelligence, Helliwell became head of the prestigious Miami law firm Helliwell, Melrose and DeWolf. His partner was Mary Jane Delrose, attorney for Resorts International, then a Lansky operation rumored to be involved in drug money laundering. Helliwell opened the Castle Bank in the Bahamas to launder drug payoffs for Thailand poppy growers.

As counsel for Miami National Bank, Paul Helliwel laundered Mob funds through Swiss Banks. Miami National Bank, now owned by Citibank, was known for many years to be controlled by Meyer Lansky. The bank financed the Outrigger Club, which became a meeting place for Philadelphia mobster Santos Trafficante Jr. and members of the Gambino crime family.

In 1960, when the CIA began plotting to overthrow Fidel Castro, they contacted heroin-cocaine kingpin Santos Trafficante Jr., who had just been kicked out of Cuba. Trafficante recruited the personnel who were trained by the CIA for the 1961 Bay of Pigs invasion and provided hundreds of Cuban exiles to work for the CIA against Cuba in the $100 million JM/WAVE operation. After 1968 Trafficante and his organization controlled the smuggling of heroin into the United States from Laos as the CIA waged a secret war on that nation.

Hasenfus's History

Among those who smuggled opium out of Laos for the CIA was Eugene Hasenfus, who was later shot down in Nicaragua with a planeload of arms for the Contras. From 1965 to 1975 Hasenfus worked in Laos for Air America, as did George Bush's friend Felix Rodriguez, alias Max Gomez, whom Hasenfus named as his CIA superior in the Nicaraguan operation.

The Hmong had agreed to supply the CIA with mercenaries in exchange for marketing their opium and, thereby, manned the CIA's war on the LAO patriotic front and its raids into North Vietnam. The village of Long Pot was completely destroyed by the U.S. Air Force on January 4, 1972, when villagers wanted out of the CIA's war. Laotian heroin continued coming into the United States until 1975, when revolutionary forces drove the United States out of Laos and Vietnam.

As a direct result of CIA operations, the number of people in the United States addicted to heroin jumped from 57,000 in 1965 to 560,000 in 1971 and to 740,000 in 1977. Thereafter, U.S. military and CIA operations shifted to Thailand, which became the world's largest heroin producer. In 1973 U.S. Customs agents broke up a Chicago-based drug ring that had smuggled one hundred pounds of pure opium into the United States from Thailand. A Thai national, Puttaporn Khramkhraun, who was in the United States for a management training course sponsored by U.S. AID (Agency for International Development), was among those arrested. The case never went to trial, for it was later revealed that Khramkhraun was a CIA agent, and the entire case was dropped at the request of the CIA. While in custody, Khramkhraun "sang" to an investigator about sixteen commando raids into China and of guarding caravans of opium from Burma to Thailand. In 1976 a CIA-backed right-wing military junta took over Thailand. The flow of narcotics from Thailand increased dramatically and continues today.

The Contras' Turn

In April 1986 Costa Rican police seized a small airplane loaded with cocaine near the Nicaraguan border; arrested was Aldolfo Chamarro, second commander of U.S.-backed Contra forces, and two anti-Castro Cubans.

This spurred an intensive investigation by Costa Rican authorities, which led to the expulsion of several CIA agents involved in drug running for the Contra operation. Among those expelled were Oliver North and Richard Secord, former head of Air America. They could not be prosecuted owing to "diplomatic immunity."

In the same way that Air America acted as a cover for covert CIA opium smuggling, the Contra arms operation was a cover for covert CIA cocaine smuggling. In the locations of both of these operations, standard military surveillance of these areas was shut down for "national security" reasons so that the CIA could conduct their "anti-Communist" operations unhindered.

"The Drug War"

Future historians will refer to the Vietnam War as "the drug war," akin to the British opium wars of the nineteenth century. Through Operation Air America, the CIA sold huge quantities of heroin to the troops at giveaway prices to get them addicted. One Vietnam veteran told this writer, "They sold it to us so cheap, I don't see how they could have made any money off us. I don't know why they did it." When the troops returned home, they discovered the price of the CIA's heroin had greatly increased. The CIA may have lost money selling heroin to the troops in Vietnam, but they more than made it back when the troops returned home.

In 1964 the number of heroin addicts had dropped to 48,000 from 60,000 in 1950. A few years later 15 percent of American soldiers would return home from Vietnam—as heroin addicts.

The number of addicts would increase, and the global drug trade was back in business.

Issue 2, Fall 1993

MEDIA MIND CONTROL

You Name the Dwarfs: Surrealism, Advertising, and Mass Mind Control

Robert Guffey

This article discusses the sexual themes used to market products to the public and illustrates a connection between the aesthetics of the surrealist movement (the transmitting of messages through art) and modern advertising, which seduces the consumer to buy products via a sexual aesthetic.

SIGMUND FREUD'S WORK had a great impact on two artistic movements of the twentieth century: surrealism and advertising. Some might suggest advertising is not an art movement. However, any poet, novelist, or painter will admit that their greatest wish is to transform the way people view the world. Ultimately this is also the wish of the advertiser, whose interest in Freud has mirrored that of the surrealist.

As the twentieth century progressed, Freud's ideas began to take hold among the general populace. No longer were his interpretations of dreams the sole interest of his professional colleagues and a few strange visionaries like the founder of surrealism, André Breton. Suddenly modern advertisers realized that the very techniques Breton glorified in his trio of manifestos, the techniques with which he hoped to shock the bourgeoisie, could be utilized in order to place a tight rein on the culture at large. It doesn't matter whether Freud's theory of dream significance is true or not. The fact is that the major corporations believe it to be true, just as the surrealists did, and exploit the symbolism in their ads. The obvious difference between the two movements is this: Breton and the surrealists wished to incite riot and revolt with their art, whereas the advertisers hope to instill obedience and stupidity and often do. I've decided to codify these two schools as "guerrilla surrealism" and "corporate surrealism."

Advertisers (corporate surrealists), like Breton and his cohorts (guerrilla surrealists), are fascinated by the magical and utilitarian aspects of art. Some of the guerrilla surrealists saw themselves as following in the footsteps of the ancient cavemen who painted the animals they wished to kill prior to the hunt in the belief that this would ensure the animal's capture. Art as invocation, in other words. With this in mind, it's interesting that Marshall McLuhan once chose to define advertising in the following manner:

> Ads are the cave art of the twentieth century. While the Twenties talked about the caveman, and people thrilled to the art of the Altamira caves, they ignored [as we do now] the hidden environment of magical forms which we call "ads." Like cave paintings, ads are not intended to be looked at or seen, but rather to exert influence at a distance, as though by ESP. Like cave paintings, they are not means of private but of corporate expression. They are vortices of collective power, masks of energy invented by new tribal man.[6]

McLuhan's mention of ESP is interesting in light of the fact that Sir Hubert Read, one of the most renowned art critics of the twentieth century, once edited a book about surrealism in which he postulated that "thought-transference or telepathy" was wholly possible and that painters like Salvador Dalí were unconsciously picking up and transmitting "messages" through their art.[9] Apparently Read was unaware of the fact that some artists consciously transmit hidden messages through their paintings. An abstract artist named John Hock once experimented with word embeds, particularly that favorite cultural taboo "fuck," hidden behind curved forms in the background of a painting. Strangely, he found that people who visited his house were "fascinated by the painting." Often, visitors could not seem to take their eyes off the canvas. The embedded word, he explained, "appeared to give a magic quality to the painting."[4]

The fact of the matter is that major corporations use the very same techniques in their advertisements, as in a *New York Times Sunday Magazine* ad for Horsman dolls where the word "fuck" was planted on the sleeve of the doll's left arm.[4] Sometimes the visual embeds are subtle, sometimes not so subtle. Either way they usually revolve around sex, the most effective Pavlovian conditioner. Not many people are aware of the fact that when behaviorist B. F. Skinner ran into some trouble from the psychological community over a silly thing like "ethics," he hightailed it straight to Madison Avenue. His experiments in thought control found a welcome home among the advertising executives there. Ever wonder why the Coke bottle is shaped the way it is?

In his 1924 manifesto Breton defined surrealism as "Thought dictated in the absence of all control exerted by reason and outside all aesthetic or moral preoccupations. . . . It leads to the permanent destruction of all other psychic mechanisms and to its substitution for them in the solution of the principal problems of life."[2]

This definition could easily be applied to advertising. The advertising man's dream is to wipe away all reason in the consumer, to force him or her to respond to the ad at a completely emotional level. Like Breton, the advertising man sees himself occupying a space outside all aesthetic and moral considerations. Certainly he does not create an ad with the thought that it might be hanging on the wall of a museum someday. The ad man is interested in "art" only if he can manipulate it to sell a product. Indeed, the examples of classical art appearing in modern advertisements are too numerous to mention. As for the morality question, the ad man claims that he doesn't sell anything the public doesn't already want. Like a heroin pusher on a street corner, he says, "I'm not making anyone do anything. It's the customer's choice, not mine." The only difference is that the ad man isn't risking twenty years in jail. Ultimately the ad man hopes the consumer will believe that the product, whether it's a cigarette or a computer or a new brand of hemorrhoid cream, is truly a solution to "the principal problems of life."

Of course, Breton intended his manifesto to be a blueprint for liberation. If only people could tap into the hidden wellsprings of creativity deep within themselves by exploring the intangible realm of dreams, they could cast off the shackles of irrational rationalism placed upon them by society. Freud's theory of dream significance was to be one of the tools for this revolt of the mind. However, in the early 1970s, when "members of the Woodstock Generation . . . were dropping out of the consumer culture that Ad Alley had taken such pains to create," Madison Avenue desperately turned to Freudian theories in order to regain control of the people, not to liberate them.[8]

Faced with a rebellious public, Ad Alley decided it needed an image overhaul. To do this, "Agency-employed psychologists and sociologists refined [an] art of emotional exploitation by using a variety of psychographic research systems."[8] One of the most widely used systems is called VALS, an acronym for Values and Life-styles. Developed by the Stanford Research Institute in Northern California, it divides the people of America into five distinct categories: Belongers, Emulators, Emulator-Achievers, Societally Conscious Achievers, and Need-Directed. The Belonger is an Archie Bunker conservative whose purchasing behaviors are old-fashioned and predictable. An Emulator is a young person searching desperately for an identity. An Emulator-Achiever is the successful American who has already "made it" and needs to buy more and more objects to remind himself of this fact.

The Societally Conscious Achiever is the most important target of the VALS system. These people are the main reason it was invented in the first place. They represent the experimental section of the populace who feel dissatisfied with materialism. Because their buying habits are constrained by their "ethics," they must be made to believe that their purchases are somehow diametrically opposed to those of the Belonger types. For example, these people will lumber into a Tower Records and buy a CD from the "alternative" section, never once stopping to consider that a category labeled "alternative" can't very well be alternative in the truest—indeed, the only—sense of that word. Alternative to what, itself? These people are actually Belongers but need to think that they're not. Finally, the Need-Directed are those Americans who live from paycheck to paycheck and can't afford leisure items. To the Stanford Research Institute these people are considered invisible and irrelevant.[8] It should be noted that the preceding is not simply my personal interpretation of the VALS system. This is exactly how the Stanford Research Institute describes the American population.

As stated earlier, the institute first initiated this system in the early 1970s. Perhaps it's merely a coincidence, but on February 3, 1974, novelist Philip K. Dick (author of such overtly surrealist books as *Ubik*, *Eye in the Sky*, and *Flow My Tears, the Policeman Said*) was infused by a mysterious pink beam of light that implanted the word "VALIS" into his brain. Is it just me or is that suspiciously similar to "VALS"? Dick took the word to mean "vast active living intelligence system," though that was only a guess on his part. This ostensibly mystical experience eventually led to a series of critically acclaimed novels, including *VALIS* (the original version of which was called *Valisystem A*), *The Divine Invasion*, and *The Transmigration of Timothy Archer*.[10] Something tells me Ad Alley was experimenting with a unique form of "product placement" on February 3, 1974. My advice: If you should suddenly wake up out of a deep sleep one night with a strange craving for Coca-Cola, ignore it. That was no dream, it was an advertisement.

Some people have dismissed Dick's 1974 experience as nothing but an episode of schizophrenia, which is strange since he was never diagnosed schizophrenic. Schizophrenia is a state of mind that fascinates both the guerrilla surrealists and the corporate surrealists. Among the former group, Salvador Dalí developed a technique intended to present the state of schizophrenia for the all-too-sane bourgeoisie. These "paranoiac" double visions were a perfect melding of two distinct images, as in his 1929 painting *Invisible Man*. The corporate surrealists also utilize visual puns to subtly manipulate the consumer. Some "hidden" sexual images are quite obvious to anyone who cares to see them. A recent McDonald's coupon ad that ran in newspapers throughout the country was a wonderful example of this technique. On the surface it depicted a Chicken McNugget being dipped in sauce, yet at the same time it looked exactly like an ejaculating penis. The viewer need not squint his eyes or stand on his head to see this image. It's quite clear. In fact, upon an initial viewing I had to squint my eyes and stand on my head in order to see the nugget. It was so blatant that the *Village Voice* reprinted the ad beneath the headline "Pecker Order" and asked, "What part of the hen is this?"[3]

The corporate surrealists don't stop at borrowing artistic techniques from Dalí. The guerrilla surrealist Pablo Picasso is equally ripe for plunder. In his painting *The Mirror* Picasso uses juxtaposition and contrast to demonstrate the unseen connections between two aspects of a woman's life. In an ad for Berkshire stockings, the corporate surrealists utilize the same technique to drive home a subtle message about female sexuality. An aloof, upper-class woman stands demurely against a pillar while wearing her "breath-taking . . . sheer . . . sheer . . . Berkshire Nylon stockings," the color for which was "borrowed from the sun-soaked gold of a stallion's satin coat." In the background a palomino is rearing up on its hind legs, in the Freudian sense suggesting out-of-control sexuality. By subtle juxtaposition, the ad man implies the "breath-taking pure sensation" lying just beneath the woman's stately, modest exterior.[7]

Whereas the guerrilla surrealists wish to use their art to transmit messages of freedom, the corporate surrealists wish to transmit messages of enslavement. Artists like Breton, Dalí, and Picasso warp reality to see it more clearly. The anonymous ad men warp reality to obfuscate its true meaning. The former is a positive fantasy, the latter a negative one.

In Western culture "fantasy" is often used as a derogatory term. "You're living in a fantasy world!" people say, never realizing that certain fantasies might transcend truth. The scenes depicted in Hieronymous Bosch's *Garden of Earthly Delights* ostensibly never occurred in real life, yet its subject matter is somehow more "true" than a thousand Norman Rockwell paintings. The corporate surrealists also employ fantastic elements in their work, but their fantasy attempts to emulate reality in a dishonest manner. The ad men show us scenes we all recognize, suburban Los Angeles, the coast of Florida, the streets of Chicago, at the same time populating them with alien beings that have eight-inch waists, hairless armpits, and teeth as white as ivory. The Belongers and the Emulators and the Emulator Achievers and the Societally Conscious Achievers and even the Need-Directed all sleepwalk through life, chasing rainbows and golden arches seen late at night on a flickering colorful box, unaware that the personable residents of the ad world are less real than the squidlike humanoids in a Max Ernst collage. They are dazed by a fantasy disguised as reality.

André Breton's idea of fantasy was laced with a desire for rebellion and anarchism. His political views were made explicit in the following statement:

> The only remedy . . . is to go back to the principles . . . of anarchism, not to the caricature that is made of it, nor the terror, but to . . . socialism, no longer conceived of as the simple resolution of political and social problems, but as the expression of the exploited masses in their desire to create a classless society where all human values and aspirations can be realized.[5]

The corporate surrealists have no respect for human values. When they speak honestly, they reveal themselves as fascists. This shouldn't be a surprise. Mussolini himself once said, "Fascism is corporatism." What are the ad men if not shills for the corporations that employ them? Their view of humanity is made clear enough in the following passage written by one of the most successful ad executives in America, Jerry Della Femina, who also happens to be a strident supporter of the Stanford Research Institute's special brand of psychoanalysis:

Advertising deals in open sores . . . Fear. Greed. Anger. Hostility. You name the dwarfs and we play on every one. We play on all the emotions and on all the problems, from not getting ahead to the desire to be one of the crowd. Everyone has a button. If enough people have the same button, you have a successful ad and a successful product.[8]

For some reason most people don't find it difficult to believe that advertising executives think this way but claim it doesn't matter because "Aw, advertisements don't affect anyone!" Apparently they believe major corporations spend millions upon millions of dollars every year on complex ad campaigns that have absolutely no effect on anyone and bring in no revenue whatsoever. Perhaps they do it out of the kindness of their hearts to give otherwise useless advertising executives a much needed source of income so they can buy Christmas presents for the kiddies. Perhaps.

However, a more rational explanation would be that corporations spend good money for these ads because they expect results. So much revenue is generated by the advertisements, it's completely illogical to think that the artists involved simply slap the images together in a couple of days without any thought at all. They spend as much time putting them together as Max Ernst does composing a painting, perhaps more so. The truth is that the visual embeds hidden in the ads are no "coincidence" or tricks of light and shadow. They've been placed there on purpose.

In Breton's novel *Nadja* the last line reads, "Beauty will be CONVULSIVE, or will not be at all."[1] The corporate surrealists might very well agree, though for different reasons from those Breton intended. After all, every advertiser depends on the convulsive, involuntary reflex to buy buy, buy, buy the manufactured "beauty" that must be instantly possessed, whether it be a pair of Berkshire Nylon stockings, a Horsman doll, an IBM computer, or a Chicken McNugget that looks like a flaccid cock dipped in honey sauce.

Beauty comes in many shapes and flavors, with attachable accessories. No batteries included. Dissatisfaction guaranteed. You name the dwarfs.

Star Trek: Sci-Fi or Psy-War?

Jerry E. Smith

This entertaining article begins with the premise that modern media is a form of psy-war waged against its targeted demographics. Analyzing the names and motifs used in the long-running television show Star Trek, *the author attempts to show that the series was a conspiratorial attack by the military-industrial-entertainment complex which aimed to subliminally convert American viewers to Catholicism. The author also suggests that* Star Trek *may have been a psy-war operation perpetrated by the Vatican to subvert the United States or may have simply been a vehicle for creating acceptance of a United Federation of Earth.*

PSY-WAR, OR PSYCHOLOGICAL WARFARE, is an admitted, if little understood, component of the U.S. military arsenal. Other powers, not limited to governments, are also known to deploy so-called psy-weapons. For example, modern media advertising is clearly a form of psy-war, one waged against "targeted" demographics by major corporations and other institutions, including religions.

In Victorian plays and novels, characters were often given significant names—names that described the character or had a special meaning in terms of the plot. Oscar Wilde's play *The Importance of Being Earnest* is an example, with the title's double meaning. Likewise, the names of the characters in the original television series *Star Trek* are pregnant, as the Victorians would say, with multiple meanings. Are these meanings of no significance beyond the spinning of a tale, or do they reveal a hidden, subliminal psy-war attack on a targeted population? In this article I will attempt to show that *Star Trek* was a premeditated attack, one whose purpose was to subliminally indoctrinate America into obeying the Roman Catholic Church.

First, let us consider the primary character, the mover and shaker, the guy in charge, Captain James T. Kirk, commanding officer of the Federation starship USS *Enterprise*. When we analyze his name, we first notice that James was the brother of Jesus. James took over the movement founded by Jesus after the crucifixion. The name means "the supplanter" and is a variant of Jacob, one of the patriarchs of the Old Testament. Kirk's middle name was Tiberius, a Roman general and emperor. "Kirk" is the most common European-language spelling of the word we know in English as "church." Put these all together: (brother of) Jesus, Roman (emperor), church, and what do you have? The Roman Catholic Church! It was the Roman Catholic Church (RCC) that was, symbolically, in control of the *Enterprise*.

In the U.S. Air Force a chaplain is referred to as a "sky pilot." Here, in the person of Captain Kirk, we have a church (a kirk) flying through outer space, the abode of God. Just a pun, or a subliminal message?

Who ran Kirk? He took orders from Starfleet Command. If Kirk represents the RCC, then Starfleet has to be God. "Fleet" can refer to a number of ships; it can also mean "swift." Is it not "God" who commands the "stars" in their "swift" passage through the heavens?

Under Kirk were two primary characters: The medical officer, Leonard McCoy, and the science officer, Mr. Spock. Let's take up McCoy first. Leonard is Teutonic, consisting of "-nard," meaning "brave or strong," and "Leo," the lion. Together they mean "strong in the Lord" or "strong in faith." No fewer than thirteen popes have taken the name Leo. The lion has been a symbol of Christianity nearly since its inception. Of course, the lion image tracks back to the lion of Judah, the totem of the Jews.

"McCoy" has two referents to American culture. Recall, if you will, that Spock and McCoy, the emotionless and the emotional, were perpetually locked in a feud. As well as being the archetypical battle of emotion vs. logic, this is also an allusion to an event in American history. In the name and character of "McCoy" we have the power of an archetype welded to the image of the bitter feud between the Hatfields and the McCoys. Dr. McCoy represents the McCoys and Spock stands in for the Hatfields—who lost.

McCoy's second connection to American culture and consciousness is in the phrase "the real McCoy." It means that the item referred to is the genuine article, not an imitation or fake. Is this an attempt to say that the RCC is the true religion, while upstart science, championed by Spock, is the impostor? So, Doctor (healer) Leonard (of the faith/faithful) McCoy (true religion) is the emotional (be as the little children, faith is from the heart) winner.

Dualities being the easiest to deal with in a sixty-minute format, we also have the equally archetypical battle of good vs. evil. If McCoy is on the (winning) side of true religion, then (the losing) Spock, and science, must be of the devil. Just so you don't miss which side McCoy is on, his assistant is Nurse Christine (a variant of Christ, Christian) Chapel (a small church). Likewise, to ensure that you saw Spock as the devil, they gave him pointy ears.

Spock has no other names (pronounceable by humans, that is). Demons, you may know, have names that humans can summon them by, as well as ones that cannot be uttered by the human tongue. Spock is a miscegenation (a biblical sin), a half-breed: part human, part Vulcan. "Vulcan" was the Roman god of fire and craftsmanship who lived in the underworld—again, an image of both science and the devil.

The only name "Spock" could refer to, in contemporary American culture, would be that of Dr. Benjamin Spock, the baby doctor. Perhaps this was intended to subliminally cause the viewer to associate science (only a little over a century old) with infants (in its infancy, as a baby) as a further denigration. Dr. Spock was a secular humanist, a progressive, and an outspoken opponent of the Vietnam War, which was just becoming a major shooting war at the time Star Trek hit the air.

Mr. Spock, as a half-human demon, associated with Benjamin Spock, the antitraditionalist, the secularist, the authoritative antiauthoritarian, would have been the very antithesis of what the RCC stood for. Of course McCoy was the "real thing." The Christian Church, and particularly the RCC, has always been an opponent of rational, free thinking and a proponent of emotional belief and blind faith. That was what the Inquisition was all about, wasn't it? Mr. Spock, the free thinker, the Faustian devil, would have been burned at the stake!

In Star Trek the RCC has won, for both Spock and McCoy were completely under the command of Kirk (church). Captain Kirk represents a face of the RCC that they would like us to believe is its true nature. Kirk is kind and almost indulgent of the "feud" between his juniors. Like a loving father, he is firm and forceful when necessary— yet never too forceful. There are no Inquisitions on the Enterprise.

There were two other principal officers on the Enterprise: Uhura and Scott. Uhura is a variant of "Uhuru," Swahili for "freedom." Uhura is the communications officer, so she could represent "freedom of speech"—but she doesn't speak for herself. She is the go-between for Kirk and the universe outside of the *Enterprise*, in particular his link with Starfleet (God).

Perhaps she represents religious freedom. Her "freedom," however, is closer to slavery. She cannot send or receive communications on her own, only as directed by her superiors. The message here could be that freedom, particularly religious freedom, is the freedom to be Catholic, to perceive, and receive, the universe with a Catholic mind-set; that the universe outside of one's own personal starship is whatever the RCC says it is.

The other main character was the *Enterprise*'s chief engineer, Mr. Scott. The Industrial Revolution (it can be argued) began in Scotland. "Mr. Scott" is a perfect Victorian novel name that exactly described this character's personality and function: the simple mechanic. Mr. Scott would then appear to embody all the elements of the Industrial Revolution that the RCC is willing to accept (useful gadgets without any challenging ideas), while Spock represents those elements that the RCC wishes to crush.

What about Chekov and Sulu, you ask? Sulu appeared early, around the third episode; Chekov, however, was not added until the last episode of the first season. I see no reason to treat them as part of the subliminal message addressed above. They were window dressing. Indeed, Chekov was added in response to viewer complaints that for a ship claiming to represent all of planet Earth, the bridge had an "all-American" look. Chekov and Sulu simply represent their nationalities and, by extension, the second world and third world, respectively. Note, though, that both were completely under the control of Kirk (the RCC). This suggests that the whole world is run by the RCC, or at least that they intend it to be so in the future, wherein *Star Trek* is set.

The show's starship, the USS *Enterprise*, with the designator number NCC 1701, had a conspiratorial name as well. We all know that in modern times military operations are given code names like "Desert Shield" and "Desert Storm," "Operation: Just Cause," and "Operation: Restore Hope." This practice is not entirely new. The Spanish Armada was code-named "the Enterprise."

What was Spain's failed attempt to invade England all about? England was then ruled by Queen Elizabeth I. During her reign she encouraged a cult of personality to grow up around her. She, and her inner circle, got into some pretty strange things—like goddess worship, demon conjuring, and all manner of un-Catholic activities. As an example of this, Sir Walter Raleigh's customary court clothing was all black, with magical symbols woven in silver thread. The Spanish "Enterprise" was an attempt to dethrone the neopagan queen and retake England for Catholicism.

The "USS" portion of the ship's name was defined on *Star Trek* as meaning United Star Ship, a transparent play on United States Ship, the designator for all U.S. Navy craft. As for the designator number, today all aircraft are required to display "N" numbers as a form of identification. This number could refer to the year 1701, which was the date of the beginning of the War of Spanish Succession. This was a war to determine who would ascend to the Spanish throne. It eventually embroiled all of Europe, becoming a precursor of the world wars to follow centuries later. In this context the date-number symbolized that with the airing of *Star Trek,* a new war of neo-Spanish,—that is, Catholic— succession (to the "throne" of planet Earth) had begun.

What about the latter generations of *Star Trek,* the seven movies and two TV shows that followed? Did they follow in this "conspiracy"? I think not. One can find some interesting meanings in some of the names, and one can arrive at some intriguing interpretations of some of the stories aired; but I don't see this system of hidden messages about the RCC continued.

However, there is the possibility that with the death of Gene Rodenberry, *Star Trek*'s creator, and the changing of personnel over the years, one or more other conspiratorial voices have begun to speak through this format. One episode of *Star Trek: The Next Generation* involved the Federation, in violation of its vaunted prime directive, sending undercover agents to a planet to shift them from a multinational political system to a one-world government. The object was to get them to have a single voice so that the planet could then be asked to join the Federation. This could well be a message from the new world order crowd (which the RCC seems to have joined). There is a growing movement to consolidate of all the nations of planet Earth under a single authority, such as the United Nations.

While the RCC may have taken a backseat, television programming continues to appear to be population programming, in this case a "plot" to move Earth's population toward accepting a real "United Federation of Earth" at some point in the near future.

So was *Star Trek* originally an attempt to subliminally convert America to Catholicism? Did it become a vehicle for creating acceptance for the creation of a United Federation of Earth? Was it actually a psy-war operation perpetrated by the Vatican or the New World Order to convert or subvert the United States? Or have I just found a series of "coincidences"?

Issue 14, Fall 1996

The Brits Bash Bubba

Webster G. Tarpley

In 1996 the White House issued a study on the "media food chain" that was responsible for much of the anti-Clinton scandal reporting. Readers of Paranoia, however, had read all about it in summer of 1995. The following was excerpted from the March 23, 1994, public testimony of Webster G. Tarpley, an associate of economist and commentator Lyndon LaRouche, to the Congressional Subcommittee on Treasury, Postal Service, and General Government of the Committee on Appropriations. It presents a unique perspective on Whitewater, Monicagate, and related scandals, painting Bill Clinton not as a villain, but as a victim. In it we learn of the media moguls behind the anti-Clinton effort and follow the trail back to its surprising origin: Great Britain!

I WOULD FIRST OF ALL like to thank the members of the subcommittee for this opportunity to testify. I would like to address a very serious threat to the national security of the United States in the form of a concerted international campaign to overthrow our current president and permanently weaken the institution of the presidency in a way which would clearly undermine the integrity of our federal Constitution. The relevance of this issue to the subcommittee's purview of appropriations oversight involves the Secret Service of the Department of the Treasury and specifically the Secret Service's mandated task of protecting the president and the institution he embodies. I wish to call these matters to the subcommittee's attention because they represent challenges for the Secret Service which may necessitate additional funding if they are to be dealt with efficiently and effectively.

My starting point is that the ensemble of events which may be grouped under the heading of Whitewatergate is not solely or even primarily a phenomenon of United States politics and public opinion. It rather constitutes the attempt by a foreign power to destabilize and overthrow the constitutional government of our country. The foreign nation which has been the prime mover in this entire affair and which has taken the lead in escalating the scandal at every critical turn has been the United Kingdom. What we know today as Whitewatergate could never have happened without a series of violent press campaigns attacking the American presidency that have been carried in the leading newspapers of London, above all the *Daily Telegraph* and *Sunday Telegraph*. The *Washington Post* and the *New York Times* have in the main followed the lead of the British newspapers and so-called investigative reporters in their attacks on Clinton.

To put the question in a slightly different way: Everyone remembers the role of the *Washington Post* as the flagship of damaging revelations during the original Watergate affair. To carry our analogy one step further, we can say that the "Woodward and Bernstein" of the current brouhaha is one Ambrose Evans-Pritchard, an investigative reporter for the *London Telegraph* newspapers and a person who makes no secret of his close relations with the British Secret Intelligence Service, also known as MI-6. Whether Evans-Pritchard is in fact himself an agent of MI-6 is [a question] the American Secret Service and our other intelligence agencies should urgently answer.

I submit that it is only because of the propaganda drumbeat coming from London that the Whitewatergate scandal has come as far as it has, all on the basis of not one single colorable allegation of any crime having been committed. The pattern observable during the unfolding of the Whitewater scandal was summed up by an article published in another British publication, *The Economist*, during the first week of March [1994]. *The Economist* is, of course, the house organ of the powerful Rothschild banking interests. Under the headline "Shhhh: The Press and Whitewater," *The Economist* compared the crisis of the Clinton presidency to the 1936–37 crisis in the British royal family which preceded the abdication of King Edward VIII in connection with his romance with the American divorcée Mrs. Wallis Simpson. In 1936, argued *The Economist,* there existed an accord among the Fleet Street barons of the British press which prevented publication in Britain of the main facts about the king's activities and their implications for the monarchy. In those days it was therefore mainly the American newspapers whose reports fed the scandal that ultimately led to Edward's abdication. Today, the magazine continued, the roles are curiously reversed, with the American newspapers seeming "peculiarly inhibited" in their "lackluster coverage" of Whitewatergate, while the London press and especially the *Telegraph* are taking the lead in publishing damaging revelations.

The *Economist* refers specifically to allegations made against President Clinton by a former Miss Arkansas named Sally Perdue, whose story was generally not given credence by the American media but who enjoyed an avalanche of sensational publicity in London. The implication of all this is clear: Clinton, like Edward, will be brought down, in this case thanks to a campaign of vilification spearheaded by the London press. Similarly, R. Emmett Tyrell Jr., who is part of the London operation against Clinton, wrote in the *London Sunday Telegraph* of January 23 [1994] that the story of this former Arkansas beauty queen had "become front-page news all over the United Kingdom and in Australia" at a time when nobody in the United States except for Rush Limbaugh and the *Washington Times* would touch it. Tyrell added that "British papers have been reporting other acts of violence relating to scandals associated with Clinton's name."

The *Sunday Telegraph* makes no secret of its commitment to overthrow the Clinton presidency. On February 6, [1994,] Ambrose Evans-Pritchard concluded a trilogy of "get Clinton" articles with the following comment: "The ordeal will not last forever. Indeed, the way documents keep popping up in Arkansas, Bill Clinton may be forced from office before the year is out."

Who controls the *London Daily Telegraph* and *Sunday Telegraph?* These papers are owned by the Hollinger Corporation, an international media conglomerate headquartered in Toronto, Ontario, Canada. The Hollinger Corporation is the descendant of the Argus Corporation, which was created by the British Special Operations Executive (SOE) during World War II. The owner of the Hollinger Corporation is Conrad Black, who was a protégé of E. P. Taylor, the head of the economic warfare branch of the SOE during the war. Hollinger owns the *London Telegraph* papers, the *Jerusalem Post*, the *Canadian Financial Post*, and the *Caymanian Compass*. Hollinger owns about eighty newspapers in the United States and has just acquired the *Chicago Sun-Times*.

The Hollinger board of directors includes Conrad Black, Peter Bronfinan (chairman of Edper, the troubled real estate conglomerate), R. Donald Fullerton (CEO of Canadian Imperial Bank of Commerce), and Paul Reichmann (a principal of another bankrupt real estate empire, Olympia and York). Allan E. Gottlieb, the current Canadian ambassador here in Washington, is also a director.

Hollinger also maintains a body it calls its "International Advisory Board." Here we find Lady Margaret Thatcher, Lord Peter Carrington, Lord Jacob Rothschild, and Sir James Goldsmith. American members of this body include Dwayne Andreas of Archer-Daniels-Midland, former Secretary of State Henry A. Kissinger, former NSC director Zbigniew Brzezinski, *National Review* editor William F. Buckley, former Defense Department official Richard Perle, former Federal Reserve chairman Paul A. Volcker, and columnist George Will.

The *Daily Telegraph* is a wholly owned subsidiary of Hollinger. There is also a board of directors of the *Daily Telegraph* as such. Here we find Rupert Hambro, the managing director of Hambro Bank, a city of London merchant bank with very close historic connections to the British intelligence community. During World War II Hambro provided many of the leading figures for the Special Operations Executive. Another director of the *Daily Telegraph* is Henry Keswick, chairman of Jardine-Mathieson, historically a British empire trading company based in Hong Kong which has been implicated in international narcotics trafficking since the time of the first opium war in the 1840s.

The most important writer for the *Daily Telegraph* is Sir Peregrine Worsthorne, a virulent racist and anti-American ideologue. Sir Peregrine is the stepson of Sir Montagu Norman, who was director of the Bank of England during the 1930s and supported Hitler's seizure of power in Germany.

Ambrose Evans-Pritchard, the would-be Watergator, has admitted in conversation with investigative journalists that he has been exchanging information with the British Secret Intelligence Service and specifically with MI-6 over a period of years. Pritchard was posted to Managua, Nicaragua, for a three-year period during the 1980s. During this time Pritchard says he was friendly to the Nicaraguan Contras as well as to guerrilla movements operating in El Salvador and Guatemala. Pritchard reported to the political attaché of the British embassy, whom Pritchard knew to be an agent of MI-6. Pritchard describes these practices as "swapping information."

Pritchard claims to believe that the late Vincent Foster was murdered by a hit team dispatched by the Clinton White House. The hit team, in his view, then made a maladroit effort to make the death look like a suicide. According to Pritchard, anyone who has any knowledge of the various nefarious activities carried out by Bill and Hillary Clinton is in danger of being eliminated by a sinister "Murder, Incorporated" based in the White House.

Pritchard's most recent article [1994], published in the *Sunday Telegraph* of March 13 and entitled "Little Rock's Mean Machine," is devoted to Pritchard's ostensible muckraking in Conway, Arkansas. He alleges that he has discovered a "Deep Throat" named Larry Nichols, a former functionary of the Arkansas State government. Nichols is well known, having begun a campaign of denigration against Clinton in 1991 with television and press interviews. Pritchard attempts to present Nichols as a goldmine of new scandals against Clinton that will be more powerful than Whitewater. In the same issue Pritchard writes that "Washington has been slow to grasp the gravity of it all" but that now the American capital is "paralyzed, and likely to remain so" until congressional hearings are held. According to Evans Pritchard, these hearings "will puncture the moral pretensions of this White House . . . at worst, they will lead to criminal indictments and bring down the whole administration."

Here in the United States, one of the most aggressive press organs attempting to whip up hysteria around Whitewater has been the *American Spectator,* a periodical of the so-called neoconservative circles. It was the *Spectator* whose scurrilous and unsubstantiated "troopergate" accusations, opened the current intensive phase of the Whitewater affair. The "troopergate" story was written by David Brock and was arranged with the help of Cliff Jackson, the Arkansas lawyer who has devoted himself in recent years to dishing up scandals against Clinton. A January 8 column in the American newspaper *Irish People* raised the relevant question when it asked whether Jackson is "part of a British cabal." But when "troopergate" first appeared, no questions were asked about it by such news organs as CNN and ABC, which gave extensive coverage to the wholly unproven charges of the disgruntled troopers.

According to the *Daily Telegraph,* "there has always been a strong British connection" to the *American Spectator.* The head of the *American Spectator* Washington, D.C., bureau is British: Tom Bethell, who is the son of Lord Nicholas Bethell of British intelligence. Lord Bethell for many years was one of the most important figures of British intelligence operations in the Balkans region.

Sir Peregrine Worsthorne, whom we have already met as the leading writer for the *London Telegraph* newspapers, is an active member of the editorial board of the *American Spectator,* as is British journalist Paul Johnson. On February 13 the *Sunday Telegraph* printed an article praising Tyrrell and the *American Spectator* for spearheading the Whitewater campaign against Clinton in a way that has "aroused admiration around the world." In the same issue of the *Sunday Telegraph,* Sir Peregrine Worsthorne praised Tyrrell as the man who is "masterminding the campaign which is beginning to look like it might do for Clinton what the *Washington Post* did for Nixon."

The *American Spectator* editorial board lists, in addition to Sir Peregrine, such leading neoconservatives as Jeane Kirkpatrick, Michael Ledeen, and Midge Decter and include writers like Daniel Wattenberg and John Podhoretz, scions of well-known neoconservatives. These figures are at the center of an American "neocon" network which includes the *Washington Times* [owned by the Reverend Moon organization—ed.], William Safire, and other exponents of what Admiral Bobby Inman has accurately denounced as neo-McCarthyism. The neocons, it would appear, are the most energetic fellow travelers of London on this issue.

Why are the British oligarchy and its intelligence agencies attempting to overthrow the president of the United States? The answer involves London's perception that the Clinton administration may be inclined to alter certain policies which London is hysterically and fanatically committed to maintain. These policies are generally those institutionalized during the Thatcher-Bush era, when the United States government was slavishly obedient to the demands of what Bush referred to as "the mother country" during the 1991 visit by Queen Elizabeth II. London currently demands that the Thatcher-Bush policies remain in force with no changes by Clinton, as if the American government were functioning on automatic pilot.

The most important focus of disagreement has been the question of International Monetary Fund conditionality as applied to Russia and the other successor states of the former USSR. Here London demands continued adherence to "shock therapy" looting arrangements. But first in March 1993 and then more clearly in December 1993, the Clinton administration has manifested great disenchantment with the dangerous strategic consequences of continued shock therapy. After the December 12 Russian elections and the emergence of Zhirinovsky, Vice President Gore attacked the IMF's handling of the Russian economic crisis. Strobe Talbott of the State Department, Clinton's personal friend, called for "less shock and more therapy" for Russia. This caused IMF director Camdessus to complain that the IMF was being made a "scapegoat" for Russian economic collapse and occasioned scathing attacks on Clinton in the British press. The essence of the British position is that the looting of Russia under IMF shock therapy must be continued at all costs, since the proceeds are necessary to support the international derivative securities bubble, to which the major London banks are irrevocably committed. The British are also interested in the advantages they could derive from a new era of Russian-American military confrontation, since London believes that a new cold war would enhance the importance of the U.S.–UK "special relationship" in the same way that the original cold war did.

The British are also angered by Clinton administration support for the Israeli-PLO efforts toward a permanent peace settlement in the Middle East. The British Foreign Office and intelligence agencies believe that Britain's position as arbiter of Middle East developments depends on a policy of divide and conquer which presupposes a continuation and exacerbation of the Arab-Israeli conflict. Since Prime Minister Rabin and Chairman Arafat appeared with President Clinton at the White House, the British have mobilized all their efforts to procure the failure of the Israeli-PLO negotiation. Indeed, many of the same international "neoconservative" networks that are implicated in the destabilization of the Clinton administration also show up as those implicated in the recent Hebron massacre. Most fundamentally, we must recall that the dominant groupings of the British elite have long been convinced that British power and influence around the world—which they are fanatically determined to maintain and even expand—cannot survive without being able to draw upon and parasitize the power and resources of the United States. Only through the ability to mobilize American muscle could the decrepit economy and minuscule military forces of the United Kingdom hope to play a role upon the current world stage, as such recent events as the Falklands War and the Gulf War demonstrate.

In the mind of London, the "special relationship" implies a passive subordination of American foreign and economic policies to British geopolitics and British monetarism. It was widely assumed that President Clinton, because of his background as a Rhodes Scholar at Oxford, was something of an Anglophile, but there are many signs that the disappointed British have concluded that the Clinton administration is less subservient to London than any in recent memory. Since London regards its ability to get its way in Washington as a matter of preeminent and overriding national interest, the response has been the blatant British orchestration of the Whitewater scandal. In conclusion, we have a very strong prima facie case that a power, certainly foreign and evidently hostile, has initiated an international conspiracy to overthrow the constitutional government of the United States with a sort of coup d'état. These proceedings may involve violations of the internal security laws of the United States currently on the books. Certainly such an attempted destabilization of our government is a matter to which American intelligence agencies, and most especially the Secret Service, must pay very close attention. We therefore urge the subcommittee to provide whatever supplemental appropriations might be needed to defray the costs of the necessary investigative effort. Thank you very much.

Issue 9, Summer 1995

CIA MIND CONTROL AND
PSYCHOLOGICAL WARFARE

Project MONARCH: Nazi Mind Control

Ron Patton

This article describes in detail a highly complex form of trauma-based mind control known as Monarch programming, which was practiced by the Nazis and carried over into our own CIA as part of MK-Ultra. Monarch programming creates dissociative structures and multiple personalities using "triggers" or commands. Subjects are used for covert operations, prostitution, and pornography. This article describes the methods with which these dispensable slaves are programmed for use as "plants" for infiltration purposes and as "sleeper assassins."

AMID THE SUBTLE CEREBRAL CIRCUMVENTION of the gullible populace, through a multitude of manipulated media, lies one of the most diabolical atrocities perpetrated upon a segment of the human race: a form of systematic mind control which has permeated every aspect of society for almost fifty years.

To objectively ascertain the following, one may need to reexamine preconceived ideologies relating to the dualistic nature of mankind. Resolving the philosophical question of whether we are inherently good or inherently evil is tantamount to shaping our perception of reality— specifically, the spiritual variable within the equation of life.

This exposition is substantiated by declassified U.S. government documents, individuals formerly connected to the U.S. intelligence communities, historical writings, researchers knowledgeable in mind control, publications from mental health practitioners, and interviews taken from survivors unwittingly subjected to a highly complex form of trauma-based mind control known as MONARCH programming.

A word of caution for survivors of intensively systematic mind control and/or some form of ritualized abuse: There are numerous "triggers" in this article; therefore, unless appropriate support systems are in place or you have a thoroughly reintegrated personality, we recommend you read no further.

A Brief History of Control

The mystery religions of ancient Egypt, Greece, India, and Babylon helped lay the foundation for occultism, meaning "hidden knowledge." One of the earliest writings giving reference to occultism is the *Egyptian Book of the Dead*, a compilation of rituals explicitly describing methods of torture and intimidation (to create trauma), the use of potions (drugs), and the casting of spells (hypnotism), ultimately resulting in the total enslavement of the initiate.[1] These have been the main ingredients for a part of occultism known as Satanism throughout the ages.

During the thirteenth century, the Roman Catholic Church increased and solidified its dominion throughout Europe with the infamous Inquisition. Satanism survived this period of persecution, deeply entrenching itself behind the veil of various esoteric groups.

In 1776 a Bavarian Jesuit by the name of Adam Weishaupt was commissioned by the house of Rothschild to centralize the power base of the mystery religions into what is commonly known as the Illuminati, meaning "Enlightened Ones." This was an amalgamation of powerful occultic bloodlines, elite secret societies, and influential Masonic fraternities with the desire to construct the framework for a "new world order." The outward goal of this utopia was to bring forth universal happiness to the human race. However, their underlying intention was to gradually increase control over the masses, thus becoming masters of the planet.

The Anglo Alliance

By the nineteenth century Great Britain and Germany were recognized as the primary geographic areas of Illuminati control. It then should be of little surprise to know the first work in behavioral science research was established in England in 1882, while much of the early medical and psychiatric techniques involved in mind control were pioneered at the Kaiser Wilhelm Institute in Germany.

The Tavistock Institute of Human Relations was set up in London in 1921 to study the "breaking point" of humans. Kurt Lewin, a German psychologist, became director of the Tavistock Institute in 1932, about the same time Nazi Germany was increasing its research into neuropsy-chology, parapsychology, and multigenerational occultism. Interest-ingly, a progressive exchange of scientific ideas was taking place between England and Germany, most notably in the field of eugenics: the movement devoted to "improving" the human species through the control of hereditary factors in mating. The nefariously enigmatic union between the two countries was bonded, partly through the Order of the Golden Dawn, a secret society which consisted of many high-ranking officials in the Nazi Party and British aristocracy.

Top SS Nazi officer Heinrich Himmler was in charge of a scientific project called Lebensborn, which included selective breeding and adop-tion of children, a peculiarly large number of twins among them.[2] The purpose of the program was to create a superrace (Aryans) that would have total allegiance to the cause of the Third Reich (New Order). Much of the preliminary experimentation concerning genetic engineer-ing and behavior modification was conducted by Dr. Josef Mengele at Auschwitz, where he coldly analyzed the effects of trauma bonding, eye coloring, and "twinning" upon his victims.

Besides the insidious surgical experimentation performed at the con-centration camp, some of the children were subjected to massive amounts of electroshock. Sadly, many of them did not survive the bru-tality. Concurrently, at Dachau, "brainwashing" was carried out on inmates, who were placed under hypnosis and given the hallucinogenic drug mescaline. During the war parallel behavioral research was led by Dr. George Estabrooks of Colgate University. His involvement with the army, CID, FBI, and other agencies remains shrouded in secrecy. How-ever, Estabrooks would occasionally "slip" and discuss his work in-volving the creation of hypno-programmed couriers and hypnotically induced split personalities.[3]

After World War II, the U.S. Department of Defense secretly im-ported many of the top German Nazi and Italian Fascist scientists and spies into the United States via South America and the Vatican. The code name for this operation was Project PAPERCLIP.[4] One of the more prominent finds for the United States was German general Rein-hard Gehlen, Hitler's chief of intelligence against Russia. Upon arriving in Washington, D.C., in 1945, Gehlen met extensively with President Truman, General William "Wild Bill" Donovan, director of the Office of Strategic Services (OSS), and Allen Dulles, who would later become the stalwart head of the Central Intelligence Agency. The objective of their brainstorming sessions was to reorganize the nominal American intelligence operation, transforming it into a highly efficient covert organization. The culmination of their efforts produced the Central Intelligence Group in 1946, renamed the Central Intelligence Agency (CIA) in 1947.

Reinhard Gehlen also had profound influence in helping to create the National Security Council, from which the National Security Act of 1947 was derived. This particular piece of legislation was implemented to protect an unconscionable number of illegal government activities, including clandestine mind control programs.

The Evolution of Project MK ULTRA

With the CIA and National Security Council firmly established, the first in a series of covert brainwashing programs was initiated by the navy in the fall of 1947. Project CHATTER was developed in response to the Soviet's "successes" through the use of "truth drugs." This rationale, however, was simply a cover story if the program were to be exposed. The research focused on the identification and testing of such drugs for use in interrogations and the recruitment of agents.[5] The project was officially terminated in 1953.

The CIA decided to expand their efforts in the area of behavior modification with the advent of Project BLUEBIRD, approved by Director Allen Dulles, in 1950. Its objectives were to (1) discover a means of conditioning personnel to prevent unauthorized extraction of information from them by known means; (2) investigate the possibility of control of an individual by application of special interrogation techniques; (3) investigate memory enhancement; and (4) establish defensive means for preventing hostile control of Agency personnel. In August 1951 Project BLUEBIRD was renamed Project ARTICHOKE, which evaluated offensive uses of interrogation techniques, including hypnosis and drugs. The program ceased in 1956. Three years prior to the halt of Project ARTICHOKE, Project MK ULTRA came into existence, on April 13, 1953, along the lines proposed by Richard Helms, deputy director of Central Intelligence CDCI with the rationale of establishing a "special funding mechanism of extreme sensitivity."[6]

The hypothetical etymology of "MK" may possibly stand for "Mind Kontrolle." The obvious translation of the German word "Kontrolle" into English is "control."[7] A host of German doctors, procured from the postwar Nazi talent pool, were an invaluable asset toward the development of MK ULTRA. The correlation between the concentration camp experiments and the numerous subprojects of MK ULTRA are clearly evident. The various avenues used to control human behavior under MK ULTRA included radiation, electroshock, psychology, psychiatry, sociology, anthropology, graphology, harassment substances, and paramilitary devices and materials (LSD being the most widely dispensed "material"). A special procedure, designated MK DELTA, was established to govern the use of MK ULTRA abroad. MK ULTRA/ MK DELTA materials were used for harassment, discrediting, or disabling purposes.[8]

Of the 149 subprojects under the umbrella of MK ULTRA which have been identified, Project MONARCH, officially begun by the U.S. Army in the early 1960s (although unofficially implemented much earlier), appears to be the most prominent and is still classified "TOP SECRET" for "national security" reasons. MONARCH may have culminated from MK SEARCH subprojects, such as operation SPELL-BINDER, which was set up to create "sleeper" assassins (such as "Manchurian candidates") who could be activated upon receiving a key word or phrase while in a posthypnotic trance. Operation OFTEN, a study which attempted to harness the power of occultic forces, was possibly one of several cover programs to hide the insidious reality of Project MONARCH.

Definition and Description

The name MONARCH is not necessarily defined within the context of royal nobility, but rather refers to the monarch butterfly. When a person is undergoing trauma induced by electroshock, a feeling of light-headedness is evidenced, as if one is floating or fluttering like a butterfly. There is also a symbolic representation pertaining to the transformation or metamorphosis of this beautiful insect: from a caterpillar to a cocoon (dormancy, inactivity) to a butterfly (new creation) which will return to its point of origin. Such is the migratory pattern that makes this species unique.

Occultic symbolism may give additional insight into the true meaning. Psyche is the word for both "soul" and "butterfly," coming from the belief that human souls become butterflies while searching for a new incarnation.[9]

Some ancient mystical groups, such as the Gnostics, saw the butterfly as a symbol of corrupt flesh. The "Angel of Death" (remember Mengele?) in Gnostic artwork was portrayed crushing the butterfly.[10] A marionette is a puppet that is attached to strings and is controlled by the puppet master, hence MONARCH programming is also referred to as the "Marionette syndrome." "Imperial conditioning" is another term used, while some mental health therapists know it as "conditioned stimulus response sequences."

Project MONARCH could be best described as a form of trauma-structured dissociation and occultic integration, in order to compartmentalize the mind into multiple personalities within a systematic framework. During this process, a Satanic ritual, usually including cabalistic mysticism, is performed with the purpose of attaching a particular demon or group of demons to the corresponding alter(s). Of course, most skeptics would view this as simply a means to enhance trauma within the victim, negating any irrational belief that demonic possession actually occurs.

Alters and Triggers

Another way of examining this convoluted victimization of body and soul is by looking at it as a complex computer program: A file (alter) is created through trauma, repetition, and reinforcement. In order to activate (trigger) the file, a specific access code or password (cue or command) is required. The victim-survivor is called a "slave" by the programmer-handler, who in turn is perceived as "master" or "god." About 75 percent are female, since they possess a higher tolerance for pain and tend to dissociate easier than males. Subjects are used mainly for covert operations, prostitution, and pornography; involvement in the entertainment industry is notable.

A former military officer connected to the DIA (Defense Intelligence Agency) told this writer, "In the 'big picture' these people [MONARCH victims] are in all walks of life, from the bum on the street to the white-collar guy." In corroboration, a retired CIA agent vaguely discussed the use of such personnel as "plants" or "chameleons" for the purpose of infiltrating a designated group, gathering information, or injecting an ulterior agenda.

There are an inordinate number of alters in the victim-survivor, with numerous backup programs, mirrors, and shadows. A division of light-side (good) and dark-side (bad) alters are interwoven in the mind and rotate on an axis. One of the main internal structures (of which there are many) within the system is shaped like a double helix, consisting of seven levels. Each system has an internal programmer which oversees the "gatekeepers" (demons?), who grant or deny entry into the different rooms. A few of the internal images predominately seen by victims-survivors are trees, the cabalistic "Tree of Life," with adjoining root systems, infinity loops, ancient symbols and letters, spiderwebs, mirrors or glass shattering, masks, castles, mazes, demons or monsters or aliens, seashells, butterflies, snakes, ribbons, bows, flowers, hourglasses, clocks, robots, chain-of-command diagrams, or schematics of computer circuitry boards.

Bloodlines and Twinning

A majority of the victims-survivors come from multigenerational Satanic families (bloodlines) and are ostensibly programmed "to fulfill their destiny as the chosen ones or chosen generations" (a term coined by Mengele at Auschwitz). Some are adopted out to families of similar origin. Others used in this neurological nightmare are deemed the "expendable ones" (nonbloodliners), usually coming from orphanages, foster care homes, or incestuous families with a long history of pedophilia. There also appears to be a pattern of family members affiliated with government or military intelligence agencies.

Many of the abused come from families who use Catholicism, Mormonism, or charismatic Christianity as a "front" for their abominable activities (though members of other religious groups are also involved). Victims-survivors generally respond more readily to a rigid religious (dogmatic, legalistic) hierarchical structure because it parallels their base programming. Authority usually goes unchallenged, as their will has been usurped through subjective and command-oriented conditioning.

Physical identification characteristics on victims-survivors often include multiple electrical prod scars or resultant moles on their skin. A few may have had various parts of their bodies mutilated by knives, branding irons, or needles. Butterfly or occult tattoos are also common. Generally bloodliners are less likely to have the subsequent markings, as their skin is to "remain pure and unblemished."

The ultimate purpose of the sophisticated manipulation of these individuals may sound unrealistic, depending upon our interpretive understanding of the physical and spiritual realms. The deepest and darkest alters within bloodliners are purported to be dormant until the "Antichrist" is revealed. These New World Order alters supposedly contain callback orders and instructions to train or initiate a large influx of people (possibly clones or "soulless ones"), thereby stimulating social control programs into the new millennium.

Nonbiological "twinning" is yet another bizarre feature observed within MONARCH programming. For instance, two young nonrelated children would be ceremoniously initiated in a magical "soul-bonding" ritual so they might be "inseparably paired for eternity" (possibly another Mengele connection?). They essentially share two halves of the programmed information, making them interdependent upon one another. Paranormal phenomenon such as astral projection, telepathy, ESP, and the like appear to be more pronounced between those who have undergone this process.

Levels of MONARCH Programming[11]

ALPHA. Regarded as "general" or regular programming within the base control personality; characterized by extremely pronounced memory retention, along with substantially increased physical strength and visual acuity. Alpha programming is accomplished through deliberately subdividing the victim's personality, which, in essence, causes a left brain–right brain division, allowing for a programmed union of L and R through neuron pathway stimulation.

BETA. Referred to as "sexual" programming. This programming eliminates all learned moral convictions and stimulates the primitive sexual instincts, devoid of inhibitions. "Cat" alters may come out at this level.

DELTA. This is known as "killer" programming, originally developed for training special agents or elite soldiers (such as the Delta Force, First Earth Battalion, Mossad, and so on) in covert operations. Optimal adrenal output and controlled aggression is evident. Subjects are devoid of fear and very systematic in carrying out their assignment. Self-destruct or suicide instructions are layered in at this level.

THETA. Considered to be "psychic" programming. Bloodliners (those coming from multigenerational Satanic families) were determined to exhibit a greater propensity for having telepathic abilities than did nonbloodliners. Owing to its evident limitations, however, various forms of electronic mind control systems were developed and introduced, namely, biomedical human telemetry devices (brain implants), directed-energy lasers using microwaves or electromagnetics. It is reported these are used in conjunction with highly advanced computers and sophisticated satellite tracking systems.

OMEGA. A "self-destruct" form of programming, also known as "Code Green." The corresponding behaviors include suicidal tendencies or self-mutilation. This program is generally activated when the victim-survivor begins therapy or interrogation and too much memory is being recovered.

GAMMA. Another form of system protection is through "deception" programming, which elicits misinformation and misdirection. This level is intertwined with demonology and tends to regenerate itself at a later time if deactivated inappropriately.

Methods and Components

The initial process begins with creating dissociation within the subject, usually occurring from the time of birth to about six years. This is achieved primarily through the use of electroshock and is at times performed even when the child is in the mother's womb. Owing to the severe trauma induced through electroshock therapy, sexual abuse, and other methods, the mind splits off into alternate personalities from the core. Formerly referred to as multiple personality disorder (MPD), it is presently recognized as dissociative identity disorder (DID) and is the basis for MONARCH programming. Further conditioning of the victim's mind is enhanced through hypnotism, double-bind coercion, pleasure-pain reversals, food, water, and sleep and sensory deprivation, along with various drugs which alter certain cerebral functions.

The next stage is to embed and compress detailed commands or messages within the specified alter. This is achieved through the use of high-tech headsets, in conjunction with computer-driven generators which emit inaudible sound waves or harmonics that affect the RNA covering of neuron pathways to the subconscious and unconscious mind. "Virtual reality" optical devices are sometimes used simultaneously with the harmonic generators projecting pulsating colored lights, subliminals, and split-screen visuals. High-voltage electroshock is then used for memory dissolution.

Programming is updated periodically and reinforced through visual, auditory, and written mediums. Some of the first programming themes included *The Wizard of Oz* and *Alice in Wonderland*, both heavily saturated with occultic symbolism. Many of the recent Disney movies and cartoons are used in a twofold manner: desensitizing the majority of the population, using subliminals and neurolinguistic programming, and deliberately constructing specific triggers and keys for base programming of highly impressionable MONARCH children.

A prime example of how subliminal programming works is the recent Disney cinematic sensation *Pocahontas*, curiously billed as their "thirty-third" (highest degree in Scottish-rite Freemasonry) animated movie. In the movie, Grandmother Willow is a mystical four-hundred-year-old tree who counsels the motherless Pocahontas to listen to her heart and helps her realize that all the answers lie within. Grandmother Willow is constantly talking in "double-speak" and using "reversals" ("Sometimes the right path is not the easiest one"); the esoteric derivative being: the left path (the path that leads to destruction) is the easiest one.

In Illuminati-structured MPD systems, the willow tree represents the occultic powers of druidism. The intrinsic imagery of the tree's branches, leaves, and root systems are very significant, as some of the dark spiritual properties associated with the willow tree programming are (1) the branches are used to whip victims in rituals for "cleansing" purposes; (2) a willow tree can endure severe weather disturbances and is known for its pliability or flexibility: victims-survivors of the programming describe the willow's branches wrapping around them, with no hope of escape; (3) the deep root system of the willow tree makes the victim-survivor feel as if he is falling deeper and deeper into an abyss while in a hypnotic trance.

Music plays an instrumental role in programming, through combinations of variable tones, rhythms, and words. Frightmeister Stephen King's numerous novels and subsequent movies are purported by credible sources to be used for such villainous purposes. One of his latest books, *Insomnia*, features a picture of King with the trigger phrase "We never sleep" (indicative of someone with MPD-DID) below an all-seeing eye.

A partial list of other mediums used to reinforce base programming are *Pinocchio, Sleeping Beauty, Snow White, Beauty and the Beast, Aladdin, The Little Mermaid, The Lion King, E.T., Star Wars, Ghost*

Busters, Trancers II, Batman, Bewitched, Fantasy Island, Reboot, Tiny Toons, Duck Tails, The Dead Sea Scrolls and *The Tall Book of Make Believe.*

A few movies which depict or portray some aspect of MONARCH programming are *Hellraiser 3, Raising Cain, Labyrinth, Telefon, Johnny Mnemonic, Point of No Return, The Lawnmower Man,* and *Closet Land.*

Programmers and Places

It's difficult to figure out the identity of the original programmer of this Satanic project, owing to the substantial amount of disinformation and cross-contamination propagated by the "powers that be." The two that went by the color-coded name of Dr. Green are a Jewish doctor named Dr. Gruenbaum, who supposedly collaborated with the Nazis during World War II, and Dr. Josef Mengele, whose trademark of cold-blooded and calculating brutality has scarred not only the souls of survivors from Auschwitz, but also a countless number of victims throughout the world. Mengele's direct involvement at the infamous Auschwitz concentration camp was suspiciously downplayed during the Nuremberg trials, and consequently no intensified effort by the United States and its allies was directed toward his capture.[12]

As a means to confuse serious investigators as to his whereabouts, U.S. officials would report that Mengele was a nonthreatening recluse in Paraguay or Brazil or that he was simply dead (the "Angel of Death" miraculously must have come back to life at least five different times). His unprecedented research, at the expense of thousands of lives, undoubtedly was a significant bonus to U.S. interests. Besides using the pseudonym Dr. Green, survivors knew him as Vaterchen (Daddy), Schoner Josef (beautiful Joseph), David, and Fairchild. A gracefully handsome man of slight stature, Mengele would disarm people with his gentle demeanor, while at other times he would explode into violent rages.[13]

Other characteristics remembered by survivors were the cadence of his shiny black boots as he paced back and forth and his "I love you/I love you not" daisy game. When he pulled off the last daisy petal, he would maliciously torture and kill a small child in front of the other child he was programming. Distraught survivors also recalled being thrown naked into cages with monkeys, who were trained to abuse them viciously. Evidently Mengele enjoyed reducing people to the level of animals. He also would purposely restrain his victims from crying, screaming, or showing any excessive emotion.

Dr. D. Ewen Cameron, also known as Dr. White, was the former head of the Canadian, American, and World Psychiatric Associations. Because of Cameron's extensive experience and credentials, the CIA's Allen Dulles funneled millions of dollars through front organizations like the Society for the Investigation of Human Ecology, which Cameron presided over ruthlessly. Experimentations were conducted at several locations in Montreal, mostly at McGill University, St. Mary's Hospital, and Allan Memorial Institute.

Besides the conventional methods of psychiatric tyranny, such as electroshock, drug injections, and lobotomies, Cameron conceived the technique of "psychic driving," wherein unsuspecting patients were kept in a drug-induced coma for several weeks and administered a regimen of electroshocks, while electronic helmets were strapped to their heads and repetitive auditory messages were transmitted at variable speeds.[14] Many of those exploited were abused children who had been run through the Roman Catholic orphanage system.

Not surprisingly, Dr. Cameron has been conveniently left out of most psychiatric journals. This may, in fact, have been due largely to the public exposure of Project MK ULTRA in 1970, through lawsuits filed by Canadian survivors and their families. The CIA and Canadian government settled out of court to avoid having to admit officially to any wrongdoing.

A former U.S. Army lieutenant colonel in the DIA's Psychological Warfare Division, Michael Aquino, is the latest in a line of alleged government-sponsored sadists. Aquino, an eccentric genius, founded the Temple of Set, an offshoot of Anton LaVey's Church of Satan. Aquino was connected with the Presidio Army Base day care scandal, in which he was accused of child molestation. However, all charges were dismissed and Aquino was never convicted. Code-named "Malcolm," Aquino is said to have developed training tapes on how to create a MONARCH slave and worked as a liaison among government-military intelligence, various criminal organizations, and occult groups in the distribution of MONARCH slaves.[15]

Heinrich Mueller was another alleged programmer who went under the code names "Dr. Blue" or "Gog." He apparently has two sons who have carried on the trade. The original "Dr. Black" was apparently Leo

Wheeler, nephew of the deceased General Earle G. Wheeler, who was the commander of the Joint Chiefs of Staff during the Vietnam War. Wheeler's protégé, E. Hummel, is active in the Northwest, along with W. Bowers (from the Rothschild bloodline).

In order to keep MK ULTRA from being easily detected, the CIA segmented its subprojects into specialized fields of research and development at universities, prisons, private laboratories, and hospitals. Of course, they were rewarded generously with government grants and miscellaneous funding. The names and locations of some of the major institutions said to be involved in MONARCH programming experimentation were or are Cornell, Duke, Princeton, UCLA, University of Rochester, MIT, Georgetown University Hospital, Maimonides Medical Center, St. Elizabeth's Hospital (Washington, D.C.), Bell Laboratories, Stanford Research Institute, Westinghouse Friendship Laboratories, General Electric, ARCO, and Mankind Research Unlimited.

The "final product" was or is usually created on military installations and bases, where maximum security is required. Referred to as (re)programming centers or near death trauma centers, the most heavily identified are China Lake Naval Weapons Center, the Presidio, Ft. Dietrick, Ft. Campbell, Ft. Lewis, Ft. Hood, Redstone Arsenal, Offutt AFB, Patrick AFB, McClellan AFB, MacGill AFB, Kirtland AFB, Nellis AFB, Homestead AFB, Grissom AFB, Maxwell AFB, and Tinker AFB. Other places recognized as major programming sites are Langley Research Center, Los Alamos National Laboratories, Tavistock Institute, and areas in or by Mt. Shasta, California, Lampe, Missouri, and Las Vegas, Nevada.

Notable Names

One of the first documented cases of a MONARCH secret agent was that of the voluptuous 1940s model Candy Jones. The book, *The Control of Candy Jones* (Playboy Press), portrays her twelve years of intrigue and suspense as a spy for the CIA. Jones, whose birth name is Jessica Wilcox, apparently fit the physiological profile to be one of the initial experiments or human guinea pigs under the government's "scientific" project, MK ULTRA.

The most publicized case of MONARCH monomania has surfaced through the book *TRANCE Formation of America: The True Life Story of a CIA Slave* by Cathy O'Brien. The back cover emphatically states, "Cathy O'Brien is the only vocal and recovered survivor of the Central Intelligence Agency's MK-ULTRA Project MONARCH mind control operation." This autobiography contains compelling accounts of O'Brien's years of unrelenting incest and eventual introduction into Project MONARCH by her perverted father. Along with coauthor Mark Phillips, her rescuer and deprogrammer, Cathy covers an almost unbelievable array of conspiratorial crime: forced prostitution (white slavery) with those in the upper echelons of world politics, covert assignments as a "drug mule" and courier, and the country-western music industry's relationship with illegal CIA activities.

Paul Bonnaci, a courageous survivor who endured almost two decades of alleged degradation under Project MONARCH, claims widescale crimes and corruption from the municipal-state level all the way up to the White House.[16] He has testified about sexually abused males selected from Boys Town in Nebraska and taken to nearby Offut AFB, where he claims they were subjected to intense MONARCH programming, directed mainly by Commander Bill Plemmons and former Lieutenant Colonel Michael Aquino.[17] After the young boys had been thoroughly tormented into mindless oblivion, they were allegedly used (along with girls) for pornography and prostitution with several of the nation's political and economic power brokers. Bonnaci recalled being transported from the air force base via cargo planes to McClelland AFB in California. Along with other unfortunate adolescents and teenagers, he was driven to the elite retreat in Northern California.

A sexually insatiable actress of marginal talent (now deceased), a morally corrupt TV evangelist, a heralded former Green Beret officer, and a popular country-western singer are a few others likely having succumbed to MONARCH madness. Lee Harvey Oswald, Sirhan-Sirhan, Charlie Manson, John Hinckley Jr., Mark Chapman, David Koresh, Tim McVeigh, and John Salvi are some notable names of infamy strongly suspected of being pawns who were spawned by MK ULTRA.

Deprogrammers and Exposers

Dr. Corydon Hammond, a psychologist from the University of Utah, delivered a stunning lecture entitled "Hypnosis in MPD: Ritual Abuse" at the Fourth Annual Eastern Regional Conference on Abuse and Multiple Personality, June 25, 1992, in Alexandria, Virginia. He essentially confirmed the suspicions of the attentive crowd of mental health professionals, wherein a certain percentage of their clients had undergone mind control programming in an intensively systematic manner. Hammond alluded to the Nazi connection, military and CIA mind control research, and Greek letter and color programming, and he specifically mentioned the "Monarch Project" in relation to a form of operative conditioning.

Shortly after his groundbreaking speech, he received death threats. Not wanting to jeopardize the safety of his family, Dr. Hammond stopped disseminating any follow-up information.

Mark Phillips, a former electronics subcontractor for the Department of Defense, was privy to some of the top-secret mind control activities perpetrated by the U.S. government. His inquisitive demeanor, strong conscience, and heartfelt concern for Cathy O'Brien, a "presidential model" under Project MONARCH, prompted him to reveal the inner workings of this grand deception beginning about 1991. As the story goes, he helped Ms. O'Brien escape from her captors and was able to deprogram her in about a year's time in Alaska. The controversial Phillips has his share of critics who are skeptical of the veracity of his claims.

New Orleans therapist Valerie Wolf introduced two of her patients before the President's Committee on Human Radiation Experiments on March 15, 1995, in Washington, D.C. The astonishing testimony made by these two brave women included accounts of German doctors, torture, drugs, electroshock, hypnosis, and rape, as well as exposure to an undetermined amount of radiation. Both Wolf and her patients stated they recovered the memories of this CIA program without regression or hypnosis techniques.[18] Wolf presently devotes much of her time to counseling such survivors.

A former labor attorney for Atlantic Richfield Co., David E. Rosenbaum, conducted a nine-year investigation (1983–1992) concerning allegations of physical torture and coercive conditioning of numerous employees at an ARCO plant in Monaca, Pennsylvania.[19] His clients, Jerry L. Dotey and Ann White, were victims of apparent radiation exposure; but as Mr. Rosenbaum probed deeper in the subsequent interview sessions, a "Pandora's box" was opened. His most astonishing conclusion was that Jerry Dotey and Ann White were likely the offspring of Adolf Hitler, based in part on the uncanny resemblance from photos (facial features, bone structure, and size were taken into consideration). Rosenbaum also states, "They both exhibit feelings and experiences that indicate they are twins." Dotey and White were allegedly subjected to torture of many kinds while under drug-induced hypnosis, with each one undergoing at least three training techniques by plant physicians.

Each victim was trained to enter into a hypnotic state upon the occurrence of specific stimuli, usually involving a "cue" word or phrase, and to "remember to forget" what transpired in the hypnotic state. They were subjected repeatedly to identical stimulus-response sequences to produce nearly automatic reactions to the particular stimulus. MK ULTRA veterans Dr. Bernard Diamond, Dr. Martin Orne, and Dr. Josef Mengele regularly visited the ARCO plant, according to Rosenbaum. The special conditioning of Dotey and White was intended for the artificial creation of dual German personalities. Rosenbaum, who is Jewish, has maintained a deep friendship with the two, despite the seemingly precarious circumstances.

Other renowned therapists involved in deprogramming are Cynthia Byrtus, Pamela Monday, Steve Ogilvie, Bennett Braun, Jerry Mungadze, and Colin Ross. Some Christian counselors have been able to eliminate parts of the programming with limited success. Journalists who have recently expounded on the subject matter in exemplary fashion are Walter Bowart, *Operation Mind Control,* Jon Rappoport, *U.S. Government Mind-Control Experiments on Children,* and Alex Constantine, *Psychic Dictatorship in the USA.*

Conclusion

The most incriminating statement to date made by a government official as to the possible existence of Project MONARCH was extracted by Anton Chaitkin, a writer for the political publication *The New Federalist.* When former CIA Director William Colby was asked directly, "What about MONARCH?" he replied angrily and ambiguously, "We stopped that between the late 1960s and the early 1970s."

Suffice it to say that society, in its apparent state of cognitive dissonance, is generally in denial when faced with the overwhelming evidence of this multifarious conspiracy. Numerous victims-survivors of Project MONARCH are in desperate need of help.

Although there has been some progress in deprogramming and reintegrating therapies, a much greater problem needs to be rectified. The Holy Bible addresses this problem as the fragmentation of the soul (Ezekiel 13:20). A spiritual restoration is what is truly needed (Psalm 23:3) but can take place only by completely trusting in Jesus Christ as the way to salvation (John 3:16; 1 Peter 3:18) and deliverance from demonic oppression or possession (Mark 16:17).

The true humility of Christ and the love of God effectively counters the pride and hatred of Satan. Statistically, the road to recovery for these survivors of unimaginable depravity is a long and tedious one, but God is the ultimate healer, and only within His time, through His strength, and by His grace can the captives be set free (Isaiah 61:1).

Issue 14, Fall 1996

Psy-Ops and Cereology: The Search for "Intelligent" Circle Makers

Joan d'Arc

Are crop circles the result of an elaborate worldwide hoax? This article discusses the facets of this phenomenon which the hoax explanation cannot address and concludes that it is very possible that the British Secret Service, MI-5, are behind the crop circle "hoaxes" in Britain in order to pass off a genuine phenomenon as fake.

ARE SWIRLED CIRCLES in cereal crops the result of an elaborate world-wide hoax? Are you one of the fooled who believes that "Doug and Dave" and others faked all the crop circles in England? Cereologist Colin Andrews believes it is very possible that the British Secret Service, MI-5, put the two aging hoaxers up to it to put an end to the crop circle fuss.

According to Michael Hesemann's book, *The Cosmic Connection: Worldwide Crop Formations and ET Contacts,* ye olde shopkeepers Doug and Dave claim to have faked about two hundred crop circles. In 1992 crop circle "spy" Jim Schnabel claimed responsibility for about thirty circles, and Robert Irving, known as "Spiderman," took responsibility for about twenty. If you split another fifty between the "Wessex Sceptics" and a mysterious UBI group active since 1991, you will come up with a figure of three hundred crop circle hoaxes. A 1993 crop circle count in England alone totaled three thousand formations. If only 10 percent are hoaxes, how do you explain the remaining 90 percent?

There are some facets of this strange phenomenon which the hoax explanation simply cannot address: the strange accompanying buzzing, clicking, and other sounds, unidentified luminous objects, balls of light, vortices, lightning, and other anomalous and psychic phenomena. This year, 1996, has been an exceptional one for crop circle formations. According to *CNI Newsletter,* notable patterns have been found in the United States, Canada, England, and Finland. Since 1990 pictograms have become a global phenomenon located in such diverse places as Germany, the Netherlands, Sweden, Belgium, Switzerland, Hungary, Romania, Bulgaria, the Czech Republic, the former USSR, Australia, New Zealand, Japan, Egypt, Brazil, Puerto Rico, and Mexico. In 1990 some four hundred crop circles were formed in northwest Victoria, Australia. However, over 90 percent of crop circle formations are discovered in southern England, in the vicinity of the mysterious ancient artifact Stonehenge. These include the most elaborate geometrical pictograms called the Mandelbrot Set, the Dharma Wheel, and the curious "insectograms." This year's British crop circles include several very mathematically complex "Julia Sets."

According to a Reuters newswire dated September 21, 1996, two crop circles were found about two miles apart in Espoo, Finland, a suburb of Helsinki, on the morning of August 25, 1996. The largest one measured ninety feet across, and both were "highly unusual." The opinion shared by observers was that the patterns were made from the air, as the surrounding field was completely untouched. However, the description of the crop formations in Helsinki's daily newspaper *Helsingin Sanomat* indicated that the grain was "pressed to the ground, the stems snapped at the roots and lying pointed in the same direction."

The main difference between crop formations considered to be of "anomalous" origin and circles which have been simply trampled by human endeavor is that the roots of the plants in the latter are snapped and broken. Thus the plant is dead. The video *Revelations: The Answer to the Mystery of the Cropcircles* explains in detail how circles are hoaxed. In a "genuine" crop circle, the roots are simply bent over and the plants continue to grow in the horizontal position. Separate stems are sometimes interwoven, and there is a chemical change in the plant. Crop circles appear in fields of wheat or barley and less often in crops of rape, rye, oats, and high grass. In the Northern Hemisphere the circles appear during the months of May and September, when the crops are at mature height. They have been noted to appear instantaneously. Genuine circles begin as a swirl in the center and reverse direction throughout the circle. Their geometrical forms have exhibited a marked increase in complexity since 1978, as though a communication were being developed over time. Fields can be revisited by the circle makers, and, oddly, uncompleted circles have been completed at a later time. Stories abound in the crop circle literature of an "intelligence" which is aware of conversations and even thoughts and has responded to wishes to place a circle at a given locale.

What "force" could cause the bizarre swirled patterns in crops? Colin Andrews states in his book, *Circular Evidence,* "It must be a strong force of short duration that induces horizontal growing into the plant, replacing its natural vertical tendency. Once these plants have been flattened by this force the head end never attempts to grow vertically again." The root end of the plant in a genuine crop circle has been bent over in a sharp, almost ninety-degree angle without breaking the plant or disturbing the growth rate.

Andrews also notes that the "force" that creates genuine crop circles must be able to "construct a flattened ring around the outside of the circle, closely following the contour of the circle wall." Besides creating circular shapes, the force must also have the ability to "flatten a dead straight pathway several metres long . . . miss narrow, arc-shaped areas of crop and so leave these stems standing . . . it must be so violent that some plants are pulled up randomly or ejected from the soil . . . and it must be quiet. . . ." In addition, some plant stems on the bottom layer are depressed into the soil surface. Andrews notes that the mysterious force could just as well be a subsurface force, with a "pulling down instead of pushing down force." The vertical walls of some circles are so mathematically precise that they give the appearance that a tubular shield is lowered onto the crop to contain and "punch out" the pattern.

Colin has also noted on occasion a "loud hissing, crackling sound" which covered a distance of about eight meters and was "similar to a high-voltage discharge but far more prolonged and with a pulsating beat" and which did not stop abruptly but faded. On another occasion, while inside a crop circle, Andrews tape-recorded a "peculiar roaring sound of fairly low frequency" which increased in volume and faded. In a British journal called *R.I.L.K.O.* (Research Into Lost Knowledge Organisation), Andrews reported "a deafening noise shook the night air, sending people running for the control vehicle. One person said it sounded like a city coming in to land." On another occasion Andrews reported that a stereophonic noise floated in from the east and swept by twice at about twelve-thirty at night. In the morning the investigators awoke to a new crop circle formation. According to a British publication called the *Cereologist,* dogs are known to bark during crop circle formations, apparently hearing a disturbance. These sounds have been associated with the "whistler" phenomenon discussed later.

Video Hoax

A video of a crop circle which appears to be forming by the intense activity of several small glowing balls of light has been shown by Colin Andrews on his speaking tour. The video has been viewed by this author and is admittedly a bizarre visual experience. As the balls travel above the field, a formation seems to be in the stages of taking shape in a process which takes only seconds. As the balls leave the scene, a large formation remains. However, Colin Andrews has recently announced that he believes this video to be a hoax. In his September 16, 1996, *CPRI Newsletter* he writes:

> Several weeks of investigation into the video supposedly showing four UFO spheres over a field while crop circles formed, reveal disturbing findings. The young man who took the film gave his name as J——— W———. . . . [he] asked me to research his footage . . . suggested giving me 10% of all monies earned by this footage if any were forthcoming . . . [and] . . . gave other details which have been checked out by agencies in England.

It turns out that the identity of W——— is in fact J——— W———. Andrews has not been successful in locating the correct W——— or W———.

Andrews writes: "Many things have not looked right with the film or the man since I met him in the Wagon and Horses pub, where he asked me to meet." Colin's analysis of the crop circle which was formed on the video are troubling, and his conclusion, which is still pending plant and photographic analysis, is that both the cereal formation and the video were hoaxed. Most disturbing is Colin's feeling that "several persons are involved in this fraud scam, and the video-television business is likely involved in it." He makes it clear that, contrary to claims of certain persons over the Internet, no money was given to him for the film, although many researchers as well as television stations showed interest in it. He suggests that this unfortunate incident was designed to damage crop circle researchers and the overall study of cereal formations as an unexplained anomaly.

Video Analyzed

In the November 1 issue of *CNI Newsletter,* Dan Drasin analyzed the same crop circle video and concluded that it was authentic. He states: "I will leave it to others to deal with the circumstances and personalities involved in making and releasing this tape" and limits his commentary to the film itself. Drasin has a background in cinematography as well as still photography and has a "solid understanding of motion picture special effects, computer graphics, and computer video techniques." The video he analyzed was at least third generational and was fairly grainy. His description of the action shots of the film follow.

Drasin explains that it appears to be early morning and the sky is overcast, lighting is uniform, no clear shadows are visible. In the second shot, the camera "starts with a wide-angle view of the largest and most central field and then zooms in as two glowing BOLs [balls of light] (three to six feet in diameter, thirty to fifty feet in altitude) appear at the far center of the frame and loop around the right side into the foreground. . . ." The BOLs continue to circle the central part of the field, circling clockwise, while a "disturbance" begins to appear in the crop. This disturbance expands in an outward, spiraling motion as the crop stalks lie down in a circular fashion. The spiraling works its way outward from the center, going "through several revolutions," and terminates at the outer edge of the circle. Only one second has passed so far, when six "satellite circles" begin to form simultaneously in the manner just described. In addition, six "spokes" connecting the satellites have formed at the same time. Three seconds at most were required to complete the entire configuration. The two BOLs which have appeared to be responsible for creating the configuration head toward the far right edge of the frame, and a third BOL enters the frame and follows a similar path. The third BOL slips out of the frame for a moment and reappears, followed by a fourth, less luminous BOL (which may have split off from the third one, although a splitting off is not viewed). The four BOLs then leave the frame, and the action is over.

The observations on which Dan bases his conclusion that the video is authentic are as follows:

(1) The light reflection pattern is consistent throughout the film, the left side of the circles being brighter than the right side; (2) the quality of motion of the BOL is "elegant" and "rhythmic," not mechanical, discontinuous, or jerky—the motion is described as "dolphins at play;"

(3) the perspective of the BOLs grows larger in the foreground and smaller in the background, consistent with real objects as opposed to light flashed from a flashlight; (4) the camera motion is somewhat irregular and jerky, characteristic of the use of a lightweight tripod.

Drasin explains: In order to hoax balls of light forming a crop circle by superimposition, the background would have to be "fixed" and the camera "stationary" while gliding lights over the area. He opines that "to hoax the BOLs and the circle over a smoothly and uniformly moving background shot would be orders of magnitude more expensive and complex," as the camera movements would need to be computer controlled, along with the "superimposed artifacts," for all motion to be in synch. He believes that to hoax (superimpose) the BOLs and the circle over the random jerkiness of the camera motion exhibited in this video would be even more difficult. He further posits that to produce the "quality of motion" exhibited by the BOLs would require sophistication, perhaps computer animation, with the formed crop circle formation being superimposed onto the field in precise position and timing with no visible cuts or dissolves in the background and no change of lighting quality or direction. "This is not to say it couldn't be done," he explains, "only that it would require a very hefty budget, topnotch expertise, and plenty of planning and lead time." The following story will suffice to explain just who might have that "hefty budget" and "top-notch expertise."

Circlegate

A young American crop circle hoaxer named Jim Schnabel has been working very hard to present the circle phenomenon as an illusion in articles published in the *Independent* and other newspapers. Schnabel's studies at Lincoln College at Oxford and the University of Bath are allegedly funded by "an American foundation." In a tape-recorded phone conversation with Schnabel, British conspiracy researcher Armen Victorian, pretending to be an African named "Mr. Ntumba," tricked Schnabel into revealing details of an "anti–crop circle plot" which involved Britain, the United States, Germany, and the Vatican. The aim of the plot was to discredit the crop circle phenomenon so it would disappear from media and public awareness. Schnabel allegedly claimed that the powers-that-be feared the circles "could bring about a change of world consciousness."

The "Circlegate" tapes caused quite a brouhaha in England after their publication in September 1992, but Schnabel claimed he had recognized Victorian on the telephone and had simply "pulled his leg." The recorded conversation is published in its entirety in Michael Hesemann's German publication *Magazin 2000* and published in part in his book *The Cosmic Connection*. In this bizarre conversation Schnabel alluded to magic, dark powers, and essentially something "sinister" at work in the crop circle phenomenon and asked Victorian if he was a Christian. He explained that organizations worldwide had pooled their resources to investigate this phenomenon and to determine who or what was causing it. He explained: "It is not quite a military thing, but there are elements of military intelligence which have loaned resources" and that it had a "spiritual warfare type of angle." Schnabel claimed "they are trying to bring about changes in world consciousness . . . for evil, you know, not for good, and there are some of us who are concerned about this and would like to see this new trend stopped." He claimed he and associate Robert Irving "have support at the highest levels" and feed their information to a "supernational organization."

Crop Circles and Cattle Mutilations

A typical cattle mutilation occurred in the San Luis Valley on September 22, 1996, near Antonito, Colorado, on the property of the Jaramillo family. According to the *Crestone Eagle*, Dave Jaramillo observed that the cuts were clean, with no jagged edges. The animal's tongue, anus, udder, and one ear had been removed. Scavengers had mysteriously avoided the carcass. As is typical of such cattle mutilations, the Jaramillo family could find no trace of tracks, footprints, or blood but did find a pattern of three circular formations pressed gently into the grass about one hundred feet away. Each circle measured about three feet in diameter arranged in a twelve-foot triangle and three smaller circles of four inches were arranged around each of the three larger circles. There were a total of twelve circles in the entire formation.

According to Christopher O'Brien, writing in the *Crestone Eagle,* "A vast majority of unusual animal death cases feature no additional clues whatsoever. Only a handful of cases on record feature these circular markings." He also explains that since August 1, 1996, six other cattle mutilations have been reported in the San Luis Valley, which runs north to south from Colorado into northern New Mexico. This area, which is considered sacred by the native tribes, has a long history of strange phenomena occurrences. In three of the six cases, sightings of unidentified craft were associated. O'Brien has logged over thirty UFO sightings in the valley during the summer of 1996. Two of those sightings are described as "extremely large objects moving at fantastically slow speeds." One of them, witnessed by five people in the early morning of August 1, 1996, near La Veta Pass, was said to be over a mile in length. This author would like to see hoaxers, or the U.S. government, get a hoax that large off the ground!

UFOs and Crop Circles

On September 16, 1994, a civilian air traffic controller recorded a strange object hovering over Metepec, west of Mexico City, for five hours. Another person used her camcorder to film the luminous disk and shortly thereafter sighted a four-foot-tall, luminous humanoid being standing ninety feet away in the middle of a sugarcane field. In the morning, a flattened formation was discovered in the field, along with footprints of the strange entity. A film taken by another person from a further locale on the same night showed the same luminous object landing in the field. Hesemann reports in *The Cosmic Connection* that "small balls of light had shot from it and whirled through the field, creating the crop formation in seconds, before returning to the mother ship. . . ." The sugarcane leaves had been burned in the area where the UFO had been filmed, and the ground temperature in the center of the circle was higher than in the rest of the field. In addition, a radioactivity reading indicated levels three and a half times above normal. Many Mexicans believe that these bizarre UFO-related events herald the "return of the gods" as prophesied over a thousand years ago in the calendars of the ancient Mayans and Aztecs.

The Whistlers

The so-called whistler phenomenon was once highly classified military information. According to a 1991 book edited by Donald Cyr, *Crop Circle Secrets,* whistler signals are echoes which follow a circuitous route through the atmosphere, caused by lightning storms within the circular bands in the magnetic hemispheres above the earth. A whistler is first heard as a click, followed by a tone which begins above the upper limit of hearing, falling in pitch within a second or two. A second later the whistler is seen as a reflection after the signal travels back and forth on a path some fifteen thousand miles long. Experimental recordings made in New Zealand provide evidence that whistlers travel high in the aerospace region where there are free electrons. It is suggested that "something associated with crop circle production is impinging on natural crystals in the ground, or even acting through the fillings in the teeth of the observer."

The science of the whistler phenomenon is explained in detail in *Crop Circle Secrets*, but for our purposes here we will say that the requirement for a whistler to form a crop circle by triggering the phosphorescent reaction in the plant would be "lightning occurring at the magnetic conjugate point in the opposite hemisphere, likely a seasonal event." Since whistlers heard in Alaska, for example, seem to be the result of lightning strikes near New Zealand, Cyr asks, "What precise spot on the impingement band in the Southern Hemisphere provides the lightning that whistles through Wiltshire?" To further pinpoint the source of the whistler which created the crop circle, he posits that "the lightning-generated whistler, projecting from the Southern Hemisphere, would have to occur in seasons where grain had grown to a proper resonant height in June, July, or August."

To further complicate the whistler hypothesis, the magnetic bands which surround the earth "vary from year to year, from decade to decade, or from century to century," as does the location of the magnetic poles. A drawing which has been dated to 1678, called *The Mowing Devil*, shows a devil forming a crop circle. Environmental phenomena related to the earth's magnetic field, sunspot cycles, solar winds, and other unknown factors can explain why the impact region would shift over the years. Since a crop circle was reported in Kent in 1918, Cyr deduces that "the whistler impact region was then offset somewhat eastward of the 1980s location." This might explain why the phenomenon disappears for decades or even centuries, since a whistler cannot swirl crops into a formation unless there are crops to swirl. Whistlers may just as well occur in cities or on crops which are not conducive to the swirled phenomenon. Donald Cyr explains that the reason crop circles are so rare is that the crop must have "stems of a given wavelength" and that circles will not form in certain crops such as heather, furze, hops, maize, or short grasses.

Cyr believes that incoming whistlers from Marion Island and Prince Edward Island are causing the dumbbell-shaped crop circles in Wiltshire. He hypothesizes that the second, smaller circle in the dumbbell pattern is caused by the second echo, and the bar between them represents the "noise coming through the conduit between successive impacts." Cyr believes other, more elaborate pictograms can be explained in the same fashion, since some seem like a "string of dumbbell patterns, more or less flipped over, almost like mirror images."

Archetypes and Crop Circles

In *The Cosmic Connection,* author Michael Heseman provides an interesting piece to the crop circle puzzle. "Sacred geometry supplies us with the last and most complex key," writes Hesemann. He posits that this geometry goes beyond "superficial understanding of a pictogram as a glyph in the sense of a symbol language" and into Carl Jung's "collective unconscious" of humanity. New theories attempting to crack the crop circle code incorporate the study of earth's "morphogenetic fields" to theorize that perhaps their meaning and purpose somehow represents a psychological re-programming of humankind. A theory propounded by John Michell, and explained in Heseman's book, is that the geometrical patterns which form crop circles are archetypal symbols "inherent in the structure of the universe as well as in man's mind. . . ." This new interpretation studies archetypal symbols, which are primeval images, as a language which speaks to the human subconscious, bypassing pure reason, in order to communicate with vision alone.

In his book *Flying Saucers: A Modern Myth of Things Seen in the Skies* (1958), psychologist Carl Gustav Jung investigated the circle archetype with respect to the UFO phenomenon. He diagnosed parallels to Buddhist mandalas: "The mandala is a path of initiation into the core of the psyche, and mandala thangkas act upon our subconscious through form and colour, without our needing to understand their symbolism intellectually." Jung saw the UFO phenomenon—and the crop circles would confirm this—as a sign of "great forthcoming changes, comparable with the end of an era," and as "agents and omens of change in the thinking patterns and psychic structures of mankind." The more people reacted to these signals, the closer this change was. Or, in C. G. Jung's words:

It is not presumption that drives me, but my conscience as a psychiatrist that bids me to fulfill my duty and prepare those few who will hear me for coming events which are in accord with the end of an era. As we know from ancient Egyptian history, they are manifestations of psychic changes which always appear at the end of one Platonic month and at the beginning of another. Apparently they are changes in the constellation of psychic dominants, of the archetypes, or "gods" as they used to be called, which bring about or accompany long-lasting transformations in the collective psyche. This transformation started in the historical era and has left behind its traces.

The psychological experience which is connected with the UFO phenomenon consists in the image or legend of circularity, of the symbol of wholeness and of the archetype, which expresses itself in mandala form . . . the latter usually appear in situations which are marked by confusion and perplexity. The thus constellated archetype presents a scheme of order, which is laid as psychological cross-threads or as four-part circles over psychic chaos, in which every detail finds its place, and the whole, tending to disperse into the indeterminate, is held together by the caring and protective circle. . . .

The division into four, the quadrature of the circle, about which Jung talks, is a very ancient alchemical symbol which he examined in his book *Psychology and Alchemy* (1943). The most important circle symbol for Jung was another "quadrature of the circle," a fivefold unit which he called a "quincunx": a circle at the center surrounded by four smaller circles, in quadratic arrangement, one of them "very different." This symbol, Jung was certain, was an unequivocal omen of coming change. Hesemann notes that Jung would have been excited to see the first "quintuplets" in 1988 near Silbury Hill, with a large, clockwise-turning central circle surrounded by three clockwise satellites—and a fourth in which the corn lies anticlockwise.

What is the message of the crop circles? Some believe they are mystical symbols which act on the collective unconscious to kick-start the evolution of humanity to the "next step." Some believe they are caused by environmental disturbances in other parts of the world which create the whistler effect. Other theories conclude that crop circles are signs of the Mayans' return and a prophecy of coming catastrophic earth changes. Some have noted they appear to be cosmic Post-it notes in a language we as yet do not understand. Others have implicated a supernational organization in a brewing terrestrial war with the evil circle makers. And, of course, there are those who believe the swirled cereal crops have all been hoaxed by Doug and Dave, two very busy little shopkeepers.

Issue 15, Winter 1997

Honey, Did You Leave Your Brain Back at Langley Again?

A Brief History of Modern Mind Control

Robert Guffey

This article describes the process that began with the CIA's experimentation with simple torture techniques, hypnosis, LSD and other mind-altering drugs, aversion therapy, psychosurgery, and intracerebral implants, eventually leading to the wireless electromagnetic variety now included in the much touted "nonlethal weaponry" of the twenty-first century.

Since 1947 the Central Intelligence Agency has been actively researching advanced forms of mind control. A process that began with simple torture techniques evolved into the use of hypnosis, LSD and other mind-altering drugs, aversion therapy, psychosurgery, and intracerebral implants. These developments eventually led to the wireless electromagnetic variety now included in the much touted "nonlethal weaponry" of the twenty-first century. Unfortunately, most Americans don't realize that the twenty-first century arrived in their country nearly fifty years too early.

In 1943, while working for Sandoz Pharmaceuticals in Basil, Switzerland, Albert Hofmann first synthesized ergotamine molecules in a unique mixture he called LSD-25. By now it should be well known that Sandoz's most enthusiastic purchaser of this strange new chemical was none other than Allen Dulles, the third director of the fledgling Central Intelligence Agency. By late 1950 Dulles had become thoroughly convinced that the North Koreans were using LSD as a truth serum on American POWs.

Adding to this conviction was Dr. Hofmann's comment to Dulles that "he would have confessed to anything to escape from the fear unleashed in his mind" by the LSD.[22] Outraged over the very notion that the drug would be used to convert helpless Americans to communism when it could be used much more ethically to convert helpless Communists to capitalism, Dulles arranged in 1952 for Sandoz to ship a large quantity of LSD to the CIA's Office of Technical Services Staff under an operation named after one of his favorite vegetables: Artichoke. However, before the miracle drug could be utilized against the enemies of America, the TSS decided it should be tested thoroughly on the closest possible subjects: in other words, fellow Americans.

Under the leadership of Dr. Sydney Gottlieb, infamous for being one of the first American mind control specialists, the TSS initiated a series of LSD experiments at respected research centers all across the country. Prisoners, psychiatric patients, mentally retarded children, and even fellow intelligence officers became unwitting guinea pigs for this "war against communism." In November 1953 Gottlieb spiked the drink of biochemist Dr. Frank Olson while they and other TSS operatives held an informal seminar at an isolated Maryland cabin. Only a few days later Olson went flying through the glass of a closed window on the tenth floor of the Statler Hotel in New York.[17]

Most of the researchers who speak about this incident parrot the Agency explanation released in 1975: that Olson committed suicide owing to the adverse effects of the LSD. As far as I know, however, even the most distraught individual will usually take the time to open a window before he leaps through it. A more likely scenario is that an angered Olson threatened to expose the Agency's Nazi-like tactics and was disposed of accordingly. Gottlieb's assistant, Dr. Richard Lashbrook, was in Olson's hotel room that night. He claimed to have been in the next bed, sleeping soundly, when Olson decided to step out for a bit of fresh air.

Since 1975 the tragedy of Frank Olson has become somewhat of an archetype for the LSD shenanigans perpetuated by the Agency, but Olson was by no means the final victim of the cryptocracy's lust for experimentation. In 1964, at a Los Angeles symposium on biological psychiatry, doctors openly discussed the results of giving 150 micrograms of LSD to thirty mentally retarded children on a daily basis over the course of two to three months.[13] Remember, in the early sixties LSD was still legal.

Across the United States medical doctors and university professors, unhindered by our current War on Drugs, were ordering LSD from Albert Hofmann for "research purposes" at the direction of MK-ULTRA (the name given to Operation ARTICHOKE when it was combined with MK DELTA, a CIA program involving chemical biological warfare). In 1962 a Harvard professor named Timothy Leary published a paper entitled "How to Change Behavior," which grew out of his research administering LSD to the inmates of the Concord Correctional Facility in Massachusetts. Of course, Leary later became the LSD Pied Piper, leading the youth movement away from political involvement and urging them instead to "turn on, tune in, and drop out." In the second edition of his book *Operation Mind Control*, researcher Walter Bowart writes:

> While Leary had received NIMH grants at the University of California at Berkeley from 1953 to 1956 and while working for the U.S. Public Health Service from 1954 to 1958, at first he denied that any of his psychedelic research projects at Harvard were funded by the government. Yet when I finally sat with him face-to-face after Operation Mind Control had been published (1979), and naively asked him if he was "witting" or "unwitting" of his collaboration with the CIA, Leary answered with: "Who would you work for, the Yankees or the Dodgers? I mean, who was I supposed to work for, the KGB?"[6]

One almost wishes he had. By the mid-sixties the CIA had concluded that LSD could not be utilized as a foolproof method for controlling the mind. LSD was too unpredictable for these cryptocrats' tastes. What they wanted was something far more reliable, something that could be used simply and quickly—at the press of a button, to be exact. Enter, stage left: Dr. Jose M. R. Delgado.

Dr. Delgado is a Yale University professor whose research in the 1960s revealed that electrical stimulation of the brain (ESB) could be used for mind control purposes. Having been born in Spain, he was quite eager to demonstrate his manhood by hopping into a bullring and controlling a bull from afar via a transmitter hidden behind his matador's cape. As the bull charged toward the good doctor, he pressed a button that stimulated the electrode in the animal's brain, causing it to step back, then forward, then back again. He even made it walk around and around in circles. With his remote-control device he was able to manipulate the bull as if it were an electronic toy.[9] In 1974, while speaking before the U.S. Congress, Delgado made the following statement:

> We need a program of psychosurgery for political control of our society. The purpose is physical control of the mind. Everyone who deviates from the given norm can be surgically mutilated. . . . Man does not have the right to develop his own mind. . . . Someday armies and generals will be controlled by electronic stimulation of the brain.[6]

Considering Delgado's penchant for brain implants, it should be noted that a suspiciously large amount of traumatic "alien" abductions occur near military bases.[21] On a recent episode of *The End of the Line*, a Santa Barbara radio show that often deals with political corruption and paranormal issues, Jeff Rense interviewed a Southern California surgeon who successfully removed three implants from two separate patients.[1] Though neither of the patients had ever met before, the implants were identical. I think it's safe to assume the implants didn't just grow there on their own. Someone must have put them there.

Personally, I consider it unlikely that advanced beings with the ability to zip through the universe at faster-than-light speed wouldn't also have access to virus-size, nanotechnology-tracking devices undetectable to the human eye. Even modern earth science is on the verge of developing such machines. In other words, why are little gray men from Zeta Reticuli using twentieth-century CIA technology to track down their subjects? That would be tantamount to the U.S. military using bows and arrows to attack Kuwait. Perhaps Jose Delgado and friends simply need a convenient cover story for their program of psychosurgery. Think about it: Are we being invaded from outer space or from Langley, Virginia?

This hypothesis becomes less farfetched after one reads the following comments made by the second director of the CIA, Walter Bedell Smith, in a declassified document addressed to the director of the Psychological Strategy Board:

> (1) I am today transmitting to the National Security Council a proposal (TAB A) in which it is concluded that the problems connected with unidentified flying objects appear to have implications for psychological warfare as well as for intelligence and operations. (2) The background for this view is presented in some detail in TAB B. (3) I suggest that we discuss at an early board meeting the possible offensive or defensive utilization of these phenomena for psychological warfare purposes.[6]

For some mysterious reason TABs A and B have been lost. As Walter Bowart says, "So much for the value of the Freedom of Information Act."

The Freedom of Information Act apparently carries as much weight in the political world as the Hippocratic oath does in the medical world. The same year Dr. Delgado was telling Congress that "we need a program of psychosurgery for political control of our society," another staunch defender of the healer's oath, Dr. Louis Jolyon West, was proposing just such a plan to the governor of California, Ronald Reagan. West hoped to create a Center for the Study and Reduction of Violence at an abandoned missile site in the Santa Monica Mountains. He stated in print that young black males were unusually violent and required special treatment.

Treatments discussed by West included chemical castration, psychosurgery, and the testing of experimental drugs on involuntarily incarcerated individuals. Furthermore, the activities of the center were to have been coordinated with a California law enforcement program that maintained computer files on "predelinquent" children so that they could be treated before they made a negative mark on society.[17]

Ronald Reagan loved this idea, of course, and was utterly perplexed when the people of California forced the state legislature to kill the program after news of it was leaked to the press.

At the exact time that West's "rehabilitation center" for African Americans was nipped in the bud, Jim Jones began moving his predominantly black "People's Temple" to the jungles of Guyana, far from the prying eyes of the California State Legislature. Jones recruited most of his followers from the Mendocino State Mental Hospital in Ukiah, California.

Strangely, every single employee of the hospital was a temple member. After release, the patients were placed in the custody of Jones, whose CIA connections are well delineated in John Judge's essay "The Black Hole of Guyana."[16]

Given the government's treatment of mental patients in the past, as victims of secret radiation tests, for example, it's really not too farfetched to consider that Jonestown may have been the perfect cover for a massive experiment. This idea is reinforced by the fact that only 408 bodies out of at least 1,100 temple members were initially discovered at Jonestown. Upon inspection of 80–90 percent of the bodies, the chief medical examiner "found fresh needle marks at the back of the left shoulder blades," while the others "had been shot or strangled."[16] Though I haven't researched this, I'm pretty certain that grape Kool-Aid is incapable of leaving puncture wounds on one's shoulder blade.

With about four hundred dead in Jonestown itself, the remaining seven hundred must have fled into the surrounding jungle. Colonel Bo Gritz claims he trained special forces that were sent to hunt them down. According to Gritz, the extermination program became necessary after Leo Ryan was killed at the Port Kaituma airstrip. Gritz states flatly, "Jonestown, I think, was an extension of MK-ULTRA from the CIA, and there are probably other experiments going on."[20]

If other experiments are indeed being conducted, then Dr. Louis Jolyon West is no doubt at the forefront of them. Dr. West has had a very interesting career. Not only did he run a CIA-financed LSD research project at the University of Oklahoma during the 1950s and early 1960s, but out of all the doctors in the United States of America, he happened to be the one chosen to examine Jack Ruby for signs of psychosis. Not surprisingly, he found them. He concluded that Ruby was "paranoid" because of his insistence that President Kennedy had been shot by a cabal of ultra-right-wingers. Perhaps the phrase "a cabal of MK ULTRA–right-wingers" would be more appropriate.

Dr. West, or "Jolly," as his friends call him, acts as a kind of dowsing rod for anyone attempting to track down government mind control experiments. In the late sixties the doctor inserted himself into the center of what one CIA agent called a "human guinea pig farm": San Francisco's Haight-Ashbury. According to authors Martin Lee and Bruce Shlain *(Acid Dreams)*, West "rented a pad with the intention of studying the hippies in their native habitat."[17] In 1993 Jolly was called in as an adviser during the massacre of the Branch Davidians in Waco, which eerily resembled the events at Jonestown.[23] On April 19, 1995, the day of the Oklahoma City bombing, Jolly appeared on Larry King's TV show to explain the mental state of the "lone nut" responsible for the destruction, just as he had done thirty-two years before with Jack Ruby. In light of this knowledge, Timothy McVeigh's assertion that a microchip was planted in his buttock becomes far less laughable.

Some researchers like Craig Hulet have denied the possibility of a conspiracy in the Oklahoma City bombing. During a recent interview Hulet said, "All of a sudden everybody's trying to paint the picture that [McVeigh's] an Oswald. If he were an Oswald, he'd be dead." In fact, attempts may very well have been made on McVeigh's life. On August

27, 1995, WTDW (a radio station in Madison, Wisconsin) reported this intriguing bit of news:

> At the Oklahoma prison where McVeigh and Terry Nichols are being held, the security chief has been fired. According to the *Muskogee Daily Phoenix,* Chuck Mildner ordered that only one officer be allowed to handle food trays for the bombing suspects . . . after syringes and other items led him to suspect food tampering.

Unfortunately, the story of Louis Jolyon West doesn't end there. The July 1995 issue of *Los Angeles* magazine contains an article entitled "The Othello Syndrome." On the cover this diagnosis is emblazoned on the forehead of O. J. Simpson. It turns out that the Othello syndrome is a term created by none other than our old friend Dr. West. Over thirty years ago he wrote a paper attempting to prove that a black man will inevitably kill his spouse if she's white. Self-loathing, he said, causes them to believe that "something must be wrong with their Caucasian mates for seeking love beyond the racial pale."[18]

In the same *Los Angeles* magazine article we learn that West has been friends with "famed Simpson defense counsel F. Lee Bailey" for twenty years. They met each other when Jolly was "a court-appointed witness at Patty Hearst's 1976 bank robbery trial," which is fascinating since the late Mae Brussell did an excellent job of tying in the Hearst kidnapping with mind control experiments performed on inmates at Vacaville Prison.[11]

Much earlier F. Lee Bailey had been the defense attorney for Albert Di Salvo, the Boston Strangler, who was deprogrammed by another CIA mind control doctor named William Joseph Bryan. Bryan considered himself to be "the leading expert in the world" on hypnosis and in 1969 was found guilty of hypnotizing four women patients into having sex with him. He once boasted to a pair of prostitutes that he "had hypnotized Sirhan Sirhan."[24]

There are numerous odd deaths surrounding the O. J. Simpson case that remain unreported in the mainstream media. For example, exactly two weeks after Ron Goldman and Nicole Brown Simpson were found murdered, Casimir Sucharskian, an old friend of O.J.'s with definite Mob connections, was murdered in Miramar, Florida, along with two young women companions, Sharon Anderson and Marie Rogers.[12] Sucharskian had previously gone to jail for possession of cocaine and guns recovered during a police raid on his residence. According to the police, O.J. just barely escaped this drug raid in the 1970s.

During a recent interview on KPFK in Los Angeles, Dick Gregory laid out the following information: While the Simpson trial was still in progress, Michael Nigg, a close friend of Ron Goldman's, was also murdered under mysterious circumstances. Early in September 1995 he was walking down the street with a woman named Julia Long when two men held him up at gunpoint, said it was a stickup, shot him, neglected to steal anything, didn't touch the woman, and then took off.[12] Unless these were a special brand of surrealist muggers, I can only conclude that something rather fishy occurred that night. Furthermore, on that same day Judge Ito broke down and cried in court because a friend of his, a deputy sheriff involved with the Simpson case, had been killed. According to Gregory, three reporters investigating the Simpson-Goldman murders were also killed under suspicious circumstances.

Perhaps most relevant to the specific focus of this essay, however, is researcher Alex Constantine's report that one of the jurors tried to commit suicide by eating glass after "hearing voices" in her head.[8] As if all that weren't enough, Nicole Simpson's next-door neighbor turned out to be Carl Colby, the son of William Colby, director of the CIA during the Nixon administration.[10 2]

Coupled with the involvement of F. Lee Bailey and Louis Jolyon West, these "coincidences" begin to point toward some form of Mob-intelligence involvement in the O. J. Simpson case. In the wake of the Simpson trial, one often sees airhead politicians staring into the TV camera with worry in their eyes, lamenting over the rise of violence in society today. They would have you believe that this is due to the eradication of family values. Meanwhile, the only values these politicians have are Manson family values, for these are the same officials backing the research of mad scientists like Jose Delgado.

In the mid-seventies Delgado abandoned his research into direct electrical stimulation of the brain in favor of electromagnetic fields (EMFs) that would affect certain areas of the brain from outside without the need of cumbersome bioimplants, as used with the aforementioned bull so bravely subdued by Dr. Delgado. The implications of this technology are quite literally mind-blowing. These electromagnetic fields could be used to instill rage, sadness, or fear throughout entire cities. On the battlefield they might force even the most dedicated enemy to fall to his knees in surrender. Preston Nichols *(The Montauk Project)* has commented on how suspicious it was when, almost before the Gulf War had even begun, "the same Iraqis who fought a Holy War against Iran for eight years" suddenly abandoned deep bunkers equipped with "electricity, entertainment, and enough food and water to last at least six months."[19] It's quite possible that one of the covert reasons for the Gulf War was to test a small-scale version of the U.S. military's Project HAARP.

HAARP (an acronym for High-frequency Active Auroral Research Program) is a $100 million air force experiment located in the wilderness of Alaska. Its ostensible purpose is to study the ionosphere. However, researchers like Dr. Nick Begich believe it's actually a ground-based Star Wars weapon derived from the classified technology of Nikola Tesla. According to Begich, HAARP has the capability of creating

> a huge coherent controllable electromagnetic field which could be compared to a Delgado EMF, except HAARP's doesn't fill a room, it potentially fills a region the size of a large western state and, possibly, a hemisphere. Basically, the HAARP transmitter in this application will emit energy of the same level as the Earth's, which is fifty times more than was needed in the wireless experiments of Dr. Delgado. What this means is that if HAARP is tuned to the right frequency, using just the right wave forms, mental disruption throughout a region could occur intentionally or as a side effect of the radio frequency transmissions.[5]

Though the project spokesman claims that HAARP will not be fully operational until 1998, some researchers believe it's already being utilized for clandestine purposes and might even have operated in conjunction with the so-called tethered satellite, which was lost by NASA in March 1996 after it mysteriously broke free from the space shuttle and burned up in the atmosphere. Richard Hoagland, former science adviser to Walter Cronkite and winner of the Angstrom Science Award, has come to the conclusion that the tether was actually a "thirteen-mile-long tuned resonator" which, upon being irradiated by electromagnetic energy from a powerful ground-based transmitter such as HAARP, was used as a dipole in the ionosphere. This dipole could be used to perform covert experiments with the hyperdimensional physics first described by scientist James Clerk Maxwell in the late nineteenth century.

The power densities required for such complex experimentation are much higher than those needed to effect mass behavioral modification. If one mapped out a true line course between Project HAARP and the possible relay transmitters needed to amplify and disperse the electromagnetic energy across a densely populated area, one might very well find himself on the West Coast of the United States, where such odd and wonderful events as the L.A. riots have occurred. Could these riots have been a mere cover for secret experiments involving HAARP predecessors such as the GWEN towers? GWEN, by the way, stands for "Ground Wave Emergency Network." It's unclear whether the GWEN towers end emergencies or help start them.

The May 10, 1992, edition of the *New York Times* reported that out of 18,230 people arrested during the L.A. riots, both the police and the city prosecutors could not account for 10,000. A prosecutor was quoted as saying, "We don't know where they are." It's a mystery to many of us in the system. Did these people dissipate into nothingness, or were they taken somewhere and disposed of like mad cattle? Consider: As I write this I'm worth as much as the change in my pocket. However, if I killed myself and managed to stick around on the material plane somehow, I could sell my own body for $2.5 million.[13] Healthy organs are always in demand. Now multiply 2.5 million by 10,000 and look at those zeros fly off the calculator screen. That could buy a lot of Patriot missiles, couldn't it?

In a document entitled "Mind Control Operations–Aquarius Group Activities" released by an anonymous team of intelligence officers known as Com-12, we are told the following:

> With a general ignorance through arrogance of most public population in the U.S., the erection of large cellular towers being carried out under HIGH TONE and XENO are largely going completely unnoticed. These projects are being carried out in private business capacities and therefore in Deep Black Operations cover. However, public populations would be wise to educate themselves in the construction of these seemingly innocent towers in large-population areas. The cellular 800 mHz waves are a constant wave. Due to the great proliferation of towers in key population areas, they will have a devastating effect.[6]

It is possible that these are the relay pylons being used in conjunction with HAARP.

Despite Com-12's cynicism, the information about such experiments is indeed reaching the general public, though admittedly at a slow pace. In 1995 a group of psychiatrists and mind control survivors spoke before President Clinton's Advisory Committee on Human Radiation Experiments. They revealed the fact that the radiation experiments were only a small part of a larger operation involving mind control. Though a number of journalists were indeed present during this groundbreaking testimony, none of the major newspapers reported the story. I wrote a letter to Ruth Faden, Chair of the Committee, and asked her if she was going to investigate any further into the mind control aspects of the radiation testing. I also asked her if she could comment on why the mainstream media chose to ignore the survivors' testimony. The letter came back stamped "Return to Sender." Though Ms. Faden was obviously somewhat less than enthused by what the survivors told her, a transcript of their testimony has nevertheless been made available to the public in Jon Rappoport's book *U.S. Government Mind Control Experiments on Children*.[3] Due to alternative publications like Rappoport's, vital information is gradually bursting free from behind the national security curtain.

Ultimately the only way to end the corruption and Nazi-like horror delineated in the preceding pages is to repeal the National Security Act, just as our grandfathers and grandmothers forced the government to repeal the Volstead Act in 1933. This country survived quite well for 171 years without the albatross of the National Security Act wrapped around our necks. Is it just a coincidence that Americans have grown more and more distrustful and cynical toward their government since 1947, the year this act was rushed through Congress without any debate whatsoever? The decline of America has nothing to do with "family values," but a great deal to do with the black cauldron of dirty secrets hidden from the eyes of most Americans, considered by the cryptocrats to be mere sheep simply because they don't have a need to know.

I think the American people should decide for themselves if they have a need to know, and the only way to do that is to organize and rip aside the façade of the military-industrial complex for all to see. This can be done by joining organizations like the Freedom of Thought Foundation,[4] whose primary goals are to "lend aid and protection to survivors of mind control, develop or discover countermeasures to electronic forms of mind control and publicize them, and conduct a tireless campaign to repeal the National Security Act."

These are concerns that should be shared by every American, mind control survivor or not, for as a pastor named Martin Niemoller once wrote:

> In Germany they first came for the Communists and I didn't speak up because I wasn't a Communist.
>
> Then they came for the Jews, and I didn't speak up because I wasn't a Jew.
>
> Then they came for the trade unionists, and I didn't speak up because I wasn't a trade unionist.
>
> Then they came for the Catholics, and I didn't speak up because I was a Protestant.
>
> Then they came for me, and by that time no one was left to speak up.

Don't lose your voice, as Pastor Niemoller did. Don't lose your voice to the politicians and the psychiatrists and the educators and the journalists who "know best," who say, "Trust us, we'll show you what reality is actually all about." If you allow yourself to trust them, you might as well pack up your brain right now, stamp it "Fragile," and ship it over to CIA headquarters in scenic Langley, Virginia. They've always got enough room for another brain. That's why they're constantly recruiting fresh ones from college campuses.

I hear if you work at the CIA, you have to leave your brain at the door along with your hat and coat. One time an employee forgot to retrieve his brain when he left for the day, remembering it only after his commute was already halfway over. Inevitably, he entered his suburban Virginia home to the smell of pot roast and the grating sound of his wife's voice as she planted her fists on her hips (having noticed her husband's sagging head) and sighed for the fortieth night in a row: "Honey, did you leave your brain back at Langley again?"

"Yes, dear," he replied, and promised to pick it up first thing Monday morning. After all, he wouldn't be needing it over the weekend. Misplacing his brain was but one of the many annoying, though necessary, risks of working for the Company. All in all, he couldn't complain. At least it's a living, he told himself doubtfully.

Yes, a living . . . but hardly a life.

Issue 17, Fall 1997

CULTS AND SECRET SOCIETIES

The Mystery of the Knights Templar

Scott Corrales

Were the Knights Templar the real "Raiders of the Lost Ark?" The Knights Templar were perhaps the world's first secret society. Scott Corrales explores the history and bloody rituals of this ancient order of warriors and mystics.

To PARAPHRASE *Star Wars'* Obi-Wan Kenobi's discussion of the Jedi Knights, the Knights Templar were the guardians of peace and justice during the turbulent centuries that spanned the Crusades. Springing out of an original order comprising nine members, the Templars swelled into a mighty multinational organization, perhaps the first to deserve such an appellation.

While colossal fortifications protected the hard-won Crusader territories in the Near East, and Templar escorts saw to the safe arrival of pilgrims on the way to Jerusalem, the order remained equally active in Europe. Its engineers and masons cleared forests, drained swamps, developed salt flats, channeled lagoons, rivers, and other bodies of water, reopened old Roman roads neglected for ages, and established new towns to populate the lands they had obtained by ecclesiastical cession or conquest. The first modern economists were also members of the Templar brotherhood who revolutionized traditional commerce and banking via the introduction of letters of credit and a primitive version of our checking account, which enabled travelers to make transactions without having to carry valuables on unprotected roads and pirate-infested waters.

Perhaps more important, the Knights Templar were quietly, gradually infusing a Europe barely emerged from the Dark Ages with the classical wisdom it had long forgotten but which had been preserved by Arab scholars and scientists. Part of this massive effort included an interest in pagan traditions and in fostering the creation of universities and cultural centers. It has even been speculated that a great deal of the silver used to pay for all these projects came from the visits of the Templar fleet in the year 1200 to Mexico, where such metal was plentiful.

According to Spanish author Ricardo Alarcon, the Templars' aim was to introduce strife-ridden Europe to the concept of synarchy—government with principles, which were sorely lacking in those medieval times. Those in control of power would be automatically subordinated to those whom, by their intelligence and moral virtue, would be in control of authority. The three vital functions of communal living—instruction, justice, and economy—would be represented by three social, rather than political, estates, elected through universal suffrage. Those truly able to guide others would therefore be able to provide them with genuine advancement and progress.

But the work of these industrious warrior-monks was halted abruptly by the greed and jealousy of a French monarch, who disrupted the order and heaped upon them unsubstantiated accusations of devil worship, homosexuality, and brutality. Many Templars were tortured, banished, or sentenced to die at the stake. The death of Jacques de Molay, last grand master of the order, in 1314, brings down the curtain on the Knights Templar and their prodigious works. But did these massive undertakings end here? What became of the order's amassed wealth, its private fleet, and all the learning it had collected over the three centuries of its existence?

Historical Background

In the year 1118, barely two decades since the conquest of Jerusalem by the Crusaders, a French knight named Hugh de Payens approached the patriarch of the Holy City with an idea: a military order that would live in strict accordance to a religious rule, much like the Benedictines or other monastic groups, but devoted to patrolling the dusty roads of Palestine and protecting the flow of pilgrims and trade. This idea was also welcomed by King Baldwin of Jerusalem, who was in desperate need of experienced men-at-arms.

One of the greatest problems in the Crusader realm was that as soon as the liberation of the holy places had been achieved, the crusading European noblemen often wished to return to their own fiefdoms rather than settling in the newly acquired territories. To this end, the monarch allowed Hugh de Payens to base his fledgling order on the ruins of Solomon's Temple, which would give the warrior-monks their name: the Knights of the Temple, better known as the Knights Templar.

The service provided by the Templars was apparently worthwhile. By the year 1127 notable figures in European history, ranging from Bernard of Clairvaux to Pope Honorius II and the count of Champagne, had thrown their full support behind the order. Land grants, money, and supplies were heaped upon the Templars, who would put them all to the best use possible: supporting their endeavors in the Near East. The land grants, which were numerous, were husbanded carefully and made to yield their maximum.

The Templars were quickly on their way to becoming the wealthiest and most formidable fighting force Europe had known since the days of the Roman legions. Then the accusations began pouring in. Ecclesiastical authorities charged the Templars with heresy and blasphemy. Rumor had it that initiation into the order called for stamping and spitting upon the cross and proclaiming: "I renounce Jesus!" The new adept was stripped naked and received kisses upon different parts of his body before being led to the presence of Baphomet. Other chronicles state that the idol worshiped was a statue of a dog or a cat (perhaps the statue of the Egyptian goddess Bastet, which the Templars had acquired during the Crusader incursions into that country), and the remains of another effigy known as the Goat were confiscated by the Inquisition. In the opinion of author Rollo Ahmed, these tokens were meant to represent the pantheistic concept of the Absolute:

> The animal head, usually that of a goat with a torch between the horns, represented the responsibility of matter and the expiation of sin in the body; the human hands of the figure, betokening the sanctity of labor, were pointed above and below to two crescents, the upper white and the lower black, corresponding to good and evil, mercy and justice. . . .

Beware the Dark Side

A substantial number of books written in the past hundred years point to the "black legend" surrounding the Templars and their works, a legend centered mainly around a belief that there was a hidden, special group within the order that adhered to thoroughly un-Christian beliefs: Satanism, homosexuality, child sacrifice, and other abominations. Less extreme versions declare that the "inner circle" was in charge of forgotten occult lore, and likely candidates were initiated into these "mysteries" when the time was right. The Templars' seal, depicting two knights riding on the same war charger, to symbolize the order's vows of poverty and modesty, has been reinterpreted by researcher Juan G. Atienza as a visible manifestation of the Knights Templar's understanding of the Cabala and Cabalistic instruction, which stated that "only two men united in meditation over the word of God can create a living being."

Gnostic dualism, the understanding of the teachings of Eastern philosophies, would play a crucial role in the order's development. In a way, the Inquisition had been correct in its assessment of the Templars as heretics: they had embraced Gnostic principles (probably through contact with the Islamic Ophites) and probably denied the divinity of Jesus, while holding him in high esteem as a prophet or avatar. Author George Andrews mentions a very interesting Templar item in his book *Extraterrestrial Friends and Foes*. It is the alleged transcript of a confession made under duress in February 1310 (read "torture") by a Knight Templar known as Brother Arnold. The tormented knight tells his inquisitor during the horrifying session that his castle held strange ceremonial articles and clay tablets with curious writing on their surfaces.

An even more curious item was kept in the Templar fastness, a chest which could respond, in an unknown language, to questions posed by a Templar chaplain. Pressed further by the inquisitor, Brother Arnold added that this chest was the Ark of the Covenant, which had been brought back from Jerusalem in 1127 and kept at the castle of Greols. The text goes on to say that the tormented man, driven insane by suffering, rambled on about time travel, the Apocalypse, and conflict between good and evil forces on worlds other than this one. Perhaps even more famous than the talking chest is the "idol" Baphomet, allegedly worshiped by the Templars in their ceremonies. This oracular statue, according to the inquisitors who single-handedly destroyed the order, was proof positive of the Templar's league with the devil. Efforts at securing this damning evidence failed miserably, and the "talking heads" remain just another tantalizing piece of Templar mystery. However, in May 1308 Guillaume Pidoye, a seneschal and custodian of the Templar chapter house in Paris, surrendered to the Inquisition a number of statues in his custody.

According to the records, a large head depicting a woman, made of gilded silver and bearing the legend "Caput LVIII," was presented to the authorities. Atienza's research has uncovered an interesting aspect to the Templars' interest in pagan items of worship. During the Christian reconquest of Spain from the Moors, the Templars requested that any land grants given to them in return for their assistance in this endeavor be located in certain chosen sites. All of these sites, with almost no exceptions, are close to megalithic complexes and prehistoric dolmens.

Something obviously attracted the order to these ignored sites, which were considered either a nuisance or bad luck by superstitious medieval peasants. Can it perhaps be speculated that these Stonehenge-like alignments harkened back to an age when prehistoric man tapped into telluric energies for different reasons? The Templars would have no doubt treasured this knowledge, along with Muslim archives that fell into their hands as the reconquest of Spain moved inexorably southward. It has also been suggested that the secret worship the warrior-monks were practicing was a pre-Christian, possibly even pre-Celtic, religion, such as the worship of the god Lug, whose name appears scattered throughout Eurasia under the guise of different place names, ranging from the city of Lugo in Spain to the Egyptian temple ruins of Luxor.

Keepers of the Lost Ark?

Did the Knights Templar find the Ark of the Covenant, then ship it to France for safekeeping once the Crusader kingdoms in the Near East crumbled before the advance of the Mamluks? Perhaps they could have saved Indiana Jones a trip to Egypt. A legend closely associated with the Templars has it that Yolande, wife of Baldwin of Jerusalem, was greatly intrigued by these stern-visaged knights whose headquarters were located over the ruins of Solomon's Temple. Entering their building by stealth, the queen found her way to a crypt, where she watched in amazement as six knights stood in silent meditation around an object that could only have been the Ark.

The available evidence suggests that the Templars' choice of the ruins of Solomon's Temple was far from random and that excavations began almost immediately in an effort to find something in particular that had been concealed centuries before the inception of the order. Before dismissing this possibility, it is perhaps worth pointing out that the oft mentioned "copper scroll" which forms part of the Dead Sea Scrolls describes an assortment of treasures and religious items allegedly interred beneath Solomon's Temple. Could the Templars have been aware of a similar source?

Some history becomes necessary at this point. When the Roman legions of Titus sacked Jerusalem in A.D. 70, they took with them all the treasures of the temple, including the sacred menorah, a golden table, and other items. These treasures were transported to Carthage after the Vandals sacked Rome and were later shipped to Constantinople when the Byzantine army of Belisarius put an end to the Vandal kingdom. The superstitious emperor Justinian, fearing that the captured "treasure of the Jews" would spell the ruin of Constantinople, had it sent to Jerusalem in A.D. 555. The treasure trove vanishes from history at this point, so it is safe to assume that this hoard remained in the city of David and was never taken by the marauding Arabs who conquered Palestine a century later.

It is bold to suggest that the Ark of the Covenant was part of this lost treasure, but the great secrecy surrounding the Templars at this point suggests that the magnitude of their findings inspired awe within the Order itself. The enigmatic "find" was sent back to Europe, possibly to the vicinity of Rennes-le-Château, which was ringed with Templar fortifications, and concealed in a specially built chamber hidden beneath the hill upon which stands Castle Hautpoul and the surrounding village. Was this the mystery at the heart of Templar riddle? Did the Order possess knowledge that the Ark was lost somewhere in the catacombs of the ruined temple, over which the Al-Aqsa Mosque had been built? Initiation into this secret would surely be as awesome and terrible as even the Templars themselves hinted, and custody of this holy item may have constituted a source of great and mysterious power.

This legend is connected to a host of others which have been handed down to our time. According to Michael Baigent and Richard Leigh, authors of *Holy Blood, Holy Grail* and *The Messianic Legacy,* the Knights Templar merely constituted the physical arm of a larger order that remained secret and which went by a number of other names, the "Priory of Sion" being one of them. This line of speculation and serious research opens the door to one of the most perplexing mysteries of our time—the enigma of the small French town of Rennes-le-Château, the nexus for a series of interlocking mysteries which have never been solved even after intensive research by American and European researchers.

One of these researchers, Lionel Fanthorpe, expressed this sentiment when he stated that investigating Rennes was comparable to the peeling of an onion, except that the researcher is within the onion, working from a smaller layer to a larger one. Fanthorpe states that the sleepy village has earned a reputation as a repository of arcane knowledge, such as the Emerald Tablets of Hermes Trismegistus, alchemical treatises, the lost treasure of the Cathar sect, which was brutally annihilated in the mid-1200s during a papal Crusade, and other rare and mystical periapts.

History tells us that while the Templars did not occupy the castle at Rennes, they surrounded the area with other massive fortifications, and it can be logically concluded that Rennes was part of their holdings. Centuries later, Bernard Sauniere, the parish priest, made a discovery at Rennes which made him wealthy. Could he have found the resting place of the Ark of the Covenant and been richly rewarded for it by an unknown, interested party, perhaps even the Catholic Church? An unsubstantiated and uninvestigated rumor has it that the Ark's final resting place is in the Vatican. Authors Baigent and Leigh's suggestion of the "Priory of Sion," followed up with brilliant detective work, proves that this secretive, politically active European association inherited the Templar legacy, perhaps even exact knowledge of the resting place of the Lost Ark.

In 1979, during an interview with Pierre Plantard de St. Clair, putative "grand master" of the priory, the authors were told that the treasures taken from Jerusalem would be returned to the Israeli government "when the time was right." We can only hope that time comes to pass within our lifetimes.

Issue 16, Spring 1997

Is There a Satanic Child Abuse Cover-Up?

Al Hidell

From the McMartin Preschool scandal to the Franklin cover-up, some have alleged that secret groups are forcing children to participate in sexual acts and horrific rituals. Do these groups exist, and are they a real threat to our children? Or is the "Satanic scare" the work of conspiracy-mongers who have gained financial benefit from various books, seminars, and talk show appearances? Al Hidell considers underground secret societies and their threat to our most vulnerable citizens.

IN THE EARLY 1980s allegations began to circulate that children in day care centers and schools were being sexually molested and forced to participate in Satanic rituals. Some religious leaders and law enforcement officials went so far as to suggest that there is a nationwide Satanic cult at work, forcing children to engage in sexual acts, drink blood, eat excrement, and watch horrible human and animal sacrifices. They warned that this and other "Satanic crime" is on the increase.

Is there any basis for these fantastic charges? First of all, it is undisputed that individual vandalisms, mutilations, and murders have been committed by self-proclaimed Satanists, perhaps the most infamous being California's "Night Stalker," serial killer Richard Ramirez. Undoubtedly the pedophile population contains its share of Satanists, as well as members of other, more conventional religious groups. It is also reasonable to assume that the public perception that Satanists are devoted to evil and violence—disputed by many in the Satanist community—would attract people of such inclination to "devil worship."

Consider that Richard Ramirez isn't the only Satanic serial killer. At least two other serial killers (Henry Lee Lucas and "Son of Sam" David

Berkowitz) have stated that they killed as part of two (unrelated) Satanic cults. However, as Arthur Lyons suggests in his sympathetic history of Satanism, *Satan Wants You,* "Even when an individual or group claiming to worship the Devil is involved in crimes, motivations are often not easy to sort out." He suggests that if a conspiracy exists, it is among the anti-Satanist conspiracy-mongers who have gained financial benefit from various books, seminars, and talk show appearances.

Baby Stealers

As Lyons points out, the idea of an underground secret society dedicated to evil and the destruction of civilization has been around at least since the second century. Interestingly, these groups have often been thought to engage in incest and cannibalism, perhaps society's two biggest taboos. As Lyons reports, it is ironic that "Christians were the first to be accused, by the Romans. But as Christianity gained power, Jews took their place. . . . being portrayed as baby-stealing monsters." Indeed, as historian Norman Cohen has found, well into the twentieth century it was a widespread belief in Eastern Europe that Jews used the blood of Christian babies to make Passover bread. Even today, according to Lyons, "We still need the bogeyman to articulate those dark, irrational forces that threaten to overwhelm us."

Secret Tunnels

Allegations of ritualistic Satanic child abuse were behind the longest and costliest criminal trial in American history, the McMartin Preschool case. Because the case resulted in no convictions, and the mother who initiated the investigation was said to have a history of mental problems, many have dismissed the possibility of Satanic ritual abuse. On the other hand, the mother later died of an apparent suicide, which led some theorists to speculate that she had been killed by the cult.

The 1992 trial of Frances and Daniel Keller, however, was a challenge to skeptics. For the first time, clear allegations of Satanic ritualistic abuse emerged; it was the first such multiple victim–multiple perpetrator case to result in convictions (of sexual assault). The Kellers were accused of forcing children to witness a baby sacrifice and drink the blood of a sacrificed dog. They were said to have buried children alive and forced them to watch as they dug up bodies in a cemetery one mile from the Kellers' day care center. During the trial, news cameras captured Daniel Keller twice making an odd hand gesture. Some believe that it was a Satanic hand signal meant to intimidate the child witnesses, but defense attorneys mock the charge as ludicrous.

The McMartin Case

Despite the Keller convictions, the McMartin Preschool case continues to define (and weaken) the case for ritual Satanic abuse in the public mind. Nearly four hundred children were interviewed during the initial investigation, and investigators believed that at least forty-one of them had in fact been molested. The children stated that they had been forced to participate in Satanic rituals, including animal sacrifices, in secret tunnels beneath the school. Some also spoke of being taken through the tunnels to be molested at other locations off school grounds.

Now, notwithstanding the denials of Charles Buckey, husband and father of two of the McMartin defendants, it has been revealed that the secret tunnels did in fact exist. The existence of the tunnels, exposed by private investigator and twenty-eight-year FBI veteran Ted Gunderson, could have led to the conviction of defendant Raymond Buckey. However, the Los Angeles district attorney failed to introduce this new evidence, and Buckey was not convicted.

Suspicion should have been aroused when two of the McMartin parents independently told the DA that they had observed Charles Buckey and others mixing and pouring cement outside the school. Furthermore, the parents had discovered new cement in a side lot alongside the school building, although the school had been closed for nearly six years since the scandal first broke.

The McMartin Preschool was established in Manhattan Beach, California, in 1966 (declared the first year of the Satanic age by Church of Satan founder Anton LaVey) by Virginia McMartin. Among the employees were her daughter, Peggy McMartin Buckey, and her grandchildren (Mrs. Buckey's children), Raymond Buckey and Peggy Ann Buckey. The first inkling something was wrong at the school came in August 1983, when Mrs. Judy Johnson reported to the Manhattan Beach Police Department that she believed her son had been molested by Raymond Buckey. Although Buckey was initially arrested, he was later released. However, the police continued the investigation and alerted the families of McMartin Preschool students that an investigation was under way. Over several months in the winter of 1983 and 1984, some four hundred children were interviewed extensively. Many of the children's stories about molestation rituals coincided.

Satanic Rituals

Many of the children described what appeared to have been Satanic rituals, including the sacrifice of animals, which accompanied the sexual molestation. The children also described having been taken away from the preschool building to the outside through "tunnels." According to the children, acts of molestation also took place in these tunnels. Investigators determined that, in their judgment, at least forty-one of the children interviewed had been victimized. This led to the formal convening of a grand jury by then Los Angeles district attorney Robert Philobosian. In March 1984 the McMartin family members were indicted, along with three other preschool employees, Mary Ann Jackson, Babette Spitler, and Betty Raidor, on charges of child molestation. Critics, however, have correctly pointed out that a grand jury hears only the prosecution's side of the case.

Death Threats

The McMartins and their employees were charged with having sexually abused at least eighteen children over a ten-year period, and it was charged they had used death threats to keep the children from talking. The preliminary hearings in the case took eighteen months—the longest preliminary hearing in California history. By January 1986 newly elected Los Angeles district attorney Ira Reiner announced that the evidence was insufficient to warrant a trial for five of the seven defendants, and charges were dropped. As a consequence, only Peggy McMartin Buckey and her son, Raymond Buckey, were turned over for trial. The trial did not formally begin until mid-1987 and then, finally, came to a close on November 2, 1989—then the longest criminal hearing in U.S. history. After twenty-one months of jury deliberations, the jury reached a verdict on January 18, 1990, and acquitted Mrs. Buckey on all counts. However, the jury deadlocked on thirteen counts involving Raymond Buckey, and the judge declared a mistrial on the Raymond Buckey case. At this point Reiner announced Buckey would be retried on eight counts.

Political Controversy

On May 7, 1990, Buckey's second trial began. Within a week a political controversy arose when it was revealed Reiner had offered a tentative plea bargain for Buckey, although Reiner initially denied a deal had been offered. Reiner, a candidate for California State attorney general, was defeated in the June 5 primary, in part because of the controversy over the Buckey case. It was during this period that private investigator Ted Gunderson and archaeologist Dr. Gary Stickel uncovered proof that the secret tunnels, described by the victimized children, did indeed exist. However, as noted above, the district attorney's office refused to use the evidence during the Buckey trial, much to the disgust and dismay of the children's parents.

By July 9, 1990, the case was ready for presentation to the jury, and after fifteen stormy days of deliberations, including a revote on two of the counts, the jurors were deadlocked. On July 27 the jurors announced they were deadlocked on all eight counts. At this point the judge declared a mistrial, and Buckey was free. According to private investigator Ted Gunderson, if the evidence relating to the secret tunnels underneath the school had been introduced at the Buckey trial, the verdict might have been different.

Celebrity Molesters?

Working with Ted Gunderson, the McMartin parents obtained permission from the new owners of the McMartin property to excavate an area beneath the cement, beginning in April 1990. According to Gunderson, "We found a thirty-five foot tunnel. We found a seven-foot tunnel. We found the bones of over two hundred animals in these tunnels." Gary Stickel, a professor of archaeology at UCLA and an associate of Gunderson, adds:

> The tunnels were exactly where the children said they were. In fact
> . . . one of the children took one of my assistants around to show
> where she had entered the tunnel, and where it ran beneath two
> rooms, classrooms three and four, and that's exactly where the tunnels turned out to be.

If such evidence has been ignored or covered up, it may be because, as Gunderson believes, "among the people [the children say molested them outside the school grounds] were household names: actors, sports figures, politicians." One child, in fact, identified one of the city attorneys as well as a famous action film star as two of their molesters (though no substantiation of the charges ever emerged). Given the allegations that have been made against pop star Michael Jackson, is this really as impossible as it first sounds?

D.C. Call Boys

Allegations made by conspiracy researcher Antony Sutton in his *Phoenix Letter* newsletter, as well as by John DeCamp in his book *The Franklin Cover-Up: Child Abuse, Satanism and Murder in Nebraska* (AWT Inc., 1992), make the McMartin allegations seem rather modest. Sutton has written about a Satanic ritual abuse scandal involving powerful Nebraska elites, a scandal that stretched all the way to the Bush White House.

The mainstream American media has reported only a small part of the scandal, though international media have been more forthcoming. The part that was reported was the convenient suicide of Craig Spence, who ran a Washington, D.C., "call boy" prostitution ring that reportedly catered to White House staffers and other D.C. insiders. The *Washington Times* reported that call boys "took midnight tours of the White House," but this is as far as the official story went.

Spence's Washington partner was Larry King Jr. (no relation to the talk-show host), a powerful Nebraska Republican and George Bush acquaintance, who attended both the 1984 and 1988 Republican National Conventions. Sutton claims that King was widely known for his pedophiliac practices and organized lavish parties involving pedophiles, drugs, and Satanic practices. According to Sutton, prominent Nebraska corporate and political figures participated in these parties. Children abused at King parties were drawn from Father Flanagan's Boys Club and the North Omaha Girls Club, the latter founded by King.

Investigator Killed

The Nebraska State Legislature had first begun a probe of King's shady financial dealings and found almost $40 million unaccounted for at the King-managed Franklin Credit Union. After the initial session, Nebraska State senator Chambers extended the probe to include charges of physical and sexual abuse of children. On December 19, 1988, Dennis Carlson and others from the Nebraska Foster Care Review Board (NFCRB) stunned Chambers's Franklin committee with the statement, "The nature of these allegations is something that is going to shock the committee. They deal with cult activities, they deal with sacrifices of small children, they deal with sexual abuse." Nebraska Foster Care Review Board personnel went on to detail these fantastic charges based on information in NFCRB files. According to Sutton, "Larry King was charged as the 'organizer' of an extensive child abuse–pedophiliac prostitution ring extending into the highest political circles."

Ominously, while state officials stonewalled the committee, committee investigator Gary Caradori was killed when his private plane exploded in midair on a flight to Chicago. Soon committee members began to resign, and the Nebraska State Legislature refused to continue its funding. Meanwhile King was indicted on financial charges only and sent to a federal psychiatric facility in Springfield, Missouri, and then on to jail. Amazingly, the child abuse victims who refused to recant their testimony were accused of perjury and also sent to jail.

Sixty Left Shoes

Like many conspiracy theories, those involving Satanic crime and ritualized child abuse incorporate more facts than skeptics would admit. On the other hand, speculations often extend beyond what even open-minded observers are willing to accept. In the end we are left with facts like the following and whatever speculation we care to make:

In 1985 Lucas County, Ohio, sheriff James Telb made headlines when he speculated that some eighty victims had been sacrificed by a local Satanic cult in a wooded area near Toledo. A two-day dig uncovered no bodies but several disturbing items, including a headless doll with nails driven through its feet, a nine-foot wooden cross with ligatures attached, sacks of folded children's clothing, assorted hatchets and knives, sixty male children's left shoes, and a dissection book.

Even if you're not particularly paranoid, this is scary stuff.

Issue 5, Summer 1994

Rock and Roll Minions of Satan

Adam Gorightly and Al Hidell

In the 1950s alarmed authorities called rock and roll "the Devil's music." In this article Adam Gorightly and Al Hidell explore the historical links between Satanism and popular music. The subject is long on speculation and short on facts, and the writers clearly have their tongues at least partially placed in cheek. However, the article is also a serious look at the way society seems inclined to turn relatively harmless teenage rebellion into something much more sinister.

IN THE LATE 1960s Black Sabbath was one of the first rock groups to break the countercultural banner of psychedelic Day-Glo colors, peace, love, and drugs. Ripping through the tattered fabric of the Summer of Love's idyllic symbolism, their dark fuzz tones and repetitive monster melodies paved the way for the occult-influenced rock of the 1970s and 1980s. This sudden shift in perspective appeared to some to be the antithesis of everything the Summer of Love had stood for.

In Abbie Hoffman's autobiography, *Soon to Be a Major Motion Picture,* he describes a Black Sabbath concert he attended in the early seventies and the dark vibes that blasted from the amplifiers. Everything that had gone wrong at the end of the sixties, says Hoffman, was embodied in the negativity and fuzz tones booming from Geezer Butler and Tony Iommi's respective guitars. Apparently the Rolling Stones' infamous 1969 Altamont concert—where the Devil at least metaphorically reared his malevolent horned head with the Hells Angels' stabbing murder of a spectator—had been a harbinger of things to come, just the tip of Satan's iceberg.

The Swingin' 6-6-60's

But did this devilish influence begin before 1969 and before the first heavy metal devil bands appeared on the scene, crooning their blasphemous ballads? If you look into the psychedelic drug culture of the surrealistic sixties, you'll soon see the hooves of Lucifer hobbling about from the very beginnings of the San Francisco Haight scene.

Anton LaVey, the high priest and founder of the San Francisco–based Church of Satan, became popular shortly before the psychedelic explosion. His church attracted a subculture of occult "weirdos" as well as "beautiful people" who had tuned in, turned on, and dropped out, dedicating their lives to better living through chemistry.

One young beauty LaVey attracted was Sexy Sadie/Susan Atkins, who appears in the book *Satan Wants You* by Arthur Lyons, joining his bevy of seductive and scantily clad women. In this high priest's "Witches' Sabbath" topless show, Atkins played the fitting role of a vampire. Three years later she would confess to licking blood from the knife that she used to kill actress Sharon Tate, when her theatrical vampire fantasy became reality during the Manson murders. Another photo from this period shows Atkins in her predestined role as vampire, wearing a long, open black robe revealing her nude body, as mock blood drips from her lips. Later, of course, she fell into the loving arms of Father Manson, and the rest is dark history.

Charles Manson—who was deep into Satan as well as Christ, Hitler, Scientology, and the Beatles—showed up on the Haight shortly after his release from prison in the mid-sixties. Manson immediately perceived the unlimited potential there: all the hopped-up impressionable minds waiting to be manipulated, including the minds of nubile teenage babes who would in good time and on his behalf commit grisly knife murders for their loving Messiah Chuck.

Bobby Beausoleil—who became one of Manson's most beloved hippie henchmen—was lead singer in a pseudo psychedelic rock band named Orkustra around the time of Manson's arrival on the Haight and also starred in occultist Kenneth Anger's experimental film *Invocation of My Demon Brother* (1969). That film also featured Anton LaVey and a brief appearance by Rolling Stones frontman Mick Jagger, who also composed the sound track. Around that time Jagger also cowrote the Stones' classic opus "Sympathy for the Devil."

After working with Anger, Bobby Beausoleil sank to greater depths, burrowing into the deep dark pit of Helter Skelter accompanied by Sexy Sadie, Tex Watson, Patricia Krenwinkel, et al. Watson is perhaps the most guilty and dangerous of the Manson clan, including Manson himself. Today Watson has found Christ as his personal savior and has a mail-order ministry which he operates from prison, apparently making serious bucks and attracting true believers.

Satan's Top 40

Aleister Crowley—the renowned occultist and drug-sex experimenter—greatly influenced late sixties rock music as well as the contemporary heavy metal devil worshipers. Crowley died in 1947, but his evil spirit made a comeback in the sixties with the resurgence of interest in the occult. In fact, he appears among the myriad famous faces adorning the cover of the Beatles' *Sgt. Pepper's Lonely Hearts Club Band.* While that is certainly not indisputable evidence that the four Liverpudlian lads were also part of the Satanic underground, the Beatles were in fact one of the first rock groups to explore backward masking and the use of subliminal and "coded" messages in their songs. Hence, the "Paul is Dead" hoax and the Beatles song that Manson said inspired him, the title of which his followers wrote in blood on Sharon Tate's wall. (Hint: It wasn't "I Want to Hold Your Hand.")

In the early 1980s Christian broadcasters Paul and Jan Crouch produced one of the first television segments on backward masking. In this fascinating broadcast they played several rock songs backward, by artists including Led Zeppelin, ELO, and Black Oak Arkansas. On one tune from the *Black Oak Live* album could be heard the words "Natas, Natas"—Satan spelled backward—raspily repeated over and over in a growl. Similarly, another researcher has demonstrated that Aerosmith's "Walk This Way" sounds a lot like "Hail Satan" when played backward. Some believe that such subliminal messages are poisoning the minds of susceptible listeners, who receive these sacrilegious missives surreptitiously and go on to perform evil deeds. Such an evil deed shook the small town of Northport, New York, in the summer of 1984. The incident involved three teenage boys, all from "good" homes: Ricky Kasso, Jimmy Troiano, and Gary Lauwers.

On the night of June 16 the three got together in a local park to do some mescaline, smoke some pot, and listen to a tape of Black Sabbath's Ozzy Osbourne, who most assuredly "ruled." Within a few hours Lauwers was dead, stabbed at least thirty times in what police called a "sacrificial" and Satanic "cult killing." Kasso, it was said, had repeatedly ordered Lauwers to "say you love Satan" as he stabbed him, while Lauwers could only cry for his mother.

The police and media labeled it a "Satanic" killing based on testimony given at the trial, as well as the presence near the scene of grafitti proclaiming such sentiments as "666" and "Satan Rules." Although there were clearly Satanic elements in the killing, as well as in the heavy metal music the boys often listened to, there is no evidence whatsoever that the music "compelled" the action or that the killing was part of organized Satanic "cult" activity. In fact, the killing appears to have had more to do with Kasso's drugged-out state and his anger at Lauwers for not having paid him for an order of mescaline. However, Kasso's jailhouse suicide, and the unexpected acquittal of Jimmy Troiano, raised the possibility that there was more to the story. (Another disturbing aspect of the killing was reported by David St. Clair in his book *Say You Love Satan.* He quotes a Northport real estate saleswoman's lament that "the worst thing" about the incident was that it "lowered property values.")

Mellow Slaves

Recently a commentator on a Christian television show was speaking on the subject "Satanism in Rock." Not surprisingly, Aleister Crowley was the first person he mentioned before launching into a devil-bashing discourse on the world of rock and roll, where everyone from screamin' demons like Judas Priest to mellow country-rock groups like the Eagles are part and parcel of the backward-masking demonic conspiracy, beguiling our misguided youth and leading them into the wicked world of drugs, sex, Satan . . . and *The Simpsons.*

To illustrate his point, the commentator showed a clip from *The Simpsons* in which Homer and God have a talk about why Homer hasn't been to church lately.

Heads Will Roll

In the 1970s *Creem* magazine was the rag to read if you wanted to keep up with the heavy metal scene. The hugely successful group Led

Zeppelin was a frequent presence on its slick yet gaudy pages, with stories of Zeppelin guitarist Jimmy Page's famous haunted castle, once owned by none other than Mr. Aleister Crowley. Page is said to have reported various creepy apparitions, including a disembodied head rolling down the stairway. It seems Page was heavily involved in the supernatural, owning at one time an occult bookstore. Another item of interest concerning Page was that he composed music, not used, for *Lucifer Rising* (1970), a film by the aforementioned Kenneth Anger.

Rumor has it that the woes which befell Led Zep toward the end of the seventies were due to a curse upon the band caused by Jimmy Page's endeavor into the dark side. Given the death of Robert Plant's son, in addition to the drinking- and drug-related demise of drummer John Bonham, some believe that the Zeppelinites were paying their just and due karma for years of reckless and deviant behavior—specifically that of Jimmy Page, who was said to be a notorious drug abuser who spent his idle hours having sex with pubescent jailbait girls usually fourteen years or younger.

Standing at the Crossroads

Other performers besides Led Zeppelin may have been victims of Satanic curses, signing pacts that came due too early in their music careers. Ironically, the guy who probably started it all was a man who inspired Jimmy Page: blues guitarist Robert Johnson. As legend has it, some time around the Great Depression, the struggling Johnson made a pact with the Devil while "standing at the crossroads." The deal provided him with awesome guitar-playing powers and a lasting influence on such rockers as Page and Eric Clapton. The catch was, as you might have predicted, an early death courtesy of a jealous husband.

Recently, guitarist Clapton experienced his share of tragedy when his toddler son apparently crawled out an open window and fell to his death. Also, Black Sabbath founder Ozzy Osbourne's fiery guitarist, Randy Rhodes—considered one of the greatest heavy metal players— died in a tragic plane crash at the height of success, while Ozzie and other band members watched from the ground.

And recall Jim Morrison, rock's premier delver into the darker side of human nature. According to Jerry Hopkins and Danny Sugarman's Morrison biography, *No One Here Gets Out Alive,* one night the Lizard King and a Scandinavian acquaintance named Ingrid Thompson snorted up a bunch of coke and shared a cup of ritual blood. They then fornicated, howling like banshees. After this wicked night of blood-drenched sex, Morrison woke up to discover the woman gone and himself and the sheets of his bed dry-caked with blood. This scared the shit out of even wildman Jim, who rushed out of the den of wickedness only to die in Paris a few years later under mysterious circumstances.

A few months previously, Morrison had married witch Patricia Kennely—while at the same time betrothed to common-law wife Pamela—in a secret Wiccan ritual. However, it is important to note that witches (or Wiccans) like Kennely are not Satanists. Rather, they worship the ancient forces of nature: the Great Mother and her counterpart, the Horned God.

Then there's Jimi Hendrix. In an interview conducted after his death, one of his female friends stated that Hendrix had been prone to fits and seizures, where, driven to the point of madness, he'd pull his hair and go nuts, thinking himself possessed by evil entities. Was Hendrix himself the "Voodoo Chile"? Was Jimi tapped into strange spirits that in the end took his life at the pinnacle of a brilliant career?

The song has remained the same for many other rock legends, from Buddy Holly to Kurt Cobain. Even country star Hank Williams and rockabilly star Johnny Horton were said to have been married to a witch (the same woman) at the time of their deaths. After all the gifts of heaven and earth were bestowed upon them at young ages, they were taken away at a snap of a finger. Does this not sound like a pact with el Diablo?

Satanic Underground

In *The Ultimate Evil,* author Maury Terry connects Charles Manson with various rock stars from the sixties who in turn were connected to a sinister Satanic underground of drugs, sex, ritual murder, and, ostensibly, the Process Church, a Satanic religious organization formed in England during the psychedelic sixties. Terry links this Satanic underground not only to the Tate-La Bianca murders, but also to the Son of Sam killings of the 1970s. Terry's thesis is that while David Berkowitz did in fact commit some of the Son of Sam murders, others were committed by this Satanic underground, namely a character named Manson 2, who is still at large. (In 1993 Berkowitz himself claimed the involvement of unnamed others, part of what he called a Satanic cult, in the Son of Sam murders.)

According to Terry, Manson 2 played a pivotal part in the drug-related murder of Roy Radin, producer of the film *The Cotton Club*. Actor Demond Wilson, of the 1970s sitcom *Sanford and Son,* appears to have also been connected with Radin and the cocaine fast lane, apparently working as a bodyguard for the producer. Soon after Radin's messy demise, Mr. Wilson found God and picked up the Bible, becoming a Baptist minister. Like Mansonoid Tex Watson and Deomond Wison, David "Son of Sam" Berkowitz is yet another Christian convert. Do you see an odd pattern here, or is it all just coincidence?

Two more rock stars alleged to have been connected to the celebrity Satanic underground were Mama Cass and John Phillips of the Mamas and Papas. After achieving phenomenal success with that group, John Phillips seemed to be the crown prince of the feel-good generation, a mover and shaker who knew all the right people and made all the right moves, financially and socially. Legendary were the parties at his posh pad in the Hollywood Hills, where a *Who's Who* of hip were known frequently to gather, getting high and cutting deals, plotting the new revolution of drugs, left-wing politics, and sexual liberation.

Author Maury Terry suggests it was at some of these parties that the paths of Roman Polanski, Sharon Tate, and the rest of the star-struck Cielo Drive crowd initially crossed with the Manson clan. In a seemingly familiar pattern, misfortune soon fell upon Sharon Tate, Mama Cass, and John Phillips: Tate, of course, was brutally killed by the Mansonites; Cass soon died, done in by a heart condition; and John Phillips's life was nearly destroyed by his growing drug addiction. (Today Phillips is clean and drug-free, owing, in part, it is said, to the encouragement of friend Mick Jagger.)

Chuck Is Chic

Surprisingly, Manson had other celebrity connections. Prior to the Tate-La Bianca murders and Chuck's ignominious fall from grace, Beach Boy Dennis Wilson is said to have been a Manson supporter. Manson and his "family" did in fact live in Dennis's house for a few months, supported by Wilson. Soon Manson was recording some songs at the home studio of Dennis's brother (and fellow Beach Boy), Brian Wilson. However, Dennis soon became frightened by Manson and fled the house, whose lease was almost up anyway. Manson and friends remained but were soon evicted by the landlord. Nevertheless, a song by Manson, with slightly altered lyrics, appears on the Beach Boys' album *20/20*. The original song was prophetically titled "Cease to Exist," but it is called "Never Learn Not to Love" on the album.

Because he dared to alter Manson's "sacred" lyrics, and also failed to get him a recording contract with producer Terry Melcher, Manson apparently grew to hate Dennis Wilson. Some believe that the Tate-La Bianca murders were actually a twisted warning to Terry Melcher, who was living at the murder scene just weeks before the killings occurred. In addition, a few days after the murders, Manson showed up at Dennis Wilson's house. Dennis was on tour, but Manson left a bullet and told the person answering the door to tell Wilson that "this is for you."

Tragically, Dennis Wilson died an early and (according to the late conspiracy researcher Mae Brussell) mysterious drowning death in 1983. Was this the result of a Manson vendetta or curse? Did Dennis Wilson possess knowledge that would have turned Satan's mighty underground upside-down if revealed? Or did he die, as friends claim, in what was nothing more than a drunken swimming accident?

Before her own untimely death, Mae Brussell was researching the military's involvement with the occult, Satanism, and child abductions. Did she discover certain secrets that led to her undoing? Some believe the cancer which killed Mae was created in a lab and injected, a scenario which Lee Harvey Oswald's killer, Jack Ruby, believed applied to his own fatal cancer. But that's another story.

In the 1990s singer Axl Rose has become Charles Manson's latest celebrity supporter. Rose has been criticized for recording a Manson song, wearing and selling Manson T-shirts at Guns n' Roses concerts, and sharing the profits with Charlie. Why is he doing this? Perhaps Rose is simply trying to attract publicity through his controversial actions. If so, he wouldn't be the first rock star to do so.

However, this might instead be a sign that a new generation of rockers has begun to play the same old dangerous game, courting forces more sinister than they or their fans can imagine.

Issue 7, Winter 1997

The Cult That Haunted River Phoenix

Al Hidell

In one of Paranoia's *most controversial articles, Al Hidell explores actor River Phoenix's little-known cult background. Phoenix's parents were active members of a religious sect known as the Family, a group accused (but never convicted) of practicing pedophilia and led by self-styled prophet Father David. Has the Family been the victim of lies and religious persecution, as they staunchly maintain, or have their friends in high places (including George Bush) been protecting them?*

IN ITS OFFICIAL OBITUARY of actor River Phoenix, the young star of *Stand By Me, Running on Empty,* and *My Own Private Idaho, Time* magazine mentioned in passing that Phoenix's parents had served in Latin America as "missionaries" for a group known as the Children of God. Like previous coverage of Phoenix's past, the mild words obscured a dark and unbelievable secret.

Some two months before Phoenix's fatal Halloween 1993 drug overdose, *Time* had carried a brief item in its "News Digest" headlined "Argentine Sex Cult," which stated that Argentine authorities had taken 170 children (nearly 60 American) into custody after allegations that many were being sexually abused by members of "the Family, an American-led cult that calls itself a worldwide Christian missionary church." The news item failed to note that the group, whose full name is the Family of Love, was formerly known by another name: the Children of God.

Missionary Man

Phoenix's father, John, had not been your average Christian missionary. He and his family had actually been followers of a cult that promoted, among other things, adult-child and child-child sex. Rather than a lowly "missionary," John Phoenix had actually been named the group's "archbishop" in Venezuela. River Phoenix himself admitted in 1991 that he spent much of his youth as a cult member and had been forced to have sex with other children until the age of ten. However, it is important to note that Phoenix's parents disassociated themselves from the group in 1977 and have never been charged with sexual abuse. Also, the group has continuously denied such charges.

Yet most reporters in our supposed tabloid media culture consistently ignored or missed this important aspect of the Phoenix family's past. The fact that his death came in the midst of a major criminal investigation of the cult (based on the Argentine raids of September 1993) has also eluded the mainstream press. And no one has told us exactly why the drug dealer who allegedly supplied Phoenix's fatal doses was never questioned by police or how Phoenix—who had no needle marks on his body—had consumed such a large quantity of heroin and cocaine.

Granted, this might be a simple case of a tragic drug overdose and the timing of the death mere coincidence. However, the more one learns about the Family of Love and its powerful allies, and the way it has repeatedly evaded criminal prosecution, the more one has to wonder.

One Big Hippy Family

Time's sister publication, *Life,* ran an article in August 1987 that is typical of past superficial and unrelentingly upbeat coverage of the Phoenix family. Entitled "One Big Hippy Family," the article mentions that John and Arlyn Phoenix once joined a "Christian commune" and traveled as "Children of God missionaries." It also quotes Mrs. Phoenix as saying, "Our strength [as a family] has always been that we could hug and cuddle." *Rolling Stone*'s Lisa Bernhard does refer to the Children of God as a "religious cult" in her October 1991 profile of River Phoenix, but she provides no details.

Bizarre History

Even without the Phoenix connection, the Family of Love has a history so bizarre that one wonders why most Americans have not heard of this American-led group. However, the cult has received considerable attention in the British and Argentine press, and the U.S. TV newsmagazine

Prime Time Live did do a story about the cult after the 1993 Argentine raids. So the news blackout is by no means complete. Nevertheless, I could find no citations for "Family of Love" or "Children of God" in the massive 1987–1993 Info-Trac database of major magazine articles.

The minimal and incomplete coverage of the cult and its Phoenix connection might well be the result of tight deadlines, limited resources, and effective PR on the part of the Phoenix family. However, the cult's ability to escape unscathed from repeated official investigations suggests that they may have enjoyed the protection of powerful friends. According to State Chief Inspector Juan Carlos Rebollo, who led the September 1993 raids against the Family of Love's Argentina compound, "We found evidence suggesting the Family is funded by influential business-men worldwide."

An earlier raid in 1989 had found cocaine, pornographic videotapes, and children's books with condoms stuck to the pages. No Family members were ever prosecuted, however, and the judge in the case questioned whether the items actually came from the group's compound. Likewise, a 1974 investigation by the New York Attorney General's Office—which accused cult members of a range of offenses, including rape, incest, and kidnapping—ended when Attorney General Louis Lefkowitz made the inexplicable declaration that the cult was protected from prosecution by the First Amendment. (Today Leftkowitz cannot recall the matter.) Even the 1993 Argentine raids led nowhere, when it was determined that a federal judge had no jurisdiction in the case, and the sex abuse charges were dropped.

The most remarkable sign of the cult's power may have come in 1992, when a chorus of Family of Love children was invited to serenade Barbara Bush in the East Room of the White House.

A Very Sexy God

The Family of Love has a shocking history that makes its apparent acceptance by the Bush White House all the more frightening.

By 1974 cult founder and leader David "Moses" Berg had established 120 Christian "communes" throughout the United States and was expanding internationally. Appealing largely to street kids and others on the fringe, Berg had approximately 250,000 converts in 60 countries by 1978. Berg's message, however, was not something most observers would associate with "Christian missionaries." Quite simply, Berg promoted child-adult and child-child sex.

Berg has written that he "found little girls as fascinated by my own erections and quite as willing to feel them as I was to explore their own more hidden recesses." In a 1973 tract titled "Come on Ma! Burn Your Bra!" he declared, "We have a very sexy God and a very sexy religion and a very sexy leader with an extremely sexy young following. . . ." In addition, videotapes and publications seized from the Family are alleged to show minors repeatedly engaging in intercourse. However, reports made after the examination of children following the 1993 raid were conflicting: Reuters news service (September 5, 1993) reported that there were "no signs of abuse," while England's *Manchester Guardian* reported on September 11, 1993, that some of the boys had rectal excoriations and that girls as young as nine had torn hymens and flayed vulvae.

Fishing Expeditions

A pamphlet written by Berg in the early 1970s titled "My Little Fish" featured a photo of an adult male stroking the penis of a boy approximately three years old. A later pamphlet written by Sara Davidito, a nurse in charge of child care for the Children of God, pictured Davidito having oral sex with a young boy, as well as the boy and a girl in a copulatory position.

Former member Abigail Berry has stated plainly that intergenerational sex has been a basic tenet of the cult. Berry, who was a prosecution witness in the 1993 Argentina trial, stated that all females in the cult, including pregnant girls, were expected to perform what cult leaders call "flirty fishing." To attract new members, the young "fishers of men" were instructed to lure men into anonymous sex.

Significantly, a January 1990 letter from cult leaders instructed female family members to restrict such outside sexual activities to men who were well-known. Nevertheless, current members, including Christine Richards, leader of the Cleveland chapter of the Family, maintain that the cult unconditionally ended the practice of "flirty fishing" in 1987, a tacit admission that such sexual activity was in fact promoted by cult leaders in the past.

Berg's own daughter, Debra Davis, a former cult member, claims, "My father was involved in incest with his own daughters, myself and my sister. It was child abuse—sex, sex, sex. There is nothing sexual [the cult] hasn't practiced."

Other former members have described frequent cult sex practices involving children and adults. Joyanne Treadwell Berg, twenty-nine, granddaughter of David Berg, claims her cousin Mene was abused by Berg and other cult leaders:

> When my grandfather [David Berg] initiated [Mene into the Children of God], he abused her sexually. She rebelled. [Cult members] hit her, tied her up in bed, and wrapped barbed wire around her body. They hit her so much—then they spread the news that she was mentally ill.

Links to Qaddafi

David Berg's teachings, contained in memoranda to his followers, extended far beyond the realm of sex. For example, he believed that Comet Kahoutek would destroy America, that the moon contains an underground city, and that he was guided by the spirits of (among others) General Douglas MacArthur and Rasputin. He also espoused a hatred of Jews and blacks, explaining, "I'm a racist because God is!"

Despite (or because of?) these beliefs, Berg and his cult have maintained bizarre associations with several political leaders and factions. Chilean dictator Augusto Pinochet is said to have been a financial and political supporter of the group. In the mid-1980s Family of Love leaders in the Philippines sympathized openly with the military leaders who plotted to overthrow Corazon Aquino. In the 1970s Berg's second in command was Barbara Canevaro, the Italian duchess of Zoagli and Castelvari.

Also in the 1970s, citing religious persecution, cult members found sanctuary in Libya. Libyan leader Colonel Muammar al-Qaddafi was, as Berg gushed in his newsletter *New Nation News*, "the savior who would ignite the young and rescue them from . . . godless Communism and American materialism." Qaddafi is said to have returned the favor by composing a song that was sung by Children of God choruses around the world. It isn't known whether they sang it for Barbara Bush or at another serenade of President Bush himself while he toured the devastation of Hurricane Andrew. In addition, Joyanne Berg has stated that through the cult she "met presidents from around the world" and that she was paired sexually with "very important" government officials. However, no one has suggested that George Bush was among those officials.

The Big Lie

This is all so unbelievable that the suspicion naturally arises that David Berg and his group are the victims of a smear campaign, perhaps one meant to discredit all nonmainstream Christians, people who express racist ideas, or particular world leaders like Pinochet and Qaddafi.

Lawyer and conspiracy researcher Linda Thompson believes that such accusations are being used by groups like the Cult Awareness Network (CAN) and Jewish Anti-Defamation League (ADL) to discredit patriotic and Christian groups and, as was the case in Waco, anyone who dares violate the nation's increasingly strict gun laws.

However, while the Family of Love, as stated previously, has been said to promote anti-Jewish sentiments, they have not been accused of any weapons violations. Also, the idea of a well-orchestrated smear campaign doesn't fit in with the fact that the Family of Love has received such limited coverage in the United States.

There are certainly some obvious similarities between the charges made against Berg and those made against David Koresh—for example, that they are nominally Christian leaders who make bizarre proclamations, have sex with children, and lead a group of brainwashed cult members. But if it is indeed all a big lie campaign, what exactly is the truth that is being covered up? What is the motive? Why would charges of child sexual abuse—a serious enough crime by itself—be augmented by charges of bizarre teachings and associations? Finally, who would have the motive and means to produce so many faked Family videotapes and publications?

Perhaps the Family of Love is just what it appears to be and has escaped criminal prosecution through the efforts of influential friends and backers. Or perhaps it is completely innocent. Another possibility is that given these apparent extensive links to politicians and businessmen worldwide, the Family of Love may actually be some sort of intelligence agency tool, whose shocking and bizarre attributes have been manufactured to divert attention from its more "traditional" covert activities. Finally, there is the question of whether River Phoenix had been contacted by, or was going to be contacted by, the Argentine prosecutors. If so, did the cult want him silenced?

Why were David Koresh and his followers—who were accused of child sexual abuse on a much smaller scale and with little (if any) evidence—killed? Meanwhile, members of a much larger cult, against which similar but far more substantial charges have been made, were invited to sing at the White House. Is the Family being smeared and set up for a Waco-like massacre? Or has the sect been protected by powerful allies?

If only for the memory of River Phoenix, that cult's most famous abuse victim, it's time to get some answers.

Issue 6, Fall 1994

The following rebuttal is excerpted from "Setting the Record Straight! The Family Replies to Misrepresentations in the Media."

THE FAMILY HAS BEEN THE SUBJECT of a number of reports in the American media recently. While some have been generally fair-minded, and presented our beliefs and practices relatively accurately, others have not. In some cases they have even insinuated that our members are guilty of serious crimes. . . . We therefore find it imperative to correct these media misrepresentations in order that our friends, supporters, and the general public may have a clear understanding of our fellowship and the work we are engaged in. Following is a brief explanation of The Family, along with a short rebuttal to some of the points which were distorted by the press.

WHO ARE THE FAMILY? We are a fellowship of independent Christian missionary communities, and our members are presently active in about 50 countries. We have a full-time membership of 3,000 adults and their 6,000 children. There are approximately 750 of us currently in the United States, 2/3 of whom are children. Generally speaking, our Family has three broad priorities. Our primary mission is to obey Christ's command to "go into all the world and preach the Gospel to every creature" (Mark 16:15). We believe that the miracle-working love and power of Jesus, as portrayed in the Bible, is the one real lasting answer to the many problems that plague mankind today. We are also active in ministering to the socially disadvantaged. Secondly, we live a cooperative, communal lifestyle, which is patterned after the early Christians as recorded in the New Testament's Book of

Acts. This has proven to be very economical, greatly facilitating our evangelical mission. . . .

OUR ORIGINS. The Family traces its origins to the Jesus Revolution of the late 1960s. Our founder, Father David, started a ministry to the hippies in southern California, many of whom were subsequently delivered from drugs and chose to work with him to reach and help others. The group grew and was given the name The Children of God (COG) by the media. By 1978, the COG had become established in scores of countries. However, when reports of abuse of authority by some COG officials began to a surface, Father David dissolved the COG and invited those interested to join him in a new fellowship, which over the years became known simply as The Family.

OUR BASIC BELIEFS. Our basic beliefs and doctrines are the same as those of millions of Christians the world over. We hold the Bible to be the divinely inspired Word of God, that Jesus is the only begotten Son of God, and that through His death on the cross redemption was brought to mankind. Salvation is a gift given freely by God to anyone who sincerely acknowledges their need for a savior and asks for Christ's forgiveness. We are persuaded by Scripture that we are living in the last generation prior to Christ's visible return to Earth.

Two of our beliefs which many mainline Christians do not agree with have fueled much of the controversy about our fellowship. We hold that Father David is a prophet of God for this generation, and that loving heterosexual relations between consenting adults is not a sin in the eyes of God, provided that it is with the agreement of all involved, and hurts no one.

OUR CHILDREN ARE SAFE FROM ABUSE. Although much has been made of our sexual beliefs and practices, our children have not been abused. We acknowledge that our sexual beliefs are controversial, but we emphasize that we do not promote nor condone any behavior that is unloving or perverted, let alone illegal. Sex is a very minor part of our lives. But rather than adopt the hypocritical double standard of much of today's secular society and even many professing Christians, we prefer to be honest and state our sincerely held religious convictions on the subject.

Our children are not permitted to engage in any sexual activity that is improper or illegal, and our teens are strongly encouraged to refrain from sexual relations until they are of legal age. If various American polls are to be believed, Family teens are much less active sexually than the average American teenager.

We cannot emphasize strongly enough that we do not tolerate any form of abuse of children within our communities. Sexual contact is prohibited between anyone over the age of 21 with anyone under 21. Offenders are expelled from our fellowship. In spite of the most determined efforts of our detractors to smear us with charges of child abuse, our members have always been completely exonerated by authorities who have examined our children and communities.

QUOTATIONS TAKEN OUT OF CONTEXT. Many of the quotations from Letters written by Father David were taken out of context in these recent articles. Over a period of 23 years, 35,000 pages of Father David's writings have been published. As he is by nature an outspoken iconoclast, it is inevitable that some of his statements can be misconstrued. . . .

Some articles have also quoted excerpts from a few of the more than 50,000 other pages of literature we have published throughout the years. Many of the controversial publications in question have long since been removed from our communities, and in no way reflect the current practices of our membership.

SUPPRESSED RESEARCH
AND SECRET SCIENCE

AIDS: A Doctor's Note on the Man-Made Theory

Alan R. Cantwell Jr., M.D.

Were gay men given experimental vaccines contaminated with the AIDS virus? The government says no, but government agencies have a long history of covert and unethical medical experimentation, particularly with minorities. This article provides an overview of such secretive medical experimentation, along with the history of AIDS and why this doctor, the author of AIDS and the Doctors of Death, *and* Queer Blood, *believes AIDS is man-made.*

WHEN AIDS OFFICIALLY BEGAN in 1981, the public was told that anal sex, drugs, and homosexuality were at the root of the new "gay plague." The first cases were all young, predominantly white, and previously healthy homosexual men from Manhattan who were dying mysteriously from "gay pneumonia" and "gay cancer" in the form of Kaposi's sarcoma. The association with homosexuality was so remarkable that the disease was initially termed GRID ("gay-related immune deficiency"). To this day, gays are still blamed for the spread of AIDS into the U.S. population.

When the disease first broke out, a new virus was suspected, but officials reassured "the general public" there was nothing to worry about. Of course, the health experts were wrong. Now most of the world's AIDS cases are heterosexuals. The AIDS virus (HIV) can also be transmitted vaginally, and one does not need to be a drug abuser, a promiscuous person, or a homosexual to contract AIDS.

The Green Monkey Theory

Where did HIV originate? Prominent cancer virologists and government epidemiologists have theorized that HIV originated in African green monkeys. Purportedly the monkey virus "jumped species" and entered the black population. From there it migrated to Haiti and Manhattan. After the virus entered the black heterosexual population in the late 1970s, it spread rapidly to millions of blacks because of transfusions with HIV-infected blood, dirty needles, promiscuity, and genital ulcers, or so the experts said.

Not all scientists believe the official monkey story, although it is rare to find people who express this view publicly. One persistent underground rumor is that AIDS is biological warfare. Proponents of the AIDS conspiracy theory believe that AIDS has nothing to do with green monkeys, homosexuality, drug addiction, genital ulcerations, anal sex, or promiscuity, but that it has to do with scientists experimenting on blacks and gays: in short, AIDS is genocide. Most African Americans have heard the theory that HIV is a manufactured virus genetically engineered to kill off the black race. Thirty percent of New York City blacks polled by the *New York Times* (October 29, 1990) actually believe AIDS is an ethnospecific bioweapon designed in a laboratory to infect black people.

Despite the general acceptance that HIV came from monkeys and the rain forest, there is no scientific evidence to prove that HIV and AIDS originated in Africa. What is true is that the first AIDS cases were uncovered in the United States in 1979, around the same time that AIDS cases were discovered in Africa. In addition, no stored African tissue from the 1970s tests positive for HIV. And scientists have a hard time explaining how a black heterosexual epidemic centered in Africa could have quickly transformed itself into a white homosexual epidemic in Manhattan.

The Gay Hepatitis-B Vaccine Experiment

Conveniently lost in the history of AIDS is the gay Hepatitis-B vaccine experiment that immediately preceded the decimation of gay Americans. Over a thousand young gays were injected with the vaccine at the New York Blood Center in Manhattan during the period November 1978 to October 1979.[1] Similar gay experiments were conducted in San Francisco, Los Angeles, Denver, St. Louis, and Chicago, beginning in 1980.[2] The AIDS epidemic broke out shortly thereafter.

The experiment was run by Wolf Szmuness, a Polish Jew born in 1919. He was a young medical student in eastern Poland when the Nazis invaded the country in 1939. His entire family perished in the Holocaust. When Poland was partitioned, Szmuness was taken prisoner and sent to Siberia. After the war he was allowed to finish medical school in Tomsk in central Russia. He married a Russian woman, had a daughter, and in 1959 was allowed to return to Poland, where he became an expert in hepatitis.

According to June Goodfield's account of his life in *Quest for the Killers*, Szmuness defected from Poland with his family in 1969, arriving in New York with $15 in his pocket.[3] Through scientific connections he found work as a laboratory technician at the New York Blood Center. Within a few years he was given his own lab at the center and was also appointed professor of public health at Columbia University. By the mid-1970s Szmuness was a world authority on hepatitis and was invited back to Moscow in 1975 to give a scientific presentation. As a defector he was terrified to set foot back in the Soviet Union, but his colleagues assured him he would have the full protection of the U.S. State Department. His return to Russia was a scientific triumph.

In the late 1970s Wolf Szmuness was awarded millions of dollars to undertake the most important mission of his life: the Hepatitis-B vaccine experiment. Szmuness specifically wanted to use gay men to avoid "serious legal and logistical problems."[4] For his study he did not want monogamous men or men with lovers. He chose only healthy, young, responsible, intelligent, and primarily white homosexuals. The experiment was costly, and he didn't want any uncooperative or hard-to-find gays messing up his experiment. Involved in the experiment were the Centers for Disease Control (CDC), the National Institutes of Health (NIH), the National Institute of Allergy and Infectious Diseases (NIAID), Abbott Laboratories, and Merck, Sharp & Dohme. Szmuness's experiment was hugely successful, and his vaccine was hailed as having tremendous global implications.

The Gay Plague

The links of the gay experiment to the outbreak of AIDS are obvious to anyone who wants to see the connection. Three months after the experiment began, the first cases of AIDS reported to the CDC appeared in young gay men in Manhattan in 1979. The first San Francisco AIDS case appeared in that city in September 1980, six months after the Hepatitis-B experiment started there.[5] In June 1981 the AIDS epidemic became "official."

Were gay men given experimental vaccines contaminated with the AIDS virus? The government says no, but government agencies have a long history of covert and unethical medical experimentation, particularly with minorities. Was it simply a quirk of nature that a virus "out of Africa" would suddenly decimate the most hated minority in America?

Why did the U.S. government choose Wolf Szmuness, a Soviet-trained doctor and a recent American immigrant, to head this dangerous experiment? Goodfield, who has written the definitive account of the Hepatitis-B experiment, claims Szmuness had a painful life. Confined as a political prisoner in Siberia during World War II, he was repeatedly interrogated and beaten by the Russian KGB for refusing to cooperate in spy activities. When he could not be broken, they warned him: "Say nothing of this to anyone, but remember. We will reach you anywhere in the world. No matter where you go, no matter where you try to hide, you will never be out of our grasp."[6]

The experimental Hepatitis-B vaccine was manufactured primarily by Merck. However, during the experiment Szmuness was concerned about possible vaccine contamination. Goodfield writes, "This was no theoretical fear, contamination having been suspected in one vaccine batch made by the National Institutes of Health, though never in Merck's."[7]

After the Hepatitis-B experiment ended, Szmuness insisted that all thirteen thousand blood specimens donated by gay men be retained at the New York Blood Center for future use. Because of space requirements, it is highly unusual for any laboratory to retain so many old blood specimens. However, several years later, when this blood was retested for the presence of HIV antibodies, government epidemiologists were able to detect the "introduction" and the spread of HIV into the gay community.

When asked why he was keeping so many vials of blood, Szmuness replied, "Because one day another disease may erupt and we'll need this material."[8] A few months after the Hepatitis-B experiment began at the center, the first AIDS cases began to appear in gay men living in Manhattan. The retesting of gay blood at the New York Blood Center proved that HIV was first introduced into the gay population of New York City sometime around 1978–1979, the same year Szmuness's gay Hepatitis-B experiment began.[9]

Was Szmuness psychic in his prediction that a new disease would appear in the gay community? Or did he actually know or suspect that a new and deadly virus was being introduced into the gay volunteers? Unfortunately, the answers to these questions can only be surmised. In June 1982 Szmuness died of lung cancer. In his eulogy, Aaron Kellner of the New York Blood Center wrote: "It is the rare physician who, like Wolf Szmuness, is given the grace to touch the lives of billions of people; those living on this planet and generations yet unborn."[10]

The African Origin of AIDS

Was HIV introduced into millions of Africans in the late 1970s during the smallpox vaccine eradication programs sponsored by the World Health Organization? It is known that animal and human cells harbor all sorts of viruses, including viruses not yet discovered, and animal tissue cell cultures are often used in the manufacture of viral vaccines. Therefore the possibility of vaccine contamination with an animal virus is a constant danger in the manufacture of vaccines.

Despite the most meticulous precautions in production, contaminating animal viruses are known to survive the vaccine process. For example, during the 1950s millions of people were injected with polio vaccines contaminated with "SV-40," a cancer-causing green monkey virus. Such vaccine contamination problems are largely kept hidden from the public. Yet in spite of the known danger, drug companies and physicians always pooh-pooh any suggestion that AIDS could have arisen from animal virus-contaminated vaccines. Animal cancer viruses are also contained in fetal calf serum, a serum commonly used as a laboratory nutrient to feed animal and human tissue cell cultures. Viruses in calf serum can be carried over as contaminants into the final vaccine product.

The problem of vaccine contamination by fetal calf serum and its relationship to AIDS is the subject of a letter by J. Grote ("Bovine Visna Virus and the Origin of the AIDS Epidemic") published in the *Journal of the Royal (London) Society of Medicine* in October 1988. Grote discounts the green monkey theory and questions whether bovine visna contamination of laboratory-used fetal bovine serum could cause AIDS. Bovine visna virus is similar in appearance to HIV. Grote, a London-based AIDS researcher, writes:

The seriousness of this becomes apparent when we consider the manufacture of vaccines requires the growth of virus in cell cultures using fetal calf serum in the growth medium. The contamination of vaccines with adventitious viruses has been of concern for many years and the presence of virus-like structures in "virus-screened" bovine serum has been reported. It seems absolutely vital that all vaccines are screened for HIV prior to use and that bovine visna virus is further investigated as to its relationship to HIV and its possible causal role in progression towards AIDS.

Millions of African blacks are reportedly infected with HIV. This large number could never have been infected by the simple act of a monkey virus "jumping" over to infect one African in the late 1970s. If that were the case, why don't we now have millions of AIDS cases in the United States? One logical explanation for the millions of Africans infected is that the vaccines used in the mass inoculation programs administered by the World Health Organization (WHO) were contaminated.

Was the contamination accidental or deliberate? It is well-known in vaccine circles that the vaccinia (cowpox) virus used in the manufacture of the smallpox vaccine is an excellent virus for genetic engineering. For example, Charles Pillar and Keith Yamamoto, authors of *Gene Wars: Military Control over the New Genetic Technology* (1988), state: "Researchers have been able to splice genes coding for the surface coats of other viruses, such as influenza, hepatitis, and rabies into vaccinia virus DNA. The result: a 'broad spectrum' vaccine with a coat of many colors."[11]

In 1985 the Russians caused an international furor by claiming that AIDS was caused by experiments carried out in the United States as part of the development of new biological weapons. Responding to this Soviet accusation, Pillar and Yamamoto admit that "although no evidence has been presented to support this claim, manipulating genes to defeat the body's immune system is quite feasible."[12]

In *Magic Shots*, Allan Chase claims that during the years 1966–1977, the WHO utilized "200,000 people in forty countries—most of them nondoctors trained by seven hundred doctors and health professionals from over seventy participating countries—spent $300 million, and used forty million bifurcated vaccinating needles to administer 24,000 million (2.4 billion) doses of smallpox vaccine."[13]

On May 11, 1987, the *London Times,* one of the world's most respected newspapers, published a front-page story entitled "Smallpox Vaccine Triggered AIDS Virus." The story suggests that African AIDS is a direct outgrowth of the WHO smallpox eradication program. The smallpox vaccine allegedly awakened a "dormant" AIDS virus infection in the black population. Robert Gallo, the codiscoverer of HIV, was quoted as saying:

> The link between the WHO program and the epidemic is an interesting and important hypothesis. I cannot say that it actually happened, but I have been saying for some years that the use of live vaccines such as that used for smallpox can activate a dormant infection such as HIV (the AIDS virus).

The *Times* story is one of the most important ever printed on the AIDS epidemic; yet the story was killed and never appeared in any major U.S. newspaper or magazine.

Despite covert human experimentation, vaccine contamination problems, and the genetic engineering of new and highly dangerous viruses, the medical establishment ignores the AIDS biowarfare issue. For example, in the prestigious *British Medical Journal* (May 13, 1989), Myra McClure and Thomas Schultz wrote a paper entitled "Origin of HIV" and quickly disposed of the idea that AIDS is connected to germ warfare. They state simply: "Lack of supporting evidence precludes serious discussion of such a bizarre hypothesis. This review deals with the theories on the origin of HIV that are scientifically plausible."

Thus medical science ignores evidence suggesting AIDS originated as a secret experiment. Most physicians and microbiologists steadfastly hold on to the illogical and improbable green monkey theory of AIDS. And the major media remain silent, often dismissing the biowarfare theory as Communist propaganda of the most malicious sort. Forgotten is the connection between the National Academy of Sciences and the military biowarfare establishment in the development of biological weapons for mass killings.

Creation of a "Supergerm" in 1969

A decade before the first cases of AIDS, Dr. Donald M. MacArthur, a spokesman for the Department of Defense, told a congressional hearing that a "supergerm" could be developed as part of our experimental biowarfare program. This genetically engineered germ would be very different from any previous microbe known to mankind. The agent would be a highly effective killing agent because the immune system would be powerless against this supermicrobe (Testimony before a Subcommittee of the Committee on Appropriations, House of Representatives, Department of Defense Appropriations for 1970, dated July 1, 1969, Washington).

A transcript of this meeting headed "Synthetic Biological Agents" records the following comments of Dr. MacArthur:

1. All biological agents up to the present time are representatives of naturally occurring disease and thus are known by scientists throughout the world. They are easily available to qualified scientists for research, either for offensive or defensive purposes.

2. Within the next 5 to 10 years, it would probably be possible to make a new infective microorganism which could differ in certain important aspects from any known disease-causing organisms. Most important of these is that it might be refractory to the immunological and therapeutic processes upon which we depend to maintain our relative freedom from infectious disease.

3. A research program to explore the feasibility of this could be completed in approximately 5 years at a total cost of $10 million.

4. It would be very difficult to establish such a program. Molecular biology is a relatively new science.

There are not many competent scientists in the field, almost all are in university laboratories, and they are generally adequately supported from sources other than the Department of Defense. However, it was considered possible to initiate an adequate program through the National Academy of Sciences—National Research Council (NAS-NRC). The matter was discussed with the NAS-NRC, and tentative plans were made to initiate the program. However, decreasing funds in CB (chemical/biological) research, growing criticism of the CB program, and our reluctance to involve the NAS-NRC in such a controversial endeavor have led us to postpone it for the past two years. It is a highly controversial issue, and there are many who believe such research should not be undertaken lest it lead to yet another method of massive killing of large populations. On the other hand, without the sure scientific knowledge that such a weapon is possible, and an understanding of the ways it could be done, there is little that can be done to devise defensive measures. Should an enemy develop it, there is little doubt that it is an important area of potential military technological inferiority in which there is no adequate research program.

Was the AIDS virus or other so-called emerging viruses, such as the Ebola and Marburg virus, created in biowarfare laboratories during the 1970s? During the 1970s the U.S. Army's biowarfare program intensified, particularly in the area of DNA and gene-splicing research. Renouncing germ warfare except for "medical defensive research," President Richard Nixon in 1971 ordered that a major part of the army's biowarfare research be transferred over to the National Cancer Institute (where HIV would be discovered a decade later by Gallo). That same year Nixon also initiated his famous War on Cancer, and offensive biowarfare research (particularly genetic engineering of viruses) continued under the umbrella of orthodox cancer research. Cancer virologists learned to "jump" animal cancer viruses from one species of animal into another. Chicken viruses were put into lamb kidney cells; baboon viruses were spliced into human cancer cells; the combinations were endless. In the process, deadly man-made viruses were developed, and new forms of cancer, immunodeficiency, and opportunistic infections were produced when these viruses were forced or adapted into laboratory animals and into human tissue cell cultures.[14]

As predicted by the biowarfare experts, new cancer-causing monster viruses were created that had a deadly effect on the immune system. In one government-sponsored experiment reported in 1974, newborn chimpanzees were taken away from their mothers at birth and weaned on milk obtained from virus-infected cows. Some of the chimps sickened and died with two new diseases that had never been observed in chimps. The first was a parasitic pneumonia known as Pneumocystis carinii pneumonia (later known as the "gay pneumonia" of AIDS); the second was leukemia.[15]

Monkey Business

Almost two decades after the first U.S. AIDS cases were diagnosed, most people still believe the government's green monkey story, and AIDS educators teach that HIV originated in Africa. However, a few cracks in the monkey theory have appeared in print.

A story entitled "Research Refutes Idea That Human AIDS Virus Originated in Monkey" appeared in the Los Angeles Times (June 2,

1988). In the process of decoding the genetic structure of the monkey virus and the human AIDS virus, Japanese molecular biologists discovered that the gene sequences of the two viruses differed by more than 50 percent—indicating absolutely no genetic relationship between the green monkey virus and HIV. The Japanese investigators specifically criticized Myron Essex and Phyllis Kanki of Harvard Medical School, who "discovered" a second AIDS virus in African green monkeys that was widely heralded in the media. Essex and Kanki's "second" AIDS virus was later proven to be a contaminant monkey virus traced back to the Harvard researchers' own laboratory.

More than a decade earlier, in 1975, Gallo reported the "discovery" of a "new" and "human" HL-23 virus he cultured from human leukemia cells. Eventually the virus was proven to be three contaminating ape viruses (gibbon ape virus, simian sarcoma virus, and baboon endogenous virus). To this day Gallo claims he has no idea how these three animal viruses contaminated his research.[16]

If HIV is not related to a green monkey virus, what is its origin? On November 13, 1988, the *Orange County Register* devoted an entire section of the newspaper to AIDS in Africa. Several African officials were interviewed; all were adamant that AIDS did not originate in Africa. The theory "is false and has never been scientifically proved, so why should Africa be the scapegoat?" declared Dr. Didace Nzaramba, director of the AIDS prevention program in Rwanda. The *Register* commented:

> From early on, scientists have speculated that the disease might have begun in Africa. Researchers in Africa tested old blood samples and said they found HIV-infected serum that went back years. In 1985, Harvard researchers, Phyllis Kanki and Myron Essex, announced the discovery of a new virus isolated in green monkeys that seemed similar to HIV. Eventually, researchers concluded that early blood tests used in Africa were not reliable, and Kanki and Essex said their blood tests probably had been contaminated and that their results were invalid. But the perception of an African link was established.

Media Disinformation

With the publication of *And the Band Played On* in 1987, the media became obsessed with author Randy Shilts's "Patient Zero" story. In the popular award-winning book, a young Canadian airline steward named

Gaeton Dugas is portrayed as the promiscuous gay man "who brought the AIDS virus from Paris and ignited the epidemic in North America." Shilts, who later died of AIDS, never explained where or how Dugas got his infection.

After a year of swollen lymph nodes and a rash, Dugas was finally diagnosed with AIDS-associated "gay cancer" in June 1980 in New York City. What Shilts probably did not know is that when Dugas was diagnosed in 1980, over 20 percent of the Manhattan gays in the Hepatitis-B experiment were HIV-positive. This 20 percent infection rate was discovered after the HIV blood test became available in 1985 and after the stored blood at the New York Blood Center was retested for HIV antibodies. Remarkably, these gay men had the highest recorded incidence of HIV anywhere in the world for that time. Even in African populations, where AIDS has been theorized to exist for decades, or even millennia, there were never reports of such a high incidence of HIV in 1980.

Shilts's sensational Patient Zero story quickly became "fact." Even the AMA-sponsored *American Medical News* (October 23, 1987) fell for the ludicrous story, claiming that Dugas "may have brought AIDS to the United States." The media continue to promote unlikely stories about the origin of AIDS, always avoiding discussion of the idea that HIV came out of a laboratory and always pointing the finger at black Africa.

In late 1987 the media widely reported an "old AIDS case" dating back to 1968. DNA testing of the blood and tissue was reported as HIV-positive.[17] For the last year of his life, "Robert," a fifteen-year-old black boy from St. Louis, wasted away with a bizarre disease that severely bloated his legs and genitalia. His sexual preference was unknown, but his doctors tried hard to insinuate the dying boy was gay. At autopsy, internal Kaposi's sarcoma of the rectum was discovered, along with anal warts and lacerations. And after fingering the dead boy's rectum, the pathologist noted "a lax anal sphincter." When newer viral identification techniques were reapplied to Robert's blood in 1990, his blood retested HIV-negative, proving that Robert never had AIDS.[18]

In 1990 the media sensationalized another "old AIDS case," this time an unmarried English sailor who died in Manchester in 1959. When his stored tissue remains tested positive for HIV, major newspapers throughout the world used this case to again discredit the persistent rumor that AIDS was a man-made disease. The *New York Times* (July 24) declared:

> The case also refutes the widely publicized charges made by Soviet officials several years ago that AIDS arose from a virus that had escaped from a laboratory experiment that went awry or was a biological warfare agent. The human retrovirus group to which the AIDS virus belongs was unknown at the time. Nor did scientists then have the genetic engineering techniques needed to create a new virus.

In a letter to the medical journal *Lancet* in January 1996, this 1959 case was ruled not to be AIDS because the DNA tests were found to be contaminated owing to a laboratory error.

Despite the denial of the *Times* regarding the laboratory creation of new AIDS-like viruses, it was common practice during the early 1970s for virologists to alter animal viruses by inserting them into other animal species and into human tissue cells in culture. Experiments performed at Harvard in the mid-1970s by Max Essex and Donald Francis (two of the best-known AIDS experts) produced AIDS in cats with the feline leukemia retrovirus. In addition, a decade before the outbreak of AIDS in the United States, Robert Gallo was engineering cancer-causing retroviruses and studying the effects of viral mutants and their ability to suppress the immune system. A full description of Gallo's animal retrovirus research activities dating back to 1967 is chronicled in *Emerging Viruses, AIDS & Ebola: Nature, Accident or Genocide?* by Dr. Leonard Horowitz, published in 1996.[19]

Secret and Covert Biological Warfare Research

It is difficult, if not impossible, to determine the truth about global biological warfare capabilities and their possible effects on world health. The American taxpayer is kept ignorant about U.S. chemical and biowarfare programs. Scientists involved in biowarfare research are sworn to secrecy and silence. Thus "classified" and "top secret" medical experimentation continues to be promoted by powerful government agencies, such as the CIA, the CDC, the Department of Defense, the military, and other institutions.

Recent revelations of horrific radiation experiments conducted on unsuspecting U.S. citizens during the cold war years up until the 1980s have shocked the nation. Some of this research was conducted at the most prestigious medical institutions in our country. None of the perpetrators have been brought to trial. In light of these revelations, it is inconceivable to think that leading AIDS scientists would be unaware of the connections between their institutional research and the biowarfare establishment.

Currently, strange and unprecedented diseases are appearing mysteriously in various parts of the world. The peculiar Persian Gulf War syndrome has sickened over fifty thousand of our vets who served in Desert Shield/Storm. Their illnesses have been largely dismissed by health experts as due to "psychological stress," even though there is evidence that this new disease is contagious and sexually transmitted. Nevertheless, government health officials remain silent on these issues.

A few scientists insist that some cases of Gulf War syndrome are related to biological warfare agents. Dr. Garth Nicholson and his wife, Nancy, formerly scientists at the M. D. Anderson Cancer Center in Houston, have discovered in the blood of some sick reservists a new infectious microbe (a mycoplasma) that has part of the AIDS virus spliced into its genetic material. The Nicholsons say: "The type of mycoplasma we identified was highly unusual, and it almost certainly didn't occur naturally. It has one gene from the HIV-1 virus—but only one gene. This meant it was almost certainly an artificially modified microbe—altered purposefully by scientists."

By censoring certain aspects of AIDS history, particularly the origin of HIV, we allow dangerous medical experimentation to continue. The New York Blood Center is now testing a new vaccine made from a "harmless" canary-pox virus that has been genetically engineered to carry parts of HIV, the AIDS virus. The center is recruiting HIV-negative gay men by funding Project Achieve, an organization designed to test and sign up young men for the new vaccine experiment. Homosexual men are lured into the program by posters that feature cute, multiethnic gay boys. According to Timothy Murphy of *HX* magazine, there is a waiting list for the center's vaccine experiment.

The enigmatic Dr. Szmuness has been erased from AIDS chronicles. His name does not appear in Shilts's *Band,* or in Mirko Grmek's *History of AIDS* (1990), or in Laurie Garret's massive tome on emerging viruses, *The Coming Plague* (1994). Although his untimely death went largely unnoticed in medical journals, he was remembered and honored on May 11, 1984, by a small coterie of medical power brokers and distinguished scientists who convened at a landmark symposium in the nation's capital. The meeting, entitled "Infection, Immunity, and Blood Transfusion," was sponsored by the American Red Cross.[20]

Paying tribute to Szmuness were top government scientists in AIDS and cancer research, the most well-known researchers in animal experimentation, the heads of the most prestigious biomedical establishments in the country, and the chief executives of drug companies tied to genetic engineering, vaccine production, and biological warfare research. Dr. Robert Gallo, who had announced the discovery of the AIDS virus to the American public three weeks earlier, was one of the most distinguished attendees.

There is an ominous link between cancer and AIDS, between animal experimentation and the genetic engineering of viruses, between biological warfare technology and drug companies, between gay experiments and AIDS, between vaccine programs and the contamination of the nation's blood supply. Why else would all these people from diverse areas of science be attending this high-level government conference?

There is also a connection that cannot be denied between Szmuness's gay experiment and the outbreak of AIDS. This connection is not coincidental or a paranoid fantasy.

It is time for serious students of AIDS to study the link between covert biological warfare research and the initial outbreak of the "gay AIDS plague." Ignoring evidence pointing to AIDS as a man-made disease makes a sham out of AIDS education.

Issue 17, Fall 1997

Saucer Kraut: Inside the German Research Project

Interview With Henry Stevens

D. Guide

Did the Nazis have their own "Area 51"? In this exclusive interview conducted by D. Guide, Henry Stevens of the German Research Project (GRP) reveals the secret UFO technology that was developed by the Germans during World War II and discusses other secret Nazi technology still being suppressed to this day.

THE GOVERNMENT PLAYS COY about Area 51. We are being bombarded with UFO-alien propaganda from every direction. Even the most "respectable" of the conventional media are solemnly intoning, "We are not alone." Obviously the mass consciousness is being primed to accept the UFO-alien doctrine. But if the UFO-alien theme is propaganda, then it cannot be true. Brainwashing is not the standard method of purveying truth.

Even more disturbing is the trend by the popular media to create an acceptable religious framework for their propaganda. During the *Nightline* ("Are We Alone?") program aired July 16, 1996, Ted Koppel's guest "expert"—with Koppel's prompting—pointedly attempted to connect religion to aliens and their spacecraft. The "expert," a physicist named Paul Davies from the University of Adelaide, was a recent recipient of the $1 million Templeton Prize for Progress in Religion, awarded annually at Buckingham Palace. Davies emphasized the "religious dimension of the UFO experience" and postulated that aliens were intermediaries between the human race and "some superior intelligence." He compared angels of the past to today's UFO-aliens and proclaimed that what we have is "essentially the same system."

Given the fact that public knowledge concerning flying disc technology has been suppressed for over fifty years, and that the media is ratcheting up the intensity of their propaganda, it seems that their awesome deception is about to bear fruit. This outer space ecumenicism has gone far enough. It's time for researchers to gird their loins and look for some real answers. And there's hardly anyone better qualified than Henry Stevens, director of the German Research Project, to dissuade us of the media's outrageous manipulations.

D. GUIDE: *Tell me about the German Research Project. How would you describe your mission?*

HENRY STEVENS: German Research Project (GRP) is about eight years old, but my interest goes back to the late 1970s. I saw an article by Renato Vesco describing the work the Germans did with saucers during the war. I could get no other information until W. A. Harbinson's book *Genesis*, which had a bibliography. It was in the German language, but I had studied German as an undergraduate and was able to do research in that language. I sent a German student, returning to Germany for the summer, to get the references cited. I read them and eventually translated them on paper. I got the idea that perhaps others who could not read German might be interested enough to purchase these articles, and with the money I could finance further research. That was the idea behind German Research Project.

And now . . . ?

GRP currently investigates all aspects of flying discs built by the Germans during World War II. This includes the technology, history, people, and organizations involved and disposition of these craft after the war. GRP also researches Nazi technology which, for whatever reason, the victorious Allies chose to conceal from the public. This is a great body of knowledge as evidenced by the fact that thirty boxcarloads of German patents were taken out of the German patent office by the Allied powers.

Finally, GRP researches the hidden history and people involved with this technology. This aspect of the research tends to humanize and personalize the work and, I think, appeals to me and to others who would not normally be interested in just the technology alone. Much of this knowledge is still secret.

In your many years of research, what is the most compelling evidence you've found that modern UFOs can be identified as flying disc technology inherited from the Nazis?

The answer is basic scientific reasoning. One does not jump to a conclusion without researching the possibilities. And one starts with the simplest possibility and exhausts it before proceeding to the next simplest possibility, and so on. The simplest possibility is that UFOs, like other metallic flying objects, are man-made. This proposition has never been properly researched.

Couple with this the claim by many German sources that they produced craft of this type during the Second World War, two years before rising to notice here in America. Personally, in researching an origin for UFOs, I never needed go beyond this paradigm.

Initially, other researchers told me that they "had researched this claim and there was nothing to it." The president of the largest national UFO organization in the world told me those exact words via telephone. It was a lie. They had done nothing, and I can prove it. Large, national UFO organizations are nothing more than black holes into which UFO information is sucked and does not have the power to escape. After fifty years of "research," can they state even one concrete fact that they have learned? I think not.

Let me state this another way. I have never seen an alien. I have never seen an alien engineer. I have never seen an alien design for a UFO. And I have never seen anyone produce any concrete proof linking UFOs to aliens. But I have seen Germans. I have seen a German saucer engineer on videotape and corresponded with him. I have seen German saucer designs and their explanations as to how they work. I have a statement of a German saucer test pilot. I have heard detailed historical information which sets German saucers in a cultural context. And at least one artifact exists linking saucer hardware with German manufacture.

These are real people with real names and real addresses who are verifiable and lay themselves and their reputations on the line. Until aliens come up with this level of proof, why are we even discussing them? No, not all UFOs are of German inspiration. But that fact alone has been used over and over as an excuse to dismiss both German-based saucers and man-made saucers in general. And in doing this, what has happened in the UFO world is that one of the few researchable problems available to us has been purposefully taken off the table. I am glad this trend is finally turning.

Without doing too much bashing of "ufology," perhaps its orientation should be problem directed, with a focus on researchable, solvable problems. Currently ufology can be described only as reactionary. As it has been done for over fifty years, researchers chase sightings or interview individuals claiming to be "contactees" or "abductees" or "implantees." This is not a problem-directed methodology.

This reactiveness leads to sensationalism and one-upmanship among those involved in the research. Information of all sorts and styles is gathered, but no basic facts have been deduced or generalizations made by the ET crowd. There is no logical reason to continue a methodology after fifty years of failure.

Another compelling aspect of German UFOs are the many old photographs, diagrams, and written statements from various sources documenting the German origin for many UFOs. And in many cases this material comes with a cultural context rather than as a random photograph.

Let me give an example. There is the famous "Kraut Meteor" in W. Mattern's book *UFO's Unbekanntes Flugobject oder Letzte Geheim Waffe des Dritten Reiches*. Mattern states that this is a photograph of the V-7. He describes it in his book, stating who built it, where, when it was test-flown and where, by whom, and who witnessed the event. Mattern even goes on to say that these objects were given the nickname "Kraut meteors" by Allied fighting men.

What's your take on Area 51?

Having said what I don't like about the UFO scene, I am glad to be able to answer a question on a positive note. There is nobody I admire more than those guys who pioneered Area 51. I am speaking of William Cooper, Sean Morton, Norio Hiakawa, and others (I am sorry if I left out your names). These guys got off their butts and did something. These are the men of action in the UFO world who literally laid their butts on the line and handed us the information on a silver platter. Their methodology employed predictability for the first time. They should be commended and admired.

The question of aliens here is really ridiculous. A U.S. military base which has been—thanks to the above individuals—caught red-handed flying UFOs is the smoking gun we have been looking for. Are we to believe this is somehow alien connected because UFOs are present? This is faulty logic. Would it not be far simpler to believe that these are secret, man-made UFOs which are being developed and tested on the very base where other secret, man-made craft have been historically developed and tested? At least, this should be the working hypothesis until shown wrong.

The point is that the real power behind our government wants you, as an individual, to be totally accountable to them. They want to know who you are, where you are, how you get and spend your money, and they want you to believe several core concepts. These are the ones pushed down your throat every time you open a newspaper or magazine, turn on the radio or television, or watch a movie. These are the ideas and values that they have selected for you to believe—and which you know deep in your gut are lies. They are issues, beliefs, and attitudes which, if you deny them publicly, will get you in trouble. They are the lies you deny in whispers, privately, only to your close friends. These are the issues some call "politically correct."

These people first push, then deny, then replant the alien-UFO connection. They feed false leads to researchers and then discredit those same researchers when their data becomes unverifiable. They keep the UFO world chasing its tail. Until we stop using government data as a primary source, stop accepting a methodology of regression hypnosis, and shed the shackles of large UFO research organizations, we will remain at the mercy of this most childish manipulation.

Why is the occult so intrinsically connected to this technology, with both Nazi and New Age occult links?

The Nazi occult is connected to this technology because it is one explanation for this technology. This explanation is being advocated by a group of Austrians who possess a mass of pictures, old documents, and general explanations concerning these craft. These people—the Tempelhof Gesellschaft, which might be called the New Templars in English—claim to have had a relationship with the Thule Society and the Vril Society during the prewar years in Germany. It was the members of the Thule Society, such as Rudolf Steiner, who would be recognized today as New Agers. Besides Steiner, there was Victor Schauberger, who worked on water and "dimagnetic" energy, which is said to cause objects to levitate. Schauberger's sympathy, as was his son Walter's, was to the movement we identify as the Greens. Few are aware of the fact that the first Greens were Nazis. Walter was active in Die Greune Front, or the Green Front.

The modern descendants of the higher-level Nazis are clearly the Green Party, and the modern descendants of the lower level are the skinheads. All the ideas contained within the beliefs of the Greens and the skinheads can be found within the Nazi Party, in spite of the fact that nothing would seem farther apart today than the Greens and the skinheads.

Besides a concern for the environment, the Thule and Vril groups greatly respected and studied the ancient knowledge of the megalithic monument builders, both in Europe and in the Near East. They studied and believed in the ancient wisdom of the East, particularly Tibet and India.

And they believed that soon a new form of energy would be discovered for the benefit of man. They called this energy *vril* and likened it to the *chi* energy of the Chinese or to the *prana* of Indian belief. Today we would call this force "free energy." It is the claim of these individuals that at least one source of information concerning this energy and technology of levitation was channeled to them exactly as channeling is done today.

And the New Templars operate in a similar fashion?

Ralf Ettl and Norbert Juergen-Ratthofer, the Austrian scriptwriters for *Secrets of World War 2 German Flying Saucers* and also *UFO Secrets of the Third Reich,* state their theory of a connection between certain extraterrestrials and the Sumerian language. They also believe a connection between Sumerian and German existed. Further, they repeat a hypothesis that certain electromagnetic German saucers were able to jump interdimensionally through time and were actually hidden in ancient Sumeria at the close of World War II.

There are several problems with these statements, but first let me say that neither Ettl nor Juergen-Ratthofer are technical people, although they do some technical writing. They are not Nazis or neo-Nazis. They are religious people. They are the Templar connection—although they are New Templars and are in no way (or so I believe) linearly connected to the Knights Templar. Aspects of their religion deal with tracing mother-goddesses under various names throughout history. In this, they seem to start with Cro-Magnon times and then jump to Sumeria, then to Egypt, and into classical times.

And how do they arrive at their conclusions?

Their extraterrestrial connection is a linguistic one and was arrived upon through channeling. Their connections with the Germanic languages are not explained in detail. Of course, Sumeria existed at 3000 or 4000 B.C. The Germanic languages did not exist until Illyrian invaders from Central Europe entered Scandinavia at about 500 B.C. There can be no relationship between the two languages unless it is assumed that Sumerian was an Indo-European language. This is not normally assumed.

Sumeria, which is in fact ancient Babylon, appears to be a popular jumping-off point for some strange reason.

The other proponent of "Sumerian ufology" is Zecharia Sitchin. His work is much worse. I say this because he is a linguist. Linguistics is a solid discipline, a subset of anthropology. Linguistics has been around for a long time and has made many, many, positive contributions to our understanding of human history. Linguistics, as an established discipline, has an extensive infrastructure, including conferences of professionals and, most important, professional journals. If Sitchin has anything worth reporting, it should be done in a linguists' journal and peer reviewed. The results of this digestion of facts within the discipline should be presented in a more general journal for public consumption.

Ufology has no methodology. Because of this, our journals lack rigor. We are not a science. We are a bunch of dilettantes. Sitchin bypasses his peer review process and presents his ideas to a bunch of UFO people who are not in a position to evaluate his presentation. If Sitchin has anything of value to say, we should hear about it from another linguist.

In this context, mention must also be made of Erich von Daniken, who is still wildly popular with the Ancient Astronaut Society.

As I recall, von Daniken was not a professional archaeologist, and so can be forgiven the sins of Sitchin since he is a nonprofessional and therefore cannot be held to the same standard. But in saying that, I am really saying he is an amateur and that his ideas are amateur, which they are.

If one searches the world, especially among hunter-gatherer societies, one will find anomalies, or seeming anomalies, concerning what we believe they knew and what they believed they knew. This is further compounded when we interpret their art, or religious art, or ritualistic art, when we have no understanding of that culture. The job is compounded if that culture is extinct. The only good thing I can say about him is that he got people thinking.

Well said, indeed. I have noticed the misinterpretation of ancient art repeatedly, always in support of dubious theories, and I find that entirely unacceptable. This kind of error only convinces me that the theory itself is worthless.

But it is important to bear in mind that this explanation is not the only explanation for the flying disks. Recently a man in New Mexico, Bill Lyne, has given us a more "nuts and bolts" solution for electromagnetically powered saucers. And as a child, he saw one of these flying saucers very near a U.S. military base where captured German technology was tested.

Lyne has given us a second avenue of attack concerning this problem, and he proposes simple solutions for what is observed, using for the most part Tesla technology readily available to the Germans. Rather than being accused of stealing his thunder, I would like to refer one and all to his book *Space Aliens from the Pentagon,* published in 1995.

How is the abduction phenomenon to be understood? Subliminal brainwashing? Mary Seal suggests that covert psychotronics are at work here, possibly through radio and television.

I am not a big abduction fan. I am sure that some abductions have taken place since we keep hearing about them from all quarters. I am not convinced that these abductions are the work of extraterrestrials. If a creature has two arms, two legs, walks bipedally, and has stereoscopic vision, it is a human or a human derivative in my book. Parallel evolution would not produce such a close analog on another world. Perhaps some of the "real" abductions are government experiments: They have done strange experiments on unwitting civilian populations before.

Many abduction tales have strong sexual overtones. This bothers me. And most abductees don't become abductees until they employ a hypnosis. This really bothers me. As far as I am concerned, hypnotherapy is not good science, it is no science. All information gathered in this way should be heavily scrutinized. But alien abductions fuel the mass media and also act as a self-verifying mechanism for the alien hypothesis in general, and so has ingrained itself in the field.

One line in your introduction to Secret German Flying Discs of World War Two *really stayed in my mind. That's the part when you wrote, "Should a UFO land on the White House steps tomorrow, our government would pray that an alien stepped out, as opposed to a former, unbowed SS man. . . ."* Now according to recent reports, a new German training center has been established at Holloman Air Force Base in Alamogordo, New Mexico. The Pentagon has stated that this is the first permanent military base to be established in America. What's the real significance of this foreign base on our soil?

This is not the first German base on our soil. Once while looking for directions, I personally entered a West German military installation in the San Fernando Valley, north of Los Angeles. It consisted of one or two old buildings in a run-down industrial area. German military personnel identified themselves openly, explained their presence as legitimate, and gave me the directions I needed. I have no idea what is going on at Holloman Air Force Base.

Are there any indications that an SS base in Antarctica is still operational?

In 1938–1939 the German ship *Schwabenland* took possession of a portion of Antarctica, calling it Neuschwabenland after their ship. They made a geologic survey of this area, finding mountains rising up to twelve thousand feet, warm-water ponds, and other evidence of geothermal activity. It has always been rumored that the Germans built a base there during the war, a vast tunnel system such as they did in the Harz Mountains and the Alps. Again, rumor has it that this was the destination of SS members who did not want to end the struggle. The base was said to be a stronghold and well supplied.

In 1946 Admiral Byrd led an expedition to Antarctica with submarines, an aircraft carrier, destroyers, aircraft, military transport vehicles, and four thousand fighting men—for purposes still unknown. He left Antarctica suddenly after the mysterious loss of several aircraft. He spent only six weeks in Antarctica, although he was outfitted for several months.

In July 1952 a whole squadron of UFOs buzzed the White House and were seen by many people as well as recorded on radar. Jet fighters were sent to intercept them, but the jets could never catch the UFOs. Once the jets left the area, the UFO squadron re-formed over the White House. In 1958 and 1959, under cover of the International Geophysical Year, three nuclear missiles were launched by the United States naval forces and detonated in Antarctica. I believe all these actions were connected to the German base somewhere in Neuschwabenland.

Does that base still exist? I don't think so. There are still plenty of UFO sightings in Antarctica, if we are to believe the South American press, but supplying the small necessities of life to Antarctica over a prolonged period would be difficult. Think of the screws, toothpaste, toilet paper, shoes, lubricating oil, spare parts, and so forth which would need to be brought there! And think of the human aspects involved. Imagine yourself in your mid- or late twenties in exile in Antarctica.

The other reason I don't think it lasted for more than a few years was that the Germans had an excellent base in the Andes, which would have proved even more secure, because in the politics of South America, security has a price. How secure you want to be is only a matter of money—and the Nazis had plenty of money.

The 1968 Report from Iron Mountain toyed with, and then seemingly discarded, the idea that an artificial invasion from outer space might produce the desired global harmonic convergence. After almost thirty years, we now see efforts to debunk this report (such as the Wall Street Journal on May 9, 1995). Nevertheless, when we consider the continuous drumbeat from the media on the alien theme, there is obviously some merit to the report, even if the idea didn't fly (no pun intended) at that time. It provides a framework for our government's involvement with these sightings and also a reason for their secrecy. It would also explain the current media hype. Do you think that this theory has any merit?

More and more, we are governed via the crisis. A crisis allows our government to evoke martial law, called euphemistically "emergency powers." They have done a lot of practice runs lately. They do this every time it rains, floods, during earthquakes and fires. In my book, they are gathering data on how much martial law citizens will tolerate, given the circumstances.

Henry Stevens and the German Research Project can be contacted at P.O. Box 7, Gorman, California, 93243-0007.

Issue 15, Winter 1997

Diet for a Zombified Planet

Mark Westion

This article reveals that sodium fluoride is a toxic by-product of alumi-num production, promoted to curb a huge waste disposal problem at the ALCOA plant owned by the Mellon family. It has been discovered that repeated infinitesimal doses of fluoride will, over time, make a person submissive and docile by slowly poisoning a certain area of the brain. This article also discusses the health horrors of irradiated food, pasteurized milk, Prozac, Olestra, aspartame, and other FDA-approved goodies. Let the eater beware.

A RECENT *New York Times* article reported the startling news that a second brain has been discovered in the human body. This second brain, dubbed the enteric nervous system, has been the subject of scien-tific investigation for a number of years and has spawned a new medical discipline known as neurogastroenterology.[1] One would think that such an important discovery would be the subject of much debate and con-jecture, yet aside from the aforementioned newspaper article, the guard-ians of the fifth estate seem strangely reticent.

According to Dr. Michael Gershon, a professor at Columbia-Presby-terian Medical Center in New York, this second brain extends from the esophagus down to the colon and has thus been referred to as the "gut brain." It consists of a network of neurons, neurotransmitters, and pro-teins, just like the brain located in the head. It is connected to the head brain through the spinal cord and uses this pathway to carry on a continuous two-way communication. For instance, when the "head brain" is upset, the "gut brain" reacts accordingly (and vice versa). This new knowledge goes far in explaining a whole range of maladies, from "butterflies in the stomach" to peptic ulcers. It also lends credence to the belief that too much to eat before bedtime causes nightmares.

Research has shown that the two brains have few, if any, connections from birth through infancy; these connections develop only when the child's motor skills start to develop. It has been theorized that this initial separation enables the baby's "gut brain" to take care of its physical needs (feeding-elimination) while freeing its "head brain" to study its environment (learning-social interaction).

All of this research would only amount to a scientific curiosity if it weren't for the discovery of two intriguing facts. The first is that the "gut brain" naturally produces a family of psychoactive compounds known as benzodiazepines.[2] We recognize some of these compounds by such brand names as Valium and Xanax. The second discovery is that the "gut brain" can be trained to react to outside stimuli.[3] These two facts ought to concern every one of us, for if our stomachs truly can control how we feel and think, then it is up to us, and to us alone, to control exactly what goes into our stomach. If our gut can be trained, then we should make sure that it is we who are doing the training. The issue of personal sanctity is paramount here. Could it be that we are purposely being fed a diet that turns us into happy little consumers, at the expense of our sense of self? Is the best way to our hearts (and minds) truly through our stomachs? What follows is a collection of evidence that this may be the case.

Sodium Fluoride

The fluoridation of the water supply was one of the first cold war conspiracies to be brought to public attention. Those who decried the spiking of one of life's essential elements were painted as right-wing "Commie under the bed" kooks. As is often the case, however, the historic record seems to lend credence to what these lone voices have been attempting to warn us about. In fact, the trail leads not to "Commies," but our government's old friends in the German Socialist (Nazi) Party.

The trail begins way back in 1924, when a cartel of American bankers, led by J. P. Morgan, made arrangements to set up shop in Germany under the "Dawes Plan."[4] Such august American business concerns as Ford, Standard Oil, Du Pont, International Harvester, and General Motors lined up to provide post–World War I Germany with all the material necessary to prosecute World War II. Hobnobbing with the visionary leadership of these companies was the Mellon family (of Carnegie Mellon University).

The Mellons were also the owners of the American Aluminum Co. (ALCOA). They had a huge waste disposal problem in the form of sodium fluoride, which is a highly toxic by-product of aluminum production. When post–World War II production of aluminum really took off, something had to be done. Imagine their good fortune when the family-owned Mellon Institute discovered that fluoride helped prevent tooth decay! So the family contracted with Proctor & Gamble in 1958 to produce Crest, the first fluoridated toothpaste. This was done in tandem with efforts to fluoridate the nation's water supply. The reason given for water fluoridation was that it was helpful in preventing tooth decay in children. If this were the real reason, then why target the whole population, young and old alike?

It should be noted here that Proctor & Gamble has financial ties (as do the other firms previously listed) with the infamous I. G. Farben, the German pharmaceutical company which was Hitler's major financial backer. This is where the Nazi connection comes in. After World War II, scientists from the United States were sent to Germany to take over the I. G. Farben plant. One of these scientists was Charles Eliot Perkins, a researcher in chemistry, biochemistry, physiology, and pathology. While there he supposedly learned the truth about fluoride. This he related to Mr. Harley Rivers Dickinson in 1987, who was at the time a Liberal Party member of the Australian Parliament. The following is the story as told by Mr. Dickinson to the *Victorian Hansard,* on August 12, 1987:

> While there he was told by a German chemist of a scheme which had been worked out by them during the war and adopted by the German General Staff. This was to control the population in any given area through mass medication of drinking water. In this scheme, sodium fluoride occupied a prominent place. Repeated doses of infinitesimal amounts of fluoride will in time reduce an individual's power to resist domination by slowly poisoning and narcotizing a certain area of the brain and will thus make him submissive to the will of those who wish to govern him. Both the Germans and the Russians added sodium fluoride to the drinking water of prisoners of war to make them stupid and docile.[5]

These statements are backed up by Mr. George Racey Jordan, who was a major in charge of the post–World War II Lend Lease airlift which brought much needed supplies from the United States to Russia. When he inquired why the Russians needed large quantities of sodium fluoride, he was informed that it was to be put into the drinking water of prisoners of war to take away their will to resist.[6]

This information should not surprise anyone familiar with our government's research into incapacitating warfare agents. One needs only to look back on MK-Ultra plans to dose the enemy's water supply with such substances as LSD, BZ (an amnesiac ten times more potent than LSD), or a schizophrenic agent known as Bulbocapine. These agents, according to the *Rockefeller Report on CIA Activities*, were "part of a much larger CIA program to study possible means of controlling human behaviour."[7]

More telling still is the fact that as of 1984, no less than 25 percent of the "major tranquilizers" listed in doctor's reference books contained fluoride. Sodium fluoride is also sold as an insecticide-rat poison.[8]

Pasteurized Milk

Modern pasteurization methods require heating the milk to a temperature of 150–170 degrees Fahrenheit for fifteen to twenty-two seconds.[9] This is done to kill pathogenic bacteria which could cause disease. Unfortunately this process also destroys enzymes in the milk. These enzymes are necessary in helping us to digest food. In the case of pasteurized milk, the enzyme phosphatase is totally eradicated. Without this phosphatase, as much as 50 percent of the milk's calcium is not absorbed into the body. This heating is also responsible for as much as a two-thirds loss of vitamins A and E, up to 80 percent of vitamin B, and better than 50 percent of vitamin C. To this list should be added a 20 percent loss of iodine. In all, pasteurization of milk is responsible for the mutation or outright destruction of at least thirty-eight food factors. It is also now a recognized culprit in such coronary ailments as thrombosis and arteriosclerosis, as well as skeletal-tooth deformities.

All of this information causes one to wonder just why milk should be pasteurized in the first place? The answer, as always, lies purely in economic considerations. Simply put, pasteurized milk lasts longer on the store shelves.[10] (This is the same reason for that latest of consumable horrors, irradiated milk.)

Prozac

Prozac, one of the most controversial drugs ever brought to market, has been described as either the end of emotional depression or the main brainwashing tool in Big Brother's medicine cabinet, depending on whom you read. If you read Peter Kramer's book *Listening to Prozac*, for instance, you will be told by this self-proclaimed advocate of "cosmetic psychopharmacology" that Prozac has power to give "social confidence to the habitually timid, to make the sensitive brash, to lend the introvert the social skills of a salesman."[11] These are personal qualities which are highly valued in a service economy. As social historian David Rothman has duly noted, Prozac is "a quintessentially American drug." While not producing any of that pesky, antisocial euphoria, it instead "promotes adroit competitiveness" and is "an office drug."[12] Still, others view Prozac simply as the drug of choice for the "take your gun to work" crowd.

But I digress. The focus of this article is the gut, which leads us back to the gut brain's discoverer, Dr. Gershon. He wanted to find out why a quarter of the people taking Prozac experienced gastrointestinal distress such as diarrhea and constipation. So he took a section of a guinea pig's colon and mounted it on a stand. If you put something in what used to be the "mouth" end, the hairlike cillia on the colon wall will force the material toward the "anus" end. When you put a small dose of Prozac in the "mouth," these cillia go into hyperdrive (diarrhea). Feed it a large Prozac dose, and the colonic system freezes shut (constipation).[13] This simple experiment demonstrates clearly that any nutrients lying in the intestines along with a dose of Prozac will be restricted from proper assimilation into the bloodstream.

Olestra

In the film *Sleeper*, Woody Allen's character awakens to find himself in a wonderful future world where "junk food" is considered by the enlightened citizenry to be an integral part of a healthy lifestyle. Doubtful as this scenario may seem, a recently developed fat substitute being marketed under the name Olestra may soon be touted as the next best thing. The Food and Drug Administration has given Olestra's manufacturer, Proctor & Gamble, the green light to produce Olestra for use in certain snack foods such as potato chips, corn chips, and crackers.

Some of these products are presently being test-marketed in Cedar Rapids, Iowa, Eau Claire, Wisconsin, and Grand Junction, Colorado.[14]

Because Olestra contains no fat or calories, products cooked in the stuff will automatically be healthier for a diet-conscious populace. Or will they? According to Ronald M. Krauss, M.D., national chairman of the Nutrition Committee of the American Heart Association (AHA), "Questions about the overall safety of Olestra have not been answered."[15] In a statement issued by the Rhode Island affiliate of the AHA, he states that "its manufacturer, Proctor & Gamble Co., will conduct studies to monitor its long-term effects." He then goes on to declare, "The AHA urges Proctor & Gamble to support a widespread effort to educate the public and health professionals in the appropriate use of this product."[16] It's the same old story: The FDA tells big business to go for it, and damn the consequences. We will be the guinea pigs to be "monitored" for "long-term effects."

Although any adverse long-term effects are yet to be observed, enough research has been made known on this product's shortcomings that one wonders if P&G is putting short-term monetary gain above any concern for long-term health concerns. What do we now know about Olestra? Quoting Dr. Krauss once again, "Olestra may cause abdominal bloating and loose stools in some individuals, and it inhibits the body's absorption of certain fat-soluble vitamins and other nutrients."[17] The vitamins in question are A, D, E, and K, and according to Dr. Krauss, "A particular concern in this regard has been the possible consequences of the reduction in absorption of carotenoids that can occur with Olestra use. The role of carotenoids in human health is not fully understood, and further research in this area is necessary. [An example of a carotenoid is the yellow pigment found in carrots and sweet potatoes that the body converts to vitamin A]."[18]

Our watchdogs at the FDA are requiring that products containing Olestra must be fortified with vitamins A, D, E, and K. One must assume that the reasoning behind such an order is that increasing the intake of these vitamins will overwhelm the intestinal system, thereby forcing absorption into the body. Whether or not this is a viable approach is left to question, as Dr. Krauss is silent on the issue.

I recall reading about research into fat substitutes in a plastics industry trade journal about twelve years ago. Why was this product ballyhooed in a magazine devoted to the plastics industry? Because the fat substitute that they were so proud of was actually made out of plastic!

Now I'm not sure if Olestra is the same product, but I do know that back then in the 1980s, word was that the product was considered perfectly safe for human consumption. The reason given for this lack of concern was that the material passed through the intestinal tract without being absorbed.

Two other issues disturb me regarding the planned vitamin fortification of products containing Olestra. Foremost is the question of the efficacy of the vitamin fortification itself. If the product inhibits absorption of these fat-soluble nutrients, then does it naturally follow that these nutrients will still not be absorbed, regardless of volume? Also, is there any perceived adverse effect stemming from introducing large quantities of these vitamins into the digestive tract? Of special concern is the introduction of vitamin K. I have long been led to believe that this nutrient is contained solely in the lower intestine, and if some trauma (such as peritonitis) should cause it to escape into the upper intestinal tract, death will be only hours away. I have also seen vitamin K used as the sole active ingredient in industrial rat poison.

Americans literally eat tons of the snack foods that will be subject to "Olestrazation." It shouldn't be long before the marketing of these "low fat," "reduced fat," and "fat free" goodies causes more traditionally prepared products to become a rare commodity indeed.

Aspartame

Following the news that the artificial sweetener saccharin caused cancer in lab animals, aspartame was presented to the calorie-conscious consumer as an FDA approved sugar substitute. And it didn't leave a bad aftertaste! Little blue packets were soon to be seen edging out the familiar pink in restaurants and coffee shops. Sold under such brand names as NutraSweet, Equal, and Spoonful, aspartame quickly became the sweetener of choice in everything from soft drinks to laxatives. Concurrent with its growing popularity however, is an equally expanding body of evidence which suggests that lab results were tampered with and bribes were paid to keep the buying public in a state of ignorance.

Erik Millstone, a researcher from Sussex University, United Kingdom, has used the Freedom of Information Act to compile evidence to demonstrate that (a) test results were falsified, (b) the FDA commissioner at the time overruled his own board of inquiry to get aspartame approved (then left to take a position at one of its manufacturer's public relations firms), and (c) two U.S. attorneys who were supposed to bring fraud charges against aspartame's manufacturers instead took positions with the manufacturer's law firm and let the statute of limitations run out.[19] This kind of nepotism appears to be standard operating procedure at the FDA. It has been reported in a recent study that out of 49 top officials at the FDA, 37 took positions at companies they had regulated. Also, 150 FDA officials owned stock in companies under their jurisdiction.[20]

Aspartame may be responsible for myriad maladies, according to Dr. H. J. Roberts of the American Diabetes Association.[21]

Aspartame has also been implicated in the occurrence of some epileptic seizures. The Massachusetts Institute of Technology recently conducted a study on eighty people whose seizures were induced by aspartame.[22] The possibility of artificially induced seizures has caused the aviation industry to set up a hotline for pilots to report adverse aspartame reactions. Some of the more than six hundred pilots who called in reported experiencing grand mal seizures while in the cockpit.[23] (Could this explain some of the mysterious crashes that occur when, all other systems appearing normal, the aircraft inexplicably corkscrews into the ground?)

The adverse reactions to aspartame previously listed, terrible as they are, can still be seen as temporary and easily avoided by not consuming it. This choice may not be available to future generations whose neurophysiology has been permanently altered by this chemical compound which science considers not only a sweetener but also a neurotoxin.[24] While it is common knowledge that alcohol is a major cause of birth defects, few pregnant women realize that the can of diet cola they are enjoying instead of their favorite alcoholic beverage contains highly poisonous wood alcohol. This is because aspartame contains 10 percent methanol (wood alcohol) by weight. Research conducted by Dr. William H. Pardridge of the University of California indicates that mothers with as little as 250 parts per million of phenylalanine in their bloodstream are likely to give birth to a child with a ten-point drop in IQ.[25] (Could this explain why Johnny can't read?) This information, combined with the results of studies conducted by Dr. Ralph G. Walton on aspartame's deleterious effects on people subject to mood disorders, bodes ill for the future. According to Dr. Walton, "Its use in this population should be discouraged."[26]

Conclusion

The discovery of the "gut brain's" relationship to our emotional and physical well-being should cause us to reconsider our relationship with the chemicals that we let pass our lips. If the tiniest traces of certain compounds are capable of severely affecting the synaptic firings of the tissue mass in our skull, then it stands to reason that the tissue mass responsible for instinctive knowledge is subject to the same kinds of influences. Is that glass of tap water turning you into an obedient automaton? Is the pasteurized milk you're drinking robbing you of nutrients that your body (and both brains) require for proper functioning? Is Prozac also blocking out the vitamins and minerals while addicting both brains to its siren's song? Will Olestra prove to be the final insult? Is the NutraSweet logo a downward spiral?

The ancient Latins employed a phrase which holds true in this case. The phrase in question is "Caveat emptor" (Let the buyer beware). Another, more modern phrase springs to mind, that being "You are what you eat." Dietary issues become more complex as new products enter the market at an increasing rate. Will the chemical tinkering of both the food supply and our brain chemistry, either through intent or bureaucratic malfeasance, create a future inhabited by malnourished robots incapable of realizing their own human potential? Or are we already there?

Issue 14, Fall 1997

The Gulf Biowar: How a New AIDS-like Plague Threatens Our Armed Forces

Alan R. Cantwell Jr., M.D.

What is the common thread which weaves through the occurrence of the highly contagious disease known as the Gulf War Syndrome, which has struck as many as sixty thousand veterans? Dr. Cantwell has found a biowarfare connection. Since the Nuremberg trials, it has been against international law to use people as guinea pigs in experiments without their informed consent. In an unprecedented legal decision, the FDA allowed the Pentagon to give unapproved drugs and vaccines to soldiers without their consent. The Pentagon also refused to identify the types of drugs and injections the troops were given forcibly, rendering them powerless against genetically altered "supergerms."

As MANY AS sixty thousand of the seven hundred thousand Gulf War vets who served in Desert Storm in 1991 are ill with a variety of symptoms lumped together as Persian Gulf War Syndrome (GWS). Symptoms include chronic fatigue, severe neurological disorders, muscle and joint pain, shortness of breath, gastrointestinal problems, memory loss, insomnia, rashes, depression, headaches, and other complaints. GWS is a sexually transmitted disease and is also contagious via the airborne route. Soldiers are passing on the illness to wives and family members, and their children appear to have an increased incidence of birth defects.

The government and the Pentagon stand accused of ignoring the vets by denying they were exposed to chemical or biological agents in the Gulf. Originally many vets were told by military doctors that their symptoms were caused by stress. The large number of sick vets led to an official inquiry.

In August 1995 a massive government study of GWS indicated no evidence of so-called Gulf War disease. Dr. Stephen Joseph, assistant secretary of defense for health affairs, claimed the soldiers were suffering from "multiple" diseases not stemming from any one cause and that their collective health was no worse than that of their counterparts in civilian life. The report denied that vets were exposed to chemical agents in the Gulf.

Reynaldo Negrete, in a letter of protest to the *Los Angeles Times* (8/20/95), wrote:

> When my son Ruben, a career Navy Seebee of 14 years, was sent to the Gulf he was a healthy young man weighing 185 pounds. When he came back four months later he had lost 20 pounds and his health. He continued to lose weight for more than a year, but the doctors at Port Hueneme and his command did nothing. Not until I had my congressman, Matthew G. Martinez, intervene on his behalf was our son admitted to the Naval Hospital in San Diego a year after arriving from the Gulf War a very sick young man. He then spent a year in the hospital, until he was medically discharged from the Navy no better off than the day he was admitted. Yet, my son continues to suffer, as does his family. My son has served his country very well, for more than 14 years. He has been deployed all over the world, and in just four short months in the Persian Gulf he comes home an invalid.

A year later, in 1996, the Department of Defense finally admitted that four hundred soldiers (later changed to five thousand; still later to twenty thousand) may have been exposed to toxic agents when, after the war had officially ended, the military blew up an ammunition storage depot in Kamisiyah in southern Iraq on March 4 and again on March 10, 1991. After the bombings, a UN inspection team informed Pentagon officials that the buildings contained chemical weapons. However, the Pentagon immediately classified the UN report, and the troops were never alerted about possible exposure to toxic chemicals.

Despite the cover-up, exposure to chemicals cannot account for so many sick soldiers. Not all sick vets were stationed in the Kamisiyah area. Many left the Iraqi war zone before the war actually started or arrived after the fighting stopped. In addition, exposure to chemicals cannot explain why some cases of GWS are contagious.

The first media reports of a Gulf illness surfaced in the spring of 1992, a year after the war ended. As time passed, the transmissibility of the disease was downplayed, as well as the fact that wives complained about miscarriages and "burning semen" after sex with their husbands. Veterans' groups now claim that a third of Gulf War babies are born with birth abnormalities. *Life* magazine (November 1996) featured a story on these Gulf babies entitled "The Tiny Victims of Desert Storm: Has Our Country Abandoned Them?" Pictured on the cover was U.S. Army sergeant Paul Hansen holding his three-year-old son, born with hands and feet attached to twisted stumps.

In the search for a cause of GWS, epidemiologists have been looking for a common factor that could have exposed so many Gulf War vets. Some sick vets were in the war zone for months, while others were stationed there for as little as nine days. And the illness has affected troops stationed in widely scattered geographic areas in the region.

One factor common to all the troops is that they were given experimental and potentially dangerous drugs and vaccines employed to protect them against Iraqi chemical and biowarfare agents. As early as December 1990, there were warnings about using our servicemen as medical guinea pigs. In an unprecedented legal decision, the FDA allowed the Pentagon to give unapproved drugs and vaccines without requiring consent of the soldiers. Claiming security reasons, the Pentagon also refused to identify the types or number of drugs and injections they forced the troops to take.

An angry serviceman stationed in Saudi Arabia maintained his civil rights were violated and sued the government in January 1991. Ever since the post–World War II Nuremberg trials, which convicted many top-ranking Nazis for crimes against human nature, it has been unethical and unlawful to use people as guinea pigs in experiments without their informed consent. This legal requirement was waived when the lawsuit was dismissed by U.S. district judge Stanley S. Harris, who cited the necessity of the military to protect the health of its troops.

Soldiers who rejected the injections were given them forcibly. Physicians who refused to cooperate with the military's experimental vaccine program were treated harshly. Army reservist Dr. Yolanda Huet-Vaughn protested it was her duty under the Nuremberg Code of Justice not to vaccinate personnel with experimental vaccines without their consent. At Huet-Vaughn's court-martial trial, a military judge ignored these considerations of international law and medical ethics and sentenced the mother of three children to thirty months in prison. Under pressure from activist groups, the doctor was released from military prison after serving eight months.

Allegations that experimental drugs and vaccines are a cause of GWS have been downplayed for obvious reasons. The Pentagon does not want to publicize the idea that GWS could be a man-made disease due to unethical experiments with dangerous and possibly contaminated vaccines. Furthermore, the military has a long history of conducting covert medical experiments on its own personnel, as well as on civilians; and the Agent Orange cover-up is still fresh in the minds of Vietnam war vets.

GWS is not limited to American soldiers. More than 1,100 British vets are ill. Many blame the injections they received against anthrax and plague. Englishman Tony Flint, associated with the Gulf War Veterans and Families Association, claims more than 100 vets have died of ailments ascribed to the inoculations. He says he was forced to take thirteen inoculations in one week and states there is no evidence of GWS among French troops who did not receive these vaccines.

The HIV Connection

Garth Nicolson and his wife, Nancy, both respected microbiologists, have recently discovered a bacterium, a so-called mycoplasma, in the blood of half the vets ill with GWS. The microbe associated with GWS has been identified as *Mycoplasma fermentans* (incognitus strain). Discovered a century ago in plants, mycoplasmas are the smallest known self-replicating microbes. Larger than viruses and much smaller than common bacteria, mycoplasmas have been implicated in a variety of diseases.

The mycoplasma in GWS could not be identified using standard lab tests. Through special genetic testing Garth Nicolson was able to discover the mycoplasma. Incredibly, the microbe had a piece of the envelope gene of the AIDS virus (HIV-1) attached to it! The HIV gene makes the mycoplasma even more aggressive, allowing it to attach to cells, which it then penetrates and poisons. According to Nicolson, a mycoplasma combined with the envelope gene of the AIDS retrovirus could never have originated in nature, but only through gene splicing in a laboratory.

Both Nicolsons contracted GWD from their daughter when she returned home from Desert Storm. Because of the contagious nature of the disease, the microbiologists suspected an infectious agent rather than a chemical weapon. When the mycoplasma was identified, the research team discovered that treatment with antibiotics, particularly doxycycline, was helpful in some cases.

In an interview on the Dave Emory radio show (10/20/96), Garth Nicolson theorizes that the microbe could have been deployed through contaminated vaccines, through the deliberate release of Iraqi bioweapons, from blowback from destroyed Iraqi bioweapon factories or possibly from Scud missile attacks. He says there has been a mycoplasma unit at the University of Baghdad for twenty-two years, manned by Iraqi scientists who were trained in the United States. Before the war, the U.S. government exported to Iraq various biological agents, both classified and unclassified, that could be used or developed as biological warfare agents.

Did this mycoplasma-HIV bioweapon originate in the United States or in the Gulf? It would be extremely helpful to know if there are cases of GWS in Iraq, Kuwait, Saudi Arabia, Jordan, and elsewhere in the Middle East. Surprisingly, the government and the media are silent on this question, although Nicolson claims three hundred thousand Iraqis have died and one million are sick since the war. It is rumored that 15–20 percent of the population of the countries surrounding Iraq are ill with GWS.

In a forty-page report entitled "Germ Warfare against America: The Desert Storm Plague and Cover-Up," Nicolson reports:

> *Mycoplasma fermentans* (incognitus) has been tested on the Texas Department of Corrections prisoners in the late 1980s prior to the Gulf War. It was tested on death row inmates as well as other inmates in Huntsville, Texas. The guards then contracted it from the inmates, and the guards then gave it to their families and community. This mycoplasma vaccine testing was funded by the U.S. Army, and today there is an outbreak of 350 people in the Huntsville area with a strange disease resembling GWS.

Garth Nicolson's important research has appeared in the underground press, but until recently his research has been ignored by the mainstream, corporate-controlled media. On the Emory show Nicolson was asked how many soldiers have died of GWS. Although there are no official figures, he estimates that up to fifteen thousand vets have died of "unusual" diseases and several thousand have died of cancer. If true, these death rates are very high considering the young age (under twenty-five) of many of our soldiers. Apparently doctors, nurses, and medical personnel are contracting GWS from sick patients, indicating another AIDS-like epidemic in the making.

Further complicating the epidemiology of GWS is that soldiers' shot records and even medical records have disappeared or are unavailable. In addition, the *Los Angeles Times* (12/5/96) reports that military logs "crucial to Gulf War veterans who believe their health problems are linked to chemical weapons" are also missing and can't be found. These important logs cover the period March 4–10, during the bombings at Kamisiyah. The Senate Veterans Affairs Committee has recently won permission to examine General Norman Schwarzkopf's personal logs.

At the request of Representative Norm Dicks of Washington State, a group of military and civilian scientists and Pentagon experts met on December 23, 1996, at Walter Reed Army Hospital in Washington, to discuss Nicolson's research. Walter Reed spokesman Ben Smith said the army would agree to study his mycoplasma research as part of its investigation into the cause of GWS.

On December 27, 1996, a story about Garth Nicolson's research appeared on the front page of the *Los Angeles Times*. However, the most significant part of Nicholson's research, namely that the mycoplasma had a piece of HIV attached to it, was not mentioned. The origin of the microbe was left in doubt, the writer simply stating that Nicolson's research suggests "the primitive bacterium, called mycoplasma, was deliberately altered for Iraqi use as a biological weapon."

Also not mentioned in the media was mycoplasma research conducted by the military a decade earlier. In 1986 Dr. Shyh-Ching Lo, a molecular biologist at the Armed Forces Institute of Pathology in Washington, D.C., reported a "viruslike agent" derived from Kaposi's sarcoma, the "gay cancer" associated with AIDS. Using highly technical methods of molecular biology, Lo's "virus" was subsequently identified as the bacterium *Mycoplasma fermentans* (also known as *M. incognitus*). In 1989 Lo also reported similar mycoplasma infection as the cause of death in six young, previously healthy military personnel from New Jersey, Virginia, Guam, and Turkey, all of whom died within one to seven weeks from a progressive and mysterious "flulike disease." In 1991 Lo found yet another mycoplasma, *Mycoplasma penetrans*, in the urine of gays with AIDS. Luc Montagnier, the codiscoverer of the AIDS virus, has confirmed Lo's mycoplasma research. The Pasteur Institute virologist believes mycoplasmas are a necessary "cofactor" that allows HIV infection to progress to full-blown AIDS.

Are mycoplasmas being developed as biological warfare weapons? Certainly all known infectious agents are screened for possible military use by biowarfare scientists around the world. As stated, there was a mycoplasma lab in Iraq. Before the Gulf War the Iraqis freely used nerve gas against the Kurds in northern Iraq, and after the war they used mustard gas against Shiite Muslim nomads in southern Iraq. And the U.S. Army conducted mycoplasma research in Huntsville, Texas.

Before the Gulf War the mixing of the AIDS virus (HIV) with mycoplasmas in the laboratory by Lo and Montagnier was recorded in the scientific literature. When mycoplasma was added to HIV-infected blood cells in test tubes, it made the AIDS virus more pathogenic. Silver-leaf monkeys experimentally infected with Lo's mycoplasma all developed infections, immunosuppression, and died within seven to nine months with an AIDS-like "wasting syndrome."

A "Mycoplasma Workshop," sponsored by the National Institutes of Allergy and Infectious Diseases, was held in San Antonio, Texas, in December 1989. Lo's research was featured. When asked if his fatal mycoplasma "flu cases" were contagious, Lo replied, "We don't know." Interestingly, some of Lo's patients improved with the antibiotic doxycycline, the same drug Nicolson has found effective in some cases of GWS.

Most physicians know little about mycoplasma infection and even less about testing for these microbes. For many years this writer has reported mycoplasmalike organisms discovered in the damaged tissue of cancer, in AIDS, and in autoimmune disease. This research has been published in medical journals and summarized in two books by this author: *AIDS: The Mystery and the Solution* (1984) and *The Cancer Microbe* (1990). Unfortunately, this research has been largely ignored by the AIDS and cancer establishments, as well as by so-called mycoplasma experts. These bacteria can be easily seen microscopically in the diseased tissue of AIDS (including Kaposi's sarcoma), cancer, and certain other diseases of unknown cause.

As some people in medical science are aware, important and valid scientific discoveries are ignored because they are "politically incorrect." Lo's mycoplasma research has been largely ignored by the leading virologists who direct AIDS research. Similarly, Lo has ignored the published research of hundreds of other researchers who have shown mycoplasmalike microbes in cancer, AIDS, and immune diseases. The inability of scientists to consider "politically incorrect" scientific findings may explain why physicians currently have such difficulty understanding and treating new epidemics like AIDS and GWS, in which these microbes are operative.

Why does the military ignore GWS and deny its existence? Undoubtedly, chemical and biological weapons were employed in the Gulf War. Was the military fully capable of detecting these bioweapons? Or was the detection of chemical agents and bioweapons ignored or covered up? Is the military capable of protecting its troops from modern-day biowarfare? Are soldiers now powerless against genetically engineered "supergerms" deployed by biowarfare scientists?

In the future, will soldiers willingly go into battle knowing that exposure to bioweapons will be ignored by their government and knowing that no one is immune from the effects of these man-made microbes of death?

Issue 16, Spring 1997

Alternative Three: The Great Brain Drain

Joan d'Arc

What would explain the sudden paralysis of the American space program along with Russian manned space flights, when everything seemed to be going so well? Why did the Russians step down when they were winning the space race? Was a sweetheart deal struck between the superpowers, culminating in a shared colony on the "dark side of the moon"? Joan d'Arc examines the disturbing speculation known as Alternative Three.

ON JUNE 20, 1977, Anglia TV aired a disconcerting special which dazed and confused its British viewers. Originally intended as an April Fools' hoax, *Alternative Three* horrified the public (not unlike Orson Welles's 1938 *War of the Worlds* radio broadcast). Complete with the vintage keyboard electronics of a young Brian Eno, real NASA space footage, and actor credits at the end, the "report" of a joint Russian-American secret space program involving migration to colonies on the Moon and Mars provoked over ten thousand phone calls.

The reaction from all over the world, including letters from people in "positions of authority," convinced *Alternative Three* television writer Leslie Watkins that he had "accidentally trespassed into a range of top-secret truths." The show was then turned into a book by Leslie Watkins and David Ambrose in 1978, now out of print; this time the premise was that the Anglia TV show had been based on fact but was presented as fiction to lighten its impact.

In his book, *Casebook on Alternative Three*, Jim Keith describes the original *Alternative Three* as "a teleplay and book which utterly lack substantiation." He considers it a contrived story stuck between a collage of film footage and news briefs with no real connections, complete with hokey interviews with characters who may or may not exist. Mr. Keith arrives in short order at the conclusion that the Alternative Three "mythos" has "no basis in fact." Why, then, did he write a book about it?

The answer is as plain as the face on Mars: Because, as well-known conspiracy researcher, Mae Brussell, stated: "The book made me nauseous . . . I wanted to vomit. I wanted to faint. I wanted to cry." In short, the Goddess of Conspiracy Theory believed *Alternative Three* to be the most dangerous document in her library and that it placed everything else she had collected into meaningful perspective. It essentially provided the clue to the big picture, the iceberg submerged below the surface, the answer to the question Why mind control?

So just what is Alternative Three? First, you have to know what the first two alternatives are, if and why they proved inoperable, and what undesirable situation spawned them. Alternative One is the "ingenious" plan to "detonate nuclear bombs in the atmosphere to allow pollution and heat to dissipate into space." Alternative Two is the construction of "vast subterranean habitats" beneath the earth's surface, where the elite would meet at the push of the dreaded "red button." Alternative Three involves the great escape to a new extraterrestrial colony, first on the Moon and later on Mars.

In *Casebook on Alternative Three*, Jim Keith investigates this profoundly existential topic. The earth calamities which would cause mass extinction on Earth are population related, environmentally related (greenhouse and the like), or nuclear related. The first two alternatives might constitute some kind of half-baked "solution" to these types of threats; however, the third alternative appears to "solve" a qualitatively different dilemma. What might be the impetus for the planet hopping of phase three? Is Alternative Three an entirely different animal?

The main gist of Alternative Three is that scientists are the necessary "advance team" for the successful colonization of an alien environment. The *Casebook* tries to prove that scientists are missing by the scores since the original *Alternative Three* book was published. In this regard, Jim Keith gets a firsthand taste of what it's like not to have "documentation" of unexplainable goings-on. His secondhand stories about people who met other people who have knowledge of the disappearance of certain scientists, who have agreed to go to an undisclosed location from which they can never return is, unfortunately, more "urban legend" than fact. Of equal concern in his book is whether a mind-controlled colony reminiscent of Kurt Vonnegut's 1959 novel, *Sirens of Titan*, may have been abducted for colonizing purposes.

The confusion surrounding the Alternative Three mythos is whether, or at which point, Apollo moon missions began to be fabricated by NASA. In the *Alternative Three* video, described here in its entirety, Bob Grodin states that "the later Apollo missions are a smokescreen to cover what's really going on out there." Others—for instance, Ralph Rene in his book *NASA Mooned America*—believe all of the Apollo moon missions were photography studio hoaxes and that earthlings have never set foot on the moon. Richard Hoagland offers some intriguing observations regarding the strange Soviet and American behavior of the late sixties.

Richard Hoagland of the Mars Mission believes that the first Apollo mission made the discovery that we were not the first to set foot on the moon, and this immediately halted further manned exploration. He offers some intriguing observations regarding the strange Soviet and American behavior of the late sixties. According to the Summer 1995 issue of Hoagland's *Martian Horizons* "inexplicable Soviet behavior vis-a-vis the Moon" began in the late 1960s simultaneously with the beginning of NASA's "now unfolding weirdness" with regard to the Moon. Hoagland writes: "This recently revealed, paradoxical Soviet behavior, so at variance with all their Cold War rhetoric, includes a major mystifying incident, which occurred at the height of the so-called 'space race.' " The mystifying incident of which Hoagland speaks is the scheduling and abrupt cancellation of the first planned Russian flight of cosmonauts around the Moon in December 1968, which would have occurred just days before the infamous Apollo 8 journey. This crucial Soviet cancellation, which has since been ascertained from KGB documents, was ordered "on the eve of an imminent 'win' in the East–West Moon race, [and] came from the very top of the Soviet leadership." Hoagland believes that the timing and illogical order of this behavior is bizarre and inexplicable.

Hoagland further observes that, "This dramatic Soviet decision occurred immediately after a major unmanned Soviet mission to the Moon . . . [which] returned its high-resolution films directly to the earth." These high resolution films were matched later by similar images that were returned to the NASA photo lab by the Apollo astronauts. Hoagland wonders if the Russian lunar analysts discovered something on their high-resolution lunar films, "Something that caused the sudden, apparent paralysis history now records regarding all further Soviet policy vis-a-vis the Moon." This sudden paralysis was later inexplicably repeated in the American space program, he writes, for, "After the stunning American success of Apollo 8, there followed a rash of equally inexplicable 'failures' of the giant Russian booster designed to take Soviet cosmonauts triumphantly to the Moon ahead of the Americans."

Hoagland wonders what went so radically wrong with these space programs and what has kept "not only the Americans and Russians, but even the Europeans, Chinese, Indians, Brazilians and Japanese so closely 'by the shore.'" Could it be, he wonders, that we simply learned that we were not the first intelligent beings to reach the Moon or to leave "a dizzying array of dazzling, monumental artifacts on satellites and planets all across this solar system?"

The Brookings Report, officially entitled "Proposed Studies on the Implications of Peaceful Space Activities for Human Affairs," was commissioned by NASA in 1959. The report recommended complete censorship of any possible future discovery of extraterrestrial intelligence based on anthropological studies of societies which have disintegrated in the presence of culture shock.

Whichever scenario turns out to be true, the short end of Alternative Three is that we will never be shown the infamous "dark side of the moon" because there, as plain as day, sits a shared U.S.-Soviet colony. In addition, since the reduced gravity of the moon makes launching easier, a launching facility on the moon would make planetary exploration easier and colonization of Mars more feasible. Therefore Alternative Three appears to include plans for a Martian colony as well. Let's now go to a play-by-play description of the original British teleplay *Alternative Three: The Teleplay,* which caused so much excitement in 1977.

The *Alternative Three* video, now distributed by Underground Video, is a copy of the British-aired special of 1977. This docudrama has an extremely contrived feel to it, and it is difficult to believe that viewers accepted it at face value. *Alternative Three* begins with interviews of family members of missing scientists. One family member states: "How can people just vanish off the face of the earth in this day and age?" As the story goes, this British team began their investigation of Alternative Three by talking with scientist Dr. Anne Clark, who explained that it was a "question of facilities." She states, "If I and people like me are going to do the job we've been trained to do, then we must be given the means to do it." It is not known by this author whether the identities are real or fabricated.

Shortly after making that statement on film, Dr. Clark told the investigative team that she could no longer speak to them. She told her friends she was going to New York, and her abandoned car was found at Heathrow. There was no record of her taking a flight, and she never returned. The docudrama goes on to discuss two other missing scientists who have similar stories. These are just three of the four hundred who make up the worldwide brain drain, twenty-four of whom are British. It is reported that some have even disappeared with their entire families.

The subject then switches to Sir William Ballantine's accidental auto death and the bizarre circumstances surrounding a tape which he had sent to a colleague the day before he died. The tape was "scrambled" and could not be accessed without NASA equipment. An unknown American called the journalists shortly thereafter and arranged a meeting. The meeting with the young American on a busy city street was videotaped by the team. The American gave the team an address for a meeting the next day. A young woman answered the door the following day. They asked for the American, and she said, "You mean Harry?" The second meeting with the American turned out worse than the first. "Harry" was lying on a couch under a blanket, telling everyone to go away. Suddenly he leapt off the couch and attacked the crew, grabbing the camera which had been taping his hysterical outburst.

Alternative Three then discusses the great world drought which began in the early sixties. Scientists became aware that the earth's climate was changing radically. People were starving all over Africa and India. There were unprecedented earthquakes, volcanic eruptions, and extreme temperatures all over the world. By the late sixties, during the Carter administration, solar heat was having a hard time escaping the atmosphere, carbon dioxide was increasing, and blizzards, floods, and storms were causing national disasters. A new "Ice Age" threatened the earth. This is purportedly when Alternative One was devised: a plan to blow a hole into the atmosphere to let some of the heat escape. (Indeed, why is there now an apparent hole in the ozone?)

One scientist interviewed in *Alternative Three* claimed that a conference of government and top scientists devised three theoretical plans for at least some of the earth's inhabitants to survive a coming global calamity. The second alternative was the building of a complex underground tunnel system where the elite could meet at the push of the proverbial red button. The third alternative was considered the best one: the establishment of sustainable communities on the moon. For this, they needed to get scientists to go to work on the moon. Interestingly, the *Alternative Three* video does not really discuss whether scientists were "abducted" or whether they agreed to go in secrecy for the opportunity to work on this project. Apparently the *Alternative Three* book, which was published after the television docudrama, did delve more into the abduction and mind control aspects which are covered by Jim Keith in his *Casebook*.

After setting the stage for the "brain drain" scenario, the players in *Alternative Three* then interview a fictitious, psychologically ravaged ex-Apollo astronaut, Bob Grodin. According to this docudrama, in the interim since his moon trip Grodin had become maladjusted to society, resulting in "breakdowns in relationships, an unstable personality," and, as dramatized, a heavy drinking problem. The investigator flew to Boston to meet with Grodin at his home. After his buxom young wife served a couple of cans of beer, Grodin began drinking bourbon. His exasperation with the repeated questioning is evident. Finally, determined not to get plastered by himself, he made the interviewer join him in a bourbon. With the bourbon talking, Grodin finally spilled the beans.

After being nudged several times with questions about what he saw on his Apollo moon mission, an angry and drunk Bob Grodin finally responded: "We had a big disappointment. We didn't get there first. The later Apollo missions are a smokescreen to cover what's really going on out there."

The dismayed British interviewer responds: "But what's going on?"

To which Grodin retorts: "I don't know. Ask the Pentagon. Have you phoned the Kremlin?"

The BBC interviewer is now on the edge of his seat: "You've got to tell me. What did you see?"

"Well," says Grodin, "we came down in the wrong place. And it was crawling."

"Are you talking about men from earth?" asks the interviewer.

Grodin angrily spilled out the fantastic story in a nutshell:

Do you think that they need all that crap down in Florida to get two guys up there on a bicycle? The hell they do. You know why we're there? To give them a good PR story for all the hardware they shoot up in space. Christ, we're nothing. You know why we're there? To keep you bums happy; to stop you from asking questions about what's really going on out there. That's it. End of story. That's a finish.

Upon his return to England with the Grodin interview, the journalist received a phone call from the young American woman concerning "Harry." When they met with her, she asked for protection, and she gave them a circuit board given to her by Harry before he disappeared. The circuit board contained a decoder to unscramble the tape which Sir Ballantine had mailed to his friend before he was killed in an auto wreck. With the two pieces of the puzzle now in custody, the investigators then viewed the cut NASA footage which apparently the missing American "Harry" and the deceased Sir Ballantine had both seen. The film shows some stock footage of Bob Grodin's moon walk. Grodin was talking on the second channel that us taxpayers don't get to hear, which is called the "biological channel" since it is ostensibly used for private discussions regarding medical and biological matters. Grodin's words "This is unbelievable" are interrupted by NASA's code words "Bravo Tango . . . Jezebel." The viewer sees nothing extraordinary besides the "moon walker" he has seen before. We are left to presume he saw, on the "dark side of the moon," a bustling colony of people, presumably of earth origin.

Grodin's later comment during the *Alternative Three* teleplay, regarding "two guys on a bicycle," indicates that what he saw consisted of a superadvanced technology which puts us, comparatively, in the stone age. Similarly, his retort that the place was "crawling" suggested a massive effort had taken place or was currently being undertaken. Where would NASA acquire such an enormous labor force? Is this the source of the nausea which overtook Mae Brussell upon realizing that *Alternative Three* put all of the research in her library "in perspective"? Considering the fact that her library consisted of newspaper clippings and documents concerning mind control, missing persons, and black budget operations, *Alternative Three* was quite possibly her bull's-eye missing link. Who would have their eye on NASA and toward an effort of such huge and existentially nauseating magnitude? Leave it to the British. And they think *we're* paranoid!

It is also asserted in *Alternative Three* that during one of his flights over the moon Bob Grodin spotted a flashing light on the edge of a crater. Was someone there before us? If so, who was it? The *Alternative Three* hosts ask a very important question: What were the space shuttles "shuttling" over the years? Grodin suggests the astronauts existed only as public relations liaisons "for all the hardware they shoot up in space." *Alternative Three* discusses the unmanned earthling attempts to get to the moon, which began with the Soviets in 1959. Of the two thousand space launches, 60 percent were Russian. By the late sixties the Russians mysteriously "dropped out" of the space race, and in 1969 Neil Armstrong became the first man to "walk on the moon." Was this some kind of sweetheart deal between the superpowers? Is this the smokescreen to which the "Bob Grodin" character alluded in this fantastic teleplay?

Alternative Three states that there is a "pattern of landings on the dark side of the moon" with "groupings of American and Soviet landings on the dark side." This television docudrama attempted to uncover something that is "operating beneath the security cover" with regard to a massive secret space program between the superpowers. As incredible as it sounds, the Alternative Three scenario suggests that there is an internationally shared space colony on the moon, utilizing the most extraordinary researchers and scientists as both builders and colonists. Underlying this bizarre scenario is the assertion that the space war, even the cold war itself, has been hoaxed all along. In addition, the Alternative Three mythos includes the concern that perhaps an army of "missing persons" constitutes the labor force of the colony. Whether these groups of moon colonists went of their own free will, or were abducted against their will, remains one of the most nagging questions of the Alternative Three scenario.

Could it be we've got some civilian MIAs on the moon?

Issue 15, Winter 1996

Four Horses of the Apocalypse:
A Color-Coded Key to the Cryptocracy

Wendy Wallace

Though not science per se, this article is an intriguing example of suppressed biblical research, the kind mainstream Christian "leaders" won't touch! Wendy Wallace decodes the timeline of biblical revelations alongside current events in this spectacular article. The Time is Now.

> When he had opened the Third Seal . . . I beheld, lo, a black horse, and he that sat on him had a pair of balances in his hand . . . saying . . . a measure of wheat for a penny, and three measures of barley for a penny; and see thou hurt not the oil and the wine. (Revelation 6:5, 6:6)

IN NOVEMBER 1992 George Bush announced that he would *not* triple the tariff on rapeseed oil and Chardonnay wine, as he had been threatening to do. To the best of my knowledge, Bush's decision not to place a triple tariff on rapeseed oil and Chardonnay wine from France, after announcing that he would do so, is the only time that oil and wine, and oil and wine only, have been the subject of international attention. Indeed, it was feared that a tariff would set off international trade wars. Because of my familiarity with the Book of Revelation, the phrase "see thou hurt not the oil and the wine" in the context of commodities and prices leaped to mind. I went immediately to my King James Bible.

Another puzzle pattern emerged, and I was given to realize that this edict from President Bush (CIA group code name Black Rose) was the clue that we are *in* the Third Seal, the third of the four horsemen of the Apocalypse, the Black Horse. I perceived the bare outlines of the First Seal, the White Horse (1776–) (Illuminati and Freemasonry), and the

Second Seal, the Red Horse (1790–) (Communist revolutions), which further confirmed our position in the sequence.

The Christian Conspiracy

My immediate reaction was to send off a three-page letter to a few of the preachers on the local Christian radio station, figuring they'd be as excited as I was about this startling but prophesied occurrence. The Bible states a number of times that the end-time prophecies will not be understood until they happen (Rev. 22:10; Dan. 12:9). It further states, "And it shall come to pass afterward that I shall pour out my Spirit upon all flesh; and your sons and daughters shall prophesy. . . ." (Joel 2:28).

Well, I'm a daughter, and I'm made of flesh, so that includes me. But the pastors didn't think so. As I continued to study, the picture became larger and more accurate, with information pouring in from previously unknown sources. An old computer and printer were given to me by a friend, and the letter became sixteen pages, then twenty, and with additional documentation, it grew to a few hundred pages. I kept sending it out to these aforementioned "Christians," who continued to dismiss it. Didn't believe in conspiracies, they said. But the Bible itself describes the conspiracy in detail!

After about a year of this, my attention was drawn to a number of chapters and verses that spelled out the situation. A friend pointed out the deeper meaning of Matthew 24:5: "For many shall come in my name (that is, calling themselves 'Christians'), saying, I am Christ, (as in 'Jesus is Lord'), and shall deceive many." If you've ever seen the shenanigans of televangelists, you've got the picture. Needless to say, the "accepted" interpretation of that verse is limited to the David Koreshes and Sun Yung Moons, who proclaim themselves to be Christ, when in fact it applies to virtually all organized "Christian churches." The modern "church" as it exists in America—all denominations—is an extremely high-level, deep-cover psy-ops agency of the shadow government. And the Bible said it would be, in Luke 13:21 and Matthew 13:31. While all religions offer false methods of "knowing [or becoming] God," "Christianity" is the most pernicious, because a counterfeit is most difficult to detect when it most closely resembles the real thing.

Check out Matthew 23 for what Jesus thinks about the religionists. Hypocrites is the word He uses most. The apostle Peter wasn't nuts about them, either. His description of the "Christian right wing," "Eagle Forum," "Moral Majority," and their ilk: "There shall be false teachers among you . . . and many shall follow their pernicious ways; by reason of whom the way of truth shall be evil spoken of." So if you have a hard time controlling a gag reflex when you think of "Christians," you and Jesus have a lot in common. He says he will vomit them out of his mouth (Revelation 3:16) after removing his people from among them (Rev. 18:4; Ezek. 34:10; Jer. 5:26–31; 10:21).

If you, like most, reflexively equate these counterfeit "Christians" with the Bible and Jesus, you're living testimony to the overwhelming success of the cryptocracy's most sub-rosa (and most crucial—it's about souls, after all) operation. Obviously it's true not only of those who have resolutely shunned the "Christian Church," but of churchgoers who are too obtuse to "Come out of her, my people" (which is the vast majority of them: Matt. 7:21; Luke 1:24–30). It was a real relief to realize I didn't have to join up with that crew, but dismaying to see that there weren't any alternatives, in terms of "Christian" leadership. Having given up on the phony pastors and priests and prophets, but still not comprehending the profound and determined (predetermined!) impenetrable blindness of the "flock," I had rewritten *The Four Horsemen Exposed* for the "layperson," still figuring that it would be the "Christians" who would comprehend it. But alas, "This people hath a revolting and a rebellious heart; they are revolted and gone." (Jeremiah 5:23) "For the leaders of this people cause them to err; and they that are led of them are destroyed." (Isa. 9:16) The Bible has also made it clear that his people are not, by and large, hanging around churches. "For the pastors are become brutish, and have not sought the Lord therefore they shall not prosper, and all their flocks shall be scattered." (Jer. 10:21) "His watchmen are blind, they are all ignorant, they are all dumb dogs, they cannot bark; sleeping, lying down, loving to slumber." (Isa. 56:10)

While many are correctly identifying the world's dramatically increasing travail with the "beginning of sorrows," in Matthew 24, Mark 13, and Luke 21, and even pointing out the parallels to the horsemen that ride in the Seals, they are utterly blind to the fact that we are now living in the Time of the Seals. Because of this, they aren't able to use the convicting prescience that God has provided in the following prophecy: "And now, I have told you before it come to pass, that when it is come to pass, ye might believe." (John 14:29)

In the parable of the Great Supper, Luke 14:15–24, Jesus tells of the master of a house who prepared a marvelous feast and invited numerous guests. At the last minute, they all decided they had "better things to do" and declined the invitation. Having gone to great trouble to prepare the feast, the host told his servants, "Go out quickly into the streets and lanes of the city, and bring in hither the poor, and the maimed, and the halt, and the blind. Go out into the highways and hedges, and compel them to come in, that my house may be filled." He then declares that none of those who were first invited will ever dine with him. That's what's happening.

We're victims not only of the elegantly planned and painstakingly applied plans of the evilarchy, but of our own deceitful hearts and fallen natures (Jer. 17:9), without which their Machiavellian machinations could not succeed. We're ever ready to embrace any "solution" that allows us to continue without confronting our own delusions of grandeur. We insist that we're special by our own merits, exalted on our own account, sovereign by our own power, perfectible by our own design. We close our eyes to the evidence that surrounds us and indwells us, and we live and die in our own virtual reality. Every day, in every way, we're getting worse and worse, and we deserve what's coming down.

Seal Three: Black Horse

The basic warning signs of the impending "end of the age" are given in Matthew 24, Mark 13, and Luke 21, in answer to the disciple's question "Tell us, when shall these things be and what shall be the sign of thy coming, and of the end of the world?" The answer, as recorded in Luke 21, is

> Take heed that ye be not deceived, for many shall come in my name, saying I am Christ; and the time draweth near: go ye not therefore after them. But when ye shall hear of wars and commotions, be not terrified: for these things must first come to pass; but the end is not by and by. . . . Nation shall rise against nation, and kingdom against kingdom: and great earthquakes shall be in diverse places, and famines, and pestilences; and fearful sights and great signs shall there be from heaven. . . . And there shall be signs in the sun, and in the moon, and in the stars; and upon the earth distress of nations, with

perplexity; the sea and the waves roaring; men's hearts failing them for fear, and for looking after those things which are coming upon the earth: for the powers of heaven shall be shaken.

Even those who limit their information gathering to the nightly television news can confirm the occurrence of all of the above, as at no other time in the recorded history of mankind. In astonishing detail and accuracy, however, the Seven Seals of Revelation 6, the first four of which are the Four Horsemen of the Apocalypse, show us precisely where we are on the timetable and what's to come next. Until now they have been only vaguely described as the white horse of conquest, the red horse of war, the black horse of famine, and the pale horse of death. But there's much more.

I believe I can conclusively demonstrate that the Four Horsemen of the Apocalypse, the first Four Seals, precede Daniel's Seventieth Week; the Fifth Seal is the first three and a half years of the last seven years of this dispensation; and the Seventh Seal, which contains the First Trumpet, begins the Great Tribulation, the time of the end, the second three and a half years of Daniel's Seventieth Week, which contains both the Wrath and the Judgment.

Further, there are two Raptures, the first of which takes place during the Sixth Seal (Revelation 6:12–17) and the second before the Vial, or Bowl Judgments (Rev. 15:2), just where the Bible says they are, as opposed to the position of the "Pre-Tribulation pillow prophets" (Ezekiel 13), who expect to be evacuated between chapters 4 and 5; a slight miscalculation. We're directed to interpret Scripture literally when the text and context warrant it, and a literal, chronological, and comprehensive understanding of the Seals is now possible, as it has not been previously. This is true of much end times prophecy, owing to relatively recent events on the world scene. The Holy Scripture has told us to expect just this phenomenon (Jer. 23:20, Dan. 12:9, Matt. 10:26).

We are in the midst of the Third Seal, and the meaning and content of the first Two Seals have been made abundantly clear, when viewed in the context of recent history and in the full context of the Bible. The remaining Seals are predictable with considerable precision in regard to both timing and circumstance. With your continued patience, I hope to demonstrate incontrovertibly that the Seals are the stages of the Antichrist system, a.k.a. the New World Order being maneuvered into place for the world monarchy of the Antichrist.

The Seals are Pre–Second Coming

The very designation "Seals" tells us that they must be opened before the event (the Great Tribulation) begins. One cannot read a letter until all the seals are broken, and we are told that the Lamb (Jesus) alone is worthy to open them. He does so from the right hand of he who sits upon the throne (Rev. 5:7) in heaven. Therefore, he opens them before his Second Coming and, thus, before the Rapture of the Church. Some expositors are insistent on referring to the "Seal Judgments," but the Bible does not. The Revelation does not label anything a judgment until Revelation 14:7, which announces that "the hour of His Judgment is come," and this judgment is foreshadowed in Revelation 11:18. The word "judgment" is not used until that point, just before the Bowl Judgments. Everything between Revelation 6:17 and Revelation 17:1 is referred to as the "wrath," and the beginning of the "wrath" is clearly announced in Revelation 6:17, the Sixth Seal: "For the great day of His Wrath is come," beginning, therefore, with the Seventh Seal, the First Trumpet.

The Seals are Pre-Judgment

Revelation 6:9, the Fifth Seal, shows us all the saints martyred to that time crying with a loud voice, "How long, O Lord, holy and true, dost thou not judge and avenge our blood on them that dwell upon the earth?" They are told they must "rest yet for a little season, until their fellow servants also, and their brethren, that should be killed as they were, should be fulfilled." This corresponds to Matthew 24:9–14, Mark 13:9–13, and Luke 21:12–19, a period of time when Christians will be martyred, many of them under the justification of "biorelativity" (John 16:2). This martyrdom precedes the Great Tribulation, which begins, in each of these books, with the following verse, referring to the Abomination of Desolation. Therefore we know that Seal Five, and the four preceding Seals, takes place prior to the Time of Jacob's Trouble and the Judgment. While this would still allow for the possibility of Seals one through five happening in the first three and a half years of Daniel's Seventieth Week (if we disregard God's precision elsewhere), as we continue I think you'll see why this is not the case.

The persecution of Christians has, of course, been continual throughout history, usually at the hands of the religionists, and is now rampant in Red China, where the state-approved "Christian Church" tortures, kills, and often cannibalizes those who own or smuggle a Bible. Much the same thing is going on in South America, Senegal, Pakistan, Mexico, and elsewhere and will soon be happening in the good ol' U.S. of A. (or Magna-Region 1).

The Four Horsemen Are Pre-Tribulation

While some wish to interpret the Seals as an overview of the Tribulation, this cannot be done even mathematically, since the Fourth Seal calls for a quarter of the earth dead, and Rev. 9:18 calls for a third dead. These must be two separate events, as one fourth cannot equal one third. Interestingly enough, the Global 2000 plan fostered by the Club of Rome during the Carter administration makes the strong suggestion that half of the world's population should be eliminated by the year 2000. I wonder if they realized that one fourth of six billion is one and a half billion dead (Fourth Seal, Revelation 6:8), leaving four and a half billion, of which one third more (1.5 billion) are killed in Revelation 9:18, the Sixth Trumpet, for a grand total of three billion dead (one-half the earth's population) by the year 2000, give or take a year or two. John the Revelator wrote the Revelation around A.D. 80. So whose plan is this, really? Truly, "The fear of the Lord is the beginning of wisdom." (Psalm 111:10)

Seal Three: The Time Is Now

With these guidelines in mind, you may come to share my conviction that in November 1992 we received notification that the Third Seal was being opened. The code signal to "hurt not the oil and the wine" went forth at that time from George Bush. Lest it seem jarring to cite a contemporary as a referent of biblical prophecy, let it be noted that biblical prophecy refers to current events and people at the time those prophecies are fulfilled. This also helps us to understand that the "oil and wine" of the Revelation does not refer to the "oil and wine" of the first century A.D., but to the "oil and wine" of "end of the age" (as in now!).

The context of Seal Three is commodities and prices, of staple foods (expensive: a day's wages for a day's food) as opposed to luxury foods (such as oil and wine [Prov. 21:17] kept affordable: "hurt not"). Both of these conditions of Seal Three are now being fulfilled. The division between the haves and have-nots has never in history been as extreme as it is today. A day's wages for a day's food is already the case over much of the globe, if there is food to be had at all. Millions are starving to death each year, and multimillions more are malnourished to the point of irreversible damage. The depopulation program is moving along right on schedule. Monetary systems of all countries are in wild flux, due to systematic looting and high-level tinkering. Unemployment and underemployment are the highest since the Great Depression, and companies are still downsizing drastically or moving to areas where slave labor wages are welcomed. Brazil has an accumulated inflation rate of 146 billion percent since 1980, according to the *New York Times.*

The Central Bank in Russia forced a ruble recall of all notes printed before 1993 and allowed each citizen only $35 of the new currency, with the rest to be deposited for six months in savings accounts that will be worthless when they can be retrieved, thanks to the inflation interest ratio. Mr. Greenspan has decided that the Federal Reserve will abandon previous yardsticks and embark on new plans for controlling our money supply. A double currency, one foreign, one domestic, is being considered. The unprecedented flooding and drought in our nation does not bode well for food prices here. Du Pont has seemingly provided a "fertilizer" (read "defoliant") that has destroyed more crop land, and according to Lindsey Williams, our country has only a three-to-five-month emergency supply of grains, if that. The "leveling process" will bring the Northern Hemisphere to the level of the third world countries: on our knees, begging for bread. ("You needn't move to the Third World. The Third World is coming to you.")

While the secular world is debating the possibility of a financial "re-adjustment," we can confidently predict a total, worldwide economic collapse, based on Seal Three. In view of the astonishing specificity of Bible prophecy, particularly in regard to our Lord's First Coming and given that God does not change (Mal. 3:6), it seems reasonable to expect that the signs of His Second Coming would have the same specificity. We can see it here. Are we not required to ask ourselves (Matt. 16:4, 11 Tim. 2:15), if this is not a fulfillment of Seal Three?

The Third Seal pictures "a black horse, and he that sat on him had a pair of balances in his hand. I heard a voice in the midst of the four beasts say: 'A measure of wheat for a penny, and three measures of barley for a penny; and see thou hurt not the oil and the wine.' " We've covered the prices and commodities factor, but the color of the horse is manifestly significant. Traditionally, the black horse has simply been portrayed as Famine, but starvation and famine are not even specifically mentioned in this Seal, though they are implied; we don't expect this sort of imprecision in God's Word. I assert that the horse is black because that color defines the oligarchy now, and we will see that the colors of the other three horses identify those particular stages of the modern New World Order conspiracy, as well. Essentially, in the Four Horsemen of the Apocalypse, we've been given a handy-dandy, color-coded key to the cryptocracy.

Black Operations

The edict to "hurt not the oil and the wine" went forth from George Bush, whose CIA group is code-named the Black Rose. The Cabalistic philosophy of the Thule Society and its obeisance to the Black Sun (son, as in Lucifer, Satan) formed the impetus for the Third Reich under Hitler, which was the pivot point between the red horse and the black (see the Nazi flag). Hitler, deeply steeped in the occult, was also planning for the false millennium, the "Thousand Year Reich." It was the Holocaust (literally "burnt offering") that was the trade-off for getting the flying disk technology into the hands of humans. "UFOs" are often associated with the "Men in Black."

Most of the current global turmoil is funded by the "black budget," garnered from black operations off the official records: huge sums of money from munitions and drug profits. The black budget also funds the black sciences of mind and weather control, chemical-biological warfare, and the underground eugenics research which picked up speed in this country when we hung a few Nazis and hired the rest, in Operation Paper Clip. (Daddy Prescott Bush was generous in funding this research during World War II, and no wonder, when we look at the products of his loins).

Black, unmarked helicopters, and black "ninja" uniforms are becoming omnipresent, as the New World Order forces are being trained and utilized. The helicopters are often seen at trouble spots before the trouble erupts and have been reported spraying gaseous substances before some new disease attacks an area. The black nobility of Europe is gaining notoriety, as the Merovingian bloodlines are being frantically traced and recorded. (And the movie *The Last Temptation of Christ* from Kazantzakis's novel of the same name, has introduced a generation to the idea that Jesus Christ survived the cross and lived to produce offspring with Mary Magdalene, supposedly forming this bloodline). Jesuits sardonically worship the black pope. Genocidal wars and famines and plagues are professionally incited on the "black" continent of Africa, and the butchery of darker-skinned peoples is spread throughout the Southern Hemisphere, as a prelude to doing away with the lighter-skinned "useless eaters" of the Northern Hemisphere. The future looks black indeed. And so it *is,* but as we shall see, its defining color will be green.

Fourth Seal: Green Horse

Revelation 6:8 reads: "And I looked, and behold, a pale horse: and his name that sat on him was Death, and Hell followed with him. And power was given unto them over a fourth part of the earth, to kill with sword, and with hunger, and with death, and with the beasts of the earth." The word that has been translated for nearly two thousand years as "pale" is in fact *chloros . . . green* as grass. Why this is a green horse will soon become apparent.

The circumstances defined by the Fourth Seal are already looming. Famine is pandemic; sixty wars are being waged (at last count) and more rumored. "Natural" catastrophes (many, in fact, due to scalar and electromagnetic weather warfare) are breaking all records, and millions have died in the floods, earthquakes, tornadoes, hurricanes, heat waves, and cold spells. Birds are feasting on the scattered dead in and around Rwanda (Isa. 18). Increasingly bizarre incidents of animals attacking humans are reported in the daily papers, along with the spread of rabies and rodent-borne viruses and bacteria. AIDS and numerous other diseases (sixty-eight STDs, malaria, bubonic plague, anthrax, cholera, tuberculosis, smallpox, and more) are now utterly resistant to antibiotics and are epidemic, and new ones are being introduced routinely through vaccinations and by aerial spraying.

Microwave ATP frequencies, Gaiandriana, or the results of fetal tissue and genetic research (both high governmental priorities) could account for the upcoming horror of Revelation 9:6. The earth and its atmosphere are dying from deforestation (less than 30 percent of the rain forest remaining), desertification (twenty-four thousand square miles a year), and pollution of air, water, and soil. Over twenty-two billion tons of chemical and radioactive pollutants are dumped legally each year from the United States alone, and this doesn't even include airborne pollutants, pesticides, herbicides, and illegal dumping. The depletion of the ozone layer is now at 8 percent conservatively, and at approximately 13–15 percent all the phytoplankton will die. They are already mutating and dying in large areas of the ocean. The algae that flourish in polluted conditions are cause for the "red tides" that are becoming increasingly more common in our oceans, and these plus the death of most of the sea's denizens, and flowing blood from the genocidal wars, may well be the phenomena of Revelation 8:8 and 16:3.

The phytoplankton which get choked out are not only the base of the food chain, but have been the primary source of oxygen in our atmosphere, even more than the rain forests. It takes an excess of oxygen to form the ozone layer and keep it in its place as a protector of the atmosphere. Whether the depleted ozone is a result of chlorofluorocarbons or whether that story is just another Du Pont concoction to corner the market for new patents and electromagnetic pulses are the real cause is moot. The ozone layer is deteriorating in either case and is irreversible for at least the next ten years. Meanwhile we are producing less oxygen, thereby depleting the buffer zone that is meant to keep the ozone in place. This will culminate in Revelation 16:8, when the sun is given the power to "scorch men with fire."

The hoofbeats of the Fourth Horseman are audible, and just a little farther in the distance is the sound of trumpets. Underground testing of massive bombs has loosened the mantle of the earth from the core, leading to the earthquakes (or pole shifts, perhaps assisted by nuclear detonations) of the Sixth Seal and throughout the Book of the Revelation. Underground testing has also heated up the volcanoes in the Pacific Rim, causing thermal pollution (attributed to a most unusual "El Niño" in California) and likely activating the volcanoes themselves. The world has had more earthquakes over 6.5 on the Richter scale in the last three years than in all recorded history combined (Matt. 24:7, Mark 13:8), now accompanied by tsunamis (tidal waves) (Luke 21:25). Revelation 8:8 could well be the result of comets or of the return of radioactive space junk we've lofted into the sky; one aerospace project is code-named Woodpecker (Wormwood), and since "Chernobyl" means wormwood in Russian, we can assume that Revelation 8:11 and Jeremiah 23:15 refer to radioactivity, and that possibly Revelation 16:2

and 10 refer to radiation sickness. We're seeing this already, in our troops returned from Iraq, where they were contaminated by their own radioactive bullet casings, and in the population at large, as a result of domestic experiments and not-so-accidental "accidents."

Numerous citizens' militias have been fueled by misguided patriots in Pavlovian response to the urgent short-wave and AM promptings of the likes of Bill Cooper and Linda Thompson and their countless panicky callers, guaranteeing a Bosnian-Rwandan bloodbath of mammoth proportions in the United States, when the move is made to designate us Magna-Region 1, if not before. As these professing "Christians" (whose actions-emotions definitively prove they aren't walking the walk: see Matt. 26:52; Isa. 8:9–20; Luke 6:46,47) squawk and cackle about the immediate threat of UN troops on U.S. soil, and the any-moment roundup of dissidents and patriots for delivery to the "concentration camps," they're witlessly paving the way for a total discreditation of anything that anyone calling himself a Christian has to say.

As a result of their premature and hyped-up hollering "Wolf," few will pay heed to the warnings when the wolf actually arrives on the scene from a totally unexpected direction. While this contingent is certainly courageous, and probably means well, their double mind (James 1:8) is apparent. They are well aware of the chemical-biological and electromagnetic capabilities of the not-so-secret government and are clearly operating under strong delusion to suppose their pop guns are going to get them anything but dead. Ezekiel 32 offers a full report on their fate.

As we have seen, the Third Seal is yet to be completed (as of February 1995). When the economic plug is pulled, the UN troops, Multi-Jurisdictional Task Force, BATF, CALIA, and other alphabet soup agencies will be made heroes by the media as they pass out soup, fight fires, and put down riots. The Christian patriots will die or dine on crow, as we are ushered into the Fourth Seal. The completion of Seal Three, by worldwide economic collapse (which will prove the necessity for a one-world monetary system) and the imminent arrival of the green horse was cleverly heralded to the cryptocracy at the Economic Summit of the Americas, December 9, 1994, when both Gore and Clinton appeared in green suits on a green-carpeted stage with a green backdrop which held a green sign. The plans they think are theirs are coming along nicely. Witness the economies of Mexico and Canada since the summit. Who is next? The U.S.-Mexico borders are being beefed up under the direction of Janet Reno, perhaps as much to keep U.S. citizens and their assets in when the collapse comes here as to keep illegals out.

The "Green" Movement

That Fourth Horseman of Revelation 6:8 has been referred to for two thousand years as the Pale Horse of Death: it is not a pale horse at all, as I stated earlier, but a bright green one. The word in the Greek is *chloros,* the root of our word "chlorophyl" and as green as grass. (Just in case we missed it, the same word is used to describe grass in Revelation 8:7.) Minor mistranslations like this one, scarce but crucial, make me wonder if Francis Bacon did do a little diddling with the Holy Writ.

The significance of the color green is immediately apparent to the conspiracy student. Already the Green Revolution is making moves to destroy all national sovereignty to facilitate the enforcement of UN treaties to save the ozone, the soil, the air, and the waters of Gaia, Green Mother Earth. Gorbachov's Green Cross organization and Benjamin Creme's Tara Institute (Tara's a Green "goddess") under the Club of Rome are waving the green flag of environmentalism with fervor. It's a very appealing idea to gather together as world citizens and save our planet, and the controllers have been steadily touting its desirability over the last thirty years. Alex Cockburn, in the September 1994 issue of *The Nation,* does a fine job of exposing promoters of environmental politics who made their megabucks by destroying the earth. And why, but to manipulate the masses by offering a false hope of an earth renewed by the power of man? "There is a way that seemeth right unto a man, but the end thereof are the ways of death." (Prov. 14:12) God has other plans for the planet He created, and He's been good enough to write them down for us. It's His planet and His disposable model, at that. (Rev. 21:1; 2 Pet. 3:10)

Green Money

Another obvious aspect of the green horse is the formation of a one-world economic and money (green) system, which is being facilitated by NAFTA, GATT, and APEC consortiums, under the leadership of the rich men of the earth (Mic. 6:12): the bankers of IMF, the Fed, World Conservation Bank, World Bank, and so on. It's likely that *Green*span will be at the top of the heap, since we're given a name in each of the four horsemen that coordinates with the color of the horse, and he's valiantly doing his part to destroy the U.S. economy.

The "MARC" of the Beast

This ongoing centralization will lead, within six years or so, to the "Mark of the Beast" of Revelation 13:16–18, without which no man will be able to buy or sell. In what would seem an impossibly brainless move were these events not foreordained, the Department of Defense in August 1994 issued a new all-purpose ID card to its employees called the multitechnological automated reader card . . . the MARC card. This is a conditioning preparation for the day when the Antichrist (also known as the first beast of Revelation 13) will "cause all, both small and great, rich and poor, free and bond, to receive a mark in their right hand, or in their foreheads" to conduct business of any kind. Sixteen thousand pages of information can now be stored in a computer chip smaller than a grain of rice, which can be injected under the skin relatively painlessly. The hand and the forehead are subject to the most temperature change, and it's the constant temperature differential that powers the minuscule lithium battery.

Interesting that the Bible is the only early prophetic work that refers to the Mark of the Beast, and it says clearly that the mark will be *in* the hand or forehead, not *on* them. The word for 666 (the basis of all bar codes and computerized data) is *chi xi stigma,* and the definition of stigma is "a mark incised or punched for recognition of ownership." Interesting, too, that if lithium leaks into the skin, the result is an infected wound. Revelation 16:2 predicts a "noisome and grievous sore upon the men which had the mark of the beast." The fact that taking it entails agreeing to worship Satan and condemning oneself to damnation will probably be perceived as an exotic and enticing fringe benefit to the hard-core tattoo-punker-S&M crowds. Given the general state of (un)consciousness in the population, and the glowing reports we're already hearing in the media about the convenience and security of microchips for pets, prisoners, and patients, it's my guess that some folks will be camping out in line to get one.

Issue 8, Spring 1995

Sources

The Center of the Labyrinth

Campbell, Joseph, with Bill Moyers. *The Power of Myth*. New York: Doubleday, 1989.

DeLillo, Don. *Libra*. New York: Viking, 1988.

Epstein, Edward Jay. *Inquest*. New York: Viking, 1966.

Kirk, G. S. *The Nature of Greek Myths*. New York: Penguin Books, 1976.

Macoby, Hyam. *The Sacred Executioner*. New York: Thames and Hudson, 1982.

UFOs: Chariots of the Damned?

1. In 1972, while visiting the Jet Propulsion Laboratory (JPL) in Pasadena, California, I learned from my tour guide—a JPL employee—that the facility had analyzed many UFO photographs. The guide told me that JPL had explained away all of them except one. That one, he said, was taken by a man who provided such good information about the time of day, location, camera, and film that JPL, after using computer enhancement of the photo, could offer only two explanations. The man who submitted the photo said he saw a UFO passing in front of the moon. The guide said JPL would not confirm it but was convinced there definitely was something real in the photo. The only trouble was that they couldn't tell if it was a small object about two feet in front of the camera or something one thousand miles long at a distance of one hundred thousand miles from earth. A mother ship?

2. These projects were reported by Jerome Clark in *Fate* magazine (April 1988) in the last of his four-part article on crashed UFO retrievals.

3. Another implication of this scenario is that MJ-12 or its successors had access to UFOs through their alien contacts. If so, it must be assumed that (1) MJ-12 or its successors took advantage of that to visit the moon and other planets in our solar system long before the Apollo 11 moon landing in 1969, and (2) the NASA space exploration program is a gigantic boondoggle whose

338

real purpose is to be another secret conduit for funding military-intelligence projects which are intended to be kept from scrutiny by Congress and the public.

4. Jacobs's lecture and the proceedings of the annual UFO Experience conference, which I produce, are available in audio- and videotape format. For details, write to Omega Communications, P.O. Box 2051, Cheshire, CT 06410-5051, USA.

5. For details, see Kenneth Ring's *Life at Death* (Morrow, 1980) and *Heading toward Omega* (Morrow, 1984), Charles Flynn's *After the Beyond* (Prentice-Hall, 1986), and George Ritchie's *Return from Tomorrow* (Chosen, 1978).

6. Another example is Fowler's interpretation of the Lucas' abduction experiences. He asks in *The Watchers,* "Are highly advanced beings from outer space god's agents of creation on this and other planets?" (p. 206) He concludes the answer is yes; "Watcher," he tells us, is translated from the Chaldean word for a class of angelic beings responsible for watching over the affairs of humanity. (p. 214) Somewhat similarly, G. Cope Schellhorn's *Extraterrestrials in Biblical Prophecy* (Horus House: Madison, Wisc., 1989) concludes, "It would appear that the present mission of the large group of assorted extraterrestrials now operating near Earth is a standby mission, or as the Gospel of Matthew put it, a gathering of eagles, 'Wherever the body is, there the eagles will be gathered together' (Matt. 24:28)." Schellhorn, like Strieber, Fowler, and Downing, indiscriminately lumps together all ETs as divinely motivated. There is a double irony in Schellhorn's use of this biblical quotation. First, the more accurate translation is "a gathering of vultures," as the revised standard version notes, since eagles are not primarily carrion eaters who look for corpses (although they do occasionally scavenge). Second, and even more important, the quotation comes in the context of Jesus' enumeration of signs to distinguish false messiahs from the true one. A gathering of vultures, Jesus clearly indicates, is a sign of false messiahship—that is, deception. Despite this and several other flaws in Schellhorn's work, his book is a very useful survey of biblical events which might be better understood as encounters with extraterrestrial societies.

FEMA: Fascist Entity Manipulating America

Cox Newspapers.
The Progressive, May 1985.

Who Framed Leonard Peltier?

Churchill, Ward, and Jim Vander Wall. *Agents of Repression: The FBI's Secret Wars Against the Black Panther Party and the American Indian Movement.* Boston: South End Press, 1988.

Messerschmidt, Jim. *The Trial of Leonard Peltier.* Boston: South End Press, [n.d.].

Vander Wall, Jim. "A Warrior Caged: The Continuing Struggle of Leonard Peltier," from *The State of Native America*. Boston: South End Press, 1991. "The Government's Propaganda War Against the American Indian Movement," Ward Churchill, *EXTRA!* Oct.-Nov. 1992.
Video: *Incident at Oglala: The Leonard Peltier Story*, 1992.

TWA 800: No Single Missile Theory

Anderson, Mark K. "The Anti-Conspiracy Conspiracy," *Providence Phoenix*, Dec. 13, 1996.
Davey, Robert. "Interested Parties: TWA Flight 800," *Fairfield County Weekly*, Dec. 26–Jan. 1, 1997.
Goddard, Ian. "TWA 800: The Facts," http://www.erols.com/igoddard/twa-fact.htm
Lewis, Ron. "How a Missile Might Have Brought Down TWA Flight 800" and "Swedish Bofors RBS 70," *EmergencyNet News Service Daily Report* (vol. 2, no. 205), July 23, 1996.
Lewis, Ron. "Reasons for Suppressing the TWA Truth," *S.A.F.A.N. Internet Newsletter* (no. 246), Jan. 13, 1997, SafanNews@aol.com
Steinberg, Jeffrey. "TWA 800 Crash: An Act of War Against the Unites States?" *Executive Intelligence Review* (vol. 23, no. 31), Aug. 2, 1996.
Shoemaker, Tom. "Atlantic Coast Military Exercises," http://www.webexpert.net/rosedale/twacasefile/default.htm
Wilson, Gary. "Did 'Friendly Fire' Bring Down TWA Flight 800?," http://www.parascope.com

Drugs and the CIA: From Ho to Hasenfus

Mullins, Eustace. *The World Order.*
McCoy, Alfred. *The Politics of Heroin.*
Smith, R. Harris. *OSS: The Secret History.*
Sonres, Bruce. *Workers World.*

You Name the Dwarfs: Surrealism, Advertising, and Mass Mind Control

1. Breton, André. *Nadja*. New York: Grove Weidenfeld, 1960.
2. Gaunt, William. *The Surrealists*. New York: G. P. Putnam's Sons, 1972.
3. Key, Wilson Bryan. *The Age of Manipulation*. New York: Henry Holt, 1989.
4. ———. *Subliminal Seduction*. New York: Signet, 1981.
5. Lewis, Helena. *The Politics of Surrealism*. New York: Paragon House, 1988.
6. McLuhan, Marshall. *Culture Is Our Business*. New York: McGraw-Hill, 1970.
7. ———. *The Mechanical Bride*. Boston: Beacon Press, 1970.
8. Meyers, William. *The Image Makers*. New York: Times Books, 1984.
9. Read, Herbert. *Surrealism*. New York: Praeger Publishers, 1971.

10. Sutin, Lawrence. *Divine Invasions: A Life of Philip K. Dick.* New York: Harmony House, 1989.

Project MONARCH: Nazi Mind Control

1. Carrico, David L. *The EgyptianMasonicSatanic Connection.* 1992.
2. Bowart, Walter H. *Operation Mind Control.* Flatland Editions, 1994, p. 216.
3. Cannon, Martin. *Mind Control and the American Government.* Prevailing Winds Research, 1994, p. 19.
4. Hunt, Linda. *Secret Agenda.* New York: St. Martin's Press, 1991.
5. *Final Report of the Select Committee to Study Governmental Operations.* U.S. Senate, April 1976, p. 387.
6. Ibid, p. 390.
7. Marks, John. *The Search for the Manchurian Candidate.* New York: Times Books, 1979, pp. 60–61.
8. *Final Report of the Select Committee to Study Governmental Operations.* U.S. Senate, April 1976, p. 391.
9. Walker, Barbara G. *The Woman's Dictionary of Symbols and Sacred Objects.* New York HarperCollins, 1988.
10. Cavendish, Marshall. *Man, Myth and Magic.* 1995.
11. Hammond, Dr. Corydon. The Greenbaum Speech, 1992; Mark Phillips and Cathy O'Brien, Project Monarch Programming Definitions, 1993.
12. Posner, Gerald L. *Mengele: The Complete Story.* New York: McGraw-Hill, 1986.
13. Lagnado, Lucette Matalon. *Dr. Josef Mengele and the Untold Story of the Twins of Auschwitz.* New York: William Morrow, 1991.
14. Thomas, Gordon. *Journey into Madness: The True Story of Secret CIA Mind Control and Medical Abuse.* New York: Bantam Books, 1989.
15. O'Brien, Cathy, and Mark Phillips. *Trance Formation of America.* 1995.
16. John DeCamp, *The Franklin Cover-Up: Child Abuse, Satanism and Murder in Nebraska.* AWT Inc., 1992.
17. Chaitkin, Anton. "Franklin Witnesses Implicate FBI and U.S. Elites in Torture and Murder of Children," *The New Federalist,* 1993.
18. Rappoport, Jon. "CIA Experiments with Mind Control on Children," *Perceptions Magazine,* Sept.-Oct. 1995, p. 56.
19. Rosenbaum, David E. *First Draft: Overview of Investigation of the Group, 1983–1993.*

Psy-Ops and Cereology: The Search for "Intelligent" Circle Makers

Crop Circle Secrets, edited by Donald L. Cyr, published by Stonehenge Viewpoint, 800 Palermo Dr., Santa Barbara, CA 93105.
Delgado, Pat, and Colin Andrews. *Circular Evidence: Detailed Investigation of the Flattened Swirled Crops Phenomenon.* Grand Rapids, MI: Phanes Press.

Hesemann, Michael. *The Cosmic Connection: Worldwide Crop Formations and ET Contacts*. Santa Rosa, CA: Atrium Publishing, 1996.

Andrews, Colin. *CPRI Newsletter,* Circles Phenomenon Research International, P.O. Box 3378, Branford, CT 06405.

Global News on Contact with Non-Human Intelligence (CNINews1@aol.com), the 2020 Group, 3463 State St., #264, Santa Barbara, CA 93105. Note: You must have an e-mail address to subscribe.

Revelations: The Answer to the Mystery of the Cropcircles. Video produced by John Macnish, Circlevision Production, P.O. Box 36, Ludlow, Shropshire SY8 3ZZ, England.

R.I.L.K.O. (Research into Lost Knowledge Organisation), 10 Kedleston Dr., Orpington, Kent BR5 2DR, England.

The Cereologist, 11 Powis Gardens, London W11 1JG, England.

Honey, Did You Leave Your Brain Back at Langley Again?

1. Radio show transcript may be ordered from BioAlert Press: 475-A Linfield Pl., Goleta, CA 93117

2. Not so incidentally, I just heard on the news that ol' William has apparently given up the ghost during a rather mysterious boating accident near his vacation home in Maryland. The police found the boat, but not the body. According to the 4/30/96 (Walpurgis Night) edition of the *Los Angeles Times:* "A neighbor who checked his home found his radio and computer still on. Investigators found dinner dishes on a table and clam shells in the kitchen sink." (All right, buddy, put down those clamshells nice 'n easy! We're goin' on a little ride.) Even as I type this, the police are scouring the riverbed for any trace of the former spymaster. Something tells me newspaper pundits from coast to coast will definitely conclude that no foul play was involved.

3. Deep River Books: 512 Santa Monica Blvd., Santa Monica, CA 90401

4. The Freedom of Thought Foundation: P.O. Box 35072, Tucson, AZ 85740

5. Begich, Dr. Nick, and Jeane Manning. *Angels Don't Play This HAARP.* Anchorage: Earthpulse Press, 1995.

6. Bowart, Walter. Interview. *Something's Happening.* Pacifica Radio, KPFK, Los Angeles, 10/6/94.

7. Boward, Walter. *Operation Mind Control.* Ft. Bragg: Flatland Editions, 1994.

8. Constantine, Alex. "The Florida/Hollywood Mob Connection, the CIA and O. J. Simpson," n.p.: *The Constantine Report,* 1995.

9. Delgado, Jose. *Physical Control of the Mind.* New York: Harper & Row, 1969.

10. Emory, Dave. *One Step Beyond.* FYI Radio, KFJC, Los Altos Hills, CA, 2/12/95.

11. "The Terror Connection, Part II: California under Ronald Reagan." Radio Free America, FYI Radio, KFJC, Los Altos Hills, CA, 9/86.

12. Freed, Donald, and Raymond P. Briggs, Ph.D. *Killing Time*. New York: Macmillan, 1996.
13. Gregory, Dick, and Jon Rappoport. Interview. *Something's Happening*. Pacifica Radio, KPFK, Los Angeles, 10/12/95.
14. Hoagland, Richard. Interview. *Coast to Coast AM with Art Bell*. CBC Radio, KOGO, San Diego, 3/7/96.
15. Hulet, Craig. Interview. *Something's Happening*. Pacifica Radio, KPFK, Los Angeles, 2/29/96.
16. Judge, John. "The Black Hole of Guyana." *Secret and Suppressed: Banned Ideas and Hidden History*. Ed. Jim Keith. Portland: Feral House, 1993.
17. Lee, Martin, and Bruce Shlain. *Acid Dreams*. New York: Grove Weidenfeld, 1992.
18. Mulgammon, Terry. "Not Wisely But Too Well . . ." *Los Angeles* magazine, July 1995: 54.
19. Nichols, Preston, and Peter Moon. *The Montauk Project*. Westbury: Sky Books, 1993.
20. Parfrey, Adam. "Bo Gritz Interrogated" *Flatland* 10 (1994): 46–51.
21. Streiber, Whitley. Interview. *Dreamland*. CBC Radio. KOGO, San Diego, 12/24/95.
22. Thomas, Gordon. *Journey into Madness*. New York: Bantam Books, 1990.
23. Thompson, Linda. "Waco: The Big Lie." Granada Pavilion Lecture, Santa Monica, 11/11/93.
24. Turner, William, and Jonn Christian. *The Assassination of Robert F. Kennedy*. New York: Thunder's Mouth Press, 1993.

The Cult That Haunted River Phoenix

Constantine, Alex. "Family Ties," *Hustler* (July 1994.)
Cain, Michael Scott. "The Charismatic Leader," *Humanist* (Nov.-Dec. 1988.)
Davis, Deborah. *The Children of God: The Inside Story*. Zondervan, 1984.
Martin, Walter. *The New Cults*. Vision House, 1984.
Other sources are indicated within the article.

AIDS: A Doctor's Note on the Man-Made Theory

1. Szmuness W., Stevens C., Harley E., et al. Hepatitis-B vaccine; Demonstration of efficacy in a controlled clinical trial in a high-risk population in the United States. *New England J. Med.* 303: 833–841, 1980.
2. Francis D., Hadler S., Thompson S., et al. The prevention of Hepatitis-B with vaccine. Report of the Centers for Disease Control multi-center efficacy trial among homosexual men. *Annals Int. Med.* 97: 362–366, 1982.
3. Goodfield J. Vaccine on Trial. In Goodfield J. *Quest for the Killers*. Boston: Birkhauser, 1985, pp. 51–97.
4. Szmuness, W. Large-scale efficacy trials of Hepatitis-B vaccines in the USA; Baseline data and protocols. *J. Med. Virology* 4: 327–340, 1979.

5. Cantwell Jr., A. The Hepatitis-B vaccine trials (1978–1981). In Cantwell Jr., A. *AIDS & The Doctors of Death.* Los Angeles: Aries Rising Press, 1988, pp. 65–80.
6. Goodfield. *Quest for the Killers,* p. 57.
7. Ibid., p. 86.
8. Ibid., p. 92.
9. Stevens, C. E., Taylor, P. E., Zang, E. A., et al. Human T-cell lymphotropic virus type III infection in a cohort of homosexual men in New York City. *JAMA* 255: 2167–2172, 1986.
10. Kellner, A. Reflections of Wolf Szmuness. In *Progress in Clinical and Biological Research* 182: 3–10, 1985.
11. Piller, C., and Yamamoto, K. *Gene Wars; Military Control over the New Genetic Technologies.* New York: Beech Tree Books/William Morrow, 1988, p. 103.
12. Ibid., p. 97.
13. Chase, A. *Magic Shots.* New York: William Morrow and Company, 1982, pp. 81–82.
14. Cantwell Jr., A. Biowarfare. In Cantwell Jr., A. *Queer Blood.* Los Angeles: Aries Rising Press, 1993, pp. 31–40.
15. McClure, H. M., Keeling, M. E., Custer, R. P., et al. Erythroleukemia in two infant chimpanzees fed milk from cows naturally infected with the bovine C-type virus. *Cancer Research* 34: 2745–2757, 1974.
16. Connor, S. AIDS science stands on trial. *New Scientist,* Feb. 12, 1987, pp. 49–58.
17. Garry, R. F., Witte, M. H., Gottleib A. A., et al. Documentation of an AIDS virus infection in the United States in 1968. *JAMA* 260: 2085–2087, 1988.
18. Cantwell Jr., A. AIDS: New or old? In Cantwell Jr., A. *Queer Blood.* Los Angeles: Aries Rising Press, 1993, pp. 61–69.
19. Horowitz, L. G. *Emerging Viruses, AIDS & Ebola: Nature, Accident or Genocide?* Rockport, MA: Tetrahedron, Inc., 1996.
20. Dodd, R. Y., Barker, L. F. (eds.). Infection, Immunity and Blood Transfusion. Proceedings of the XVIth Annual Scientific Symposium of the American Red Cross, Washington, D.C. New York: Alan R Liss, Inc., 1985, pp. xiii–xv.

Diet for a Zombified Planet

1. *New York Times,* Jan. 23, 1996.
2. Ibid.
3. Ibid.
4. *Nexus* magazine, Aug.-Sept. 1995.
5. Ibid.
6. Ibid.
7. Ibid.
8. Ibid.
9. Ibid.

10. Ibid.
11. *Issues* magazine, Spring 1996.
12. Ibid.
13. Ibid.
14. *New York Times,* Monday, May 20, 1996.
15. *East Side Monthly,* letters section, Feb. 1996.
16. Ibid.
17. Ibid.
18. Ibid.
19. *Nexus* magazine, Dec. 1995-Jan. 1996.
20. Ibid.
21. Ibid.
22. Ibid.
23. Ibid.
24. *Extraordinary Science* magazine, April-May-June 1995.
25. Ibid.
26. *Nexus* magazine, Dec. 1995-Jan. 1996.

The Gulf Biowar: How a New AIDS-like Plague Threatens Our Armed Forces

"Government study of veterans finds no evidence of a Gulf War disease," Art Pine, *Los Angeles Times,* Aug. 2, 1995.

"Gulf War toxins: Pentagon's credibility sinks even lower," editorial, *Los Angeles Times,* Oct. 24, 1996.

"U.N. aide fears Iraq could turn imported medicine into weapons," Paul Lewis, *New York Times,* Nov. 11, 1990.

"Troops may get unlicensed drug," Gina Kolata, *New York Times,* Jan. 4, 1991.

"Guinea pigs and disposable GIs," Tod Ensign, *Covert Action Bulletin,* Winter 1992–1993.

"Gulf War veterans seek restitution for ailments," William D Montalbano, *Los Angeles Times,* Nov. 30, 1996.

"Were biological weapons used against our forces in the Gulf War?," Garth and Nancy Nicolson, *Townsend Letter for Doctors & Patients,* May 1996.

"Papers on Gulf War missing," *Los Angeles Times,* Dec. 5, 1996.

"Army to review link between germ, Gulf War syndrome," Renee Tawa, *Los Angeles Times,* Dec. 27, 1996.

"Isolation and identification of a novel virus from patients with AIDS," Shyh-Ching Lo, *American Journal of Tropical Hygiene,* vol. 35(4), 1986, pp. 675–676.

"Mycoplasma and AIDS: what connection?," *Lancet,* Jan. 5, 1991.

Dave Emory's *One Step Beyond* interview with Nicolson, available from Spitfire, P.O. Box 1179, Ben Lomond, CA 95005.

Cantwell Jr., Alan. *The Cancer Microbe,* Los Angeles: Aries Rising Press, 1990.

————. *AIDS: The Mystery & The Solution,* Los Angeles: Aries Rising Press, 1986.

Alternative Three: The Great Brain Drain

Hoagland, Richard. *Martian Horizons,* 322–333 (Summer, 1995).
Keith, Jim. *Casebook on Alternative 3,* IllumiNet Press, P.O. Box 2808, Lilburn, GA 30226.
Alternative 3: The Video.

Index

347

About the Editors

AL HIDELL HAS BEEN INTERESTED in conspiracies ever since he saw the Zapruder film on PBS in the late 1970s. In 1992 he and Joan d'Arc—proprietor of an alternative bookstore and organizer of a conspiracy discussion group there—founded *PARANOIA: The Conspiracy Reader,* the world's most popular conspiracy publication. It was heralded by the *Village Voice* as "Weirdness on a grand scale . . . a dizzying web of connections!" In 1996 Hidell and d'Arc served as moderators of "Konspiracy Korner" on America Online, and in 1997 they began work on *The Conspiracy Reader.* They live in New England and Washington, D.C., respectively.

About Paranoia

Paranoia: The Conspiracy Reader is the largest-selling conspiracy publication in the world and is distributed to bookstores throughout North America, the United Kingdom, Australia, and New Zealand. One of *Playboy*'s Top Ten 'Zines, it has been covered in the *Los Angeles Times Book Review*, the *Village Voice*, the *New Yorker*, and the *Atlantic Monthly*. A one-year (four-issue subscription) is $20 (U.S. $28 International), available from PARANOIA, P.O. Box 1041, Providence, RI 02901.